Azure SQL Revealed

A Guide to the Cloud for SQL Server Professionals

Bob Ward
Foreword by Scott Guthrie

Apress®

Azure SQL Revealed: A Guide to the Cloud for SQL Server Professionals

Bob Ward
North Richland Hills, TX, USA

ISBN-13 (pbk): 978-1-4842-5930-6
https://doi.org/10.1007/978-1-4842-5931-3

ISBN-13 (electronic): 978-1-4842-5931-3

Managing Director, Apress Media LLC: Welmoed Spahr
Acquisitions Editor: Jonathan Gennick
Development Editor: Laura Berendson
Coordinating Editor: Jill Balzano

Cover image designed by Freepik (www.freepik.com)

Distributed to the book trade worldwide by Springer Science+Business Media LLC, 1 New York Plaza, Suite 4600, New York, NY 10004. Phone 1-800-SPRINGER, fax (201) 348-4505, e-mail orders-ny@springer-sbm.com, or visit www.springeronline.com. Apress Media, LLC is a California LLC and the sole member (owner) is Springer Science + Business Media Finance Inc (SSBM Finance Inc). SSBM Finance Inc is a **Delaware** corporation.

For information on translations, please e-mail booktranslations@springernature.com; for reprint, paperback, or audio rights, please e-mail bookpermissions@springernature.com.

Apress titles may be purchased in bulk for academic, corporate, or promotional use. eBook versions and licenses are also available for most titles. For more information, reference our Print and eBook Bulk Sales web page at http://www.apress.com/bulk-sales.

Any source code or other supplementary material referenced by the author in this book is available to readers on GitHub via the book's product page, located at www.apress.com/9781484259306. For more detailed information, please visit http://www.apress.com/source-code.

Printed on acid-free paper

This book is dedicated to all at Microsoft who have worked tirelessly over the last decade to make Azure the world's computer.

Table of Contents

About the Author

Bob Ward is a Principal Architect for the Microsoft Azure Data team, which owns the development for all SQL Server versions. He has worked for Microsoft for more than 27 years on every version of SQL Server shipped from OS/2 1.1 to SQL Server 2019, including Azure SQL. Bob is a well-known speaker on SQL Server and Azure SQL, often presenting talks on new releases, internals, performance, and Azure SQL fundamentals at events such as PASS Summit, Red Hat Summit, Microsoft //build, SQLBits, SQLIntersection, Microsoft Inspire, and Microsoft Ignite. You can follow him at @bobwardms and linkedin.com/in/bobwardms. Bob created and produced training for Azure SQL including Azure SQL Fundamentals, Azure SQL for Beginners, and the Azure SQL Bootcamp. Bob is the author of the Apress books *Pro SQL Server on Linux* and *SQL Server 2019 Revealed*.

About the Technical Reviewer

Joe Sack is a Principal Program Manager at Microsoft, focusing for the last four years on the Intelligent Query Processing feature family for Azure SQL Database and SQL Server. He has worked as a SQL Server professional since 1997 and has supported and developed for SQL Server environments in financial services, IT consulting, manufacturing, retail, and the real estate industry.

Over the years, Joe has published and edited several SQL Server books and white papers. His first book *SQL Server 2000 Fast Answers for DBAs and Developers* was published in 2003. He also started the T-SQL Recipe series, including *SQL Server 2005 T-SQL Recipes* and *SQL Server 2008 Transact-SQL Recipes*. He recorded 13 Pluralsight courses, including "SQL Server: Troubleshooting Query Plan Quality Issues," "SQL Server: Transact-SQL Basic Data Retrieval," and "SQL Server: Common Query Tuning Problems and Solutions."

His Twitter handle is @JoeSackMSFT, and you can find Joe speaking at most major SQL Server conferences.

Foreword

Cloud computing has become a pivotal part of business and our world. Azure, the world's computer, is at the forefront of delivering cloud computing at the scale the world needs. Azure SQL has been part of Microsoft's cloud lineup since the beginning. From SQL Services to SQL Azure to the powerful lineup of Azure SQL cloud services, databases have always been a core part of Azure.

In this book, Bob Ward, an architect on my team who for 27 years has been an integral part of the SQL Server story for Microsoft, leads you on a journey to learn Azure SQL starting with the compelling history of Azure and Azure SQL. Then he describes in detail the Azure SQL lineup, including SQL Server for Azure Virtual Machine, Azure SQL Managed Instance, and Azure SQL Database. A complete chapter is available for you to understand the details of using SQL Server in Azure Virtual Machine.

The heart of the book gives you what you need to deploy and configure Azure SQL to meet your requirements. You will then learn how to secure your data, maintain performance, and achieve high availability with your Azure SQL investments. I love how Bob compares and contrasts our SQL Server product you know so well to Azure SQL deployment options. But you will also learn the innovation of Azure SQL that can truly provide your business new value, including built-in High Availability, Automatic Tuning, Advanced Threat Protection, Serverless computing, and Hyperscale databases.

With 60+ Azure cloud regions around the world and more coming every quarter, Azure is everywhere you need it with scale, compliance, and resiliency for even the most demanding applications. Azure SQL services are a core element of our strategy to provide databases at scale. I believe this book will give you the knowledge you need to translate your skills with SQL Server to maximize the capabilities of the Azure SQL data platform and meet the needs of your migrations or new database applications.

—Scott Guthrie, Executive Vice President, Microsoft, Cloud and AI

Acknowledgments

I want to first thank God for giving me the endless gift of grace through his son Jesus Christ. God's grace blesses me every day, including the honor of being married to Ginger Ward. My wife Ginger continues to show me the example of what it is like to show kindness, grace, and respect to everyone she meets. Her support throughout my time writing this book kept me going. My sons, Troy and Ryan Ward, bless me every day as I see them carry on what I've taught them about integrity and responsibility.

Publishing a book is not easy, and without Jonathan Gennick and Jill Balzano from Apress, I could not have made it. Thank you both for your professionalism and kindness. I owe a huge thanks to my technical reviewer Joe Sack. If you have never met Joe Sack, I hope someday you do. Not only is he one of the nicest people I know, but a brilliant engineer. He brought the right balance of pointing out what could work better with compliments on many of the chapters.

I want to also thank my leadership at Microsoft for giving me this opportunity, including Scott Guthrie for writing the foreword, Rohan Kumar for all his guidance and wisdom, and to my manager Asad Khan who always supports me in everything I do at Microsoft.

They say "it takes a village" to build something big, but to write a book like this it takes an army. It is hard to call out every individual who helps you as you create a book like this, so I'll first start by thanking all the software engineers and program managers across the Azure SQL team in Redmond, Israel, and Serbia. I do want to mention a few specific individuals, and it all starts with Anna Hoffman. Anna and I worked together the entire calendar year of 2020 on Azure SQL, all remote. Her patience with what she calls my "hyperfocused" work amazes me every day. But more important, she possesses what I call an "old school" work ethic at a very young age. I find that hard to see these days. I also want to thank my colleagues Buck Woody and Marisa Brasile for all their guidance, encouragement, and help promoting our work in Azure SQL. I want to pay special thanks to the folks I interviewed for the first chapter of the book to tell you the history of Azure SQL, including Ted Kummert, Rohan Kumar, Ajay Kalhan, Peter Carlin, Brian Chamberlain, Conor Cunningham, Ron Matchoro, Guy Bowerman, Drazen Sumic, Morgan Oslake, Cristian Diaconu, Steve Lindell, Mark Russinovich, Evan Basalik, and Keith Elmore.

ACKNOWLEDGMENTS

There were many members of the Azure SQL and other engineering teams that helped me with quotes and questions that I want to thank, including Dimitri Furman, Denzil Ribeiro, Sanjay Mishra, Emily Lisa, Joachim Hammer, Andreas Wolter, Girish Mittur Venkataramanappa, Alain Dormehl, Abdul Sathar Sait, Mine Tokus, Ajay Jagannathan, Borko Novakovic, Hans Olav Norheim, Misha Kolianko, Pratyush Rawat, Scott Kim, Stojan Rakic, Venkata Raj Pochiraju, Yadi Reyes, Jovan Popovic, Sherif Mahmoud, Tomer Rotstein, Andrey Karpovsky, Rohit Nayak, Vassilis Papadimos, Dejan Krakovic, Craig Freedman, Silvano Coriani, Davide Mauri, Hanuma Kodavalla, Ebru Ersan, and Srini Acharya.

Our marketing team has always been very supportive of my work, so a big thanks to John "JG" Chirapurath, Wisam Hirzalla, Eric Hudson, Debbi Lyons, and Miwa Monji.

And finally thanks to you, the community, who supports and helps us promote the amazing story of SQL Server. Many of you are now engaging with Azure, so my hope is the timing of this book is perfect for you to begin your journey with Azure SQL and empower you to put the same energy and passion behind it as you have with SQL Server for so many years.

Introduction

In November of 2019, I had just released my second book on SQL Server called *SQL Server 2019 Revealed* (my first book was *Pro SQL Server on Linux* which was released in 2018). It was only one week after we had also just launched the SQL Server 2019 release. I had also delivered some eight sessions at the recent PASS Summit conference in Seattle. Therefore, near the end of calendar 2019, I wanted to reflect back on what was successful but also look toward the future.

I found myself sitting in a room with my manager Asad Khan reviewing the work I had done over the last year and what might be the next focus for me (that is how we will roll at Microsoft; yes, we were celebrating the release of SQL Server 2019, but we are always looking at what is our next big thing). We agreed that for at least the foreseeable future I needed to focus on delivering the message of SQL Server 2019, Containers, Linux, and Kubernetes to customers and our internal teams.

I then asked a very dangerous question: "What about Azure?" Asad owns the program management for SQL Server and Azure SQL. He paused for a few seconds and then asked me, "Bob, what do you mean? Do you mean you want to get involved in Azure?" I had been thinking about this for some time. Back in the fall of 2019, I did a roadshow with Buck Woody and Anna Hoffman called "Ground to Cloud" (see the workshop for yourself at `https://github.com/microsoft/sqlworkshops/tree/master/SQLGroundToCloud`). During the roadshow, I was also thinking ahead despite the fact that I was still finishing the *SQL Server 2019 Revealed* book and part of our overall launch work for SQL Server 2019. So I told Asad, "I think one thing I can help with the cloud is to do an assessment of Azure SQL from the perspective of a SQL Server expert." Why not take my 27+ years of experience on SQL Server and see how it lines up with the cloud? Asad in his usual calm demeanor said that he thought this would be an excellent idea, but I think he was privately excited to see my involvement.

Roll forward to early January of 2020. I had spent time over the holiday break in December of 2019 talking to my wife Ginger and my sons Troy and Ryan. "Should I go for a third book?" Ginger replied with her usual wry smile "Why not? Don't you have a hang for this book writing thing now?" I thought it over for a bit and then decided to dive in. After all, 2020 marks the tenth anniversary of Azure and Azure SQL. I thought this introduction would include all the places I travelled while writing this book, as I had with my previous two books. However, there was a historic worldwide event you may have heard of called COVID-19 which disrupted not only my travel but has also affected so many people. I grieve and pay respects to all of those reading this book for themselves and any of their loved ones affected. The time not travelling did allow for me to have more focus to write this book, so I hope you like the final result. All of this book was written in my home office in North Richland Hills, Texas, but I was connected to the world throughout the writing.

This book is the culmination of work for an assessment of Azure SQL from the perspective of SQL Server. However, even if you don't know SQL Server, I believe you will gain much knowledge to learn Azure SQL. The book has many examples embedded into the text you can use, but you can also download code examples from my GitHub repository at `https://github.com/Microsoft/bobsql`.

The book starts out with a history of Azure and Azure SQL. I think understanding the history of something can help you gain knowledge of current capabilities and what is possible. I had fun writing the first chapter as it involved some fairly intensive research and interviews with some names you will find familiar.

I then will take time to explain what Azure SQL means. This is a great chapter to get started so you understand what is possible with Azure SQL cloud services, including the Azure ecosystem. This chapter will also help guide your decisions as you choose which Azure SQL option best fits your requirements. I recommend anyone reading this book to review this chapter.

One of the choices for Azure SQL is Azure Virtual Machine. Since the experience of Azure Virtual Machine (VM) inside the guest OS is very much like SQL Server on-premises, I chose to dedicate a single chapter to the subject instead of including Azure VM in the rest of the book. This chapter is great though if Azure VM is your target as I talk about deployment, networking, storage, and performance. The rest of the book covers Azure SQL Managed Instance and Azure SQL Database as Azure SQL.

One of the first things you do with SQL Server is install the software and configure it. Therefore, that is where your Azure SQL journey begins: learning the details and options to deploy and configure Azure SQL. I think you will find this is a fairly thorough discussion of the topic, because in some cases, making the right decisions during deployment will save you time and money. Even if you are familiar with the basics of deploying Azure, I recommend you review these chapters. You might find some interesting details you didn't know about.

The heart of the book then takes you on a journey to learn the core of Azure SQL, which are security, performance, and availability. Every customer I've talked to that has mastered SQL Server knows these three areas, and they represent the core of the SQL Server engine. Therefore, when you read these chapters, you will understand the capabilities and tasks of Azure SQL compared to SQL Server. These chapters are the largest in the book and contain the most examples.

You will finish the book learning "What else." There are some topics like Job Management that don't fit into security, performance, and availability, so you will round off your knowledge in the second to last chapter. One of the goals of this book is to get the SQL Server professional comfortable with Azure SQL. However, I want readers to end their journey with the book in the last chapter to see what is possible beyond the fundamentals because you are now in the world's computer, Azure.

This book is intended to help you get to Azure SQL, stay on Azure SQL, and use Azure SQL to its maximum potential. So gear up and start learning. Welcome to the world's database: Azure SQL.

Bob Ward
North Richland Hills, Texas

CHAPTER 1

SQL Server Rises to the Clouds

In late 2005, Microsoft as a company was humming (I'm a little biased here) in the enterprise space and so was the SQL Server product. In October of 2005, we were close to releasing SQL Server 2005 (code name Yukon) which was unfortunately 5 years in the making (that is a story for another book; just ask Paul Randal). I was in Microsoft Support in those days, and despite the delay in getting SQL Server 2005 to market, I was very proud of the release. Windows, Windows Server, Office, and Xbox 360 were all popular products from Microsoft.

In October of 2005, an architect new to Microsoft named Ray Ozzie sent an internal email to several executives at Microsoft (which eventually was sent to all employees including a 12-year veteran named Bob Ward) called *The Internet Services Disruption* (the email leaked to the Web fairly quickly which you can read at `www.cnet.com/news/ozzie-memo-internet-services-disruption/`). I remember hearing about the email leak and some of its contents as an employee but didn't pay much attention. Wasn't the Internet just for email and web browsing? In that email, Ray Ozzie painted a picture of Microsoft becoming a *cloud provider* vs. just a "traditional software company." Microsoft only really had a few "Internet services" offerings at the time which included the legendary Hotmail email service (which had existed since 1997), the Bing Search Service, and Xbox Live. The email from Ray Ozzie painted a picture for something far bigger.

One of the key statements from this email was "...All Business Groups have been asked to develop their plans to embrace this mission and create new service offerings that deliver value to customers and utilize the platform capabilities that we have today and are building for the future." Little did I know how much behind-the-scenes work would kick in within the SQL Server team to develop plans for this statement.

1

© Bob Ward 2021
B. Ward, *Azure SQL Revealed*, https://doi.org/10.1007/978-1-4842-5931-3_1

Ray Ozzie became the Chief Software Architect of Microsoft in the summer of 2006 (taking the role held by Bill Gates), and this email would set the stage for what would become known as *Azure*. SQL Server was destined to become a huge part of it.

CloudDB

In early 2006, Paul Flessner, Vice President of the Data Storage and Platform division of Microsoft, decided to step down as the leader of SQL Server and turn over the reins to Ted Kummert. When Ted took over to lead SQL Server, a project was already underway to look at cloud services led by Technical Fellow Peter Spiro, who was a chief architect for several SQL Server releases, including SQL Servers 7.0, 2000, and 2005. Peter formed a team which included several engineers. Among them were two architects still at Microsoft today: Ajay Kalhan and Tomas Talius. The team embarked on a project to build a cloud-based service to host databases. They called it *CloudDB*. As Ted tells it, "We needed to build a cloud version of SQL. Our goal was to build a *serverless* or Platform as a Service (PaaS) SQL. A customer wouldn't worry about a server or VM, just a database."

In order to build a cloud-based database service, the team needed to build out a robust design to support the concept of hosting multiple customers or "databases" isolated from each other using shared resources. This concept is called *multi-tenant*.

Note   The term *tenant* can mean many things in the cloud. For CloudDB, in the beginning, a tenant referred to a database owned by a customer. You will see throughout this book the word tenant, but I'll be clear about the scope of what I mean when using the term.

According to Ajay Kalhan, from the beginning the CloudDB team started working out designs to incorporate concepts such as failure detection, logical master (think of a "metadata" master, not physical), load balancing, and deployment. Early designs even looked at the idea of a "key-value store" instead of traditional relational database concepts. Not long after the team was building out the design for CloudDB, Ted assigned David Campbell to also work on the project and lead the team toward a true mission of "SQL Server in the Cloud."

The team believe it needed an internal customer to help *dogfood* the project and prove they could host customers. That internal customer would become a public-facing cloud service called **Exchange Hosted Archive** (**EHA**) (an email archive solution in the cloud predating Office 365). For this internal customer, early designs to support multi-tenants (which in this case even though there was one internal customer, that customer serviced the needs of multiple customers) used a concept called *silos* where a SQL Server could host multiple databases, but tenants were partitioned within the database itself. EHA became one of the first *Software as a Service* (**SaaS**) services at Microsoft to use our cloud-based database service. Think of SaaS as purchasing software on a subscription basis and using the software from a hosted solution, like in Azure. You just focus on using an application hosted somewhere other than your computers. Since SQL Server hosted the back-end databases, the team forked the codebase of SQL Server 2005 to use for the service.

While the CloudDB team was working on their project with a goal to support EHA and other customers, another team at Microsoft was chartered by Ray Ozzie to look at how to host *compute services* in the cloud.

The Red Dog

In 2006, Ray Ozzie enlisted Microsoft veteran Amitabh Srivastava to lead a "Cloud OS" project in the attempt to move forward the "Internet services disruption" he had talked about a year ago. One of the first actions Amitabh took was to bring out of retirement Dave Cutler, the "father" of DEC VMS and Windows NT operating systems. As part of their initial project work, Srivastava and Cutler visited groups at Microsoft that were providing "cloud services," including Xbox Live, Hotmail, and Bing. On one of the trips to visit Hotmail in San Jose, California, the team drove by a club called the Pink Poodle. It was Dave Cutler who famously said, "Maybe we should name our project the Pink Poodle?" The project team all agreed that would not go over well so named the project instead "Red Dog." The name stuck (you can read more about the great history of the beginning of Red Dog at `www.wired.com/2008/11/ ff-ozzie/?currentPage=7` and `www.zdnet.com/article/how-the-red-dog-dream-team-built-a-cloud-os-from-scratch/`).

From the beginning, the Red Dog team did things differently at Microsoft to build the "Cloud OS." They built their own "data center" in the heart of the Microsoft campus, even taking reserve power from neighboring buildings. Their goals were ambitious and still resonate today. Their main overall goal was to *build a cloud service for developers to build scalable web applications*. They also had a massive theme from the beginning: *reliability*. As Dave Cutler said back in 2008, "One of the things you did not ask is why aren't we saying more about Azure and in the process filling the marketplace with sterling promises for the future? The answer to this is simply that the RD group is very conservative, and we are not anywhere close to being done. We believe that cloud computing will be very important to Microsoft's future and we certainly don't want to do anything that would compromise the future of the product. We are hypersensitive about losing people's data. We are hypersensitive about the OS or hypervisor crashing and having properties experience service outages. So, we are taking each step slowly and attempting to have features 100% operational and solidly debugged before talking about them. The opposite is what Microsoft has been criticized for in the past and the RD dogs hopefully have learned a new trick."

The RedDog and CloudDB teams were marching together as separate projects (ironically on the same campus only buildings apart) to support cloud services for web applications and hosted databases in the cloud. These projects were on a path to come together in 2007 and 2008 for a launch of a unified cloud service.

The Azure Services Platform

In October of 2008 at the Microsoft Professional Developers Conference (PDC) in Los Angeles, California, Ray Ozzie announced **Windows Azure**. The PDC was the pre-cursor to today's Microsoft //Build conference (`https://en.wikipedia.org/wiki/Build_ (developer_conference)`). PDC was a huge event for Microsoft for developers.

Windows Azure was launched as part of the **Azure Services Platform**. Figure 1-1 shows a snapshot of the Azure Services Platform offerings.

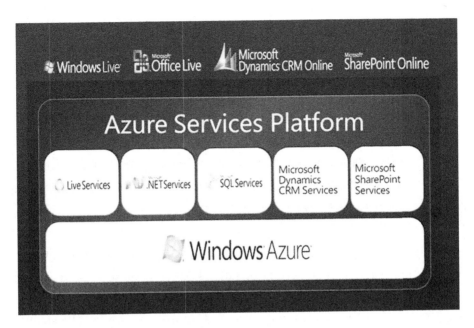

Figure 1-1. *The Azure Services Platform in 2008*

The Red Dog team had been cranking away since 2006 with the goal of releasing a cloud service for developers. Ray Ozzie called Windows Azure a "new Windows offering at the web tier of computing" (watch the video for yourself at `www.zdnet.com/article/ray-ozzie-announces-windows-azure/`). He also called Azure "Windows in the cloud." Microsoft now would offer customers Windows on your laptop (at that time, it was Windows Vista), servers for your enterprise (Windows Server), and Windows in the cloud (Azure).

Note   I sought out many folks at Microsoft on why our cloud service was named Azure. As Buck Woody, who is my colleague now but worked on Azure in the early days, tells the story, "Azure means clear blue sky with no clouds. The name just seemed right without using the word cloud in our name."

Like the goal of the CloudDB project, when Windows Azure first released, the goal was all about scalability and availability targeting web applications in the form of a *Platform as a Service* (**PaaS**). Think of PaaS as purchasing a platform to host your application or database based on a subscription where the platform is *managed* by a provider, like Azure. With PaaS, you are typically abstracted from a host computer or virtual machine. Therefore, *Cloud Services* was the first service in Windows Azure. This type of service was known internally as PaaS V1.

Note   Cloud services is still offered today in Azure. You can read more about cloud services at `https://azure.microsoft.com/en-us/services/cloud-services/`. A new service for web applications has become popular today called Azure App Service which you can read more about at `https://azure.microsoft.com/en-us/services/app-service/`.

Even though a cloud service application ran in one or more Virtual Machines, the idea was to support easy-to-scale web applications in the cloud where developers didn't focus on the details of the virtual machine but more on the application. Developers at this time for Windows were used to the Internet Information Server (IIS) feature of Windows Server. While developers didn't have to worry as much about deploying and configuring IIS, they typically had to have an administrator within their organization. While developers had some access to the Virtual Machine native OS environment for cloud services, that access was limited. It would be a few years later that Microsoft would introduce the concept of *Infrastructure as a Service* (**IaaS**) through Azure Virtual Machine. Think of IaaS as purchasing an infrastructure to host your virtual machine based on a subscription. You worry about the guest VM and the provider manages the host, hardware, networking, and storage.

One of the other promises of PaaS and cloud services is to create an easy-to-use concept of application deployment, configuration, and updates. Furthermore, providing capabilities for scalability, built-in high availability, and load balancing made the concept of cloud services extremely appealing to web developers. These same concepts you will see are a part of the appeal as well for Azure SQL and databases.

In order to host PaaS cloud services, an *underlying hosting system* had to be built. The Windows Azure team took the designs from the RedDog project to build this hosting system to support deployment, networking, high availability, scale, and security, as cloud services abstracted all these details from the developer. This software hosting system was known as the *Windows Fabric*. Providing the underlying hosting system for services consumed by users is the *power of the cloud*. I found this interesting slide from a talk at the PDC 2008 conference that talks about all the details required for someone to run their own *fabric* in a data center as seen in Figure 1-2.

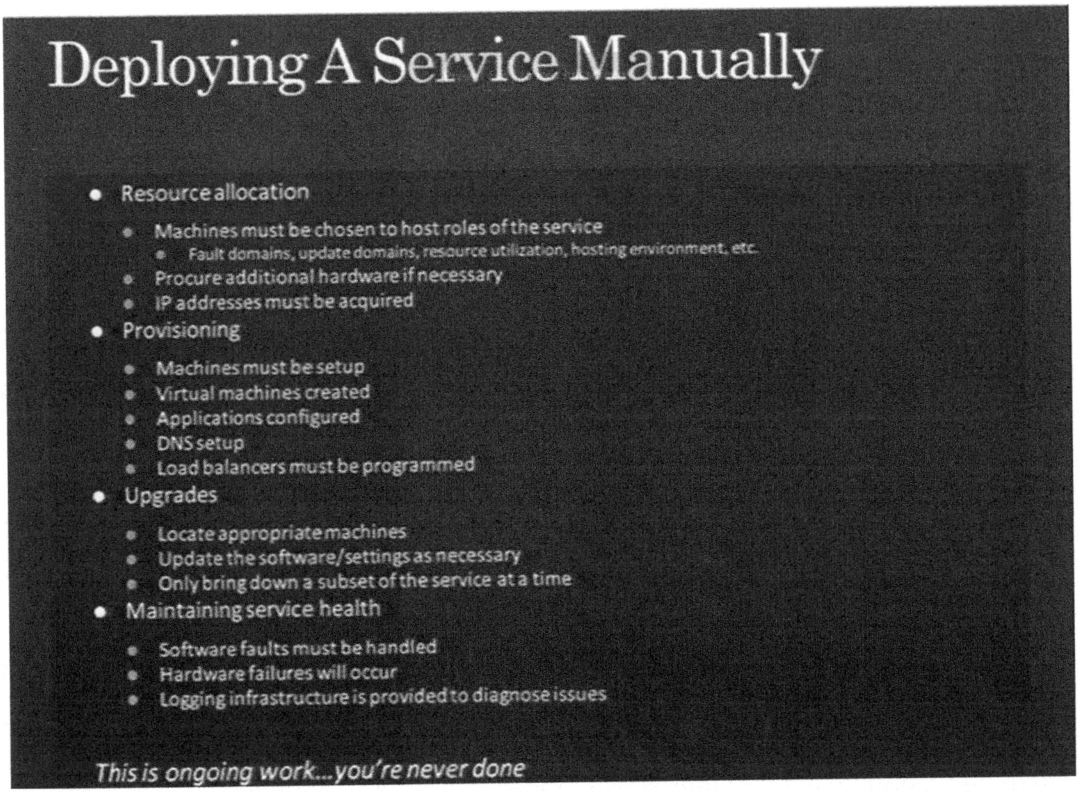

Figure 1-2. *Building your own fabric in a data center*

This slide speaks volumes for what a fabric must support for cloud services at scale. A highly available *fabric controller (FC)* is key to the system. The FC maintains a graph of the inventory of what it manages: computer, Virtual Machines, load balancers, and switches with edges being objects like network cables. One key to the fabric system is the use of a declarative model so the FC takes what you declare and implements it. Very early on, the Windows Fabric in Azure had concepts of high availability such as fault and update domains (I'll describe the importance of these in Chapters 2 and 3 of the book).

Tip   The slide from Figure 1-2 comes from an excellent presentation from the PDC 2008 event which talks about Windows Fabric and the hosting environment of the original Windows Azure service. You can watch this presentation at `https://channel9.msdn.com/blogs/pdc2008/es19`. Another good resource I found on some basics of hosting and Windows Fabric comes from an interview with Azure CTO Mark Russinovich at `https://searchcloudcomputing.techtarget.com/blog/The-Troposphere/How-Azure-actually-works-courtesy-of-Mark-Russinovich`.

Windows Fabric is today known as **Service Fabric**. The usage of service fabric is also exposed to applications to host their own services in a Service Fabric cluster. You can read more about Azure Service Fabric at `https://azure.microsoft.com/en-us/services/service-fabric/`.

Note   As you read more about service fabric in this chapter in the book, you will likely see some similarity to another *fabric system* called Kubernetes. If you want to read more about differences between these two systems, this blog post is a good place to start: `https://techcommunity.microsoft.com/t5/azure-developer-community-blog/service-fabric-and-kubernetes-community-comparison-part-1-8211/ba-p/337421`.

To round out the set of *Azure Services*, Microsoft announced the data platform or **SQL Services**, thus beginning the first public announcement of the journey that would become Azure SQL.

The Road to SQL Azure

A big part of the announcement for Windows Azure at PDC in 2008 involved data. Since the CloudDB project in 2006, Peter Spiro, David, Campbell, Ajay Kalhan, Tomas Talius, and the rest of the team had built out a set of cloud services for SQL Server to now host *multi-tenant databases* (or multiple customers in a shared set of SQL Servers).

The first name announced at PDC 2008 was **SQL Data Services (SDS)**. While the news of this service made buzz in the industry, so many customers were focused on on-premises enterprise deployments and our team overall were heavily focused on SQL Server (e.g., shipping SQL Server 2008 code-named Katmai). But internally, the leadership of the company was making a major push for the cloud but not just because they were "told to do this." Ted Kummert said, "We were believers. We believed PaaS was the future, but we were early in the industry for a service like this."

SQL Data Services

SQL Data Services was announced as part of a broader set of services called *SQL Services* which would include DataSync, Reference Data, Reporting, Data Mining, and ETL as seen in Figure 1-3.

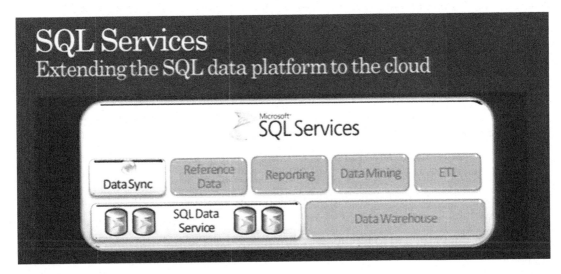

Figure 1-3. *SQL Services at PDC in 2008*

This image came from a slide from a talk presented by David Campbell back at PDC in 2008.

Note   It is interesting to see our intention was to also provide "data warehouse" services which we do today with Azure Synapse and "ETL" which is now Azure Data Factory. "Reporting" never really panned out in SQL Services (but there were attempts), but Microsoft eventually created a very powerful Reporting service called Power BI.

SQL Data Services embodied the ability for developers to host databases for their applications and be completely abstracted from the details of computers, virtual machines, and SQL Server itself. Basically, you create a database; populate it with tables, data, and indexes; and then just start using it. No machine, Operating System, or machine installation required.

Note   The announcement of SQL Data Services can be seen in this blog post: `https://azure.microsoft.com/en-us/blog/microsoft-announces-windows-azure-and-azure-services-platform/`.

The other concept that SDS provided was "database as a utility" or "pay-as-you-go service." That was really the same concept across all of Windows Azure. It represented a shift for customers to use a subscription service to pay for database usage (and the compute and storage that went behind it) vs. a license for SQL Server.

The team learned a quick lesson when it introduced the programming interface as REST API instead of T-SQL. REST stands for **Representational State Transfer** and is a common protocol used for web services. Customer feedback quickly changed that model (but REST API interfaces remain to this day for many aspects of Azure SQL which you will see throughout the book). You can see from this blog post in March 2009 (`https://web.archive.org/web/20140411144147/http://blogs.msdn.com/b/sqlazure/archive/2009/03/10/9469228.aspx`) that the SDS team needed to provide developers and users a "relational data experience" which includes programming interfaces through Tabular Data Stream (TDS). Translation: T-SQL. Other basic features you expect from a SQL Server database had to be there, including indexes, stored procedures, triggers, views, and so on.

Since the SDS and Windows Azure teams were innovating at the same time, the SDS team had to figure out a hosting system for databases and SQL Server. The Windows Fabric was being built as the SDS team was innovating. The decision was made to use a hosting system that already existed at Microsoft instead of using Windows Azure. That platform was called *AutoPilot* (you can read more about the AutoPilot system at `www.microsoft.com/en-us/research/publication/autopilot-automatic-data-center-management/?from=http%3A%2F%2Fresearch.microsoft.com%2Fapps%2Fpubs%2Fdefault.aspx%3Fid%3D64604`) built by the team running the Bing Search Service. AutoPilot was effectively a platform to provision "bare metal" computers in a scaled fashion. SDS *clusters* would physically be co-located with Windows Azure clusters, but SDS managed their own systems.

AutoPilot just provided software services to deploy and maintain applications on bare-metal servers at scale. The SDS team had to build their own set of services for fault tolerance, high availability, and connectivity. The SDS team built their own *fabric* to deploy, run, scale, and maintain SQL Server instances to host their customer databases. The original design of silos was replaced by "database per tenant" model called *partitions* (not the same as SQL Server partitions), but multiple databases could be hosted on a single SQL Server. Each bare-metal server could also host multiple SQL Server instances.

The other piece of this design to support the concept of a "database service" was to abstract users from the SQL Server instance itself (even though SQL Server instances were used to host databases). Thus, the concept of a "master node" was built into the service to host metadata about the "data nodes." These data nodes had the concept of replicas and fabric controllers. In addition, a front-end service was built where applications would connect instead of connecting to the back-end SQL Server. This would be the early design of what is now known as *Gateway Server* for Azure SQL.

Figure 1-4 shows the original design of the SDS hosting system or *cluster* (this comes from the PDC talk at `https://channel9.msdn.com/Blogs/pdc2008/BB03` from Gopal Kakivaya).

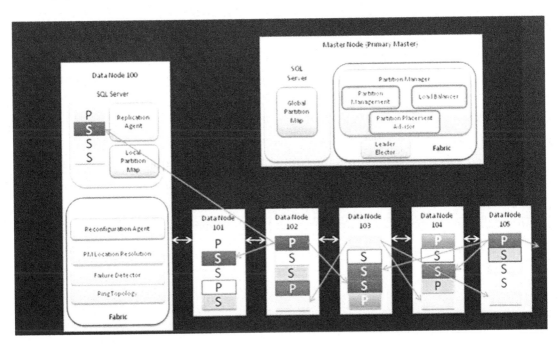

Figure 1-4. *Original SDS hosting design for SQL Services databases*

Fabric processes help coordinate with the overall cluster for failover purposes. So early on, we needed to provide

- The ability to isolate customers with our partition concept but share SQL Servers for density

- Failover logic within the fabric

- Replica sets of data. Sound familiar? (kind of like an Availability Group)

- Access for our databases to underlying storage and networking across the data center but abstracted from users

- A logical "master" database for application databases to support logins and store other metadata

- The ability to collect metrics to gain insight into telemetry and health

- *Watchdog* processes for health detection

The team learned a lot in these early days. Ted Kummert described the challenges of now not just enhancing and building the software but owning all aspects of a "live service," including hardening, quality, availability, development velocity, telemetry, outages, security, and even things like Cost of Goods Sold (COGS) and capacity planning. These early learnings would eventually allow Microsoft to scale to the levels the original team had dreamed about. As Ted described it, "...we were now not just evolving a codebase, but we were evolving as a team and our capabilities all at the same time. It was both an exhilarating and humbling experience."

Another important event in Microsoft's company history happened in 2008. Steve Ballmer then asked a leader within the company to re-invent another cloud service, the Bing Search Service. That leader was a man named Satya Nadella. According to Satya in his book *Hit Refresh*, "Ultimately, Bing would prove to be a great training ground for building the hyper-scale, cloud-first services that permeate Microsoft today."

SQL Azure Is Born

It was a massive effort to move to a market release. Along the way, SQL Data Services just didn't have the right name to many. Therefore, in the summer of 2009, while the service was still in Community Technology Preview (CTP), a branding name change was made from SQL Data Services to **SQL Azure**. The SQL Azure name is still what many call Azure SQL today (just ask Conor Cunningham). The programming and usage model were the same as SDS (except T-SQL and the TDS protocol were adopted instead of REST), the hosting was the same, but the name SQL Azure was the go-to market brand.

On February 1, 2010, it all became official. Windows Azure was officially launched and, along with it, the first truly PaaS relational database service in the industry, SQL Azure (you can read the official blog announcement at `https://blogs.microsoft.com/blog/2010/02/01/windows-azure-general-availability/`). Along with the announcement was a new logo (changing the current SQL Server 2008 logo from red to blue) as seen in Figure 1-5.

Figure 1-5. *The original SQL Azure logo*

In order to interact with Windows Azure, the team had to also snap into a user interface experience called a *portal*. The first version of the Windows Azure portal used HTML, but quickly after this, a new portal experience based on Microsoft Silverlight was adopted. This also included a separate Silverlight "administration" experience for SQL Azure.

Figure 1-6 shows an example SQL Azure management portal based on Silverlight.

Figure 1-6. *The SQL Azure Management Portal*

When Windows Azure launched, the concept of an *Azure datacenter* was introduced to our customers. A datacenter is a physical set of buildings in a specific geographic location where Microsoft hosted Azure services. The names of the datacenters were based on a geographical region (we have since shifted to a concept of *regions* and datacenters which I'll explain later in this chapter and in other places in the book). At the original launch of SQL Azure, customers could deploy databases in datacenters with names of North Central US, South Central US, East Asia, and North Europe.

The original SQL Azure had some interesting characteristics:

- We launched with a business model that had two *editions*: Web and Business. The basic difference was the maximum database size: 1Gb for Web and 10Gb for Business (as you will see in this book, you can create sizes much larger than this now). We quickly bumped this up to 50Gb by June 2010.

- In order to deploy a database, you would deploy first a *logical database server*. Multiple databases could be associated with a logical server. The logical server also contained other metadata such as logins and firewall rules for security.

- Any table in a database was required to have a clustered index.

- We used our own internal "replica system" but ensured that we always kept three replicas available. We also automated processes like backups and kept multiple copies.

- We updated the software for SQL Server through a concept called a Service Update (SU) and made announcement about these updates in blog posts (an example blog post for a service update can be found at https://web.archive.org/web/20140420195848/http://blogs.msdn.com/b/sqlazure/archive/2010/02/17/9965464.aspx).

- We introduced the concept of a Service-Level Agreement (SLA) to ensure a level of database availability.

- Early on we developed an integrated experience with the popular tool SQL Server Management Studio (SSMS).

- Customers struggled with concepts like application retry logic, new error messages, logical master, throttling, and inequality with the T-SQL surface area of SQL Server.

Note   If you want to step back in time and see some older blogs about SQL Azure, visit https://web.archive.org/web/20140410165353/http://blogs.msdn.com/b/sqlazure/default.aspx?PageIndex=1 and traverse the links at the bottom of the page.

In these early days for both Windows and SQL Azure, it was even a new world within Microsoft. Buck Woody worked on the original Windows Azure teams. He told me that working on Azure was in a group at Microsoft called "Incubation" – a startup-like culture. "One of the most interesting parts of that," he said, "was seeing everything getting built in the technology, and in the business side. It was probably the best MBA I ever got." In Incubation, you were "walled off" from the rest of Microsoft, having your own engineers, sales, marketing, and the like. When the product showed a profit and all the business processes were established, it "graduated" to the rest of the field at Microsoft. Some products graduated, and others didn't – so there was a lot of pressure to succeed.

The SAWA Project

To this point in time, SQL Azure still was deployed and ran using the AutoPilot cluster system with SQL Server instances hosted on bare-metal servers (Brian Chamberlain, one of the principal engineers for Azure SQL, calls this internally SQL Azure v1).

We knew as a team we needed to snap into the Windows Azure hosting system which uses virtual machines to deploy services. We needed to take more advantage of what Windows Azure offers for deployment, networking, and storage without making wholesale changes to the SQL Azure architecture. Therefore, a project was born called **SAWA** (SQL Azure on Windows Azure). Brian calls this SQL Azure v2. In order to help abstract the team from having to deploy on both AutoPilot and SAWA systems, we built a software layer code-named **Blackbird**.

The SAWA project was important because it would allow the team to eventually become a full-fledged Azure service, taking advantage of everything internally that Windows Azure provides to services. But for a few years, the team operated and managed SQL Azure databases deployed on both AutoPilot and SAWA. Users didn't see the difference. The service still looked and behaved the same.

For the next few years, Windows Azure offered compute services through Cloud Services and database services through SQL Azure. The SQL Azure team had also added other engineering leaders to the team including Nigel Ellis and Peter Carlin. It was the beginning of the journey, but Microsoft leadership was behind the scenes already working on changes and bigger things to push Azure further in the public cloud.

The Virtual Machine Initiative

When Windows Azure first released, among the primary target solutions were scalable web applications in the cloud. Therefore, Cloud Services was the first compute service in Windows Azure. As I described in the preceding section on Windows Azure, Cloud Service applications ran in virtual machines and had the ability to store data in SQL Azure or in Azure Blob Storage using APIs. But application developers did not have access to any local storage or full virtual machine access. The concept of a virtual machine in the cloud as a service, also called **Infrastructure as a Service (IaaS)**, had been introduced by Amazon in 2006 called Amazon Elastic Compute Cloud (EC2) as part of their overall Amazon Web Services (AWS) suite. EC2 was literally a virtual machine where you can deploy your choice of operating system and application.

For many, Cloud Services in Windows Azure was still thought of as Platform as a Service (PAAS) since developers didn't really have access to the entire guest VM or concepts like local storage. Our Windows Azure team knew we needed something to compete with EC2 and make IaaS a big part of Azure.

In 2011, Microsoft decided to make a bold move in leadership. Steve Ballmer wanted to make big bets in the cloud including Azure. He asked Satya Nadella to move from his current position leading the Bing team to run the division at Microsoft called Server Tools and Business (STB). This was the chief enterprise software group at Microsoft that ran Windows Server, SQL Server, and Windows Azure. As part of his role in taking over STB, Satya did several key things. First, he hired Scott Guthrie to lead the engineering efforts for Azure. Scott is now the leader of Cloud and Enterprises, also known as C&E, which used to be STB. Second, he hired Jason Zander to lead the Azure core infrastructure team. Jason is now the leader for all of Azure. And third, he empowered Azure CTO Mark Russinovich to build the road map for the future. And one of the first bold moves of this team was to launch into preview Azure Virtual Machine (VM) to provide a true IaaS service offering for Windows Azure.

One of the first key workloads to showcase Azure Virtual Machine would be SQL Server. I remember these early days of Azure VM as I was assigned in Microsoft support to look at the supportability of SQL Server in this environment. It was at that point I met the lead program manager for SQL Server on this effort, Guy Bowerman.

When Guy joined the SQL team around June of 2010, he found out about Cloud Services with worker and web roles, but also saw we had announced the concept of a *VM role*. A VM role allowed a user to upload a Virtual Machine image (VHD) and run their VM. However, the VM role didn't provide the richness of a true IaaS solution. The VM role, for example, did not provide local persistent storage for the operating system or attached persistent drives.

Throughout 2011 and 2012, the Windows Azure team worked with groups like SQL Server to launch a new Azure Virtual Machine preview program (you can read more about the preview launch at Preview of VM announced in June 2012, `https://azure.microsoft.com/en-us/blog/announcing-new-windows-azure-services-to-deliver-hybrid-cloud/`). Azure Virtual Machine was officially launched in April of 2013 (you can read more about the launch at `http://up2v.nl/2013/04/16/windows-azure-virtual-machines-is-now-general-available/`). Azure Virtual Machine was a significant move for Microsoft. "Opening up" the Virtual Machine now allowed users to deploy the operating system of their choice including Linux (this move would set the stage for a little project you may have heard about called Helsinki or SQL Server on Linux).

The new Azure Virtual Machine platform provided all types of benefits for running SQL Server including a dedicated "OS disk," a temporary disk for storing files like tempdb, and persistent storage for SQL Server database and log files called *data disks*. Even though the choices were limited, there were various Virtual Machine *sizes* customers could choose to deploy SQL Server, including the number of CPUs, memory, number of disks, and maximum capacity. In addition to providing these choices for the virtual machine configuration, the Windows Azure team provided a system where teams like SQL Server could provide customer choices for a fully deployed virtual machine with SQL Server pre-installed through a concept called *gallery images* or a *marketplace*. Now a user could choose a virtual machine configuration, a version of SQL Server, make a few other choices, click a button, and within 10–15 minutes have access to a fully deployed SQL Server in a virtual machine hosted in Azure. You could then use a program like Remote Desktop, connect into the VM, and off you went. In addition, Azure Virtual Machine services included SLAs and availability sets (update and fault domains).

The initial launch of Azure Virtual Machine used the same Windows Fabric that hosted Cloud Services. The SQL Server team was effectively an "internal customer" of Windows Azure to deploy virtual machines. The main interface and system in place for the SQL team to deploy was called RDFE (Red Dog Front End). This system later affectionally became known as *classic* Virtual Machines. Today, the classic system is rarely longer used in favor of the Azure Resource Manager (ARM) system, which you will learn more about in various places in the book.

While the initial Azure Virtual Machine classic system was popular with customers, it presented issues for the SQL Server team. Disk performance stood out as an issue and I remember in the early days of Azure VM as a Microsoft support engineer working with customers on trying to solve these problems. In addition, using RDFE presented some challenges to deploy virtual machine with SQL Server and provide robust programming interfaces to deploy and manage virtual machines.

Still the service was popular and important to the success of SQL Server in Azure. Now customers who didn't feel that SQL Azure could meet their requirements had another choice. They could still host a SQL Server in the public cloud in Azure with Virtual Machines. As Guy told me, "The SQL Server on Azure VMs offering proved to be one of the most popular and successful offerings after the announcement of Azure VM."

Becoming Azure SQL Database

By the summer of 2012, Microsoft started branding SQL Azure as **Windows Azure SQL Database**. There was no official branding news that I could ever find. My research and internal discussions on our teams were that we just decided to start calling the service **SQL Database** to highlight the fact that the service is all about "Database as a Service" abstracting the details of SQL Server instance from the user.

In 2014, Microsoft changed the branding of Windows Azure to **Microsoft Azure**, or just Azure, so the current name of Azure SQL Database came to life.

Note   The branding of Microsoft Azure was significant to the future of Azure. Windows was and still is a dominant force for operating systems. However, since the launch of Azure Virtual Machine, we had seen an uptick in the number of deployments for virtual machines running Linux. With the branding of Microsoft Azure or just Azure, we were sending a signal to the industry that Azure is more than just a Windows cloud.

As SQL Azure started to mature, other engineers from the "traditional" SQL Server team started to come on board including Conor Cunningham. One of Conor's goals was to work directly with customers to make them successful with SQL Azure. This included internal customers such as **Team Foundation Services** (TFS). Conor to this day still works with TFS (which has morphed into Azure DevOps) and their success with Azure SQL. According to Conor, "They are one of our best ISVs using the platform and they help us make SQL Azure better every day."

There were also important external customers who wanted to harness the power of Azure. One of the largest and most notable customers Conor and many on the team worked with was **Pottermore**. Around 2012, all the Harry Potter movies had been released, but the popularity of the books and movies was massive. Therefore, the Pottermore company decided to build a website experience for fans. And they chose Windows Azure and SQL Azure to power the website experience (see the full story at
`https://news.microsoft.com/2012/06/06/pottermore-new-website-based-on-the-hugely-popular-harry-potter-books-uses-windows-azure-to-scale-up-to-1-billion-page-views-in-first-two-weeks/`).

Note   Pottermore (see `https://en.wikipedia.org/wiki/Pottermore`) is actually a company, and the previous Pottermore website is now officially wizardingworld.com.

Pottermore was an interesting test for the SQL Azure team. This project involved many databases and concurrent users. As Conor tells it, "We clearly didn't want to disappoint all the Harry Potter fans of the world, but we also learned a lot about how to design things that scale." As with any innovation, projects like these were ambitious but also became a foundation of knowledge to improve the future.

Microsoft support also experienced big shifts to deal with the cloud. My longtime colleague and friend Keith Elmore (the famous author of the popular ostress tool), now a Principal Engineer for Microsoft CSS, was involved in Azure support from beginning. He told me that supporting Azure had some interesting challenges but also opened new possibilities. Keith said, "There was a major shift in how we could troubleshoot. We no longer had to ask customers to capture a lot of troubleshooting data as we did in the on-premises environment, but could immediately access a large set of Azure telemetry to assess the general nature of their problem, and often narrow down the specific issue." Supporting the cloud though presented a new expectation from customers to deliver a solution fast. Microsoft now owned the "back end" so data that customers normally had completely control over obtaining was not possible for them in Azure. According to Keith, "the expectation of resolving a large percentage of your support cases in a day or less was radical. The team rallied around how we could organize ourselves and leverage this Azure telemetry to resolve most issues in one day." You will learn about some of the resources Azure provides customers for support and troubleshooting later in this book.

The Sterling (SAWAv2) Project

By 2013 and 2014 timeframe, Azure SQL Database had many different successful customers, but the legacy architecture even running on SAWA was starting to show its age through different problems and customer experiences like TFS and Pottermore:

- As much as we made changes in the infrastructure, one thorny problem cropped up all the time, called the *noisy neighbor* problem. A customer could consume resources for one database that could adversely affect another. We needed a solution where each tenant (database) had their own SQL Server instance. This would allow us to use features like SQL Server Resource Governor.

- We also felt a lot of pressure to open more of the T-SQL surface area for SQL Azure customers. Since multiple tenants shared a SQL Server instance, this was a major problem. For example, how do we present a Dynamic Management View (DMV) of just your database when they by design show anything on the underlying instance?

- We also needed a model where customers would expect more predicable performance since they had no way of choosing things like the number of CPUs, memory, or I/O speed.

- Our codebase for Azure SQL Database was still forked from SQL Server 2005 (yikes!). For the SQL team to become truly *Cloud First*, we needed to merge the codebase of SQL Azure and SQL Server.

- We still used local disks for everything (including user databases, telemetry, etc.) with our own custom replication system. Even with SAWA we were using custom hardware to support large disk needs as all our storage was local using spindles (non-SSD drives). We needed to move toward hardware generations that were aligned with all of Windows Azure. However, the generation of hardware at this time only supported very small local SSD drives. Therefore, we needed a strategy that allowed for "remote" databases using Azure storage.

- The *Windows Fabric* which hosts and powers most Azure services internally has many built-in capabilities to support deployment, scaling, networking, storage, high availability, and fault tolerance. We knew to enable new models and options like Azure Storage for databases, Azure SQL Database needed to become a *WinFab application* (or Windows Fabric application).

As early as 2011, team members including Morgan Oslake were looking to solve the noisy neighbor problem with concepts like *resource reservations* and *node isolation*. Resource reservations were implemented with a concept called a **Service-Level Objective (SLO)**. Even today, you can see the term SLO in some of the diagnostics for Azure SQL. This work led to several innovations which would shape the future.

As Morgan tells it, "The initial solution also set the stage for enabling true scaling elasticity. Incidentally, this project is also where IO Resource Governor was born in partnership with Microsoft Research and the solution was eventually integrated into the SQL Server boxed product."

As SQL Server 2014 was being developed and launched, the Azure SQL Database team internally started working on a project called **Sterling** (also known as project Dearborn or SAWAv2). At this time, SQL Azure was known as *v11* (the @@VERSION string had 11.x in it).

Note   The name of Sterling comes from an interesting source. As Peter Carlin tells it, "The name of the project was supposed to be after Stirling, a well-known efficient heat engine invented by Robert Stirling in the 1800s. Ironically, the project name got misspelled to Sterling, but the name stuck."

For the team, Sterling effectively became a rewrite of the architecture of the service while still maintain the principles of a database service for customers. The next generation of Azure SQL Database would also get a "version bump" to highlight this new architecture called **v12**. v12 also included a merge of the SQL Server codebase. Code fixes and new features could be done in a single branch that would be used for both SQL Server and Azure SQL Database. The v12 name was confusing for customers because it did not line up to a specific version of SQL Server. We named it v12 because with this new architecture, we opened more SQL Server features like columnstore and instance-level diagnostics. We didn't want to break applications so changed the major version to v12 (which corresponded to the SQL Server version number 12.x of SQL Server 2014). Since this time, Azure SQL Database has become a *versionless* SQL Server, which I'll describe more in Chapter 5 of the book.

Rohan Kumar, the current Vice Present of Azure Data Engineering, was leading engineering efforts in Azure SQL around this period. He says about the codebase merge, "Probably the most important decision technically we made was to unify the codebase." In fact, Rohan was assigned to lead this project which took some 18 months while we were maintaining and running the service and delivering releases of SQL Server at high quality.

The Sterling architecture involved running the SQL Server instance (and other needed programs) as a WinFab application or effectively as worker roles in the Windows Azure nomenclature. One interesting aspect to the deployment of Azure SQL Database for Sterling was that only a single virtual machine is used per host with one or more SQL Server instances, each hosting a tenant database. The Sterling architecture is in use today for Azure SQL Database.

Note   You will see later in Chapter 4 of the book that Azure Managed Instance can combine more than one virtual machine per host.

Figure 1-7 comes from a diagram Peter Carlin built to show the primary difference between the SAWA (and AutoPilot) and Sterling architectures from a SQL Server instance, logical server, and database perspective.

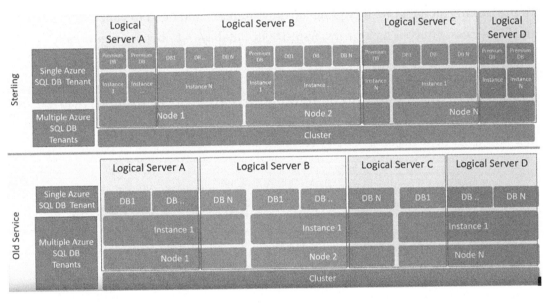

Figure 1-7. *Sterling architecture database isolation*

In this diagram, a Node is a virtual machine or server. An Instance is a SQLSERVR. EXE instance. The Cluster is a logical collection of machines hosting virtual machines. A logical server is a really a set of metadata describing the collection of databases.

Notice in the "Old Service" (SAWA and AutoPilot) that databases from two different logical servers could be deployed on a single SQL instance. With Sterling, each instance was reserved for a single logical server, but multiple instances could (but don't have to) be deployed on a single virtual machine (or node).

Note   Today almost every Azure SQL Database has its own dedicated SQL instance with a few exceptions, which I'll cover in Chapter 4.

Using the Windows Fabric also allowed us to provide better resource governance closer to the operating system, provide direct connections to the back-end SQL Servers, and leverage Azure Storage for databases and backups. The Windows Fabric also provided architectures for fault tolerance and networking in the form of *clusters, nodes,* and *rings.* You will learn more about these concepts as well as other aspects of the Azure SQL Database architecture throughout the rest of this book. You will also learn in this chapter and the rest of the book how we have created other deployment options based on the Sterling architecture including Elastic Database, Managed Instance, Hyperscale, and Serverless. After a long journey, Azure SQL Database V12 becomes generally available in the spring of 2015.

In addition to work on Sterling, Microsoft Azure had pivoted to a *new portal experience* based on HTML (moving away from Silverlight) for all Azure services including Azure SQL Database. Figure 1-8 is a snapshot of Scott Guthrie showing off the new portal in one of his blog posts' archives.

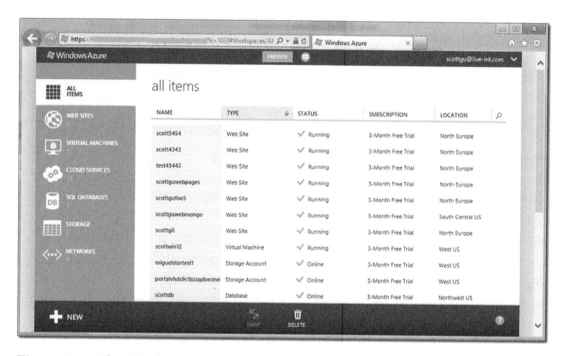

Figure 1-8. *The Windows Azure admin portal*

Tip   Given Scott Guthrie's long role in Azure, the archives of his blog are incredible to tour the history of Azure! You can find them at `https://weblogs.asp.net/scottgu/archive`.

New Editions, the DTU, and Previews

Independent of the new V12 architecture, we also had realized the current editions of Azure SQL Database, Web and Business, were outdated both from a payment model and a predictable performance and choice perspective.

The SLO work that had started before Sterling ultimately led to a preview of a new edition called **Premium**. In some cases, Premium customers were isolated to a single node to provide maximum performance. Along with the Sterling architecture, the concept of resource reservations and node isolation pave the way for a new edition suite and a self-service method to choose *sizes*.

In April of 2014, we announced a new pricing model based on new editions, **Basic, Standard, and Premium** and concept to materialize sizes called *performance tiers*. Performance tiers offered granularity within an edition for maximum database size and a SLO. In order to support a SLO, we introduced a new concept called a **Database Transaction Unit (DTU)**. We started this new model with a preview of these editions and tiers in April 2014. By this time, we allowed up to a 500 GB for Premium editions.

See the blog post and video of ScottGu talking about these new models at `https://weblogs.asp.net/scottgu/azure-99-95-sql-database-sla-500-gb-db-size-improved-performance-self-service-restore-and-business-continuity`.

A DTU was a logical concept of measurement for a combined resource usage of CPU, I/O, and memory. The idea was to provide a metric to obtain more predictable performance and pay for resource usage. You will learn more details about SLO, tiers, and DTU throughout the rest of the book. By spring of 2015, we had also announced the retirement of Web and Business editions and had fully rolled out Basic, Standard, and Premium editions.

With these new editions, we also introduced the concept of self-service database restore (Point-In-Time restore or PITR) and active geo-replication (our way of introducing Always On Availability Group replicas in the cloud). See more information about this capability and the new tiers announcement with this Channel 9 video featuring former Microsoft program managers Tobias Ternstrom and Tony Petrossian (instrumental during these years for Azure SQL), `https://channel9.msdn.com/Series/Windows-Azure-Storage-SQL-Database-Tutorials/Scott-Klein-Video-01`.

Another concept introduced during these years (and across all of Azure) was **private** and **public preview**. The SQL Server team had already shifted to the term Community Technology Preview (CTP) vs. "beta" builds before they released a version of SQL Server. New Azure services and enhancements to existing services started rolling out in previews. Since Microsoft hosted the software in the public cloud, they had the ability to *whitelist* specific customer subscriptions to use specific services and even features for services. A private preview required a customer to sign up to gain access to a new service or enhancement. A private preview was often free, limited in availability, and involved direct interaction between engineering and a customer (and the customer was in a non-disclosure agreement with us). A public preview was often open to the public. For a new service, it was sometimes free but most often involved a significantly discounted price. In most cases, for a new feature for a service, public preview was free. Previews allowed Azure teams to move agile and fast, gain customer adoption and feedback very quickly, and eventually move to *General Availability (GA)*. You will learn in this book as a customer how to keep up with previews and announcements for Azure services and enhancements.

Note   You will read terms in the book like "went GA" or "went public preview" to note when a service or feature was released.

The preview system also was a great example of a new approach for the SQL team, namely, a *cloud first* approach. Cloud first means that the SQL team could build out a new service or feature first in the cloud and then eventually allow that feature to appear in the next major release of SQL Server. Previews combined with a merged SQL codebase allowed for these types of motions to happen.

As Peter Carlin tells it, with the cloud first approach, "...we use service telemetry to learn what is wrong and needs to be improved, use that telemetry as we build and refine it via iterative deployments and then when we know it works well for the scenarios."

Intelligent Performance and the MDCS

By the 2013 timeframe, the SQL Engineering team had hired resources outside of Redmond. Microsoft had built a development center in Serbia called the Microsoft Developer Center Serbia (MDCS). You can read more about MDCS at `www.microsoft.com/sr-latn-rs/mdcs`. Our Azure SQL Database team assigned engineers from MDCS to form a data science team. One of the first tasks for this team was to investigate how to provide *value-added services* for Azure. Azure SQL Database was launched as a true PaaS service. Abstracting the developer from the details of SQL Server was important, and providing built-in HA and predictable performance were critical. However, our team wanted to see what type of additional services we could offer customers as part of the platform.

Performance is perhaps one of the toughest problems within SQL Server to solve given how vague an issue can be (ever heard of "it is just slow"). Add to that the open nature of T-SQL and databases (bad indexes + bad queries = poor performance). Engineers Vladimir Ivanovic and Miroslav Grbic embarked on a project to see how Machine Learning at scale could improve performance for Azure SQL Database. As current team member Miodrag Radulovic tells it, "the original intention was to leverage data science and ML at Azure scale to find a way to improve customer experience of using Azure SQL Database. Performance optimization was identified as one of the areas where the team could deliver pretty impactful improvements, especially for those novice users who are not that skilled in perf optimizing SQL Server engine." Vladimir specifically said that index recommendation for performance was an area the team felt important to tackle. SQL Server had technologies to assist with index recommendations, namely, Dynamic Management Views and a tool called Database Tuning Advisor (DTA). Vladimir says, "We picked index recommendations since the technology was already partially available via missing indexes DMV and also DTA, and our initial analyses showed that a significant number of SQL DB customers could benefit from this."

The work for this project took some time to get it right. The work started in 2014 and was released for public preview in July of 2015 known as *Database Tuning Advisor*. The functionality would use Machine Learning combined with existing SQL Server resources (including the Query Store) to recommend and even auto-create/drop indexes. In January of 2016, the experience went GA and was named Automatic Tuning. You will learn more about the details of Automatic Tuning in Chapter 7 of this book.

Advanced Data Security and the ILDC Team

In addition to adding services for Azure SQL Database for performance, the team wanted to create new experiences for security. Microsoft had formed the first Research and Development Center outside the United States in 1991 in Israel called the Microsoft Israel Development Center (ILDC). You can read more about the ILDC at `www.microsoftrnd.co.il/`.

In 2014, the Azure SQL team turned to the ILDC to look more into security to form a group called the *Azure Security Center for SQL*. When first formed, this group, according to one of the original members Ron Matchoro, was chartered to look at security topics like auditing, data masking, vulnerability assessments, and threat protection techniques.

This work led to several innovations for both Azure SQL and SQL Server. The team first landed the concept of *Dynamic Data Masking* in Azure SQL in 2015 and in the SQL Server 2016 release (read more about Dynamic Data Masking today at `https://docs.`
`microsoft.com/en-us/sql/relational-databases/security/dynamic-data-masking`).

The team then accelerated further by enhancing auditing (SQL Server already had a concept called SQL Server Audit) for Azure SQL, delivering on a method to perform vulnerability assessments (which would also land in SQL Server Management Studio). The ILDC also invested in a concept for data classification which now exists in Azure SQL and SQL Server 2019.

Perhaps the biggest area of investment was in *threat protection*. The concept was to use the power of the cloud to detect possible threats to an Azure SQL deployment and alert administrators. This included concepts like detecting *SQL injection* attacks. This capability went GA with Azure SQL in 2017 as **Advanced Threat Protection (ATP)**. In 2019, the team grouped together a series of capabilities including ATP, Vulnerability Assessment, and Data Classification called **Advanced Data Security (ADS)**. You will learn more about ADS in Chapter 6 of this book. Today, the ILDC continues to work with our teams in Redmond to deliver on new security capabilities for Azure SQL.

A Pane for the Future Called Ibiza

Microsoft also decided around the 2014 timeframe the current Azure portal experience needed a new look (yes again). Project **Ibiza** was a new Azure portal with a completely new look and design. This was effectively the fourth generation of the Azure portal. The Ibiza portal was also known early on as the "Preview Portal." This new portal used a concept called *blades* as a user interface experience. Users reported very early on this portal was more reliable, faster, and an overall better user experience that included a dashboard and pins and supported all the various Azure services.

Figure 1-9 shows the Ibiza portal at launch in 2015. Today it is simply known as the **Azure Portal** (accessed by almost anyone from portal.azure.com).

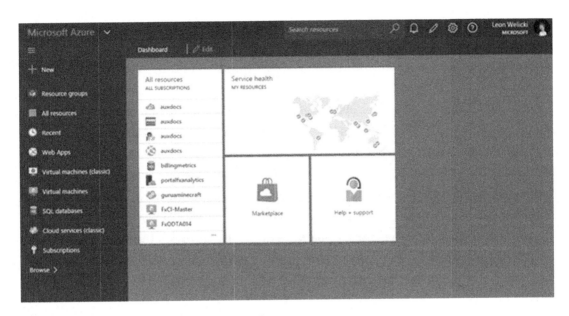

Figure 1-9. *The original Ibiza portal*

You can read more about the launch of the Ibiza portal at `https://azure.`
`microsoft.com/en-us/blog/announcing-azure-portal-general-availability/`. This
portal serves as the foundation of the current Azure portal which you will see throughout
the chapters of this book.

A New Engineering Model for Azure

Even since the launch of SQL Azure, a unique experience existed within Microsoft. For
SQL Server, the engineering team mostly focused on designing and building a new
release. They absolutely take in customer feedback as they build new features or resolve
problems, but their lenses mostly came from feedback forums or Microsoft Technical
Support.

With the launch of a service, the engineering team now owned the operation of SQL
Server in the cloud. They built the software but also managed the operation of a data
center. While other teams owned the overall operation of data centers, the SQL Azure
engineering team owned the health, cost, and operations of the Azure SQL Database
service. This involved all types of proactive monitoring for health and reliability. But it
also meant the team owned updating all the software behind the scenes that powered
the service.

SQL Azure engineers were now involved in *Live Site* experiences (a good reference to read more about Live Site can be found at https://docs.microsoft.com/en-us/azure/devops/learn/devops-at-microsoft/live-site-culture-and-reliability). If an outage occurred, the SQL Azure engineering team was directly involved in resolving the problem. These experiences over time drove innovation and automation. Much of the functionality behind the scenes that is part of the Azure SQL Database ecosystem was built to avoid manual intervention of problems. Even new features introduced both for Azure SQL Database and SQL Server came from Live Site experiences for the team ensuring the service was healthy, applications were performant, and databases were reliable and available. Peter Carlin describes the benefits of Live Site "...basically everything we have built in the last 5 years are driven by learnings from live site. In many ways, we didn't know how to run our own product, and once we realized how hard we had made it, could make the changes to make it much easier to operate - benefiting all SQL DBAs."

As Rohan Kumar tells it, "One of our biggest challenges was team culture. We needed to create a team that could not only build great software but also operationally run it."

By 2015, Azure SQL Database had a robust architecture for the future with v12 and innovation to add value for both performance and security. As new customers built applications with the service, feedback and LiveSite experiences drove future innovation, both for the architecture and new deployment models.

Bending Azure SQL Database

As we announced the introduction of Basic, Standard, and Premium editions and were phasing out Web and Business editions, we had some customers, mostly ISVs, that brought us a dilemma. Web and Business editions charged only for storage, not for compute, but there was no predictable performance. Basic, Standard, and Premium editions were paid by DTU, not just storage. Some ISVs wanted to host many databases, sometimes 1000s, to support their application, many of them Software as a Service (SaaS) applications. The new edition model with DTUs would now become cost prohibitive. Not all 1000 databases needed the same DTU capacity, but more importantly, the needed DTU usage could vary widely across these databases. The only way to support all these databases to provide required performance would be to pay for the maximum DTU needed for any database.

Around the 2014 timeframe, program managers Morgan Oslake and Tobias Ternstrom were assigned to come up with a solution where, according to Morgan, "We (SQL DB) needed a price-perf optimized solution for SaaS ISVs with apps containing 10s, 100s, 1000s, or more databases." Tobias proposed the project named *Malmo* (as Morgan recalls, "...the name was motivated by the observation that Malmo, the city in Sweden, was growing rapidly and bursting in population size. In any case, a concept of Malmo is to more efficiently accommodate bursting episodes of multi-database apps"). The team moved fast to a private preview of the capability for databases to be grouped together called an **elastic pool**. We moved to public preview in April of 2015 and General Availability in 2016. Read the announcement at `https://azure.microsoft.com/en-us/updates/azure-sql-database-supports-large-numbers-of-databases-for-saas-providers/`.

Elastic pools allowed a developer to group databases together in a pool and consume and pay for usage as an elastic DTU or *eDTU*. You will learn more about how elastic pools work in Chapter 2 of the book. Having elastic pool as an offering also helped pave the way to deprecate and remove the Web and Business edition model.

With new editions, the Sterling architecture, DTUs, and elastic pools, many of what customers needed to adopt Azure SQL Database were in place. However, some customers using the SQL Server "box" product were resistant. As we polled and talked to these customers, we discovered the *surface area* of Azure SQL Database didn't meet their core requirements. By 2016, we determined we needed to develop another option to enable more customers to adopt Azure SQL.

Lifting Customers to the Cloud

With the success of the MDCS team working on Automatic Tuning, our team turned to them to work on another project to help reduce the friction from migrating SQL Server instances to Azure. One of the leaders in MDCS, Drazen Sumic, told me the origin of the project. He said, "Lindsey Allen, one or our leaders in Azure SQL, was on a flight back from Microsoft Ignite in 2016 after receiving tons of feedback on Azure SQL and came up with an idea to *lift* customers to the cloud." By December of 2016, the MDCS team was working on project *CloudLifter*.

By 2016, Azure Virtual Machine offered many choices to deploy a full instance of SQL Server. However, a user must still own the management and every aspect of the guest OS and SQL Server. No Azure service existed to provide some of the benefits of PaaS but also *feel* like a SQL Server instance. That is what Lindsey proposed to Drazen and the MDCS team. The team had to find a way to deploy and *expose* a SQL Server instance within the PaaS architecture of Azure including integration with Service Fabric. Users would then connect to the SQL Server instance and use it just like a regular SQL Server on-premises or in Azure Virtual Machine. In addition, the new service still needed to provide the benefits of PaaS, such as built-in high availability and SLAs.

The team spent almost the entire 2017 year in a private preview program for a new service called **Azure SQL Database Managed Instance** (or often called just Managed Instance). Many folks in MDCS worked on this project, including Borko Novakovic, Jovan Cukalovic, Branko Kokanovic, and Milan Novakovic. Public Preview of Managed Instance landed in March of 2018, and General Availability for the first set of tiers was announced at the Microsoft Ignite conference in September 2018 (you can read the announcement at `https://azure.microsoft.com/en-us/blog/azure-sql-database-managed-instance-general-purpose-tier-general-availability/`).

Even though many folks in Redmond were instrumental in this project, including Lindsey Allen, Peter Carlin, and Alexander Vorobyov, this project was an important milestone for the MDCS team for SQL. According to Drazen, "Yes, this was the largest project to date to be driven from the Serbia team. We're proud of it, and thankful for the trust. Previous efforts were also important (e.g., Query Store for the SQL 2016 wave) but were smaller features compared to this one."

Managed Instance solved another aspect for increased cloud adoption, but the ability to handle very large enterprise workloads was still an issue for the team.

Project Socrates Goes Hyper

In the fall of 2015, Rohan Kumar, who effectively owned engineering teams for both SQL Server and Azure SQL at the time, was holding a meeting with many in his senior staff talking about a recent Live Site incident involving a customer when he asked the question to the room "If we had to build an architecture for Azure SQL Database from scratch what would that look like?" It was not like the current Sterling architecture was not good. In fact, the Sterling architecture had allowed Azure SQL to grow significantly.

However, if we wanted to truly run very large sized mission critical workloads, the team thought something different might be needed. Something we could build on top of the existing Sterling architecture. "How can we provide no-limits scale to SQL in the cloud" was the mission Rohan gave the team.

One of the people in that room was Cristian Diaconu, one of the principal engineers who had been instrumental in the Hekaton project for SQL Server (In-Memory OLTP). Cristian talks about those early meetings with Rohan, "So Rohan kept at it saying that he wants us to think about building for the longer term, with more architectural durability and something that we'd be hanging our name to because it was differentiated in the industry."

That meeting led to a series of discussions about a possible new architecture with engineering leaders like Hanuma Kodavalla, Tomas Talius, Donald Kossman, Justin Levandovski, Phil Bernstein, Peter Byrne, Peter Carlin, and eventual engineering leader Naveen Prakash.

Note   You can see a more comprehensive list of team members and contributors from the white paper written for this project at www.microsoft.com/en-us/research/uploads/prod/2019/05/socrates.pdf.

By May of 2016, the team had funding to move forward with their designs into a full-fledged project. They called it *Socrates* (Cristian says that "...as I was meeting a lot of folks with a ton more experience doing this than I, so it dawned on me that all I had were questions – hence Socrates").

The Socrates concept was to build a very scalable architecture in Azure through separation of services like logging and caching services (e.g., page servers). The original Socrates architecture can be seen in Figure 1-10 (from the paper www.microsoft.com/en-us/research/uploads/prod/2019/05/socrates.pdf).

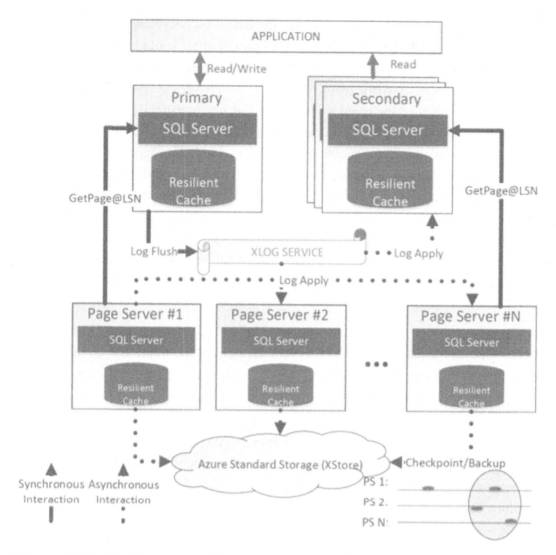

Figure 1-10. *The Socrates architecture*

The team moved quickly to turn their design into working code. By December of 2016, they had a working prototype. However, this architecture was not a trivial project to get right, so it took until September of 2018 to launch a public preview. The name of the new offering would be called **SQL Database Hyperscale** (we technically call this *Hyperscale Service Tier*). By May of 2019, Hyperscale was a generally available service (you can read the announcement at https://azure.microsoft.com/en-us/updates/azure-sql-database-hyperscale-support-for-single-databases-is-now-available/).

Hyperscale literally put Azure SQL on the map at a new level even within Microsoft. Watch Rohan Kumar demonstrate Hyperscale at the keynote with Satya Nadella at the Microsoft Inspire 2019 conference, `https://youtu.be/WtoU8gugP5g`. You will learn more about Hyperscale in other chapters in the book including Chapters 4, 7, and 8.

Azure SQL Today

The evolution of Azure SQL from CloudDB to Hyperscale has been an amazing journey for the SQL team and Microsoft. February 1, 2020, marked the official tenth year of Windows and SQL Azure. However, as the story I've told in this chapter unveils, the origins of Azure go back much farther. Figure 1-11 shows the timeline of significant events in the history of Azure SQL.

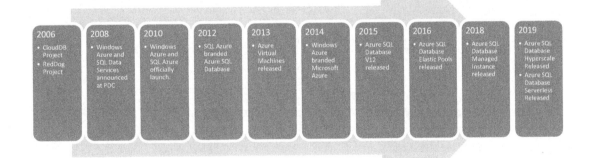

Figure 1-11. *Significant events in Azure SQL history*

What started as shared databases on bare-metal servers supporting only a maximum of 10Gb is now a powerful force in the industry and the future of data services in the cloud called Azure SQL. Azure SQL today even supports the concept of a *serverless database* which you will learn about more in the next chapter. New purchasing models and tiers are available in the form of vCores with new hardware generation options (you can read the

announcement of vCore purchasing models at https://azure.microsoft.com/en-us/
updates/general-availability-vcore-based-purchasing-model-for-azure-sql-
databases-and-elastic-pools/). New security models and monitoring options are now
available. You will learn throughout the rest of this book how to navigate all the flavors and
options of Azure SQL.

Azure itself has grown from a few datacenters in three countries to 58 regions
available in 140 countries worldwide (that number will likely be obsolete by the time you
are reading this book!). Figure 1-12 shows the incredible vastness of Azure across the
globe.

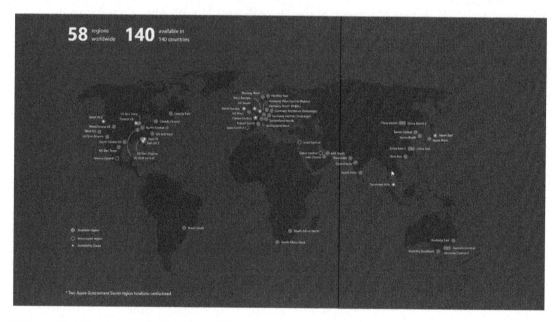

Figure 1-12. *Azure regions worldwide as of early 2020*

Tip   If you want to see an interactive visual map of Azure regions across the
globe, visit http://map.buildazure.com/.

Azure is chartering new territories including Project Natick for a self-sustaining
underwater datacenter (read more about Natick at https://news.microsoft.com/
features/under-the-sea-microsoft-tests-a-datacenter-thats-quick-to-deploy-
could-provide-internet-connectivity-for-years/).

Azure experiences include a robust cross-platform command-line interface called **az** cli (you will see the usage of az cli throughout the rest of this book), enhancements to the Azure portal, and new portal experiences as both a Windows and mobile application (try out the Windows Azure Portal application from `https://portal.azure.com/App/Download`).

Azure and Azure SQL are poised for the future for even bigger things. Azure SQL can be a destination for SQL Server in the cloud. I believe it which is why I decided to write this book. This book is intended to help you navigate how to make Azure SQL a successful destination. The first step in that road to success is to further understand the scope and options for Azure SQL. What do I mean when I say the word Azure SQL? What are all the options for Azure SQL? When and why would I choose one over the other? Read on to get answers to those fundamental questions and more.

CHAPTER 2

What Is Azure SQL?

"Bob, what is the cloud?" I vividly remember over a year ago my beautiful and talented wife Ginger asking me this question when I walked in our kitchen after coming home from work. I paused for a second, getting ready to present my incredible and thoughtful answer, and said, "Well, you see the cloud is...." Fifteen minutes later (as Ginger recalls; I thought it was just a few minutes), Ginger politely interrupted me and said, "Uh...I was kind of looking for the CliffNotes answer?" I was taken back. How can anyone define the cloud as something so simple when it is such a complex topic and provides so much. I couldn't let this go so spent the next few days researching a simpler answer that still defined the cloud. But I also wanted to make sure Ginger knew the answer to the question "What is Azure?"

Turns out Microsoft has an answer for this in the documentation at `https://azure.` `microsoft.com/en-us/overview/what-is-azure/`. **Azure** is defined as "...an ever-expanding set of cloud services to help your organization meet your business challenges. It's the freedom to build, manage, and deploy applications on a massive, global network using your favorite tools and frameworks." I proudly showed this to my wife thinking I have now provided the simple answer she wanted. With a twinkle in her eye (she does that), she said, "That is impressive of course but what?" Leave it to my CEO, Satya Nadella, to save the day for me. He says simply, "Azure is the world's computer" (see the exact quote from the keynote he presented at Build 2018 at `https://news.microsoft.com/` `speeches/satya-nadella-build-2018/`).

I then showed this quote to my wife. She responded "Yes. I get it. If you don't have your own computer just use Azure. Just use the cloud" (maybe, we should hire her). That is what Azure is in a nutshell. Azure defines and provides the promise of **cloud computing** including the following:

- Scale out instead of having to scale up.

- Add and remove capacity on demand.

- Pay for what you use as you go.

- Double down on automation to reduce cost.

© Bob Ward 2021
B. Ward, *Azure SQL Revealed*, https://doi.org/10.1007/978-1-4842-5931-3_2

Note   Microsoft provides a free training course on the concepts of cloud computing at `https://docs.microsoft.com/en-us/learn/modules/ principles-cloud-computing/?WT.mc_id=azureportalcard_ Category_overview_-inproduct-azureportal`. You should also know that this course is part of a suite of free Azure training (400+) you can find at `https://docs.microsoft.com/en-us/learn/browse/?products=azure`.

If this is Azure, then *what is Azure SQL?* This is the chapter to set the foundation for the rest of the book to answer that question. In this chapter, I'll define in more detail Azure SQL and all the "what, why, and how" behind it. However, first, I feel it is important for you to know more about some of the basic elements of Azure.

The Azure Ecosystem

In order to properly understand all the elements of Azure SQL and go through examples in the book, it is important to know certain aspects of Azure independent of Azure SQL. I call this the *Azure ecosystem*. This includes Azure accounts and subscriptions, interfaces such as the Azure Portal and APIs, resource management, regions, and Service-Level Agreements (SLA). This section is not a comprehensive discussion on the topic. I'll provide you enough information (with references) so you can understand terms and systems that Azure provides as you deploy and use Azure SQL services.

Azure Accounts and Subscriptions

One of the most fundamental concepts you need to get started in Azure SQL is an Azure **account**. An Azure account is required to do anything with Azure. You may be working for a company that has already created an account for you. If not, you can create one yourself by following the documentation at `https://azure.microsoft.com/en-us/ account/`. Azure offers a free trial account which you can read more about at `https:// azure.microsoft.com/en-us/free/`.

Note   While you can deploy Azure SQL resources with a free trial account, the credits for this account may not be enough to complete all examples in this book.

Accounts are used as a mechanism for billing and are used to assign owners or members of one or more **subscriptions**. In this book, I will not focus on the details of billing in Azure, but I will talk about various aspects of how Azure SQL services are charged. You can read more about management costs and billing in Azure at `https://docs.microsoft.com/en-us/azure/cost-management-billing/cost-management-billing-overview`.

Subscriptions are a very important concept in Azure. Azure resources and access rights to resources are managed through a subscription. You will learn how to access resources and use an Azure subscription throughout this book. It is possible in your organization you are members of many different subscriptions but have different levels of access within each subscription. You will find out that many Azure resource names are unique within the scope of a subscription (while other names are unique to a scope of an Azure resource or global to the entire Azure system).

Subscriptions also provide a very convenient method to organize resources within an organization (such as production vs. non-production). The Azure documentation has very good instructions on using subscriptions at `https://docs.microsoft.com/en-us/azure/cloud-adoption-framework/ready/azure-best-practices/initial-subscriptions`.

There are also various **subscription offers** that determine how you pay for Azure services. The most basic subscription offer is **Pay-As-You-Go** which you can read more about at `https://azure.microsoft.com/en-us/offers/ms-azr-0003p/`. There are other offers including Free Trial, Enterprise Agreement (EA), Cloud Service Provider (CSP), Enterprise Dev/Test, Pay-As-You-Go Dev/Test, and Monthly Azure Credits for Visual Studio subscribers. You can learn about all of these options at `https://azure.microsoft.com/en-us/pricing/purchase-options/`.

Azure also has the concept of **Management Groups** which allow you to organize and set policies and access to a group of subscriptions in your organization. You can read more about Management Groups at `https://docs.microsoft.com/en-us/azure/governance/management-groups/overview`.

One important security concept in the Azure ecosystem that applies to accounts, management groups, and subscriptions is Azure *Policy*. **Azure Policy** is a system that allows you or your organization to establish policies for management groups and subscriptions (or at a lower level like resource groups which you will read about in the following section called "Azure Resource Manager (ARM)"). Example policies are built into Azure, and others can be created by you. An example of a built-in policy is to require all Azure SQL Databases to enable Transparent Data Encryption (TDE). You can read more about Azure policies at `https://docs.microsoft.com/en-us/azure/governance/policy/overview`.

The Azure Portal

If Azure is the world's computer, then the **Azure Portal** is the *user interface* for the world's computer. You may have read in Chapter 1 the interesting evolution of the Azure Portal over the years. Today the Azure Portal is available through a web browser (`https://portal.azure.com`), Windows application (in preview at `https://portal.azure.com/App/Download`), or mobile application (`https://azure.microsoft.com/en-us/features/azure-portal/mobile-app/`). The Azure Portal is supported on multiple browsers (see the latest supported list at `https://docs.microsoft.com/en-us/azure/azure-portal/azure-portal-supported-browsers-devices`).

Figure 2-1 shows the **Home** page from the latest Azure Portal experience for my account.

Figure 2-1. *The Azure Portal Home page*

Note   In this book, I'll be showing various screenshots of the Azure Portal. Microsoft employees by default use a *preview* of the Azure Portal to help test the latest updates. For the most part, your view of the Azure Portal should look similar, but there could be some differences.

There are several features of the Azure Portal I think you will find important as you see it used in this book and in your own experiences. Figure 2-2 highlights some of these.

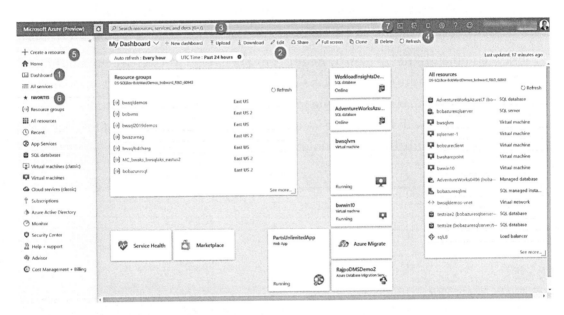

Figure 2-2. *Highlights to use the Azure Portal*

Following the number sequences in the preceding figure, consider these Azure Portal features:

1. **Dashboard** – Select the dashboard to see important resources you have *pinned* (you can pin almost anything in Azure to your dashboard).

2. **Customize** your dashboard – Select Edit to move your pinned resources around and organize them in your dashboard. You can have multiple dashboards.

3. **Search** – You will use this often to search for and find resources and Azure services.

4. **Notifications** – As deploy and manage Azure resources, notifications are provided for progress, failures, and completion events.

5. **Quick create** an Azure resource – Choose this to quickly create a resource from a popular Azure service.

6. **Navigate** to popular Azure objects – Navigate to favorite resource or Azure services.

7. **Azure Cloud Shell** – Open a command prompt for PowerShell or bash within the portal experience.

I'm a "command-line" person by nature (most of us who worked in computers from the 1980s are). The Azure Cloud Shell is simply amazing! The Azure Cloud Shell comes with your subscription, is accessible via the Portal, has many tools pre-installed (e.g., sqlcmd), and comes with free storage for a personal "hard drive" for your files. Figure 2-3 shows an example Azure Cloud Shell for my account using PowerShell.

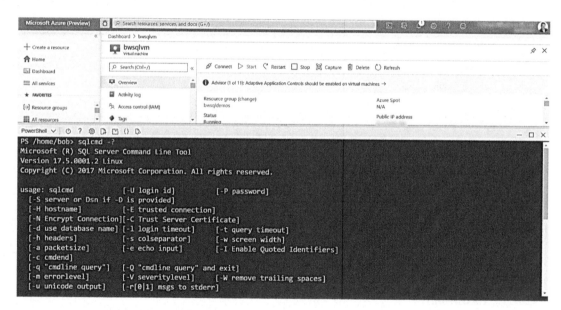

Figure 2-3. *The Azure Cloud Shell*

You can read and learn more about the Azure Cloud Shell at https://azure. microsoft.com/en-us/features/cloud-shell/.

> **Note**   Microsoft offers a free online training course on how to use the Azure
> Portal at `https://docs.microsoft.com/en-us/learn/modules/tour-`
> `azure-portal/?WT.mc_id=azureportalcard_Category_Overview_-`
> `inproduct-azureportal`.

The Azure Marketplace

To deploy or consume an Azure service, you use the **Azure Marketplace**. The
marketplace is a collection of services you can deploy, consume, and pay for. Microsoft
provides many of the services in the marketplace as *publisher* (not all but many
Microsoft services start with the word Azure). The marketplace also has solutions
provided by other publishers, known as partners.

To see a list of services in the Azure marketplace provided by Microsoft, you can
choose the *QuickStart* Create Resource option in Portal as seen in Figure 2-4.

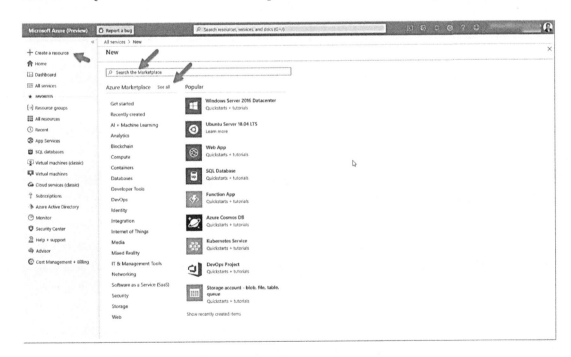

Figure 2-4.   *The Azure marketplace in the portal*

At this point, you can search the marketplace with keywords, pick from categories, or choose from popular services. If you select **See all**, you will get a list of all Azure services in the marketplace by all publishers organized by categories.

Azure services published by Microsoft are also known as **products**. You can see a list of Azure products on the Azure documentation site from `https://azure.microsoft.com/` as seen in Figure 2-5.

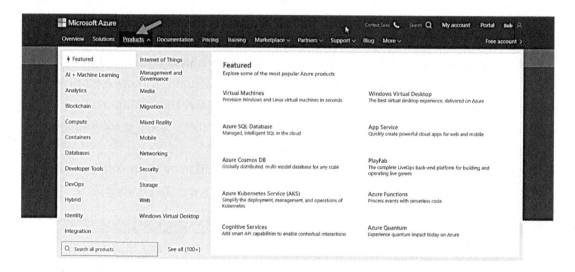

Figure 2-5. *Azure products*

Azure API and CLI

Almost every Azure service has its own application programming interface (API), protocol (TDS, e.g., for Azure SQL), and tools (sqlcmd or SSMS for Azure SQL).

However, a common thread across all Microsoft Azure services is a Representational State Transfer (REST) API. **Azure REST APIs** are service endpoints that support sets of HTTP operations (methods), which provide create, retrieve, update, or delete access to the service's resources. You can think REST APIs are a *low-level core layer* of API across many different Azure services and base functionality (like Azure Resource Manager). You can find more information about the fundamentals of Azure REST API at `https://docs.microsoft.com/en-us/rest/api/azure/`.

Your API usage with Azure services most likely will be at a higher layer using programming languages such as .Net, Java, or Python. Or you may use the Azure command-line interface (CLI) called **az** CLI. The az CLI is cross-platform program used for many different types of operations across a wide variety of Azure services and core operations such as accounts and subscriptions. You can get all the latest information on the az CLI at `https://docs.microsoft.com/en-us/cli/azure/?view=azure-cli-latest`. The az CLI uses Azure REST APIs under the covers.

Tip   You can see a trace of Azure REST API from az CLI by using the --debug option for any az CLI command.

Azure also provides a series of **PowerShell** cmdlets for managing Azure services. You can go to the central hub for Azure PowerShell at `https://docs.microsoft.com/en-us/powershell/azure`.

Azure Resource Manager (ARM)

I've described an Azure service as something you consume or *deploy*. An instance of an Azure service you have deployed can be thought of as a *resource*. Technically, some Azure services result in multiple resources being created as part of a deployment. For example, you might deploy an Azure Virtual Machine, and the result is a virtual machine resource plus other resources associated with the VM such as networks and storage.

The system that supports management of Azure services as resources is called the **Azure Resource Manager (ARM)**. You can read all about the Azure Resource Manager at `https://docs.microsoft.com/en-us/azure/azure-resource-manager/management/overview`. ARM is not a service you consume. Rather it is a system to support your deployment and management of services across Azure.

Every system like ARM is based on *interfaces*. ARM exposes an interface both in and outside of Azure. You might remember the RDFE interface from Chapter 1 that was used previously in Azure (also referred to as the *classic* model). ARM is today the primary system used by tools and APIs including the Azure Portal. Figure 2-6 from the Azure documentation at `https://docs.microsoft.com/en-us/azure/azure-resource-manager/management/overview#consistent-management-layer` shows the interfaces of ARM.

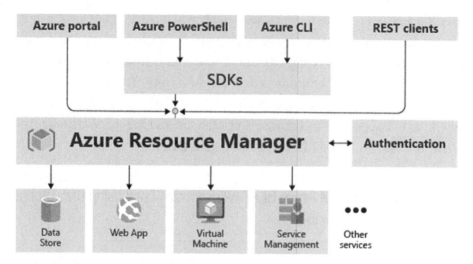

Figure 2-6. *Azure Resource Manager interfaces*

ARM provides many benefits of consistency and management across all Azure services including

- **Resource Groups**

    One of the objects in the Azure ecosystem you will use often are **resource groups**. Resource groups are a logical collection of resources you can manage as a unit. Every Azure resource (e.g., a Virtual Machine or database) must exist in a resource group and can only be a member of one resource group. Resource groups have metadata including a region location (but resources in a group can be in different regions). You can read more about resource groups at `https://docs.microsoft.com/en-us/azure/` `azure-resource-manager/management/overview#resource-` `groups`.

    A resource group is always associated with a specific Azure subscription. Remember that earlier I mentioned that Azure subscriptions are associated with an account and possibly management groups. You can therefore apply Azure policies at the account, management group, subscription, resource group, or resource level.

One nice advantage of managing resources at the group level is deletion. If you delete a resource group, all resources associated with the group are also deleted. You could therefore associate all resources for a proof-of-concept (POC) project with a resource group and then delete the group when you are done, thereby avoiding any unnecessary costs.

- **Role-Based Access Control (RBAC)**

  RBAC is an authorization system that provides access management to Azure resources. RBAC is based on security principals, roles, and scope. Security principals are objects like users associated with an Azure subscription. Roles are collections of permissions based on types such as owners or contributors. Scope is the level of access such as management groups, subscriptions, resource groups, or resources. You will see examples of RBAC throughout this book including Azure SQL specific RBAC objects. You can read more about RBAC at `https://docs.microsoft.com/en-us/azure/role-based-access-control/overview`.

- **Locks**

  Azure locks allow you to prevent users from accidentally deleting or modifying critical resources. For example, you could create a resource group and apply a lock that prevents any user from deleting resources in the group. Valid lock types are CanNotDelete and ReadOnly. You can read more about locks at `https://docs.microsoft.com/en-us/azure/azure-resource-manager/management/lock-resources`.

- **Templates**

  ARM is a *declarative* system. You use ARM by stating your intentions and ARM does the rest. You declare your intentions through interfaces such as the Azure Portal or APIs. ARM also provides an interface mechanism to declare your intentions through a JSON file called a **template**. Templates provide a method to deploy resources consistently, repeatedly, and at scale. I'll show you example templates you can use with Azure SQL throughout the book. You can read more about templates at `https://docs.microsoft.com/en-us/azure/azure-resource-manager/templates/overview`.

- **Activity Logs**

  As you use the Azure Portal or APIs to interact with ARM to deploy and manage resources, your activities or operations are logged in a store called the **Activity Log**. Each subscription has a single activity log that records operations against resources associated with the subscription. Subscription-level events in the activity log are general (like an Azure Policy action) or specific to a resource (like updating an Azure SQL Database). You can read more about Azure Activity Logs at `https://docs.microsoft.com/en-us/azure/azure-monitor/platform/activity-log-view`.

Azure Monitor

SQL Server professionals are used to look at metrics and logged events in tools like Windows Performance Monitor, Windows Event Log, Linux systemd logs, or Grafana dashboards. You will see in this book that Azure Virtual Machine will give you access to all these tools *inside* the Guest Operating System.

However, given Azure is the hosting system for all your Azure resources, it would be nice to have a centralized system for hosting, viewing, and analyzing *metrics* and *logs* of events for all your Azure resources. That in a nutshell is what **Azure Monitor** provides.

You will learn more about how to use Azure Monitor with Azure SQL services throughout this book. You can read more about Azure Monitor at `https://docs.microsoft.com/en-us/azure/azure-monitor/overview`.

Azure Regions and Datacenters

Where does the world's computer exist? While it is perhaps fun to think of Azure existing literally in the clouds, Azure services are hosted in physical buildings called a **datacenter**. You might have remembered in the first chapter of the book that Azure started with four datacenters around the world.

Today, datacenters are not the choice you make to deploy Azure resources. Instead, datacenters are organized around the globe into **regions**. Regions are a group of datacenters connected through a low-latency network. You will see in this book, as you deploy Azure SQL services, you will choose a region as the target for deployment. At the time of writing this book, Azure has 58 regions worldwide available in 140 countries. I have no doubt that by the time you are reading this chapter those numbers will be higher. Some regions have special purposes for specific customers such as *government* or *national* regions. For example, Azure provides special regions throughout the United States called Azure Government regions (you can learn more about Azure Government at `https://azure.microsoft.com/en-us/global-infrastructure/government/`).

A **geography** is a market of two or more regions that preserve *data residency* and compliance boundaries. To ensure further resiliency, regions are sometimes located close enough to be *paired* but far enough in distance for scenarios like natural disasters.

In addition, within some regions, one or more datacenters are grouped in an **availability zone** to prove further high availability for Azure resources. You can learn more about regions, geographies, and zones at `https://azure.microsoft.com/en-au/global-infrastructure/regions/`.

Azure Service-Level Agreement (SLA)

Formal documents called **Service-Level Agreements** (SLAs) capture the specific terms that define the performance standards that apply to Azure.

SLAs describe Microsoft's commitment to providing Azure customers with specific performance and availability standards. There are SLAs for individual Azure products and services. SLAs also specify what happens if a service or product fails to perform to a governing SLA's specification. Azure SQL has specific SLAs that apply to availability and performance which you will learn about throughout this book. You can read more about Azure SLA at `https://azure.microsoft.com/en-us/support/legal/sla/`.

Note   Microsoft provides free training on Azure regions and Service-Level Agreements (SLA) at `https://docs.microsoft.com/en-us/learn/modules/explore-azure-infrastructure/?WT.mc_id=azureportalcard_Category_overview_-inproduct-azureportal`.

What Is the Azure SQL?

Azure SQL represents a suite of Azure services for databases. It is both a collection and a *brand*, including virtual machines, managed instances, and database services. It spans both Infrastructure as a Service (IaaS) and Platform as a Service (PaaS). If Azure is the world's computer, then **Azure SQL is the world's database**.

IaaS vs. PaaS

Infrastructure as a Service (IaaS) is a computing system hosted by a cloud service provider like Microsoft Azure. Users of IaaS deploy and manage a virtual machine while Azure provides the hosting infrastructure for the hardware, including host server, storage, and networking. Azure IaaS services are surfaced through Azure Virtual Machines. Azure SQL has specific options for IaaS customers. You can read more about Azure IaaS at `https://azure.microsoft.com/en-us/overview/what-is-azure/iaas/`.

   Platform as a Service (PaaS) provides all the benefits of IaaS with additional benefits of cloud services usually abstracted from an underlying Operating System or Virtual Machine. The concept is for the developer or user to focus on the application or in the case of Azure SQL a database or instance instead of details of the OS or VM. Typically, a PaaS service provides other benefits to the user, including built-in scalability, high availability, and security. Azure SQL provides two PaaS services, including Managed Instances and Databases. You can read more about Azure PaaS at `https://azure.microsoft.com/en-us/overview/what-is-paas/`.

   One other pivot to the cloud service model is **Software as a Service (SaaS)**. A SaaS user takes advantage of using application software hosted by a cloud service provider. Many SaaS providers use IaaS, PaaS, or some combination of cloud services to support their service. Azure IaaS or PaaS services make the perfect system for many SaaS vendors. SaaS applications were the early pioneers of cloud services in the form of email systems like Hotmail. Today, Microsoft SaaS applications include the famous Microsoft 365 application suite. You can read more about SaaS with Azure at `https://azure.microsoft.com/en-us/overview/what-is-saas/`.

The Azure SQL Lineup

With the concepts of the Azure ecosystem and IaaS/PaaS in mind, Azure SQL consists of the following Azure services: SQL Server on Azure Virtual Machines, Azure SQL Managed Instance, and Azure SQL Database. Figure 2-7 shows a visual of the Azure SQL *lineup*.

Azure SQL

SQL virtual machines	Managed instances	Databases
Azure manages the host and hardware	Azure manages the host, hardware, and Virtual Machine	Azure manages the host, hardware, virtual machine, and SQL Server
You manage the Virtual Machine	You manage the SQL Server	You manage the database
Azure provides value-add services	Azure provides PaaS services	Azure provides PaaS services

Figure 2-7. *The Azure SQL lineup*

There is a purpose to the order of the Azure SQL lineup left to right. As you move left to right, the *friction* is higher to migrate an existing SQL Server application to Azure and your *control* over all aspects to the underlying SQL Server is less. However, this is not a negative thing. As you move right, you *increase capabilities for PaaS or managed capabilities* for databases. There are benefits to abstracting the details of a SQL Server as you will see when you learn all about Azure SQL Databases. As you read about each of these options for Azure SQL, keep in mind these common threads:

- The same SQL Server engine powers each of these options.

- The same T-SQL language you know and love works with each of these options.

- The tools and APIs that you use today with SQL Server all work with each of these options.

SQL Virtual Machines

Officially called **SQL Server on Azure Virtual Machines**, this is your IaaS option to deploy SQL Server in Azure. You should think of this option as the *same as you are using SQL Server in a virtual machine today* except Azure hosts your virtual machine. Azure manages the host servers and hardware system. It provides interfaces for you to deploy a complete virtual machine running Windows or Linux and your choice of SQL Server. SQL Server is a complete edition (Enterprise, etc.) as you would deploy in a virtual machine in Hyper-V or VMware. Your responsibility is to manage all aspects of the Guest Operating System and SQL Server environment. However, because the virtual machine runs in Azure, there are benefits to assist you in managing the SQL Server and Virtual Machine. Instead of providing any further details in this chapter, Chapter 3 is a complete discussion of SQL Server on Azure Virtual Machines.

Managed Instances

Officially called **Azure SQL Managed Instance**, this is an Azure service one level *up* from Azure Virtual Machine. Managed Instance is a *full* SQL Server database engine *instance* deployed as a PaaS service, hence the term *managed*. Azure provides the host server, hardware system, and virtual machines allowing you to focus on deploying and managing a SQL Server instance and set of databases. You will see in this book the benefits of Azure PaaS for Managed Instance, especially in the areas of security, scale, and high availability.

Databases

Officially known as **Azure SQL Database**, this is an Azure PaaS service up another level from managed instance. Azure provides a method to deploy one or more databases and takes care of the host, hardware system, virtual machine, and SQL Server instance. You will see that Azure SQL Database provides many different deployment options to meet some unique database application scenarios. Azure SQL Database provides PaaS benefits in the areas of security, scale, intelligent performance, and high availability.

We are always innovating database services in the cloud. Chapter 13 will discuss new innovations to the Azure SQL lineup.

Azure SQL Managed Instance

I described the history and purpose behind Azure SQL Managed Instance, or **Managed Instance**, in Chapter 1 of the book: make it easier to lift SQL Server applications to Azure (a.k.a. CloudLifter). You should absolutely think of a Managed Instance like a SQL Server *Database Engine instance* today you install on-premises. The install or deploy experience will be completely different as you will learn in Chapter 4 of the book. The experience of setting up the infrastructure to connect and network with the instance will also be different. However, once you have completed these tasks, your experience with Managed Instance will *feel* like a SQL Server instance today.

Note   A Database Engine instance is one type of instance for the SQL Server product. Another type is SQL Server Analysis Services (SSAS) as described at `https://docs.microsoft.com/en-us/analysis-services/instances/analysis-services-instance-management`. A PaaS version of SSAS is Azure Analysis Services which you can read more about at `https://azure.microsoft.com/en-us/services/analysis-services/`.

Today, when you install SQL Server, you have a single *database engine instance* of SQL Server running (see a definition of a database engine instance in the documentation at `https://docs.microsoft.com/en-us/sql/database-engine/configure-windows/database-engine-instances-sql-server`). You also have options to install multiple instances (on Windows; for Linux, you would use containers).

For a Managed Instance, you also will have a database engine instance running in the Azure infrastructure after a successful deployment. You then are free to perform instance-level configuration tasks, create databases, load data, and start connecting and use the instance. You are abstracted from the infrastructure details of how a managed instance is deployed. However, it can be important to know some aspects of how a managed instance is deployed in the Azure infrastructure. You will learn more about the architecture of a managed instance deployment in Chapter 4 of the book.

Managed Instance Capabilities

Since a managed instance is like a **database engine instance of SQL Server**, the *surface area* of the database engine is almost 100% like SQL Server. If these capabilities of SQL Server are important to you, then a Managed Instance may be the best choice:

- SQL Server Agent Jobs

- Database Mail

- Cross-database transactions

- SQL Server Replication and Change Data Capture

- Resource Governor

- Service Broker

These capabilities are not exposed with Azure SQL Database.

Note   We are always updating the capabilities of Azure SQL Database so some options on this list may be available for Azure SQL Database at the time of the publication of this book.

That is not the complete list, and we are constantly adding new features to get Managed Instance as close to a complete 100% SQL Server database engine instance as possible. You can see the latest complete list of differences between Managed Instance and SQL Server at https://docs.microsoft.com/en-us/azure/sql-database/sql-database-managed-instance-transact-sql-information.

Note   This is an exhaustive list of T-SQL differences. Consider in some cases it may not matter. For example, the T-SQL syntax to create and manage availability groups doesn't exist for managed instance. However, this may be just fine for your requirements since managed instance can automatically deploy and manage an availability group for you.

There are major benefits in using a managed instance because it is a PaaS service:

- Built-in high availability (including availability groups), automated backups, Point-In-Time restore, and recovery of deleted databases.

- A 99.99% uptime SLA.

- HADR across Azure regions with Auto-Failover Groups.

- Security isolation with Virtual Network Integration.

- Azure Active Directory Integration.

- Simple and easy-to-use scaling options for resources.

- A *versionless* SQL Server constantly updated with the latest updates and features.

Note   You will learn more details on what a versionless SQL Server means in Chapter 5 of this book.

- Abstraction from the details and maintenance of the host and virtual machine environment.

- Integration with Azure Monitor.

- PaaS security capabilities such as Advanced Data Security (ADS). You will learn more about ADS in Chapter 6 of this book.

As you go through this book, you will be learning in more details about many capabilities of a managed instance. To see a complete list in our documentation, read more at https://docs.microsoft.com/en-us/azure/sql-database/sql-database-managed-instance#key-features-and-capabilities.

Managed Instance Options and Limits

When you install a SQL Server in a Virtual Machine or bare-metal server, you typically have pre-configured CPUs, memory, and storage resources (size and speed).

When you will deploy a managed instance, you will have similar choices to make to meet your resource needs. These choices start with a concept called a **service or pricing tier**. For Managed Instance, the two service tier choices are **General Purpose** and **Business Critical**.

These tier choices will dictate your performance capabilities, resource limits, and in some cases feature capabilities. You will see more details about how to pick these tiers in Chapter 4 of the book (and you will also see the same service tier names, plus more, with Azure SQL Database). Here is a quick tour of each of these service tiers for an Azure SQL Managed Instance.

General Purpose

General Purpose is a service tier choice for most Managed Instance deployments, hence the term *general*. General Purpose service tier supports *vCores* from 4 to 80 (remember numbers like these can change over time as we add more capabilities for Azure). You should think of vCore as a logical CPU for your Managed Instance. Managed Instances are charged based on your vCore choice (at a fixed cost per hour).

Your choice of vCore affects other capacity choices or limits for General Purpose, including maximum memory, maximum storage for databases for the instance, and resource rates such as Input/Output Per Second (IOPS) or Log Write throughput.

General Purpose tiers also provide *basic* built-in high availability using Azure Storage (think of Failover Cluster Instance) which you will learn more about in Chapters 10 and 11 on Availability.

Even though a managed instance has an almost full feature set of a SQL Server, a General Purpose service tier does not support In-Memory OLTP. One of the reasons behind this is the storage requirements for In-Memory OLTP that can be only met on local storage.

You can read all the capacities and limits for a General Purpose Managed Instance at https://docs.microsoft.com/en-us/azure/sql-database/sql-database-managed-instance-resource-limits#service-tier-characteristics.

Note   Columnstore indexes, which are considered another in-memory technology, are available with General Purpose tiers.

Business Critical

Business critical has all the maximum capacities you need for a managed instance. Business critical choices have the same number of vCores as General Purpose but have these unique characteristics:

- Built-in High Availability with replicas using Always On Availability Groups (1 read replica is included)

- High-speed low-latency I/O using local storage

- In-Memory OLTP

- Higher IOPS and I/O throughput rates than General Purpose

It is important to know that today since Business Critical uses local storage, your maximum database size is less than a General Purpose service tier.

There are a few limits for managed instances for a given subscription in a region (e.g., total number of vCores). You can read about these limits at `https://docs.microsoft.com/en-us/azure/sql-database/sql-database-managed-instance-resource-limits#regional-resource-limitations`.

You will learn various aspects of both service tiers for managed instance throughout the rest of this book.

Managed Instance Pools

One of the interesting aspects of Managed Instances is the deployment architecture, which is a *virtual cluster* built for a new managed instance. You will learn more about the architecture of a Managed Instance in Chapter 4 of the book. For now, know that this type of deployment can result in a much longer time to deploy new managed instances than an Azure SQL Database. In addition, because of the nature of deployment, the smallest CPU choice for a Managed Instance is 4 vCores.

Therefore, we now allow the concept of a **Managed Instance Pools** (in Public Preview at the time of writing of this book; you can read the announcement at `https://azure.microsoft.com/en-us/updates/azure-sql-database-instance-pools-are-now-in-preview/`).

A Managed Instance pools provide all the same capabilities as a Managed Instance except they allow for smaller instance deployments (2 vCores) and provide a method to deploy instances much faster. You will learn more about the architecture differences between a Managed Instance and a Managed Instance Pool in Chapter 4 of the book. To read more now about a Managed Instance Pool, you can read the documentation at https://docs.microsoft.com/en-us/azure/sql-database/sql-database-instance-pools.

Managed Instance vs. SQL Server on Azure Virtual Machine

As you have read about SQL Server in an Azure Virtual Machine and Azure SQL Managed Instance, it might be clear to you the main differences between these Azure SQL options. However, let me provide a quick summary so you can make decisions on which option you might choose.

SQL Server on Azure Virtual Machines is your best choice

- If you need to **migrate quickly** to Azure from an existing SQL Server installation. This is really a *lift and shift* of your SQL Server (which most likely is already installed in a VM) to a different VM hosting system. You will learn more in Chapter 3 about optimizing this experience and configuration.

- If you need **full SQL Server box** capabilities like Filestream, Distributed Transactions (DTC), Simple Recovery databases, and SQL Server Analysis Services (SSAS).

- If you want **complete control of the Operating System and SQL Server**. This includes SQL Server versions back to SQL Server 2008 and choice of Windows, Linux, or Containers.

Tip   Before you think you absolutely need full control of the version of SQL Server, *carefully study all the capabilities of a Managed Instance*. It may have everything you need for your SQL Server; moving away from having to depend on a version of SQL Server or having to manage the Guest OS can be a good thing!

- **Capacity can be a factor**. If you need more than 80 vCores (remember this could increase as we improve Managed Instance), 400Gb memory, or a database bigger than 8TB. In addition, Managed

Instance may limit things like transaction log rates depending on your deployment choices. SQL Server on Azure Virtual Machine has no limits on transaction log rates within the engine. The only limit would be the I/O rate applies to storage for the virtual machine.

Note   Azure SQL Database can offer more vCores, memory, and database size which you will learn about in the section of this chapter called "Azure SQL Database."

If these factors are not critical for your requirements, there are big advantages to use Azure SQL Managed Instance since this is a database engine instance with almost full SQL Server engine capabilities combined with the power of PaaS.

Customers Using Managed Instance

One question I often receive about our technologies is "Who else is using this?" For Managed Instance, it is a good question. Is anyone using Managed Instance and why? A great customer case study (and a cool story) I found is **PowerDetails** (www. powerdetails.com/). PowerDetails provides an easy-to-use platform for police officers to find part-time security opportunities that they can pursue off duty. Originally, PowerDetails wanted to build a SaaS model and needed the "power of the cloud." So, they moved their SQL Server on-premises instances to SQL Server on Azure Virtual Machine. This model worked great, but PowerDetails needed more. They needed the full extent of a SQL engine instance but wanted to not spend as much time on management tasks like backups and configuring HADR. They made the move to Azure Managed Instance which now gave them the feel of SQL Server with new PaaS capabilities and ever better SLAs from Azure. As Andy Rivera from PowerDetails says it, "When Managed Instance first came out, we were excited because it felt like we knew how to use it already. Because Managed Instance has near 100 percent compatibility with SQL Server, our team was very comfortable with everything we were seeing." You can read the full customer case study at https://customers.microsoft.com/en-us/story/powerdetails-partner-professional-services-azure-sql-database-managed-instance. It is an interesting evolution of migration story. This customer first moved to Azure with Virtual Machines, and then to get more efficient, they moved to Managed Instances.

Azure SQL Database

As you read in Chapter 1 of the book, **Azure SQL Database** (formerly SQL Azure) is *where it all started*. Even though a database for an Azure SQL Database deployment is installed on an actual SQL Server instance, the concept is to abstract you away from details of the instance and focus on the database. An Azure SQL Database is sometimes called a **single database**. It doesn't mean you won't get exposed to the feel of a SQL Server as you will see throughout the book.

Azure SQL Database Capabilities

Azure SQL Database offers you the most complete PaaS capabilities including the *most options for deployment*. Like an Azure Managed Instance, an Azure SQL Database gives you access to core SQL Server database engine capabilities. However, not all database engine instance features are available. For example, columnstore indexes are available with an Azure SQL Database, but you cannot create SQL Server Agent jobs.

There are major benefits in using an Azure SQL Database because it is a complete PaaS service:

- Built-in high availability (including availability groups), automated backups, long-term backup retention, Point-In-Time restore, and recovery of deleted databases.

- Up to 99.995% uptime SLA.

- HADR across Azure regions with Active Geo-Replication and Auto-Failover Groups.

- Virtual Network Integration and security isolation with Private Link Support.

- Azure Active Directory Integration.

- Simple and easy-to-use scaling options for resources.

- A *versionless* SQL Server constantly updated with the latest updates and features.

Note   You will learn more details on what a versionless SQL Server means in Chapter 5 of this book.

- Abstraction from the details and maintenance of the host, virtual machine environment, and SQL Server instance.

- Intelligent Performance capabilities such as Automatic Tuning. You will learn more about Automatic Tuning in Chapter 7 of the book.

- Integration with Azure Monitor.

- Azure Portal visualizations for query performance analysis.

- PaaS security capabilities such as Advanced Data Security (ADS). You will learn more about ADS in Chapter 6 of this book.

- Integration with other Azure and Cloud services such as Azure Data Sync, Azure Search, Azure Stream Analytics, and Power Platform. You will learn more about these Azure integration options in Chapter 10 of the book.

Azure SQL Database Options and Limits

You have similar but more choices to deploy an Azure SQL Database than a Managed Instance along with different sets of resource limits. Even though you will see more details of how to pick these options and various resource limits in Chapter 4, it is worth reviewing these choices as you evaluate whether Azure SQL Database is the right option for you.

Figure 2-8 shows a high-level decision flow for Azure SQL Database Options.

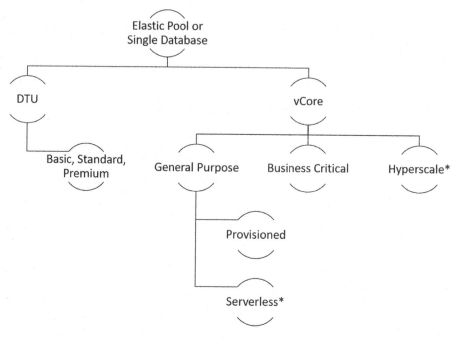

Figure 2-8. *Azure SQL Database Options*

Let's explore the options and each part of this decision process.

DTU vs. vCore

One of the first decisions you will make is a concept called a *purchasing option* for Azure SQL Database. Even though this option will also dictate your resource capacity and limit, it greatly affects how you pay for the Azure SQL Database service.

One option you can choose **Database Transaction Unit (DTU)**. As I described in Chapter 1 of the book, we introduced the DTU concept as a logical concept of measurement for a combined resource usage of CPU, I/O, and memory. Your choice of resource limits and capacities for the DTU choice are DTU levels called Basic, Standard, and Premium (with multiple levels for each of these). Microsoft recommends for most customers to use the vCore model, so I won't spend any other time in this book on the DTU model. You can read more about the DTU model should you want to choose this option at https://docs.microsoft.com/en-us/azure/sql-database/sql-database-service-tiers-dtu.

The vCore model is very similar to the model for Azure SQL Managed Instance and the recommended purchasing model. In fact, using the Azure Portal will show you the vCore options by default. The vCore model gives you more choice of choosing different resources you pay for including CPU and storage. In addition, the vCore model allows you to take advantage of cost savings options such as Azure Hybrid Benefit (AHB) licensing (which you can read more about at `https://docs.microsoft.com/en-us/azure/sql-database/sql-database-azure-hybrid-benefit`) and Reserved Capacity (which you can read more about at `https://docs.microsoft.com/en-us/azure/sql-database/sql-database-reserved-capacity`).

What is different about the vCore model from an Azure SQL Managed Instance is that you now have three *service tier options*: **General Purpose, Business Critical, and Hyperscale**.

General Purpose

Like a Managed Instance, General Purpose is a service tier choice for many Azure SQL Database deployments, hence the term *general*. Unlike a Managed Instance, Azure SQL Database supports two General Purpose options called *Compute Tiers*: **Provisioned and Serverless**.

A provisioned General Purpose choice is very much like General Purpose for a Managed Instance. General Purpose provisioned service tiers support *vCores* from 2 to 80 (remember numbers like these can change over time as we add more capabilities for Azure). You should think of vCore as a logical CPU for your Azure SQL Database. Azure SQL Databases are charged based on your vCore choice (at a fixed cost per hour).

Your choice of a provisioned vCore affects other capacity choices or limits for General Purpose, including maximum memory, maximum storage for databases for the instance, and resource rates such as Input/Output Per Second (IOPS), I/O latency, or Log Write throughput. You can see the details of these limits for a General Purpose provisioned service tier at `https://docs.microsoft.com/en-us/azure/sql-database/sql-database-vcore-resource-limits-single-databases#general-purpose---provisioned-compute---gen5`.

There is another choice for General Purpose provisioned tier called a **Hardware Generation**. At the time of the writing of this book, hardware generation options for General Purpose provisioned tiers are Gen5 and Fsv2 (in Preview). This choice can also affect resource options such as number of vCores. You can read more about hardware generation choices at `https://docs.microsoft.com/en-us/azure/sql-database/sql-database-service-tiers-vcore?tabs=azure-portal#hardware-generations`.

Note   At the time of writing this book, the Gen4 hardware generation was being phased out. Microsoft is constantly looking at providing the best hardware choices that power Azure SQL Databases. By the time you read this book, there could be new hardware generation choices.

General Purpose tiers also provide *basic* built-in high availability using Azure Storage (think of Failover Cluster Instance) which you will learn more about in Chapters 10 and 11 on Availability.

Like Azure SQL Managed Instance, engine features like In-Memory OLTP are not available for General Purpose (but columnstore indexes are supported).

Serverless

The other compute tier option for General Purpose is Serverless. You may remember the story behind Serverless from Chapter 1 of the book. The vCore model still applies to Serverless but in a different way.

You will choose a *range* of vCores which includes a min and a max value (the min can be < 1 vCore). Azure SQL Database will *autoscale* your application to the number of vCores required by the application within this range. One of the advantages of Serverless is that you pay for resource compute usage *by the second* vs. a fixed vCore cost per hour with provisioned.

In addition, Serverless supports the concept of *pausing* the database when it is not in use. If activity for the database is *inactive* within an **autopause delay** interval (which you can configure), no compute charges are billed, only storage costs. This provides an amazing cost savings opportunity for a user who has an application that does not use Azure SQL Database 24/7. We found some customers who are building new applications have natural complete idle times or natural times of different compute scale needs. Serverless provides a natural fit for those customers. Although the capabilities of Serverless are the same as Provisioned, the resource capacities and limits are different. You can read the specific resource limits for Serverless at `https://docs.microsoft.com/en-us/azure/sql-database/sql-database-vcore-resource-limits-single-databases#general-purpose---serverless-compute---gen5`. I personally believed the Serverless model will become one of the most popular choices for many applications using Azure SQL Database.

You will learn how to use Serverless throughout this book. For now, you can read more details about Serverless at `https://docs.microsoft.com/en-us/azure/sql-database/sql-database-serverless#serverless-compute-tier`. You can also see a nice comparison to decide between Serverless and Provisioned at `https://docs.microsoft.com/en-us/azure/sql-database/sql-database-serverless#comparison-with-provisioned-compute-tier`.

Business Critical

Just like with a Managed Instance, Business Critical service tiers are designed for applications that need maximum performance and availability. The differentiators for Business Critical are

- Built-in High Availability with replicas using Always On Availability Groups including read scale-out (with 1 read-only replica).

- Provide further availability protection using Azure Availability Zones. You will learn more about this capability in Chapter 8 of this book.

- High-speed low-latency I/O using local storage.

- In-Memory OLTP.

- Higher IOPS and I/O throughput rates than General Purpose.

- A new compute option called M-Series which offers more vCores and Memory than any other Azure SQL Database option (including Hyperscale).

The SQL Server surface area and T-SQL support (other than In-Memory OLTP) are the same as for General Purpose.

Hyperscale

As you read in Chapter 1 of the book, the Socrates project was a milestone of innovation for the Azure SQL engineering team which launched as Hyperscale.

Hyperscale is an appropriate name given that the reason to consider using Hyperscale is about *scaling*. Consider these facts about why Hyperscale could be your best service tier choice over General Purpose or Business Critical:

- First and foremost is database size. The current documented maximum size of a Hyperscale database is **100TB** and **1TB** transaction log (as with other Azure options, I expect these to change and get bigger over time). Automatic database sizing for Hyperscale database is also extremely fast.

Note   We built the Hyperscale architecture so that it could theoretically support *limitless* database and transaction log sizes.

- The vCore support limits are the same as General Purpose or Business Critical, but the time required for **scaling operations is constant**.

- Read scale is truly *scale*. You get up to **four read replicas** with Hyperscale.

- **Restore** operations are **incredibly fast regardless of size**. Hyperscale uses snapshot backups of database files to provide fast backups and very fast restores.

- Your **transaction log throughput is independent** of your vCore configuration or the fact that Hyperscale has replicas. This is because the replica architecture doesn't rely on Always On Availability Group technology.

- **I/O operations can be extremely fast** especially if they are served by caching systems implemented with Hyperscale.

There are some limitations as of the time of this writing on Hyperscale you should know as you make decisions. For example, Automatic Tuning is not available for Hyperscale. Keep track of the latest known limitations with Hyperscale at `https://docs.microsoft.com/en-us/azure/sql-database/sql-database-service-tier-hyperscale#known-limitations`.

Being a lifelong SQL Server engine internals geek, I believe Hyperscale is one of the most innovative engineering efforts for the SQL team (right along the amazing story of SQL Server on Linux which you can read more about in Pro SQL Server on Linux) in its history. Talking about Hyperscale just in this section doesn't give it due justice so you will read more about Hyperscale throughout this book. But take a few minutes and watch this video where Kevin Farlee, my colleague in the SQL Server engineering team, shows the Microsoft Mechanics team why Hyperscale is so special at `https://youtu.be/Z9AFnKI7sfI`.

Elastic Pool Databases

As I told the story in Chapter 1 of the book, Project Malmo turned into the popular option for software vendors called **SQL Elastic Pools**. Elastic Pools are simply the concept of grouping a collection of Azure SQL Databases for the purpose of lower cost and management of databases.

Think of a scenario where you are a Software as a Service (SAAS) vendor and want to use Azure SQL Database. You decide to build a database for each customer to partition and isolate their performance and experience. You may need to deploy thousands of databases.

Here is your problem. How do you decide which pricing tier to use for each database for each customer when they may not all have the same usage across time? You have two choices:

- Provision all databases with the maximum resource capacity (such as vCores) you think may be needed. In this scenario, you may be overpaying across all databases.

- Provision all the databases with a lower resource capacity which can save you money but might cause issues for you to have to scale up and down specific databases depending on their usage leading to downtime.

Elastic pools allow you to provision (serverless is not available) a General Purpose or Business Critical service tier with a vCore choice (DTU is also possible) and database size that will be used across a group of databases that are added to the pool. This way, you pay for the resources of the entire pool and databases can share resources across the pool.

Databases in an elastic pool can use all Azure SQL Database options except for Serverless or Hyperscale. I won't spend a lot of time in the rest of the book with details or usage of Elastic Pools. I recommend you look at the following resources should you want to use this deployment option:

- Read an **overview of Elastic Pools** at https://docs.microsoft.com/en-us/azure/sql-database/sql-database-elastic-pool.

- Read about **guidance** to pick the right sizes for the pool at https://docs.microsoft.com/en-us/azure/sql-database/sql-database-elastic-pool#how-do-i-choose-the-correct-pool-size.

- Read about how to **manage elastic pools** at https://docs.microsoft.com/en-us/azure/sql-database/sql-database-elastic-pool#using-other-sql-database-features-with-elastic-pools.

Azure SQL Database vs. Azure SQL Managed Instance

As you have read and seen all the options for Azure SQL Managed Instance and Azure SQL Databases, you might have enough information to start making choices. Many customers choose a combination of these options depending on their application needs.

As you make this decision, consider these major factors as differences between an Azure Managed Instance and Azure SQL Database:

- If you need a **database > 8TB**, **Hyperscale** today is your only choice.

- If your deployment requires **Database Engine Instance features** such as SQL Server Agent jobs, Database Mail, Resource Governor, or Transactional Replication, **Azure Managed Instance** is your only choice.

- If your application is very **sensitive to I/O latency**, **Business Critical** service tiers or **Hyperscale** may be your best choices.

- If you need the **highest level of availability and resiliency**, then **Business Critical** service tier is your best choice.

- If your application has a very **intermittent usage patterns** including periods of almost complete idleness, then **Serverless** may be a very good choice for you.

As you look at these factors and still may not be sure whether an Azure SQL Managed Instance or Azure SQL Database fits your requirements, then I would first recommend you look at Azure SQL Database. Azure SQL Database has most of the core database engine features you likely need and provides the highest level of managed service capabilities. I've also found that Azure SQL Database has the fastest deployment and scaling operations across various deployment options.

You still may find that Azure SQL Database does not have the feature set you need. Therefore, I highly recommend you look at this feature comparison in the documentation (which we are always updating) at `https://docs.microsoft.com/en-us/azure/sql-database/sql-database-features`.

A really nice comparison between service tiers across Azure SQL Database General Purpose, Business Critical, Hyperscale, and Azure SQL Managed Instance can be found at `https://docs.microsoft.com/en-us/azure/sql-database/sql-database-service-tiers-general-purpose-business-critical#service-tier-comparison`.

Customers Using Azure SQL Database

Azure SQL Database has been a popular customer choice across a single database, Hyperscale, Serverless, and Elastic Pools.

For example, a great example of a Software as a Service (SaaS) vendor using the power of the cloud including Azure SQL Database is **Teledoc**. Teledoc provides a complete virtual healthcare delivery system. Without Azure, this could not be a viable business operation. Teledoc uses many different Azure services including Azure SQL Database. You can read more about the Teledoc customer case study at `https://customers.microsoft.com/en-gb/story/teladoc-health-provider-azure`.

ClearSale helps major online brands accurately detect fraud and reduce false declines on their ecommerce channels. They wanted to move to the cloud to handle their expanding business but needed the familiarity of SQL Server. The **Hyperscale** option of Azure SQL Database was a perfect choice for them. According to ClearSale, "Working in the Azure SQL Database hyperscale tier helps us streamline upgrades to new and existing applications, and with instant, unlimited scaling, customers can rely on us when it counts." You can read the complete ClearSale story at `https://customers.microsoft.com/en-us/story/773410-clearsale-partner-professional-services-azure`.

The true power of **Serverless** is cost savings for applications that don't need a high level of compute usage 24/7. **CampBrain** is a software company that offers a service to help camps run their operations. When CampBrain discovered Microsoft Azure SQL Database serverless, a compute tier for databases with intermittent, unpredictable usage, it cleared one of its biggest hurdles: managing compute costs despite the highs and lows created by extreme usage, plus reducing performance management complexity and risk. You can read the full CampBrain customer story at `https://customers.microsoft.com/en-us/story/779861-campbrain_professionalservices_azure_canada`.

Paychex serves some 650,000 businesses across the United States and Europe. They chose Azure SQL Database to gain the availability and performance they needed. However, they wanted to isolate customers per database. Therefore, using **Elastic Pools** became the natural choice to deliver on performance but optimize costs. You can read the full story about Paychex at `https://customers.microsoft.com/en-us/story/paychex-azure-sql-database-us`.

Interfaces for Azure SQL

At the beginning of this chapter, I described the various interfaces in the Azure ecosystem: Portal, API, and CLI. Azure SQL integrates with all these interfaces but also with traditional SQL Server interfaces.

Azure Portal

We have created an Azure SQL experience in the Azure Portal to snap to the Azure SQL lineup. Figure 2-9 shows the Azure SQL options after using search in the portal.

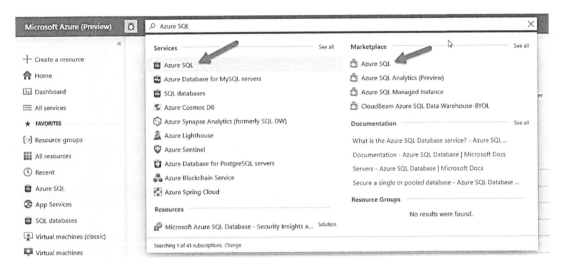

Figure 2-9. *Azure SQL Services and Marketplace*

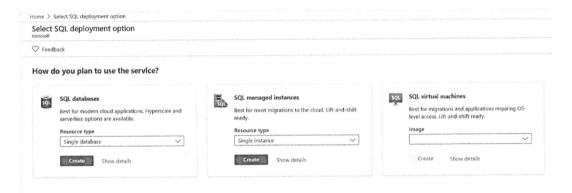

Figure 2-10. *Azure SQL deployment options*

If you choose Azure SQL Services, you will see a list of resources you have created for Azure SQL (including registered Virtual Machines). If you choose the Azure SQL Marketplace option, you will see choices to create Azure SQL Services as seen in Figure 2-10.

You will also see that after you have deployed Azure SQL resources, there are specific integrations for virtual machines, instances, and databases. You will see the examples throughout the rest of the book.

Even though we will not use it in the book, the Azure Portal includes a Query Editor to submit T-SQL queries to an Azure SQL Database. Figure 2-11 shows the Query Editor (which was in Public Preview at the time of the writing of this book).

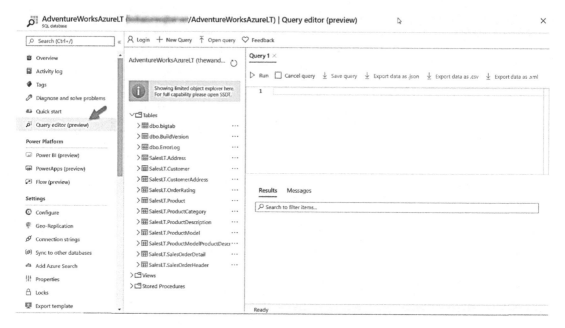

Figure 2-11. *The Query Editor in the Azure Portal*

az CLI

There are specific options for the az CLI cross-platform utility for virtual machines, managed instances, and databases. Don't forget az is installed by default in the Azure Cloud Shell. You can find a complete list of az commands specifically geared toward Azure SQL at `https://docs.microsoft.com/en-us/cli/azure/sql?view=azure-cli-latest`.

- Here is a reference for how to use the az for SQL Server on Virtual Machines: `https://docs.microsoft.com/en-us/cli/azure/sql/vm?view=azure-cli-latest`.

- You can find a list of az options specifically for managed instances at `https://docs.microsoft.com/en-us/cli/azure/sql/mi?view=azure-cli-latest`.

- You can find examples for using the az with databases at `https://docs.microsoft.com/en-us/azure/sql-database/sql-database-cli-samples?tabs=single-database`.

Don't forget about ARM templates. You can find many examples of ARM templates specific to Azure SQL. A great resource is *QuickStart* templates all found on GitHub. To see the complete gallery, visit `https://azure.microsoft.com/en-us/resources/templates/`.

PowerShell

The PowerShell Azure cmdlet suite includes specific options for Azure SQL:

- The following link contains an example of how to use Azure PowerShell to provision a SQL Server on Virtual Machines: `https://docs.microsoft.com/en-us/azure/virtual-machines/windows/sql/virtual-machines-windows-ps-sql-create`.

- You can find examples for PowerShell for Azure SQL Database at `https://docs.microsoft.com/en-us/azure/sql-database/sql-database-powershell-samples?tabs=single-database`.

- You can find a complete list of Azure PowerShell cmdlets for Azure Managed Instance and Databases at `https://docs.microsoft.com/en-us/powershell/module/az.sql`.

REST API

It may be rare you use the REST API interfaces for Azure:

- If you do, there are some specific REST API operations for Azure SQL Database which you can see at `https://docs.microsoft.com/en-us/rest/api/sql/`.

- You can find REST API references for Azure SQL Managed Instance at `https://docs.microsoft.com/en-us/azure/sql-database/sql-database-managed-instance-create-manage#rest-api-create-and-manage-managed-instances`.

- You can also manage Azure Virtual Machines through REST which you can read about at `https://docs.microsoft.com/en-us/rest/api/compute/virtualmachines`.

TDS and T-SQL

All Azure SQL services are powered by the SQL Server Engine. This means all Azure SQL services support the Tabular Data Stream (TDS) protocol. The full TDS specification can be found at https://docs.microsoft.com/en-us/openspecs/windows_protocols/ms-tds/b46a581a-39de-4745-b076-ec4dbb7d13ec.

This also means that all Azure SQL services support a variety of programming languages, drivers, and providers. Use the website https://aka.ms/sqldev to learn how to develop programs for SQL Server and Azure SQL. In some cases, a provider may provide specific options only applicable to Azure SQL. For example, the .Net provides modules for Azure SQL Management which you can read at https://docs.microsoft.com/en-us/dotnet/api/microsoft.azure.management.sql.models?view=azure-dotnet.

Because all Azure SQL services are powered by the SQL Server database engine, the engine programming language for all is T-SQL. As described throughout this chapter, not all Azure SQL options support all 100% T-SQL statements supported in SQL Server. Here is a summary guide for you to use:

- SQL Server on Azure Virtual Machine is a 100% support of T-SQL.

- Azure SQL Managed Instance is close to 100% T-SQL support. You can read the differences at https://docs.microsoft.com/en-us/azure/sql-database/sql-database-managed-instance-transact-sql-information.

- Azure SQL Database has the largest difference in T-SQL support from SQL Server, but *core database engine* T-SQL statements are supported. The documentation provides a guide for you at https://docs.microsoft.com/en-us/azure/sql-database/sql-database-transact-sql-information.

In some cases, there are new T-SQL options only applicable to a Managed Instance or Database. For example, CREATE DATABASE has option to specific service tiers for Azure SQL.

Tip   The Microsoft documentation for the T-SQL reference has a concept called "Applies To." This guide will help steer you whether a T-SQL statement applies to SQL Server, Azure SQL Database, or both. You can read about this guidance at `https://docs.microsoft.com/en-us/sql/t-sql/language-reference?view=sql-server-ver15#applies-to-references`.

SQL CLI

All common SQL Server command-line interfaces (CLI) support all options for Azure SQL, including **sqlcmd** and **bcp**. You can read about these tools at `https://docs.microsoft.com/en-us/sql/tools/overview-sql-tools?view=sql-server-ver15#command-line-tools`.

SQL Server Management Studio (SSMS)

SSMS is perhaps the most popular SQL Server tool in the world. SSMS fully supports all options for Azure SQL. In fact, SSMS detects the specific Azure SQL type and only provides options that work for that type. For example, if you connect SSMS to Azure SQL Database, it will not show you options in Object Explorer (e.g., SQL Server Agent) that are not supported for Azure SQL Database. Download the latest SSMS version (typically updated monthly) at `https://docs.microsoft.com/en-us/sql/ssms/download-sql-server-management-studio-ssms?view=sql-server-ver15`.

When you connect with SSMS to an Azure SQL Database, the icon in Object Explorer will look like Figure 2-12.

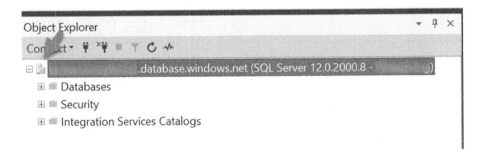

Figure 2-12. *SSMS Object Explorer connected to Azure SQL Database*

When you connect with SSMS to an Azure SQL Managed Instance, the icon in Object Explorer will look like Figure 2-13.

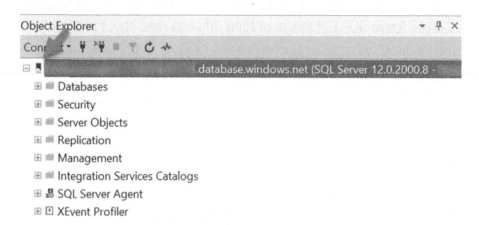

Figure 2-13. *SSMS Object Explorer connected to Azure SQL Managed Instance*

Azure Data Studio (ADS)

Azure Data Studio (ADS) is a new, modern, cross-platform database tool that works with SQL Server and all the Azure SQL services. You can download the latest ADS (typically updated monthly) from https://docs.microsoft.com/en-us/sql/azure-data-studio/download-azure-data-studio?view=sql-server-ver15. ADS includes the concept of extensions. Figure 2-14 shows an example of ADS connect to both an Azure SQL Database and an Azure SQL Managed Instance using an extension built to operate specifically against an Azure SQL Managed Instance.

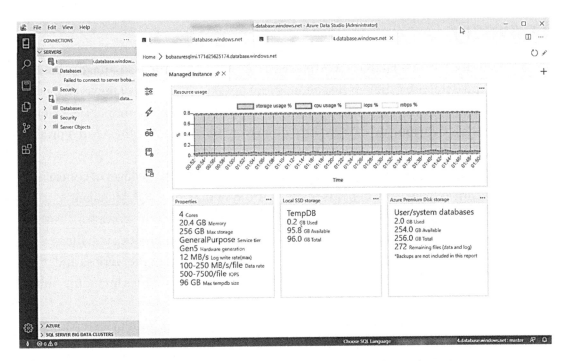

Figure 2-14. *Azure Data Studio connected to Azure SQL services*

One of the most interesting features of ADS are *Notebooks*. Notebooks give you the power of markdown documentation code embedded with language code such as T-SQL, PowerShell, Python, and other languages. You will be using ADS with notebooks in several examples of this book. There is no better way to get started with notebooks than to watch this video from my colleague Vicky Harp, the Group Program Manager for SQL Server tools, at `https://youtu.be/Nt4kIHQoIOc`.

Visual Studio Tools

The popular SQL **Server Data Tools (SSDT)** fully supports Azure SQL Database. You can read more about SSDT at `https://visualstudio.microsoft.com/vs/features/ssdt/`. **Visual Studio Code** supports an extension called **mssql** which supports Azure SQL Database and Managed Instance. You can see an example of using the mssql extension with Azure SQL Database at `https://docs.microsoft.com/en-us/azure/sql-database/sql-database-connect-query-vscode`.

Summary

Azure SQL is the world's database. With services for virtual machines, managed instances, and databases, there is just about every option you need – all powered by the same database engine for one of the world's most popular database products SQL Server.

Azure SQL is fully integrated with the Azure ecosystem including the Azure Portal and popular interfaces and tools.

SQL Server on Azure Virtual Machines provides you the ultimate level of control while taking advantage of the benefits of the Azure system. Azure SQL Managed Instances provide you a database engine instance combined with the power of a PaaS service including built-in high availability. Azure SQL Database provides you the most deployment options for a modern cloud application including serverless and Hyperscale. Azure SQL Database gives you maximum PaaS capabilities including built-in HADR and Automatic Tuning.

The rest of this book is a deep dive into the Azure SQL lineup. Your first stop in that journey is SQL Server on Azure Virtual Machines.

CHAPTER 3

SQL Server on Azure Virtual Machine

In Chapter 2, I described the Azure SQL lineup which includes SQL Server on Azure Virtual Machine (VM). SQL Server on Azure VM represents the primary IaaS deployment option for SQL in Azure.

In this chapter, I will cover all aspects of deploying, configuring, optimizing, and managing SQL Server on Azure Virtual Machine. To get you started, read the overview of SQL Server on Azure Virtual Machine in our documentation at `https://docs.microsoft.com/en-us/azure/virtual-machines/windows/sql/virtual-machines-windows-sql-server-iaas-overview`.

You will go through several examples in this chapter. You will need the following to complete these examples:

- An Azure subscription.

- A minimum of Contributor role access to the Azure subscription. You can read more about Azure built-in roles at `https://docs.microsoft.com/en-us/azure/role-based-access-control/built-in-roles`.

- Access to the Azure Portal (web or Windows application).

- Installation of the **az** CLI (see `https://docs.microsoft.com/en-us/cli/azure/install-azure-cli?view=azure-cli-latest` for more details). You can also use the Azure Cloud Shell instead since az is already installed. You can read more about the Azure Cloud Shell at `https://azure.microsoft.com/en-us/features/cloud-shell/`.

© Bob Ward 2021
B. Ward, *Azure SQL Revealed*, https://doi.org/10.1007/978-1-4842-5931-3_3

Deploying

As a longtime SQL Server user, I have never really used the term *deploy*. I have always used the term install or setup. Deploy is a term I will use for the rest of this book to talk about installing a SQL Server on Azure Virtual Machine, Managed Instance, or Database. There is a good reason to snap to the term deploy. When you create a resource for an Azure service (whether that is through the Portal or CLI), Azure Resource Manager will create a **deployment**. You will learn how to view information about deployment history in this chapter and in Chapter 4 of this book. You can read more about a deployment history at `https://docs.microsoft.com/en-us/azure/azure-resource-manager/templates/deployment-history`.

The basic process to deploy SQL Server on Azure Virtual Machine is

- ✓ Decide to use a SQL Server Gallery Image or "deploy on your own."
- ✓ Choose a Resource Group, Region, and Availability option.
- ✓ Choose a Virtual Machine Size, admin account, and port rule.
- ✓ Optionally supply other configuration choices.
- ✓ Deploy it!

Note   This chapter assumes virtual machines deployed using Azure Resource Manager. I do not recommend using *classic deployment*. You can read more about deployment models at `https://docs.microsoft.com/en-us/azure/azure-resource-manager/management/deployment-models`.

Pricing

Before I get into the details of deployment, you should understand more about how you pay for Azure Virtual Machines. Since you are deploying in Azure, you are paying Microsoft a fee on a regular basis (billed monthly) for resource usage such as compute and storage. This is referred to as *pay as you go*. In addition, you will pay for the license for the operating system (if that OS requires a paid license such as Windows Server) and the license for SQL Server. You will have options to *Bring Your Own License* (BYOL) for both the OS and SQL Server to utilize licenses you have already paid for. This is referred to as Azure Hybrid Benefit (AHB). You will also learn that there are other ways in this chapter to save money such as Reserved Instances and stopping the VM when you do not need it. Read more about pricing at `https://azure.microsoft.com/en-us/pricing/details/virtual-machines/windows/`. You can also use a very nifty website called a pricing calculator at `https://azure.microsoft.com/en-us/pricing/calculator/?service=virtual-machines`.

SQL Server Gallery Images

To deploy a SQL Server on Virtual Machine, you can choose from a set of pre-installed images of an Operating System/SQL Server version/Edition combination called *Gallery Images*. When you choose a SQL Server Gallery Image, you are making a conscious decision to pay for a SQL Server license using your subscription. There are all types of choices here. For all the details for pricing of SQL Server on Azure Virtual Machines, look at the documentation at `https://docs.microsoft.com/en-us/azure/virtual-machines/windows/sql/virtual-machines-windows-sql-server-pricing-guidance`. In addition, there is a good FAQ resource on SQL Server images at `https://docs.microsoft.com/en-us/azure/azure-sql/virtual-machines/windows/frequently-asked-questions-faq#images`.

Think of using a SQL Server Gallery Image like a *sysprep installed SQL Server* (read more about sysprep and SQL Server at `https://docs.microsoft.com/en-us/sql/database-engine/install-windows/considerations-for-installing-sql-server-using-sysprep?view=sql-server-ver15`). You can also choose to deploy a Virtual Machine with an Operating System from a Gallery Image and then install SQL Server from your own media inside the Guest OS of the VM. I call this method "deploy on your own." I will discuss this option in the following section titled "Deploy on Your Own."

Let us explore using the Azure Portal a deployment of SQL Server 2019 on Azure Virtual Machines using a Gallery Image.

In your Azure Portal, search for Azure SQL in the **Marketplace** using the Search box at the top of your portal as in Figure 3-1.

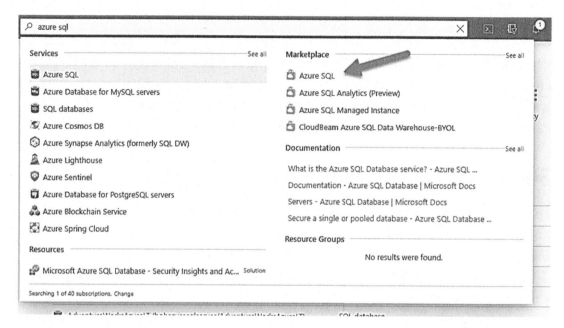

Figure 3-1. *Azure SQL from the Marketplace*

You are now presented choices on the type of Azure service to deploy. Use the drop-down list under SQL virtual machines to choose **SQL Server 2019 Enterprise Windows Server 2019** as in Figure 3-2.

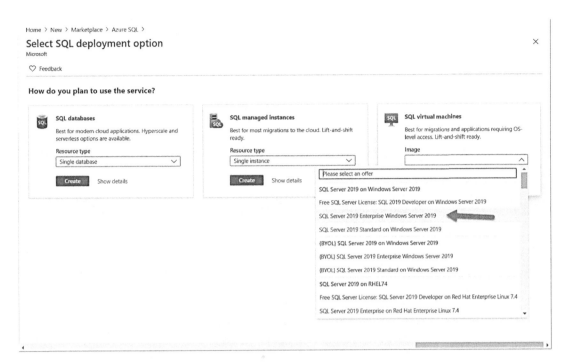

Figure 3-2. *SQL Server 2019 Gallery Image from Azure SQL*

For purposes of this example, I am going to choose SQL Server 2019 Enterprise. This allows me to show you a few configuration choices in the rest of this chapter. You could have easily picked Free SQL Server 2019 Developer on Windows Server 2019. For this image choice, the SQL Server license is free, but you can only use the VM for development purposes.

Choose this option and click the **Create** button. You are now presented a screen for a series of required fields and choices to deploy the VM as seen in Figure 3-3.

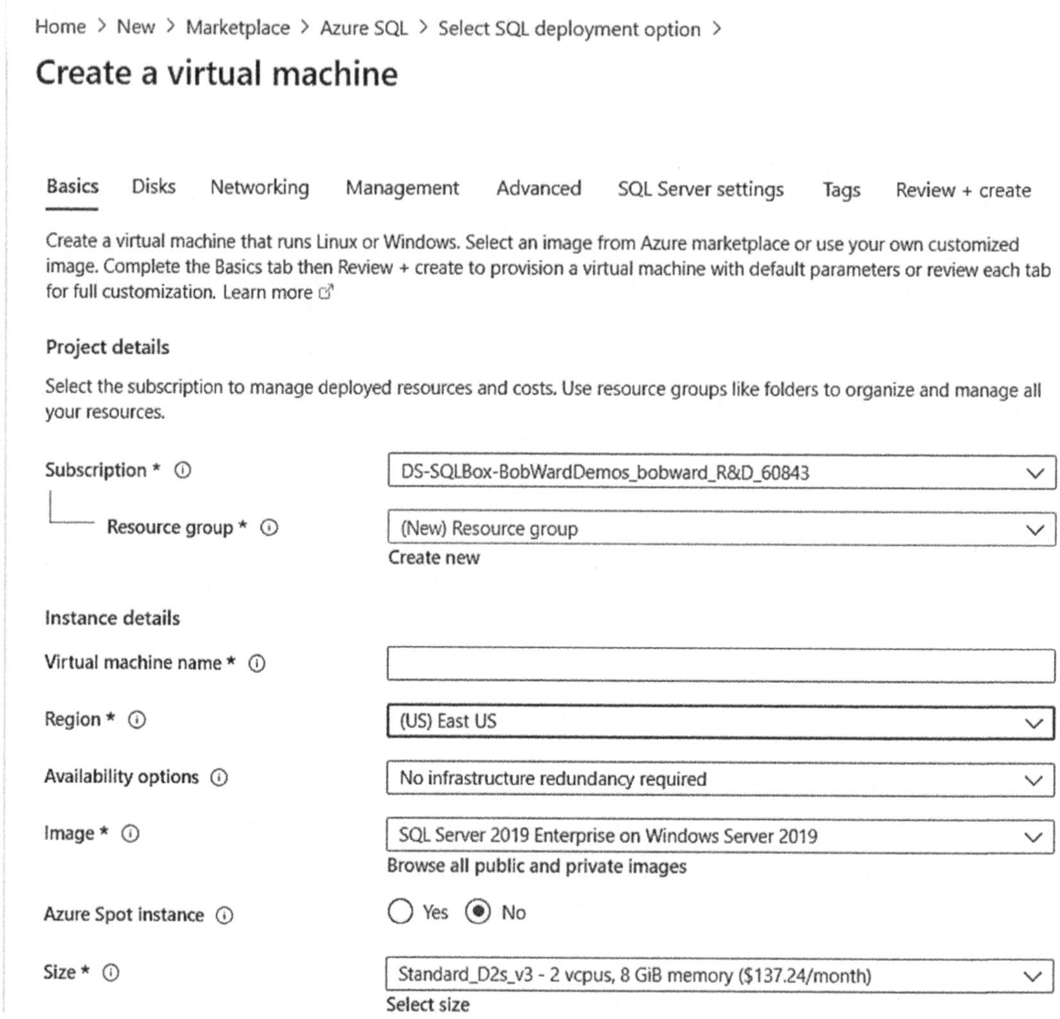

Home > New > Marketplace > Azure SQL > Select SQL deployment option >

Create a virtual machine

Basics   Disks   Networking   Management   Advanced   SQL Server settings   Tags   Review + create

Create a virtual machine that runs Linux or Windows. Select an image from Azure marketplace or use your own customized image. Complete the Basics tab then Review + create to provision a virtual machine with default parameters or review each tab for full customization. Learn more ⬀

Project details

Select the subscription to manage deployed resources and costs. Use resource groups like folders to organize and manage all your resources.

Subscription * ⓘ   DS-SQLBox-BobWardDemos_bobward_R&D_60843   ⌄

└── Resource group * ⓘ   (New) Resource group   ⌄
                                     Create new

Instance details

Virtual machine name * ⓘ   [   ]

Region * ⓘ   (US) East US   ⌄

Availability options ⓘ   No infrastructure redundancy required   ⌄

Image * ⓘ   SQL Server 2019 Enterprise on Windows Server 2019   ⌄
                                     Browse all public and private images

Azure Spot instance ⓘ   ◯ Yes ⦿ No

Size * ⓘ   Standard_D2s_v3 - 2 vcpus, 8 GiB memory ($137.24/month)   ⌄
                                     Select size

Figure 3-3. *The initial Create SQL VM screen*

Some of your defaults will be different (e.g., your Azure subscription will be listed as a default. If you have more than one subscription, change it here to the desired target subscription for the VM deployment) and you will be making various choices. Let us walk through all your choices during the deploy process and create screens.

Resource Group, Region, and Availability

Your first several options are required fields to provide, including a resource group, name, and Azure region. In addition, you have an option to choose an availability option.

Resource Group

As I have described in Chapter 2 of the book, a resource group is a great way to organize and manage Azure resources together. You will see in this chapter that, by default, a virtual network is created for a new resource group you specify and the VM is automatically added to the virtual network. For the purposes of this exercise, choose **Create New** and give it a name. I called mine **bwsqlvmsrg**.

Virtual Machine Name

This is both the name of the Azure resource and the guest host name inside the VM (you can change the host name in the VM after deployment). Note some special characters are not allowed and the name must be no longer than 15 characters. This name must be unique within the resource group. For this exercise, I put in the name **bwsql2019**.

Region

This is the region where Azure data centers are located. I described Azure regions and data centers in Chapter 2 of the book. There are several factors for the region you choose including available VM sizes, compliance, price, and latency to users and applications. You can read more about choosing the right region at `www.cloudelicious.net/azure-region-and-datacenter-find-your-best-match/`. Note it is also possible that your subscription does not support certain Azure regions. Check with the owner of your account associated with your subscription. I will choose East US for my region.

Availability Options

This is an optional field during deployment. This choice will only make sense to choose if you plan to connect your SQL VM to other VMs for HADR purposes (such as Availability Groups, Failover Cluster Instance, etc.). Unfortunately, it is best to decide which option to use here during deployment. For the purposes of this example, leave this as "No infrastructure redundancy required." I will discuss more on when to use certain options here under the section titled "HADR" later in this chapter.

> **Note**   This does not mean you do not get basic High Availability for a *stand-alone* SQL Server. Azure can handle migrating your VM to a host within a data center for failures (using live Migration). In addition, there is built-in redundancy for Azure storage for your databases.

Image

This will be filled in with the choice you made from the Azure SQL screen. It is possible for you to change it at this point before you deploy. Leave the choice SQL Server 2019 Enterprise Windows Server 2019 for now.

> **Note**   You can get a complete list of SQL Server Gallery Images available in a specific region using the following PowerShell command (substitute in your region name of choice):
>
> **Get-AzVMImageOffer -Location 'East US' -Publisher 'MicrosoftSQLServer'**

Spot Instance

An Azure Spot Instance is a concept to save you money on Virtual Machines that are not used consistently. This is a great concept but probably not applicable to your use of SQL Server in Azure Virtual Machine. You can read more about Spot Instance at `https://docs.microsoft.com/en-us/azure/virtual-machines/windows/spot-vms`.

After making these choices, my screen looks like Figure 3-4.

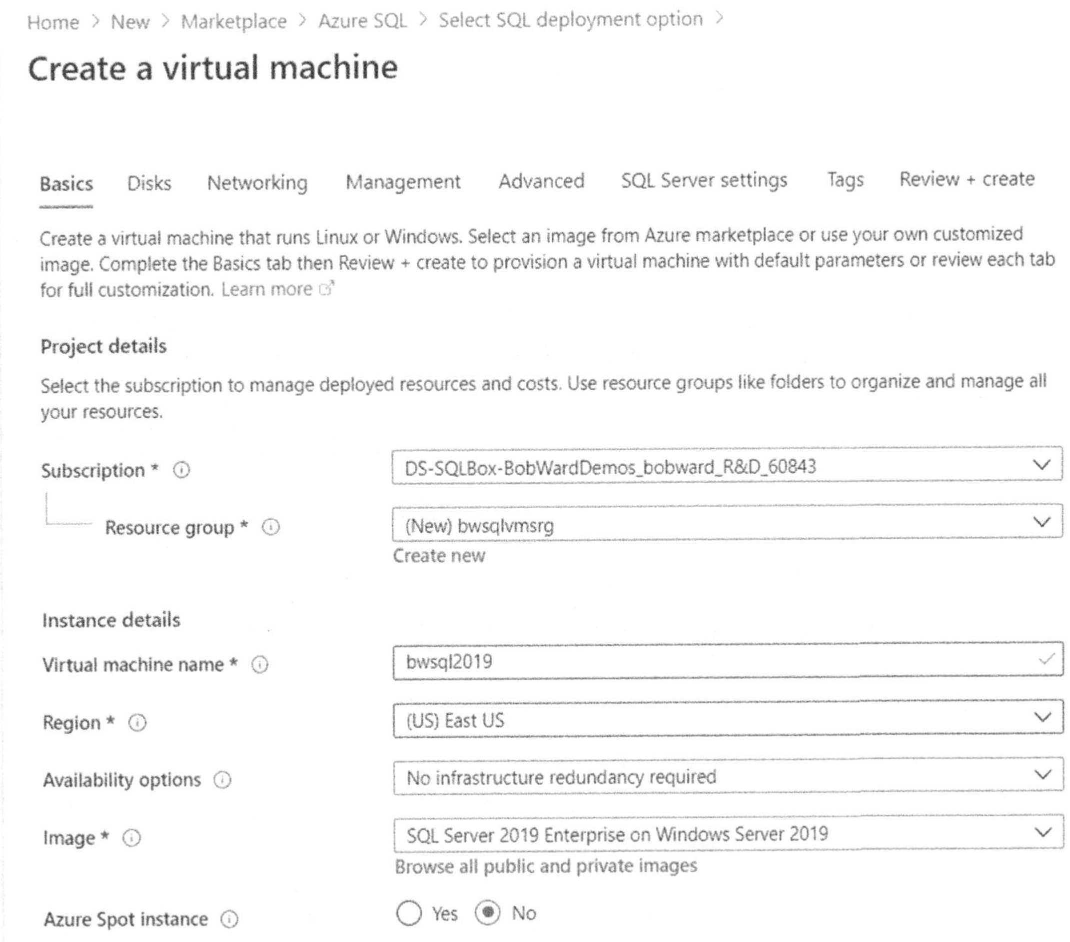

Home > New > Marketplace > Azure SQL > Select SQL deployment option >

Create a virtual machine

Basics   Disks   Networking   Management   Advanced   SQL Server settings   Tags   Review + create

Create a virtual machine that runs Linux or Windows. Select an image from Azure marketplace or use your own customized image. Complete the Basics tab then Review + create to provision a virtual machine with default parameters or review each tab for full customization. Learn more ⬀

Project details

Select the subscription to manage deployed resources and costs. Use resource groups like folders to organize and manage all your resources.

Subscription * ⓘ

    DS-SQLBox-BobWardDemos_bobward_R&D_60843   ⌄

Resource group * ⓘ

    (New) bwsqlvmsrg   ⌄
    Create new

Instance details

Virtual machine name * ⓘ

    bwsql2019   ✓

Region * ⓘ

    (US) East US   ⌄

Availability options ⓘ

    No infrastructure redundancy required   ⌄

Image * ⓘ

    SQL Server 2019 Enterprise on Windows Server 2019   ⌄
    Browse all public and private images

Azure Spot instance ⓘ   ◯ Yes ⦿ No

Figure 3-4. *Specifying Resource Group, Region, and Availability*

Virtual Machine Sizes

One of the most important decisions you will make is what *size* to make the Virtual Machine for SQL Server in Azure. Size is effectively a combination of CPU, memory, and I/O choices. You make these choices today in your data center when you deploy SQL Server to a Virtual Machine or bare metal. You select out how many CPUs, CPU speed, RAM, size of disks, and disk speed.

Azure Virtual Machine sizes are categorized by *type* and are known with a letter designation (B, D, etc.). If you are just trying to get started and try out SQL Server in Azure Virtual Machine, my recommendation is to pick a reasonable size to test out SQL Server vs. cost. If you are choosing a size for production, you need to carefully review size options. As you can imagine, the higher the *horsepower*, the higher the cost.

Tip   I use Azure VMs a great deal in my job even when demonstrating SQL Server "box" capabilities. Therefore, I must carefully consider the costs of deploying in Azure. If you are using Azure for demonstrations, development, or just testing, be sure to stop your Virtual Machine through the Portal or CLI when you are not using it. My colleague Anna Hoffman also gave me the great tip of using *burstable* or B-series which you can read more about at `https://docs.microsoft.com/en-us/azure/virtual-machines/sizes-b-series-burstable`.

As Azure data centers bring in new models of computers to support virtual machine and Azure resources, new sizes support different hardware *generations*. Therefore, you will see Virtual Machine sizes called Dv2 or Dv3. Rather than trying to explain all the sizes, take some time to review the documentation for Azure Virtual Machine sizes for Windows at `https://docs.microsoft.com/en-us/azure/virtual-machines/windows/sizes` and Virtual Machine sizes for Linux at `https://docs.microsoft.com/en-us/azure/virtual-machines/linux/sizes`.

I will talk more about the performance ramifications of sizes in the section of this chapter called "Maximizing Storage Performance." For now, look at our documentation best practice guidance for choosing VM sizes better suited for SQL Server's unique CPU, memory, and I/O characteristics at `https://docs.microsoft.com/en-us/azure/virtual-machines/windows/sql/virtual-machines-windows-sql-performance#vm-size-guidance`.

For the purposes of our example, I want to show you a few specific options that are only available with certain sizes. Therefore, I will use the **Select size** option as seen in Figure 3-5 to bring up a list of choices.

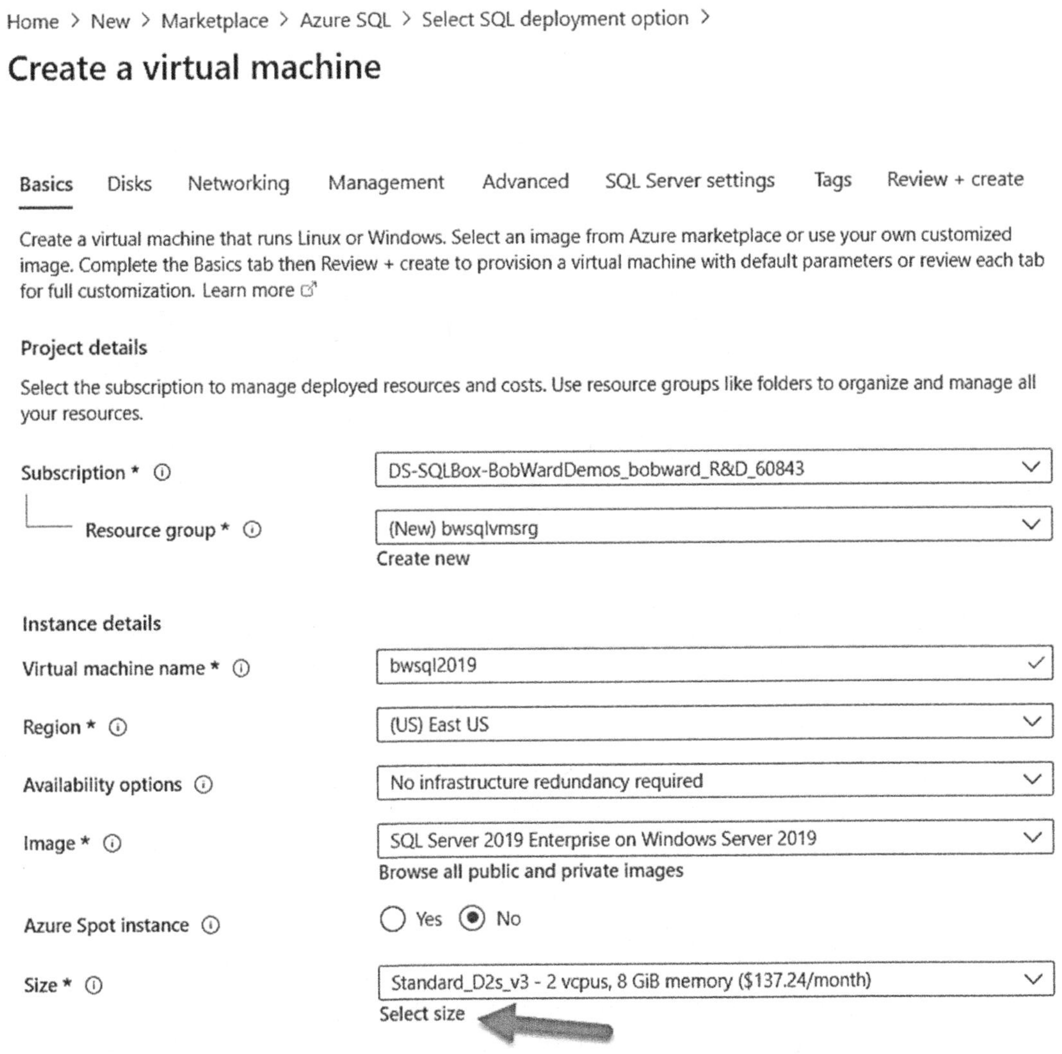

Home > New > Marketplace > Azure SQL > Select SQL deployment option >

Create a virtual machine

Basics   Disks   Networking   Management   Advanced   SQL Server settings   Tags   Review + create

Create a virtual machine that runs Linux or Windows. Select an image from Azure marketplace or use your own customized image. Complete the Basics tab then Review + create to provision a virtual machine with default parameters or review each tab for full customization. Learn more ⌐'

Project details

Select the subscription to manage deployed resources and costs. Use resource groups like folders to organize and manage all your resources.

Subscription * ⓘ | DS-SQLBox-BobWardDemos_bobward_R&D_60843 ∨

Resource group * ⓘ | (New) bwsqlvmsrg ∨
Create new

Instance details

Virtual machine name * ⓘ | bwsql2019 ✓

Region * ⓘ | (US) East US ∨

Availability options ⓘ | No infrastructure redundancy required ∨

Image * ⓘ | SQL Server 2019 Enterprise on Windows Server 2019 ∨
Browse all public and private images

Azure Spot instance ⓘ | ○ Yes ● No

Size * ⓘ | Standard_D2s_v3 - 2 vcpus, 8 GiB memory ($137.24/month) ∨
Select size ⬅

Figure 3-5. *Choosing a VM size*

You should now be presented with a screen that gives you choices on VM sizes. These tables can look daunting, but it gives you a feel of the why you would pick a specific size because it dictates the number of CPUs, RAM, disks, IOPS, and so on you get for your VM deployment. Figure 3-6 shows results after I have typed in the "Search by VM size..." the string v3 which shows me some of the latest hardware for VMs.

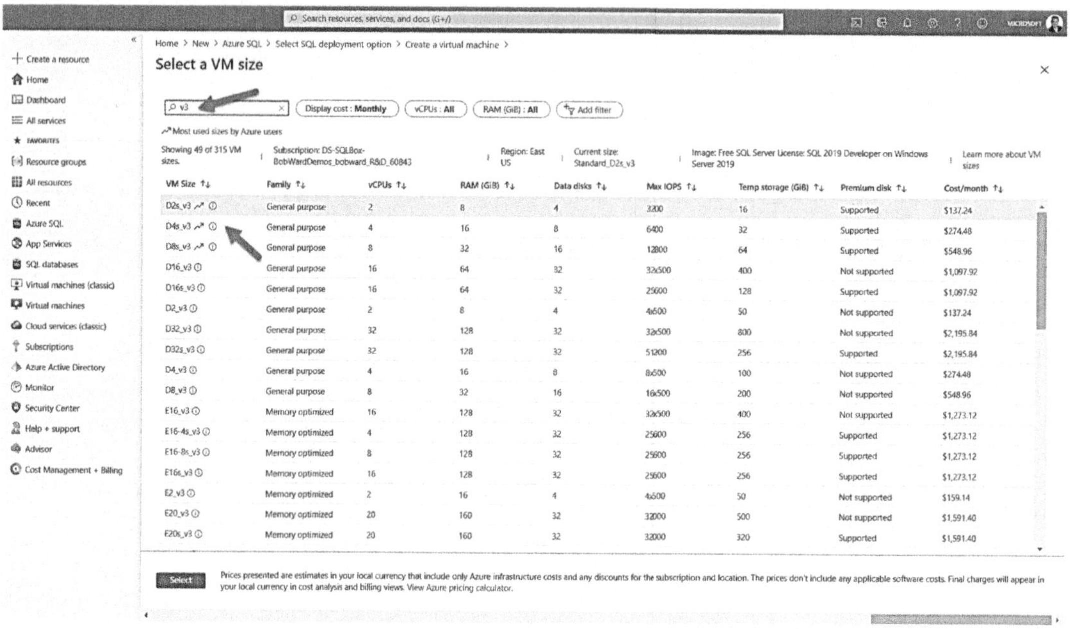

Figure 3-6. *VM size choices for Azure*

I am going to choose D4s_v3 because it has plenty of CPUs and RAM for my purposes and enables a few options I need which I will describe shortly. Notice on this screen a tag that shows my choice is used by many Azure users.

You can also see a cost factor in the VM size list so this could be a factor in your choices. Even though I will mention sizes throughout the rest of this chapter in various situations, keep these important points in mind:

- You can read more about VM sizes for Windows and Linux at `https://docs.microsoft.com/en-us/azure/virtual-machines/windows/sizes`.

- You can change the VM size after you have deployed without having to delete and recreate it. This is called *resizing* a VM. There are limits here and it will require some downtime, but you can read more about resizing VMs at `https://docs.microsoft.com/en-us/azure/virtual-machines/windows/resize-vm`.

Account, Port, and OS Licensing

To finish off the default screen to deploy SQL Server in a Virtual Machine, I must provide an administrator account and password. For Windows, this becomes the local admin account and for Linux a root user. For a SQL Server Gallery Image deployment on Windows, this local admin account is automatically added to the sysadmin role (just like you would add yourself during SQL Server setup). The password for the admin account can be between 12 and 123 characters and must be a strong password with at least 3 of the following characters: 1 lowercase, 1 uppercase, 1 number, and 1 special character.

The next choice is to decide whether any ports for the virtual machine will be opened and available for inbound traffic. By default, port 3389 which is used by the Remote Desktop Connection (RDP) protocol is selected (for Linux, this would be port 22 which is the default port for the ssh protocol). Using this option is the most flexible but not the most secure option. I will leave this option for now, but later in this chapter in the section called "Connecting to Your VM," I will talk about using different security options.

The final choice involves licensing for Windows deployments. When you choose a SQL Server Gallery Image with Windows, your license will be a *pay-as-you-go* subscription for both SQL Server and Windows. This basically means you pay each month for a fixed cost of using Windows and SQL Server. You also pay cost for resource usage based on CPU usage and storage. If you own existing licenses for Windows Server, you can apply those licenses to your Azure Virtual Machine cost. You can read more about using Azure Hybrid Benefit for Windows Server at `https://docs.microsoft.com/en-us/azure/virtual-machines/windows/hybrid-use-benefit-licensing`.

Figure 3-7 shows the rest of the portal screen to fill out these options.

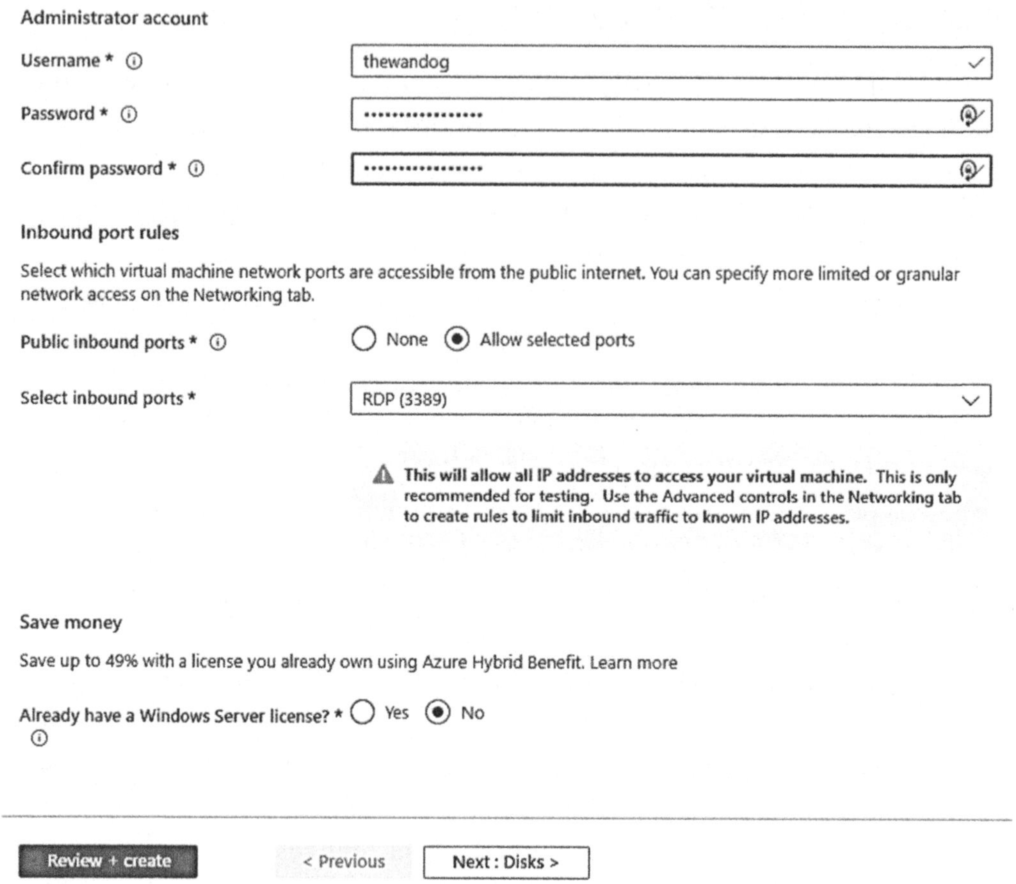

Administrator account

Username * ⓘ

thewandog ✓

Password * ⓘ

•••••••••••••••• 👁

Confirm password * ⓘ

•••••••••••••••• 👁

Inbound port rules

Select which virtual machine network ports are accessible from the public internet. You can specify more limited or granular network access on the Networking tab.

Public inbound ports * ⓘ

○ None ● Allow selected ports

Select inbound ports *

RDP (3389) ⌄

⚠ **This will allow all IP addresses to access your virtual machine. This is only recommended for testing. Use the Advanced controls in the Networking tab to create rules to limit inbound traffic to known IP addresses.**

Save money

Save up to 49% with a license you already own using Azure Hybrid Benefit. Learn more

Already have a Windows Server license? * ○ Yes ● No
ⓘ

[Review + create]   < Previous   [Next : Disks >]

Figure 3-7. *Choosing account, port, and license*

At this point in the deployment process, you can click **Review + create** and deploy your VM with other default options. And if you want to get up and running quickly, just select Review + create. However, there could be reasons for you to choose other options to configure how the Virtual Machine is deployed.

Making Configuration Choices As Part of Deploy

Let us look at the other options you can select as part of deploying SQL Server for Azure Virtual Machine.

OS Disks

Select **Next: Disks >** to see the following options as seen in Figure 3-8.

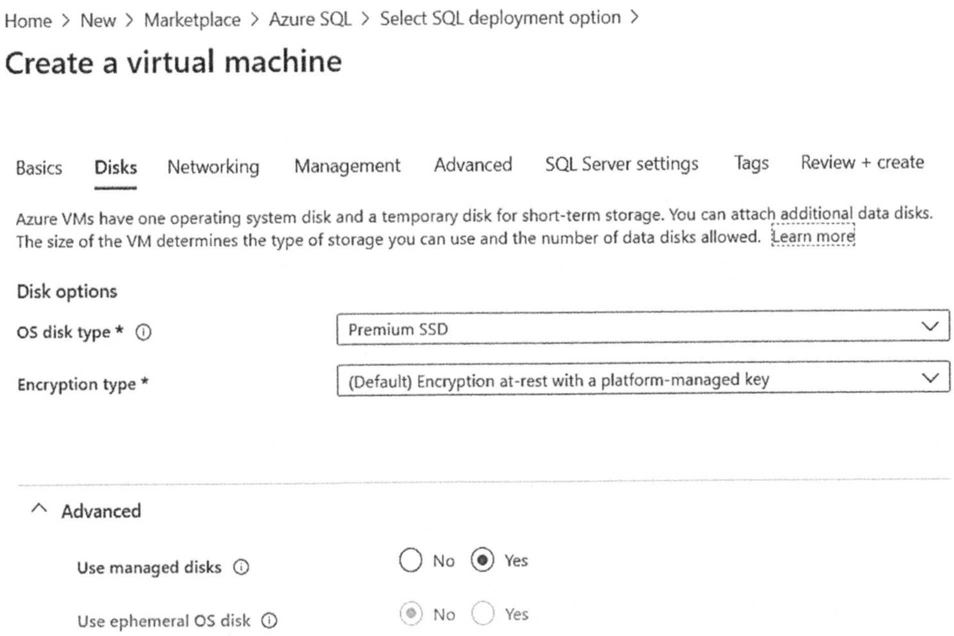

Home > New > Marketplace > Azure SQL > Select SQL deployment option >

Create a virtual machine

Basics   **Disks**   Networking   Management   Advanced   SQL Server settings   Tags   Review + create

Azure VMs have one operating system disk and a temporary disk for short-term storage. You can attach additional data disks. The size of the VM determines the type of storage you can use and the number of data disks allowed. Learn more

Disk options

OS disk type * ⓘ

Premium SSD	⌄

Encryption type *

(Default) Encryption at-rest with a platform-managed key	⌄

∧ Advanced

Use managed disks ⓘ   ○ No ⦿ Yes

Use ephemeral OS disk ⓘ   ⦿ No ○ Yes

Figure 3-8. *Disk options for Azure Virtual Machine during deployment*

The disk options presented here (note I expanded the Advanced option) are for the disk supporting the Operating System and other system files. For all SQL Server deployments, I recommend you choose the default options provided here including Premium Managed disks. I will talk more about different types of Managed disks you can use with SQL Server for Azure Virtual Machine in the section called "Maximizing Storage Performance." I will recommend you take advantage of Managed disks with SQL Server for the simple advantage of fault tolerance, but you may want to read more about unmanaged and ephemeral disks. You can read more about Managed Disks at `https://docs.microsoft.com/en-us/azure/virtual-machines/windows/managed-disks-overview`. You can read more about ephemeral disks at `https://docs.microsoft.com/en-us/azure/virtual-machines/windows/ephemeral-os-disks`.

Note   If you install just an operating system image from the marketplace (e.g., Windows Server), you would get options here to add data disks. For SQL Server marketplace images, you will be able to add data disks in the following configuration section called "SQL Server Settings" or after you have deployed.

Networking

Now click **Next: Networking** >. Here you are going to be presented with a set of choices to configure various aspects of networking for your virtual machine as seen in Figure 3-9.

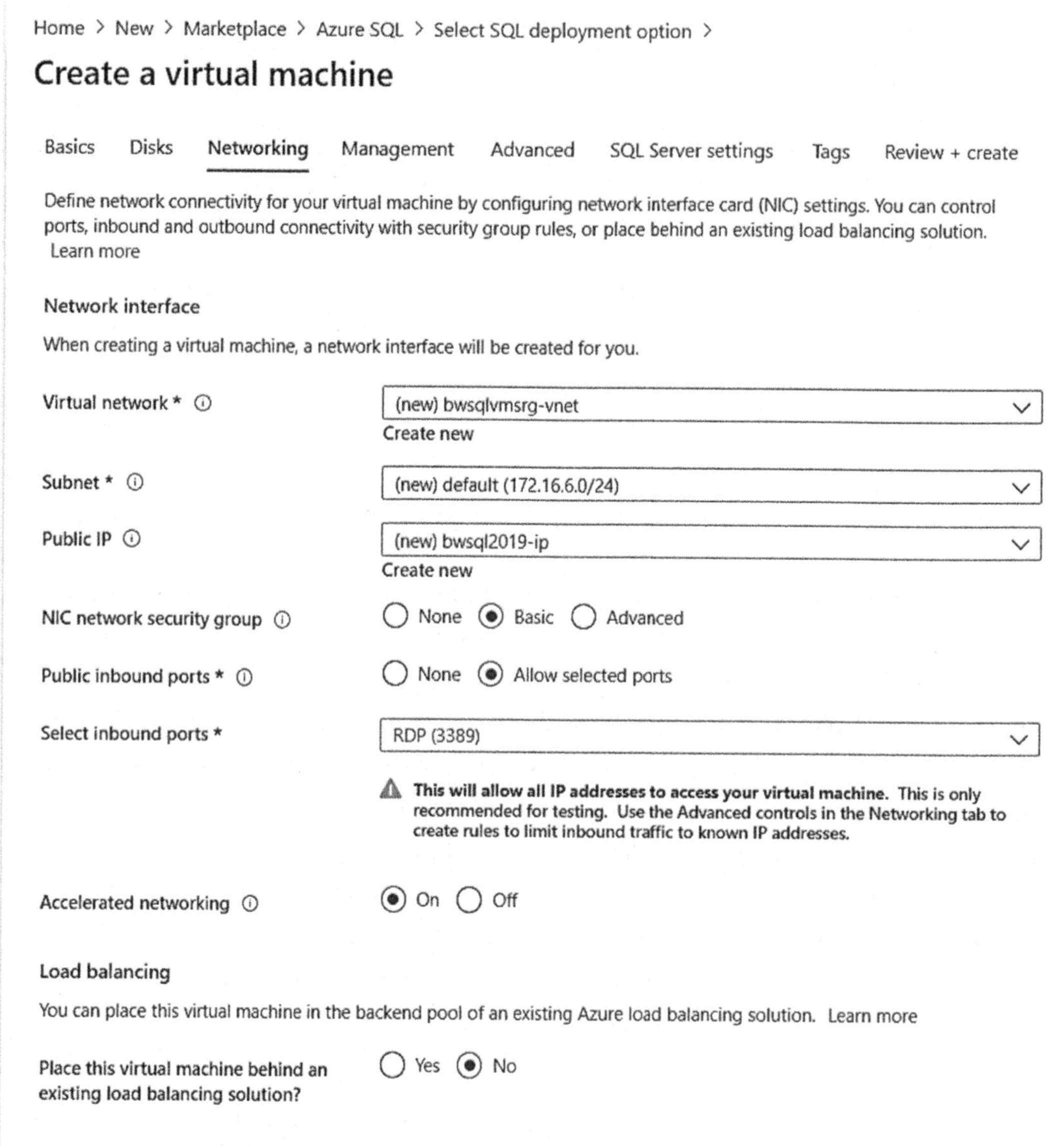

Home > New > Marketplace > Azure SQL > Select SQL deployment option >

Create a virtual machine

Basics   Disks   **Networking**   Management   Advanced   SQL Server settings   Tags   Review + create

Define network connectivity for your virtual machine by configuring network interface card (NIC) settings. You can control ports, inbound and outbound connectivity with security group rules, or place behind an existing load balancing solution. Learn more

Network interface

When creating a virtual machine, a network interface will be created for you.

Virtual network * ⓘ	(new) bwsqlvmsrg-vnet ⌄
	Create new
Subnet * ⓘ	(new) default (172.16.6.0/24) ⌄
Public IP ⓘ	(new) bwsql2019-ip ⌄
	Create new
NIC network security group ⓘ	◯ None ⦿ Basic ◯ Advanced
Public inbound ports * ⓘ	◯ None ⦿ Allow selected ports
Select inbound ports *	RDP (3389) ⌄

⚠ **This will allow all IP addresses to access your virtual machine.** This is only recommended for testing. Use the Advanced controls in the Networking tab to create rules to limit inbound traffic to known IP addresses.

Accelerated networking ⓘ	⦿ On ◯ Off

Load balancing

You can place this virtual machine in the backend pool of an existing Azure load balancing solution. Learn more

Place this virtual machine behind an existing load balancing solution?	◯ Yes ⦿ No

Figure 3-9. *Networking options during deploy for Azure Virtual Machine*

The two options you may want to consider changing are the Virtual Network and Subnet if this virtual machine needs to be included in an existing Azure Virtual Network. Notice in this example, a new virtual network will be created including a name that contains my new Resource Group. If you would have selected an existing Resource Group on the first screen to deploy, the virtual network associated with that resource group (if one exists) would be selected. I will discuss more about networking options for Azure Virtual Machine in the section later in this chapter called "Networking."

The only other option I want to call out on this screen that I believe applies to your SQL Server on Azure Virtual Machine deployments is **Accelerated Networking**. Accelerated networking can be extremely beneficial for SQL Server deployments where client applications must communicate across a virtual network to SQL Server. Therefore, you may want to choose a VM size (or a VM size with the required number of CPUs) that supports accelerated networking. If you plan to just deploy SQL Server in a virtual machine and do everything inside the virtual machine, you do not need to worry about this option. You can read more about the benefits of Accelerated Networking at `https://docs.microsoft.com/en-us/azure/virtual-network/create-vm-accelerated-networking-powershell#benefits`.

Note   You can later change the size of the virtual machine and then enable Accelerated Networking using PowerShell. You can read more about how to do this at `https://docs.microsoft.com/en-us/azure/virtual-network/create-vm-accelerated-networking-powershell#enable-accelerated-networking-on-existing-vms`.

Management

Select **Next: Management >**. Figure 3-10 shows some options that may be interesting to your deployment and use of SQL Server with Azure Virtual Machine.

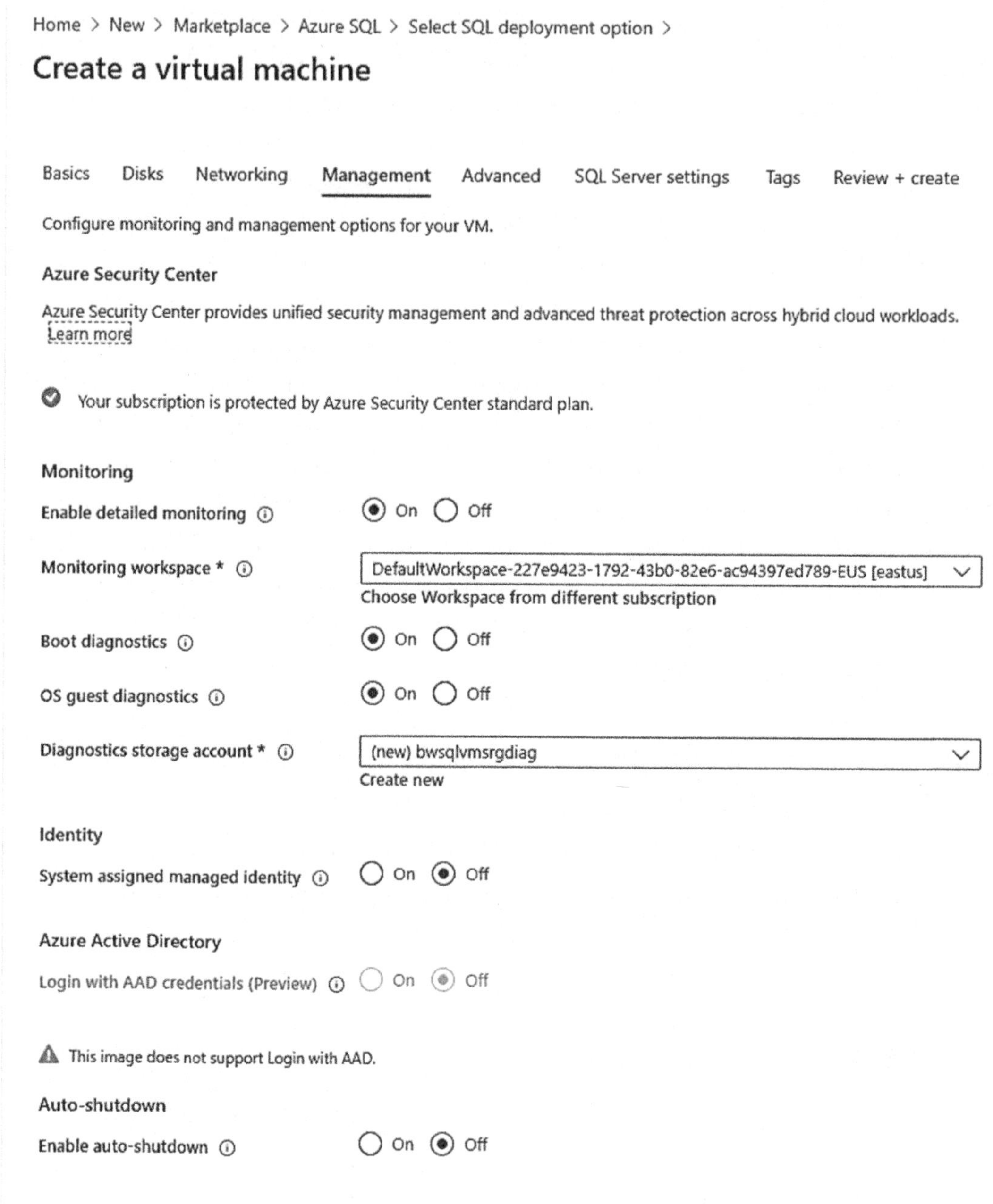

Home > New > Marketplace > Azure SQL > Select SQL deployment option >

Create a virtual machine

Basics   Disks   Networking   **Management**   Advanced   SQL Server settings   Tags   Review + create

Configure monitoring and management options for your VM.

Azure Security Center

Azure Security Center provides unified security management and advanced threat protection across hybrid cloud workloads.
Learn more

✓ Your subscription is protected by Azure Security Center standard plan.

Monitoring

Enable detailed monitoring ⓘ   ⊙ On ○ Off

Monitoring workspace * ⓘ

| DefaultWorkspace-227e9423-1792-43b0-82e6-ac94397ed789-EUS [eastus] ⌄ |
Choose Workspace from different subscription

Boot diagnostics ⓘ   ⊙ On ○ Off

OS guest diagnostics ⓘ   ⊙ On ○ Off

Diagnostics storage account * ⓘ

| (new) bwsqlvmsrgdiag   ⌄ |
Create new

Identity

System assigned managed identity ⓘ   ○ On ⊙ Off

Azure Active Directory

Login with AAD credentials (Preview) ⓘ   ○ On ⊙ Off

⚠ This image does not support Login with AAD.

Auto-shutdown

Enable auto-shutdown ⓘ   ○ On ⊙ Off

Figure 3-10. *Management options during deploy for Azure Virtual Machine*

You can see on this example screen I have turned on **Enable detailed monitoring**, **Boot diagnostics**, and **OS guest diagnostics**. Perhaps it is my nature from having worked in technical support, but I want as much diagnostics available to me.

Enabled detailed monitoring will allow you to choose an existing or *new log analytics workspace*. I will show you later in this chapter how you will use this workspace for performance monitoring. You can read more about what **Enable detailed monitoring** provides you at `https://docs.microsoft.com/en-us/azure/azure-monitor/insights/vminsights-overview`.

Boot diagnostics are very helpful to see the serial output screen of your virtual machine on the host. This is like seeing the boot screen using a tool like Hyper-V Manager. You can read more about boot diagnostics at `https://azure.microsoft.com/en-us/support/legal/support-diagnostic-information-collection/`.

I personally recommend you select **OS guest diagnostics**. This will allow you to see performance information from the guest OS in systems like Azure Monitor and even get alerts. I will discuss how to use this in the section titled "Performance Monitoring" later in this chapter.

Two other options worth talking about but that I do not personally use much are **System assigned managed identity** and **Enable auto-shutdown**.

System assigned managed identity is an interesting option allowing you to create an identity in Azure Active Directory to use for authentication without having to put credentials in your code or application. One nice example to use this capability with Azure Virtual Machine is to connect to an Azure SQL Database from a virtual machine using Azure Active Directory without prompting for any passwords. You can read more about managed identities at `https://docs.microsoft.com/en-us/azure/active-directory/managed-identities-azure-resources/overview`. You can see the example of using this with Azure SQL Database at `https://docs.microsoft.com/en-us/azure/active-directory/managed-identities-azure-resources/tutorial-windows-vm-access-sql`.

Enable auto-shutdown provides an option where the virtual machine will be shut down daily on the time of your choosing. Why would you ever select this for a SQL Server deployment? The primary reason is that you have a SQL Server deployment and you have some downtime you can afford and want to save money. When a virtual machine is shut down, you only pay for your licensing and storage costs. I will talk more about stopping and starting virtual machines in the section titled "Configuration and Managing" later in this chapter.

Advanced

With these options selected, click **Next: Advanced >**. As the name implies, these are advanced options that may interest you as seen in Figure 3-11.

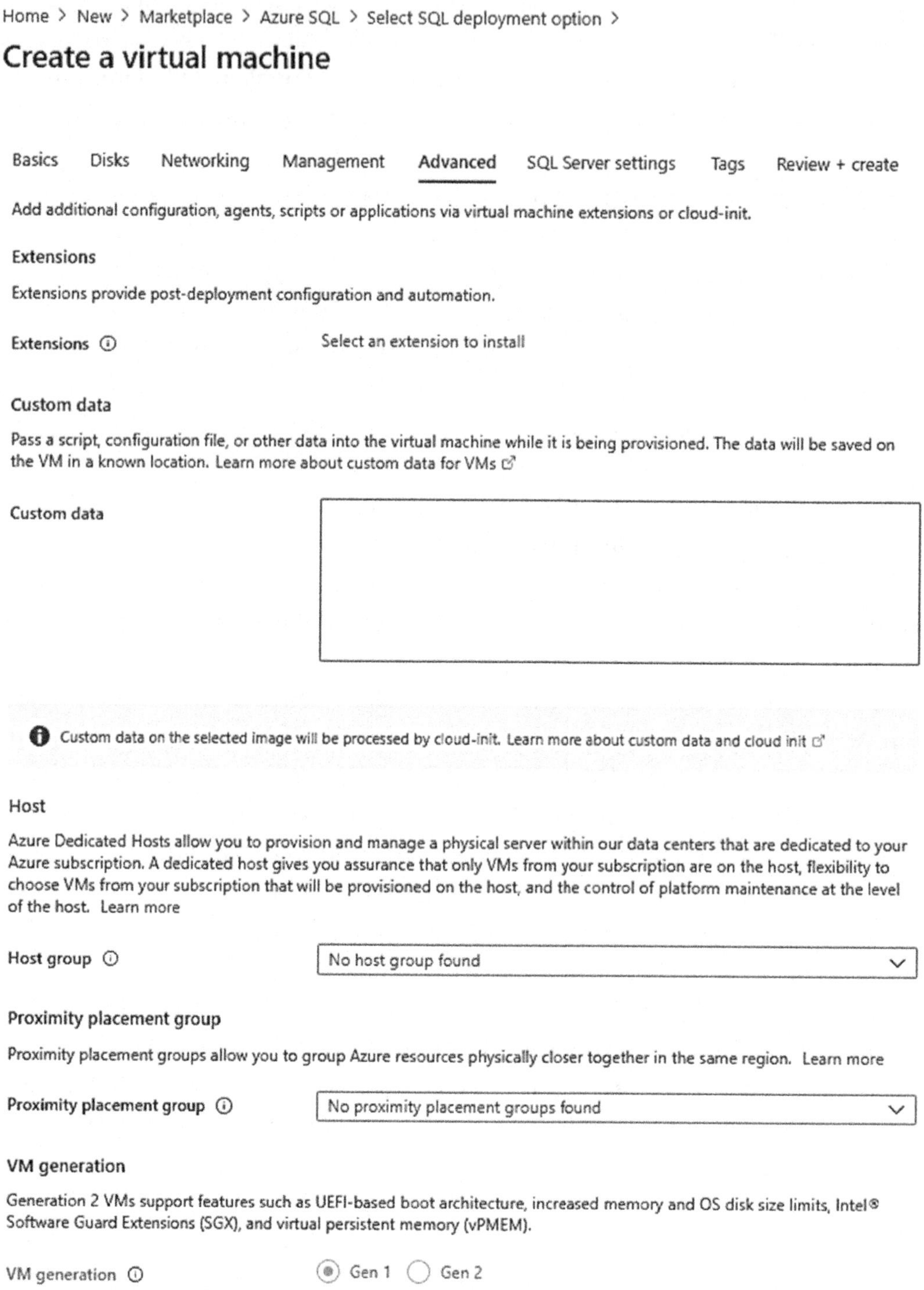

Home > New > Marketplace > Azure SQL > Select SQL deployment option >

Create a virtual machine

| Basics | Disks | Networking | Management | **Advanced** | SQL Server settings | Tags | Review + create |

Add additional configuration, agents, scripts or applications via virtual machine extensions or cloud-init.

Extensions

Extensions provide post-deployment configuration and automation.

Extensions ⓘ   Select an extension to install

Custom data

Pass a script, configuration file, or other data into the virtual machine while it is being provisioned. The data will be saved on the VM in a known location. Learn more about custom data for VMs ⌕

Custom data

ⓘ Custom data on the selected image will be processed by cloud-init. Learn more about custom data and cloud init ⌕

Host

Azure Dedicated Hosts allow you to provision and manage a physical server within our data centers that are dedicated to your Azure subscription. A dedicated host gives you assurance that only VMs from your subscription are on the host, flexibility to choose VMs from your subscription that will be provisioned on the host, and the control of platform maintenance at the level of the host. Learn more

Host group ⓘ | No host group found   ⌄ |

Proximity placement group

Proximity placement groups allow you to group Azure resources physically closer together in the same region. Learn more

Proximity placement group ⓘ | No proximity placement groups found   ⌄ |

VM generation

Generation 2 VMs support features such as UEFI-based boot architecture, increased memory and OS disk size limits, Intel® Software Guard Extensions (SGX), and virtual persistent memory (vPMEM).

VM generation ⓘ   ◉ Gen 1   ○ Gen 2

Figure 3-11. *Advanced options for Azure VM*

Extensions are applications that run inside the VM that can provide post deployment and automation tasks. The SQL Server gallery images have an extension used to configure SQL Server after deployment called **the SQL Server IaaS Agent Extension** which you can read about at `https://docs.microsoft.com/en-us/azure/azure-sql/virtual-machines/windows/sql-server-iaas-agent-extension-automate-management`. You do not need to select this extension on this screen, but there are others you may be interested in.

Host group defines an Azure Dedicated Host used for your virtual machine. I will discuss more about Azure dedicated hosts in a later section of this chapter titled "Reserved Instances and Dedicated Hosts."

Proximity placement groups are an interesting concept in Azure that allows you to request multiple Azure resources be located as close as possible within an Azure datacenter to provide the lowest network latency possible. This may be an option to consider if the application to connect to SQL Server in Azure Virtual Machine will be hosted in Azure.

Note   I would not recommend using proximity groups for a HA solution for SQL Server in Azure Virtual Machines such as Availability Groups. In this scenario, you will use a concept called Availability Sets or Availability Zones. I will discuss these concepts later in the chapter in a section titled "HADR."

VM generation allows you to specify a new VM architecture which can provide you some benefits (e.g., faster boot and install times). We do not enable all SQL Server gallery images with this option. You can read more about support for Generation 2 VMs on Azure at `https://docs.microsoft.com/en-us/azure/virtual-machines/windows/generation-2`. If you need this option and the SQL Server gallery image does not support it, you can use the "deploy on your own" technique.

Click **Next: SQL Server Settings** > to see the next set of options.

SQL Server Settings

Up to this point, all the configuration choices are independent of SQL Server. This screen provides specific configuration choices for deployment specific to SQL Server. Let us look at these choices in more detail. Figure 3-12 shows choices for Networking, Security, and Storage.

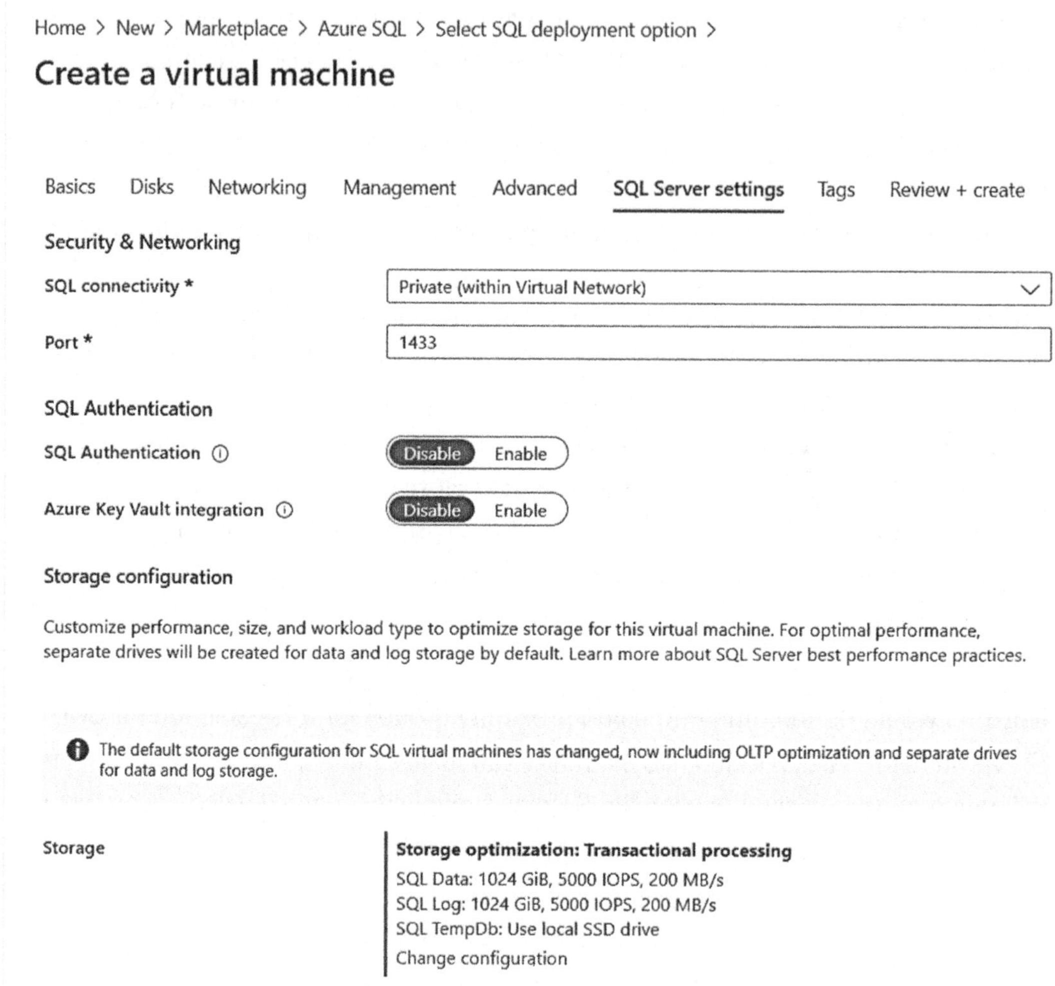

Home > New > Marketplace > Azure SQL > Select SQL deployment option >

Create a virtual machine

Basics   Disks   Networking   Management   Advanced   **SQL Server settings**   Tags   Review + create

Security & Networking

SQL connectivity *

| Private (within Virtual Network)   ∨ |

Port *

| 1433 |

SQL Authentication

SQL Authentication ⓘ   (**Disable**   Enable)

Azure Key Vault integration ⓘ   (**Disable**   Enable)

Storage configuration

Customize performance, size, and workload type to optimize storage for this virtual machine. For optimal performance, separate drives will be created for data and log storage by default. Learn more about SQL Server best performance practices.

> ⓘ The default storage configuration for SQL virtual machines has changed, now including OLTP optimization and separate drives for data and log storage.

Storage

Storage optimization: Transactional processing
SQL Data: 1024 GiB, 5000 IOPS, 200 MB/s
SQL Log: 1024 GiB, 5000 IOPS, 200 MB/s
SQL TempDb: Use local SSD drive
Change configuration

Figure 3-12. *SQL Server settings for network, security, and storage*

Note   As of the time of writing this book, SQL Server Linux images do not support SQL Server settings during deployment.

Networking provides a choice on how to expose the SQL Server instance default TCP port 1433. Think of this choice like using a firewall. *Private* means any Azure source within the virtual network of the VM can access this port. This is the default and one I recommend you use. *Local* means the only access is allowed inside the VM. *Public* means the TPC port is exposed on the Internet. As tempting as it may be to use the public option so you can connect with a tool like SSMS from your laptop to this deployed VM, I do not recommend using this option.

Note   The first time I deployed a SQL Server in Azure VM using the public option, I immediately got attacked from outside intruders trying to log in using the sa account guessing password. I found this out when I saw my ERRORLOG flooded with login failed messages. This occurred almost immediately after deploying the VM.

The choice for **SQL Authentication** is identical to enabled Mixed Mode security for SQL Server. Even though the sa login is disabled by default if you choose to enable this option, you will be prompted for a SQL login that will be granted SQL Server sysadmin rights for your deployment.

Azure Key Vault integration is a choice you might want to enable, but do not worry you can enable this post deployment. Azure Key Vault integration may be helpful to ease your use of Azure Key Value for scenarios like Transparent Data Encryption (TDE). You can read more about Azure Key Vault integration with SQL Server in Azure Virtual Machine at https://docs.microsoft.com/en-us/azure/azure-sql/virtual-machines/windows/azure-key-vault-integration-configure#enabling-and-configuring-key-vault-integration.

Storage configuration is perhaps one of the most important choices you will make for SQL Server in Azure Virtual Machine especially for performance. While I will talk more about storage performance in the section titled "Maximizing Storage Performance" later in this chapter, let us take a brief look at your options to configure storage during deployment.

The default settings for storage configuration are to configure **two data disks** using Azure Premium storage: one intended for database files and one for transaction log files. Tempdb will be kept on a local SSD drive. The default configuration as you see on the screen is intended for typical OLTP type workloads. If you click Change configuration, you will see options such as seen in Figure 3-13.

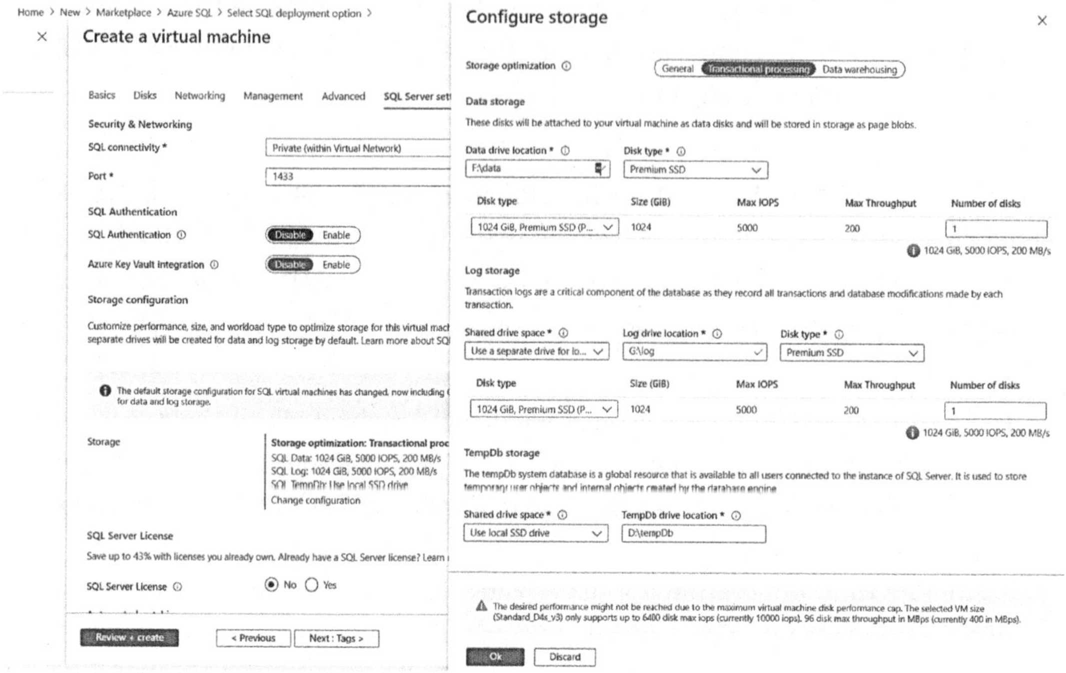

Figure 3-13. *Configuring storage for SQL Server in Azure Virtual Machine*

You can see at the top of this screen three options for **Storage optimization**: General, Transactional processing, and Data warehousing. The General option will help create a single data disk where you can place database, transaction log files, and tempdb (in different folders). The Transaction processing and Data warehousing options help you spread out your database and transaction log files on different data disks and store tempdb on the local SSD drive of the VM. This screen is provided to aid you in configuring storage to optimize performance or cost for your SQL Server deployment.

Note   We are looking to make some changes to these options in the future so this screen may be different when you view it.

For my deployment, I am going to use the defaults which deploy two data disks for database and transaction log files and use the local SSD drive for tempdb. You must choose some disk options here, but you can totally reconfigure or change this after deployment.

Notice the warning at the bottom of the screen. It says the configured disks have a performance vector that is greater than what the VM size supports. You could either choose a disk type for each that lines up more with the VM size selected or choose a larger VM size. Again, you can change these after you deploy. SQL Server does not place any databases or files on these data disks. System databases such as master, model, and msdb are placed by default on the operating system disk.

Figure 3-14 shows the additional options for SQL Server Settings.

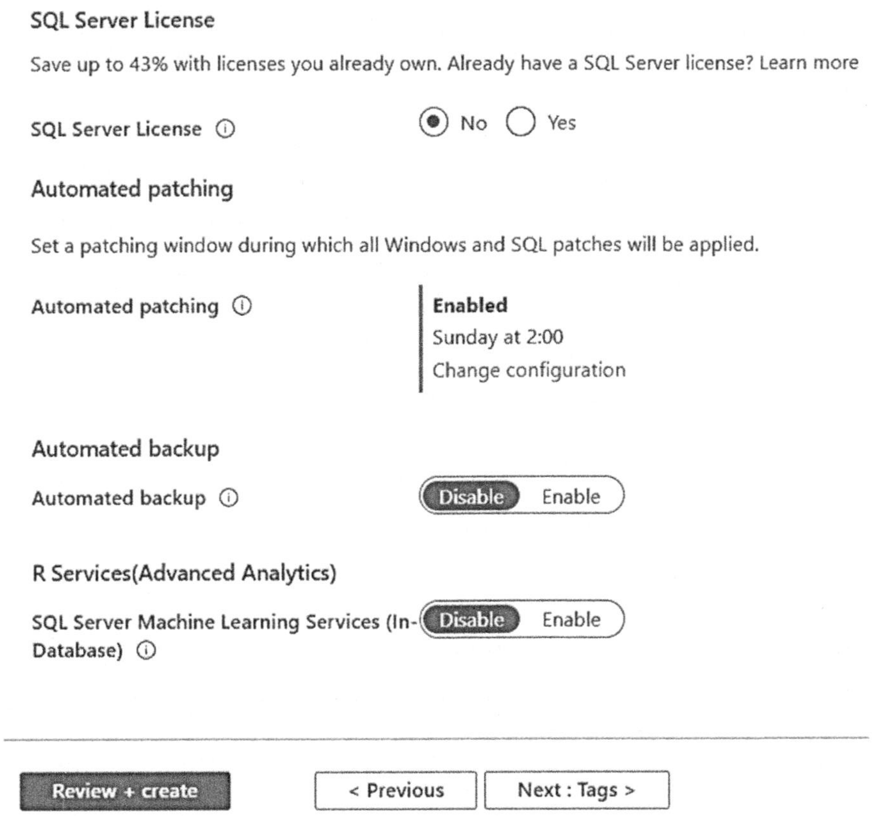

Figure 3-14. *Additional SQL Server Settings*

SQL Server License allows you to testify that you have an existing SQL Server license that allows you to apply it for Azure Hybrid Benefit (AHB) like the choice for Windows. This can be a significant cost savings to you when using SQL Server for Azure Virtual Machine. You can learn more about AHB at `https://azure.microsoft.com/en-us/pricing/hybrid-benefit/`.

Note   If you do not see this option available, it is because you picked a SQL Server image choice where this option cannot be or is already selected. For example, images that start with the title BYOL (this means Bring Your Own License) already imply you are stating you can use AHB. Developer Edition is free, so no license applies.

We also announced in 2019 new licensing benefits for HA and DR scenarios when using Azure Virtual Machine. You can read more at `https://cloudblogs.microsoft.com/sqlserver/2019/10/30/new-high-availability-and-disaster-recovery-benefits-for-sql-server/`.

Automated patching provides specific configurations on when how to deploy important and critical updates for Windows and SQL Server. Other updates for Windows and SQL Server will depend on how you configure Windows Update inside the VM. You can read more about automated patching at `https://docs.microsoft.com/en-us/azure/azure-sql/virtual-machines/windows/automated-patching`. If you do not select this during deployment, you can configure it later. You can also provide your own customer automation for updates as found in our documentation at `https://docs.microsoft.com/en-us/azure/automation/automation-tutorial-update-management`.

Automated backup uses the Managed Backups to Azure capability that was shipped as part of SQL Server 2016. Your needs may vary, but many users might find this option very useful to provide a simple automated backup solution for SQL Server. When you enable this option, you have several choices to configure how backups are executed. You can also configure this option after deployment. You can read more about automated backups at `https://docs.microsoft.com/en-us/azure/azure-sql/virtual-machines/windows/automated-backup`.

Note   Automated patching and Automated backup options may not show up as enabled immediately after deployment. The SQL IaaS extension runs in the background after deployment.

R Services (Advanced Analytics) is an option to install the SQL Server Machines Learning services feature as part of deployment. I will describe in the next section called "Deploy!" what exactly is installed with the SQL Server gallery image.

Click **Next: Tags >** to see the last option.

Tags

The last option before you deploy your virtual machine is to potentially use a *tag*.
Tags are a concept supported by the Azure ecosystem to assign a string value to a
resource in Azure, like a virtual machine, to organize your resources. Tags have many
different purposes. As you can see in Figure 3-15, you can see I used a tag of a Name =
Environment and Value = Development, assigned to a Virtual Machine resource.

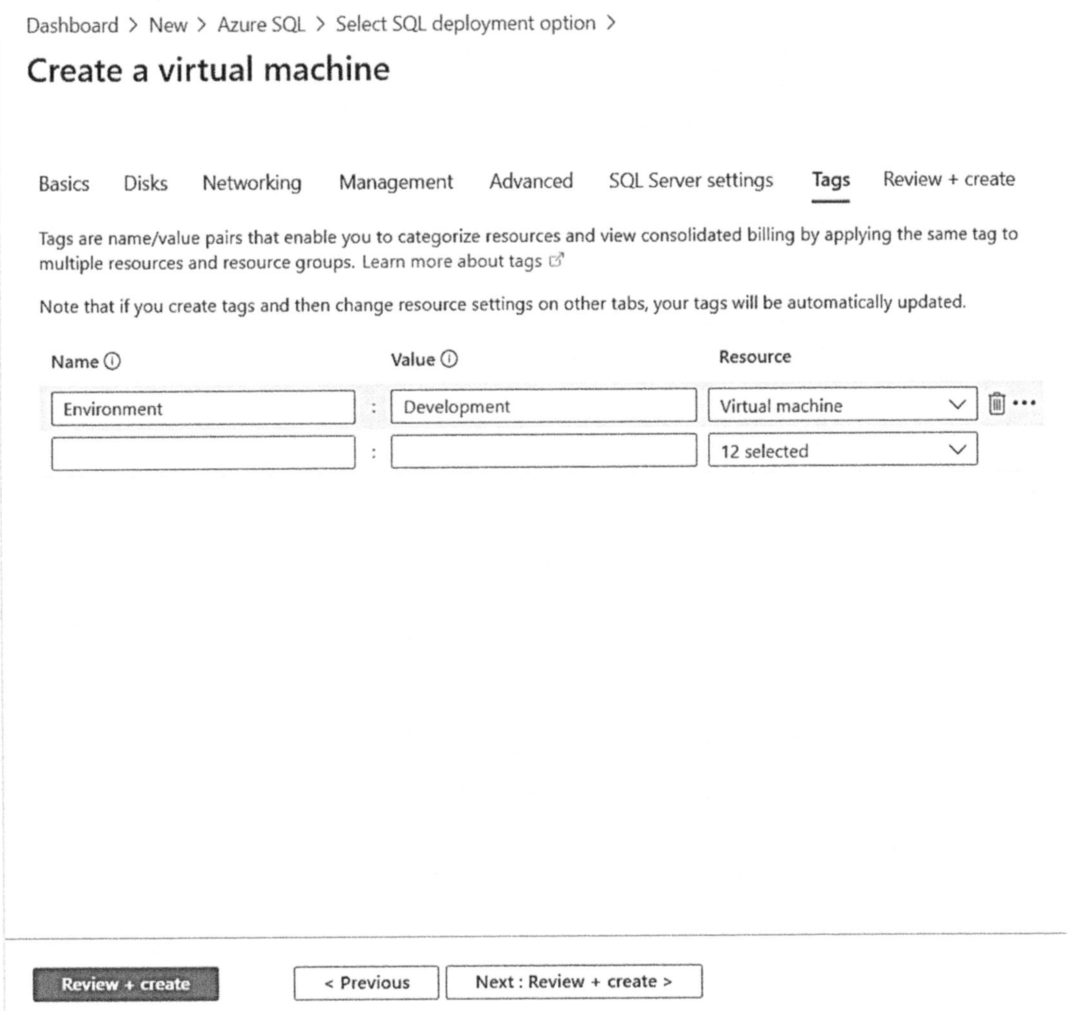

Dashboard > New > Azure SQL > Select SQL deployment option >

Create a virtual machine

| Basics | Disks | Networking | Management | Advanced | SQL Server settings | **Tags** | Review + create |

Tags are name/value pairs that enable you to categorize resources and view consolidated billing by applying the same tag to
multiple resources and resource groups. Learn more about tags ⤢

Note that if you create tags and then change resource settings on other tabs, your tags will be automatically updated.

Name ⓘ		Value ⓘ		Resource	
Environment	:	Development		Virtual machine	⌄ 🗑 •••
	:			12 selected	⌄

Review + create   < Previous   Next : Review + create >

Figure 3-15. *Assigning tags to an Azure resource*

Now I can use the Azure portal, CLI, or APIs to "find all resources or virtual machine that is part of my development environment." You can learn more about how to use Tags at https://docs.microsoft.com/en-us/azure/azure-resource-manager/management/tag-resources.

Click **Next: Review + create** > to validate and deploy the virtual machine.

Deploy!

The portal will take all your options, perform validation steps, and then present you the ability to create the virtual machine. Figure 3-16 shows some interesting information on the final validation screen before you click Create.

Figure 3-16. *Validation before creating the virtual machine*

At the top of this screen, you can see the size of the VM you chose plus estimated costs per hour. Also notice *Terms of use* and *Privacy policy*. The End User Licensing Agreement (EULA) that comes with SQL Server still applies to Azure Virtual Machine since this is a fully licensed SQL Server. However, since you are deploying the virtual machine in Azure, there are terms and privacy policies you should review. You can read more about Azure terms of use at `https://azure.microsoft.com/en-us/support/legal/`. Privacy is a very important topic, and since Microsoft is hosting your virtual machine in the cloud, you need to understand all the details of what information Microsoft collects. Read more at `https://privacy.microsoft.com/en-us/privacystatement`. Your usage of a gallery image for the operating system and/or SQL Server also has terms called Azure Marketplace Terms. You can read more at `https://azure.microsoft.com/en-us/support/legal/marketplace-terms/`.

You will also notice on this screen a warning about allowing the RDP port to be exposed to the Internet. You will learn more about how to control access and limit any issues in the following section titled "Connecting to Your VM." If you scroll down on this screen, you will see all the details of the options you chose to deploy the virtual machine. Notice also at the bottom of the screen the option to **Download a template for automation**. I will discuss using an option for automation with a template in a section later in this chapter called "Using a CLI and ARM Template."

Click the **Create** button when you are ready to launch! The deployment of the virtual machine is asynchronous so you can even exit the portal and the deployment is done in the background. However, if you leave the portal screen open, you can track progress live. Within seconds of clicking Create, my screen looks like Figure 3-17 to track the progress of the deployment.

Figure 3-17. *Azure virtual machine deployment in progress*

Not only does the main screen refresh as the virtual machine is being created but you can click the Notifications icon on the title bar of the portal to also track progress. In my example, in about 10 minutes my deployment was complete. Figure 3-18 shows all the details including status from the Notifications icon.

Figure 3-18. *Deployment complete for SQL Server in Azure Virtual Machine*

You will notice for Deployment details that it is not just a virtual machine deployed but many different resources including network interfaces, disks, storage accounts, virtual networks, and security groups. If you want more details about the deployment, you can click **More events in the activity log**. Figure 3-19 shows an example of activity log output. Remember the activity log is your "event log" for all operations as part of the Azure ecosystem.

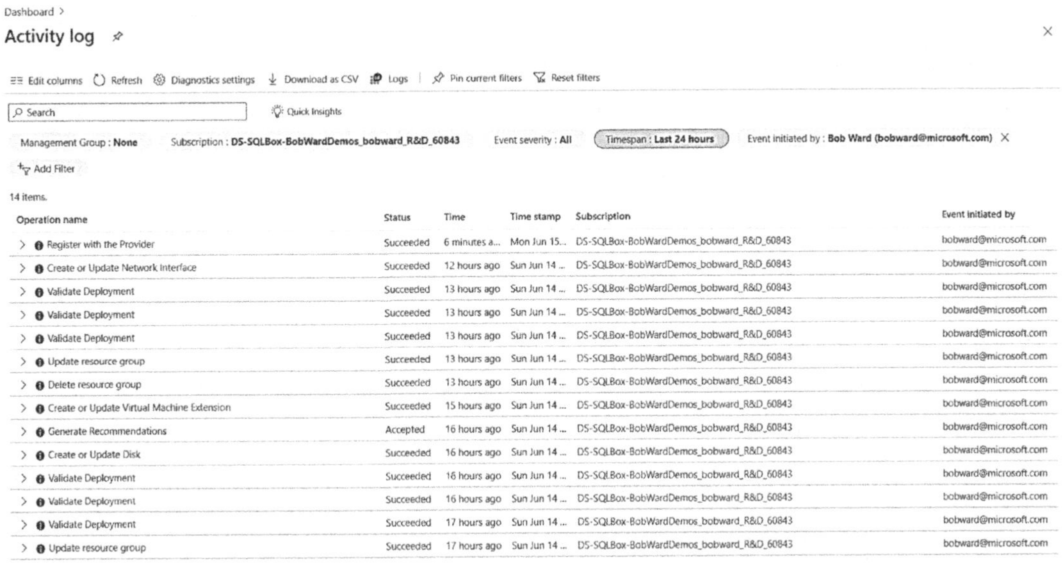

Figure 3-19. Azure activity log for a virtual machine deployment

If you click **Go to resource**, you will be presented with the overview screen for the virtual machine. Let us take a brief moment to talk about how to navigate the *overview* screen for a virtual machine.

Navigating in the Portal

You will find yourself often using several aspects to the overview screen for Azure virtual machine and all Azures resources in this book. Let us examine the main areas of the overview screen as seen in Figure 3-20.

Figure 3-20. *The overview screen for Azure virtual machine*

1. **Resource Menu**

   Each Azure resource provides a series of options to manage the resource. The very top of the Resource Menu is the same for all resources. You will want to use the **Overview** option to "find your way back" if you are deep into using *blades* for details on the virtual machine. This is super important as I often have hit the X at the top right of a screen and completely lost context of my VM. By clicking Overview on the Resource Menu, I can keep that context.

   Other options exist on the Resource Menu for virtual machines including Settings, Operations, Monitoring, and Support + Troubleshooting.

   I will not go over each option here but will use several of these options throughout the rest of the chapter.

2. **Command bar**

   These are buttons that allow you to operate the virtual machine. Every Azure resource has buttons unique to the resource. The most common buttons you will use are Connect, Start, and Stop.

3. **Working Pane**

   This area displays key information about your virtual machine including resource group and status but also lets you navigate to certain aspects of the virtual machine such as virtual network.

4. **Monitoring Pane**

   Technically, this is part of the Working pane as there are options to look at Properties (this is the default, so you need to choose Monitoring here) and choose Capabilities, but I mainly use this for Monitoring. You can see in Figure 3-20 some of the key performance metrics typically viewed for a virtual machine such as CPU, Network, and I/O. Think of this as your "Task Manager" but viewed outside of the VM. This is one of the benefits of Azure Monitor in the Azure ecosystem. Explore more about how to navigate around the portal at `https://docs.microsoft.com/en-us/azure/azure-portal/azure-portal-overview#getting-around-the-portal`.

Connecting to Your VM

Now that you have deployed, one of the first things you will want to do is connect to the VM. For a Windows VM, the most popular way to connect and use the VM is with the Remote Desktop Protocol (RDP). You saw in the VM deployment example that I chose the option to open the RDP port (3389) to the Internet.

To use RDP, click the Connect button in the Command bar and choose RDP. You will see now a screen giving you the option of downloading an RDP file to use with your Remote Desktop program (typically Remote Desktop client on Windows machines) as seen in Figure 3-21.

Figure 3-21. *Connecting with RDP to Azure virtual machine*

By default, the RDP file will be copied to your *Downloads* folder on your client machine. The public IP address for the VM is also posted here if you just want to take any valid RDP client and connect directly to the VM. Once you connect, just like any VM or Windows computer, you will be prompted to enter your credentials (which you supplied as part of deployment) which by default is a member of the Administrators group.

Note   If you notice under Download RDP File, there are options to help you troubleshoot any RDP connectivity issues which I highly recommend you look at should you encounter any issues.

You can also see on this screen a recommendation to enable *just-in-time access* to the VM to improve security. Just-in-time access is a way to gain RDP access to the VM "on-demand" so that the RDP port is not opened to the Internet when you are not using the VM. This is a way to allow you to connect to the VM from any client yet limit the exposure of the RDP port to everyone. I use this method within Microsoft for all my Azure VMs. You can learn more about just-in-time access at `https://docs.microsoft.com/en-us/azure/security-center/security-center-just-in-time`.

There are two other methods to restrict access to RDP for the VM. One method is to set a more restrictive *Inbound port rule* for port 3389. You can click Networking on the Resource on the Resource Menu to access these rules. Check out the documentation at `https://docs.microsoft.com/en-us/azure/virtual-machines/windows/nsg-quickstart-portal` to learn more how to do this. The other method is to use a more secure method called Azure Bastion which you can learn more about at `https://azure.microsoft.com/en-us/services/azure-bastion/`.

You may also connect with standard SQL tools from another Azure VM that you have deployed in the same Azure virtual network. Keep in mind that if anytime you deploy an Azure VM in the same resource group as another VM, they are both part of the same virtual network by default. I use this method a lot when using many different VMs in Azure.

Exploring the SQL Server Installation

I thought you might find it interesting to know exactly what we install and how we configure the SQL Server instance when you deploy with a SQL Server gallery images.

What Is Installed

A SQL Server gallery image installs the entire database engine, SQL Server Analysis Services, SQL Server Integration Services, MDS, and DQS. In addition, we install the following engine features:

- SQL Server Agent

- SQL Server Replication

- Full-text search

We also install client, tools, SDK, and SQL Server Management Studio. We do not install Polybase by default. As I have described earlier in this chapter, you can install R Services as part of the deployment based on an option you choose.

For a SQL Server gallery image, we copy the SQL Server media so you can install or remove any features you want. You can find all the setup files in the **C:\SQLServerFull** folder in the VM. Figure 3-22 shows an example of what features are installed by default using a SQL Server gallery image.

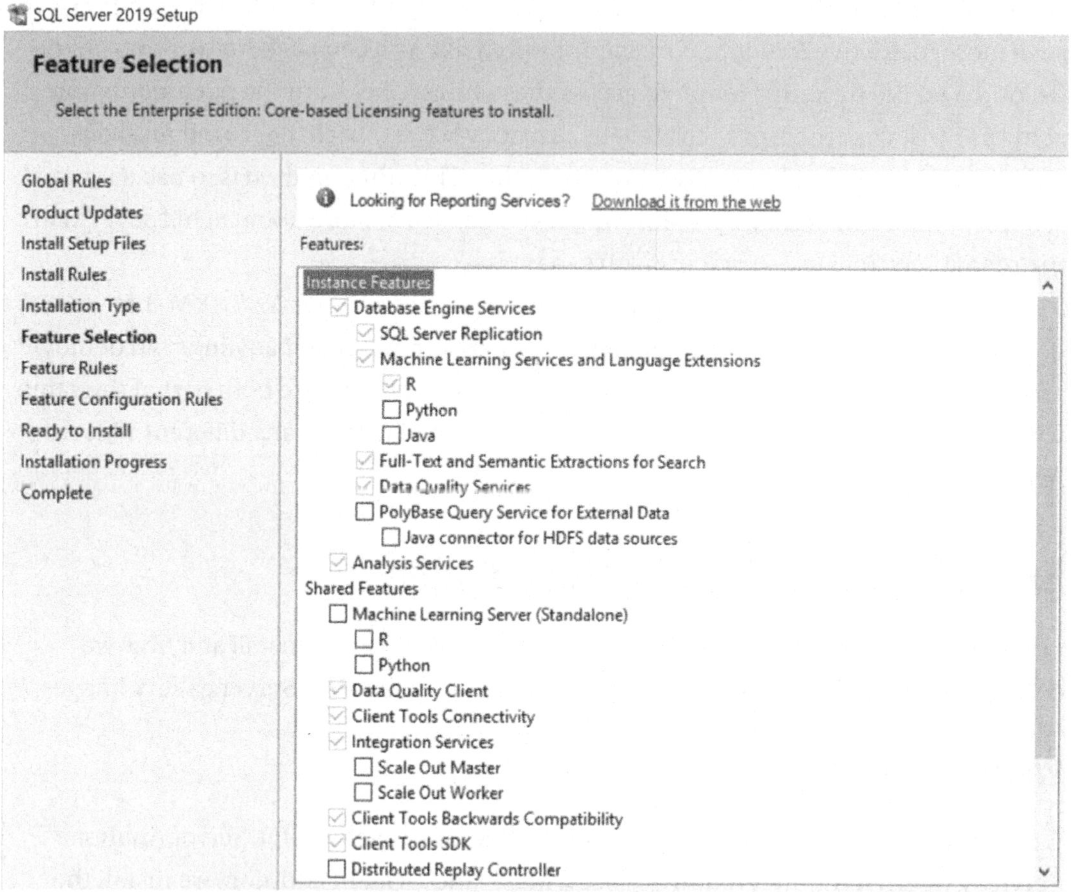

Figure 3-22. *SQL Server features installed by default*

What Is Configured

The following is a list of configuration choices we make as part of a SQL Server gallery image installation:

- SQL Server, SQL Server Agent, and SSIS services are set to Automatic and are running after deployment. Service SIDs are used for all services.

- The VM admin account you specify during deployment becomes a SQL sysadmin.

- The # of tempdb files is to a default of 2. MAXDOP is also configured for 2 for the instance.

Note   Why? Because the gallery images are "images" that are predefined, and they were built on a two-core machine. This is an important thing to note and make sure you adjust post deployment. We are looking toward the future for a better way to help integrate these choices to align with your VM size vCore deployment.

- The filestream feature is disabled by default (but can be enabled and supported).

- Always On Availability Groups are disabled by default (but can be enabled and supported).

- The TCP/IP protocol is enabled for SQL Server (even for Developer Edition).

- We typically have a recent Cumulative Update installed, but it may not be the exact latest cumulative update. You can read more about how we keep our images up to date at `https://docs.microsoft.com/en-us/azure/azure-sql/virtual-machines/windows/sql-server-on-azure-vm-iaas-what-is-overview#lifecycle`.

- Locked pages and Instant File Initialization are not enabled by default (they are supported, and I personally recommend you use these when possible).

- CEIP is enabled by default, but you can disable it. Read more at `https://docs.microsoft.com/en-us/azure/virtual-machines/windows/sql/virtual-machines-windows-sql-server-iaas-overview#customer-experience-improvement-program-ceip`.

- I also observed the Microsoft VSS Writer for SQL Server is installed. You can read more about the SQL Writer Service at `https://docs.microsoft.com/en-us/sql/database-engine/configure-windows/sql-writer-service`.

Deploy on Your Own

Today when I deploy a SQL Server instance in a Hyper-V virtual machine (often just on my laptop), I go through the process of choosing certain options for the VM (like number of logical CPUs, memory, location of disks) and then install an operating system like Windows Server or Linux (typically from an .ISO file). When this is done, I usually connect to the VM with Remote Desktop (Windows) or ssh (Linux). For Windows, I will download the installation media for SQL Server to my local drive and then "copy and paste" it into a folder in the VM. I then run setup and am off and running to deploy SQL Server. For Linux, I just make sure my VM is connected to the Internet and run the SQL Server on Linux installation which downloads packages as part of the installation process.

This same process is almost identical to the "deploy on your own" option for SQL Server on Azure Virtual Machine, with one exception. You will configure the VM and deploy an Operating System by *using one of the gallery images just for the operating system*. You can use the portal, az cli, or PowerShell to choose your VM size and Operating System very similar to using a SQL Server gallery image, except all the options for SQL Server will not be part of the process.

This technique is one I sometimes use because I have complete control of how and what is installed with SQL Server vs. what Microsoft chooses from a gallery image. If you use this method, there is one downside. You do not immediately get to take advantage of the options you get with a SQL gallery image such as automated backups and security updates. Fortunately, there is a solution to use this customized method for deployment but take advantage of automated features and licensing options. This solution is called the **SQL Virtual Machine resource provider**. I will discuss more about the SQL VM Resource Provider in the following section called "SQL Virtual Machine Resource Provider."

Keep in mind that using this method is one way to install SQL Server Reporting Services which you still have access to in your installation media files and can be part of your SQL Server license.

Using a CLI and ARM Template

Azure provides other ways to deploy SQL Server on Azure Virtual Machine besides the Azure portal using a command-line interface (CLI) with the **az vm** CLI.

Here is an example of using az vm to create a virtual machine like the VM example I showed you in the portal (I ran this using the Azure Cloud Shell):

> **Tip**   To use az vm, you must first create the resource group using az group create. In addition, to find the name of the SQL gallery images, you need to first run the command `az vm image list-offer -l <region> -p MicrosoftSQLServer`.

```
az group create -l eastus -n bwsqlvmsrg
az vm create -n bwsql2019 -l eastus -g bwsqlvmsrg --image
MicrosoftSQLServer:sql2019-ws2019:enterprise:latest --size Standard_D4s_
V3 --admin-username thewandog --admin-password <password> --nsg-rule RDP
```

> **Tip**   If you want to only install SQL Server Engine components (basically not SSAS and SSIS), you can use the image MicrosoftSQLServer:sql2019-ws2019:enterprise dbengineonly:latest.

A few thoughts about this example are as follows:

- You can add more options for the VM independent of SQL Server as you saw from the portal.

- You cannot configure SQL Server Settings but can use the az sql vm command or the portal to do this post deployment. In fact, you need to do this to have this VM registered with the SQL Resource Provider.

- You will also need to configure storage (including moving tempdb to the local SSD drive).

You can read all the options for az vm at `https://docs.microsoft.com/en-us/cli/azure/vm?view=azure-cli-latest`.

PowerShell also has a module to create an Azure Virtual Machine with the **New-AzVM** command. In addition, a PowerShell command called **New-AzSqlVM** can be used to add the SQL IaaS extension and choose a license type (you could then configure auto-backup and auto-security settings post deployment). While az CLI accepts many parameters, PowerShell expects you to run various commands to set properties of the VM before you execute New-AzVM. You can see a great example of using PowerShell to create a SQL Server in Azure Virtual Machine at `https://docs.microsoft.com/en-us/azure/azure-sql/virtual-machines/windows/create-sql-vm-powershell`.

While you can script out the usage of az CLI or PowerShell with all the parameters and option, there is a better way. Azure provides a mechanism for any Azure resource to automate the use of Azure CLI tools with a concept called an *ARM template*. An ARM template is a JSON file that describes in a declarative fashion the configuration and infrastructure of a deployment.

While you can try to learn how to build templates from scratch, I recommend you get an example. If GitHub is your thing, you can download and edit an example of an azure template to create a new SQL Server in Azure Virtual Machine from `https://github.com/Azure/azure-quickstart-templates/tree/master/101-sql-vm-new-storage`. Azure templates not only configure all the properties to create the virtual machine but support *parameters* so you can use a template and then supply the parameters you want to customize the deployment at runtime.

The az CLI command **az deployment** can be used to deploy based on a template. You can even export a template based on a current deployment using this command. You can also download a template from an existing resource, resource group, or past deployment from the Azure Portal. You can read more about how to deploy using az CLI and templates at `https://docs.microsoft.com/en-us/azure/azure-resource-manager/templates/deploy-cli`. You can read how to download a template from the portal at `https://docs.microsoft.com/en-us/azure/virtual-machines/windows/download-template`.

Reserved Instances and Dedicated Hosts

To save money on Azure Virtual Machines, you can prepay for a period (one to three years) and then save on the compute costs of the Azure Virtual Machine as you deploy. This option is called **Azure Reserved VM Instances**. If you plan to deploy many SQL Server Azure Virtual Machines, you probably should investigate this option. Learn more about reserved instances at `https://azure.microsoft.com/en-us/pricing/reserved-vm-instances/`.

You might remember there was an option during the deployment example in the portal called a *dedicated host*. An **Azure Dedicated Host** allows you to reserve physical servers dedicated to you and your organization. While normal virtual machines are dedicated to your deployment, you are typically sharing the underlying hosts with other users. A dedicated host may give you the option you need for specific compliance requirements. In addition, you have more control over maintenance events of the infrastructure hosting your VM deployment. You can read more about dedicated hosts at https://docs.microsoft.com/en-us/azure/virtual-machines/windows/dedicated-hosts.

Migrate Using Azure Migrate

You might be considering a migration of an existing SQL Server installation to Azure Virtual Machine. Here are a few tips that might help your migration plans.

Restoring a Database

Since SQL Server in Azure Virtual Machine is a full SQL Server engine, one simple way to migrate an existing SQL Server is to just restore a backup of existing databases.

Since the target SQL Server is in the Azure Infrastructure, you have a few ways to do this:

- Copy the backup file with "copy and paste" over RDP. RDP clients allow you to copy and paste files, and I have done this a bunch of times for Azure VM. Of course, this only makes sense for small backup files (although I have done this with backup files even 1Gb in size).

- Back up the database to Azure Storage using the backup to URL functionality within SQL Server. Then in the Azure VM, restore the backup from the same Azure Storage account. You can read more about SQL Server Backup to URL at https://docs.microsoft.com/en-us/sql/relational-databases/backup-restore/sql-server-backup-to-url?view=sql-server-ver15.

- Use **Azure Files**. Think of this like creating your own file share in the cloud. You can use az CLI or tools to copy your backup file to the Azure file share. Then you can mount the Azure file share within the Azure VM (i.e., it will look like a network share in the VM). Read more about how to do this at https://docs.microsoft.com/en-us/azure/storage/files/storage-files-introduction. I have used this method several times for both Azure VMs for Windows and Linux.

- For large backup files, consider the **Azure Import/Export service**. You literally will securely ship a hard drive to Microsoft (we can supply you these with Azure Data Box Disk), and we will import this to Azure Storage or Azure files. You can read more about this at https://docs.microsoft.com/en-us/azure/storage/common/ storage-import-export-service.

Using Data Migration Assistant (DMA)

The Data Migration Assistant (DMA) is a free tool that can be downloaded from www. microsoft.com/en-us/download/details.aspx?id=53595. I will discuss the importance of DMA more with Azure SQL in Chapter 4 of the book. But know that you can use DMA to migrate a database from SQL Server into a deployed SQL Server in Azure Virtual Machine. The tool will use a backup/restore method and requires you to be able to connect to the SQL Server Azure Virtual Machine in a virtual network connected to the computer where you are running DMA.

Using Azure Migrate Server Migration

What if you would like to migrate the installation of an entire physical server or virtual machine to Azure instead of just your data? Azure supports this concept with a service called **Azure Migrate Server Migration**. This is perhaps a true *lift and shift* operation. Think of this like taking a snapshot of your machine or VM and creating an entire VM from the snapshot. Then you configure and optimize after the fact. You can read more about Server Migration at https://docs.microsoft.com/en-us/azure/migrate/ migrate-services-overview#azure-migrate-server-migration-tool. A great example of how this works for VMware installation can be seen at https://aka.ms/ mechanicsazuremigrate with legendary Windows guru Jeff Woolsey.

Deploying SQL Server on Linux with Azure Virtual Machine

Up to this point, my examples and discussion have centered around deploying SQL Server in Azure Virtual Machines based on Windows Server.

The options and deployment process are very similar for SQL Server on Linux with some notable differences:

- The gallery images are offered for Linux distributions Ubuntu, Red Hat Enterprise Server, and SUSE. You pay for licenses if the Linux distribution requires it (e.g., Ubuntu is a free license).

- We do not support any SQL Server Settings. This is because the SQL Resource Provider does not exist for Linux (yet; we are working on it).

- This means Azure Hybrid Benefit, special storage recommendations, automated backup, and automated security updates are not available.

After using a SQL Linux gallery image, you will find the mssql-server, mssql-tools, and mssql-ha packages have been installed.

SQL Agent is not enabled, but you can do this yourself. You can enable SQL Server Agent on Linux with the mssql-conf script which you can read more about at `https://docs.microsoft.com/en-us/sql/linux/sql-server-linux-setup-sql-agent`.

Post deployment, you can use documented methods to install other SQL Server Linux packages. For example, you can read `https://docs.microsoft.com/en-us/sql/linux/sql-server-linux-setup-machine-learning` to learn how to install SQL Server Machine Learning Services for Linux.

Deploying SQL Server Containers

There is no special gallery image or process to deploy SQL Server Containers in Azure Virtual Machine. You will use the same process you use today to deploy a SQL Server container in a virtual machine. You can read more about this process at `https://docs.microsoft.com/en-us/sql/linux/quickstart-install-connect-docker`.

Tip   If you need to deploy SQL Server containers in a Windows 10 VM with Docker, you may need to deploy a VM that supports nested virtualization. You can read more about this at `https://docs.microsoft.com/en-us/azure/virtual-machines/windows/nested-virtualization`. You can read more about how to run Linux Containers on Windows Server at `https://success.docker.com/article/how-to-enable-linux-containers-on-windows-server-2019`.

Another option in Azure to deploy SQL Server containers is with **Azure DevOps** and **Pipelines**. I did a demonstration of this capability at the virtual Build 2020 conference which you can watch at `https://mybuild.microsoft.com/sessions/61cd7d08-115b-4ff5-b1a7-5df70649863e?source=sessions`. The code for the demo can be found at `https://github.com/microsoft/bobsql/tree/master/demos/build2020`. This capability is so powerful including the ability for Azure to automatically deploy your containers without you needing to deploy a VM.

Finally, **Azure Kubernetes Service** (AKS) provides a method to deploy containers at scale using the power of Kubernetes. You can see a tutorial of how to do this at `https://docs.microsoft.com/en-us/sql/linux/tutorial-sql-server-containers-kubernetes?view=sql-server-ver15`.

SQL Virtual Machine Resource Provider

You have seen several examples in this chapter of special options and advantages of deploying a SQL Server in Azure Virtual Machine with a gallery image, including licensing, configuration, and automation. This is all made possible through the **SQL Virtual Machine Resource Provider** in coordination with the SQL IaaS Extension.

If you deploy using a SQL Server gallery image, you just take advantage of what the resource provider does, and no action is required from you. However, if you deploy on your own and want these advantages including licensing, you have some steps you need to do.

First, you need to ensure your Azure subscription has the Microsoft. SqlVirtualMachine resource provider registered. You can do this from the Azure Portal as part of your Azure subscription. Or you can use the following PowerShell command:

```
Register-AzureRmResourceProvider -ProviderNamespace Microsoft.
SqlVirtualMachine
```

Next, you need to register your virtual machine with the resource provider. Registering your VM installs the SQL Server IaaS Agent Extension. The default mode to install this agent is called *lightweight mode*. This provides you the capability of taking advantage of Azure Hybrid Benefit (AHB) and does not require a restart of the VM.

You can then register the VM for *full management mode* which gives you all the capabilities as you do when using a SQL Server gallery image. This does, however, require a restart of the VM.

Note   For older releases of SQL Server such as SQL Server 2008, you can even use a "NoAgent" mode so you can register your SQL Server to take advantage of licensing.

You can read about all of the steps at `https://docs.microsoft.com/en-us/azure/azure-sql/virtual-machines/windows/sql-vm-resource-provider-register`. Mine Tokus, the lead program manager for SQL Server on Azure VM, wrote an excellent blog describing the SQL VM Resource Provider at `https://azure.microsoft.com/en-us/blog/sql-server-on-azure-virtual-machine-resource-provider/`.

Once your VM is registered or if you used a SQL gallery image, your VM is now considered both an Azure virtual machine resource and also a SQL virtual machine. This means your VM will show up when searching for **Azure SQL** resources. Additionally, the portal will show additional properties as seen in Figure 3-23 based on the deployment I did earlier in this chapter.

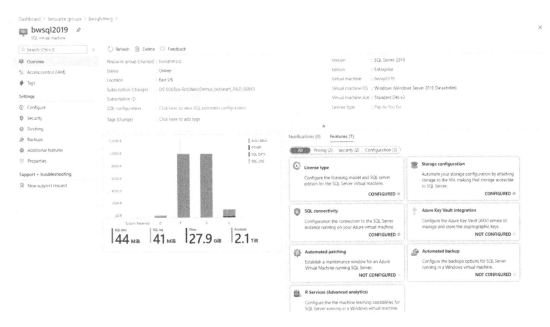

Figure 3-23. *A registered SQL virtual machine*

Note   One easy way to get to this overview page is to go to the Resource Menu of your virtual machine and select SQL Server Configuration. Then click Manage SQL virtual machine.

In addition to using the portal, we have added to the az cli a special option called **az sql vm**. This allows you to register your VM or change SQL Server properties. You can read all these options at `https://docs.microsoft.com/en-us/cli/azure/sql/vm?view=azure-cli-latest`.

Configuration

Inside the VM, your configuration of SQL Server is completely identical to a virtual machine you deploy in your data center. There are some aspects to configuration of the virtual machine from the Azure infrastructure you should be aware of.

Stopping vs. Deallocating

There could be several reasons to shut down your virtual machine in Azure. If you shut down the virtual machine inside the VM (e.g., Windows shutdown), the VM is stopped but compute resources are reserved for the VM, which means you are still billed for compute. The VM status will show as **Stopped** in the portal and CLI interfaces. To shut down the VM and ensure you are not billed for compute, you need to use the interfaces outside the VM (such as the portal or az CLI) to stop the VM. In this case, the status of the VM is listed as **Stopped (deallocated)**. Depending on your requirements, you can even automate the process of starting and stopping VMs using Azure interfaces. Read more at `https://techcommunity.microsoft.com/t5/educator-developer-blog/azure-virtual-machine-auto-shutdown/ba-p/379342`.

A related topic is maintenance windows for the infrastructure hosting virtual machines. Read more about updates and maintenance of Azure virtual machine hosts at `https://docs.microsoft.com/en-us/azure/virtual-machines/maintenance-and-updates`.

Resizing

What if you did not pick the right Azure virtual machine size during deployment? You can use the Azure portal (choose Size from the Resource Menu) or CLI interfaces to change the size of the virtual machine. This process is called *resizing* an Azure virtual machine. Resizing is much like you being able to change the resources available (CPU, storage, memory, etc.) for a VM within your data center. While you can resize a running Azure VM, a reboot of the VM is required for the resize operation. The sizes available to your choice to resize depend on whether your VM is running or stopped (deallocated). This difference is because there may be only certain sizes available on the current host of your VM (the running case). To see the full complete list of VM sizes, I recommend you stop (deallocate) your VM first. Read the overall Azure virtual machine resize story at `https://azure.microsoft.com/en-us/blog/resize-virtual-machines/`.

You can use Azure Migrate to move Azure virtual machines to other regions. Read more at `https://docs.microsoft.com/en-us/azure/site-recovery/azure-to-azure-tutorial-migrate`.

In addition, to change the resource group or subscription of your virtual machine, read the documentation at `https://docs.microsoft.com/en-us/azure/azure-resource-manager/management/move-resource-group-and-subscription`.

Security

There are a few areas you can configure related to security for SQL Server on Azure Virtual Machine outside of the standard SQL Server security options for the database engine.

RBAC

Role-Based Access Control (RBAC) allows you to assign privileges to other Azure accounts to have permissions to manage the Azure virtual machine. Learn more at `https://docs.microsoft.com/en-us/azure/role-based-access-control/quickstart-assign-role-user-portal`.

Advanced Data Security

Advanced Data Security (ADS) represents a series of capabilities for security for SQL Server in Azure. You will learn more about these capabilities in Chapter 6 of this book.

For now, understand that ADS has been expanded to support Azure Virtual Machine. Learn more at `https://azure.microsoft.com/en-us/updates/advanced-data-security-for-sql-servers-on-azure-virtual-machines/`.

Other Config Options

There are other options to configure your Azure Virtual Machine using the portal from the Resource Menu or CLI interfaces.

Examples include resetting the password for the admin user, viewing Security recommendations, and redeploying the VM to another host. Read more about some of these options at `https://docs.microsoft.com/en-us/azure/virtual-machines/windows/tutorial-config-management`.

Maximizing Storage Performance

Getting the right size for your Azure Virtual Machine is the number one factor in ensuring you have the right performance you need for SQL Server (except for standard SQL Server performance optimization practices).

You saw earlier in this chapter the example of how a SQL Server gallery image will create additional managed *data disks* based on Azure Premium storage. To achieve your best, I/O performance *and availability* SQL Server on Azure Virtual Machine, you should keep these principles in mind:

- Do not create any user databases on the OS disk. The system databases (except for tempdb) are there which should not pose a problem.

- Put tempdb on the local SSD drive which is also called temporary storage. If your VM needs to be failed over to a different host, the contents of tempdb are lost but who cares since tempdb is recreated at startup time.

- Separate your database and log files on different *managed* disks.

- Use read caching for disks hosting database files (available with Premium Storage). If you need more disk space and IOPS than a given managed disks supports, use multiple data disks with concepts like Storage Spaces.

- Use no caching for disks hosting transaction log files.

- Use Premium managed disks at minimum (also called Premium SSD). Recently, a new disk type called Ultra is also available for the most demanding latency-sensitive workloads.

- Choose disks and VM sizes that support your IOPS, throughput, and latency requirements.

You of course must balance these choices with cost. All the managed disks are based on Azure Blob Storage. An entire chapter would be needed to give you all the internals of how Azure Blob Storage and managed disks work. For now, look at these resources:

- Details on Azure Managed Disk Types can be found at `https://docs.microsoft.com/en-au/azure/virtual-machines/linux/disks-types`. You will see in these tables what sizes, IOPS, and throughput each type supports.

- We have guidance in our documentation specific to choosing the right storage for SQL Server for Azure VM at `https://docs.microsoft.com/en-us/azure/azure-sql/virtual-machines/windows/performance-guidelines-best-practices#storage-guidance`.

- This documentation provides nice guidance on choosing the right sizes for Azure Premium storage along with VM size. You can read this at `https://docs.microsoft.com/en-us/azure/virtual-machines/windows/premium-storage-performance`.

- Check out this excellent blog post by Mine Tokus on why Azure VM can provide the performance you need. This blog post talks about the importance of how Azure Blob Storage Read Cache improves OLTP performance. There are some good performance numbers as well in this blog post at `https://techcommunity.microsoft.com/t5/sql-server/optimize-oltp-performance-with-sql-server-on-azure-vm/ba-p/916794`.

- An independent study on performance for SQL Server on Azure Virtual Machine was published by GigaOm in early 2020. You can read the report at `https://azure.microsoft.com/en-us/resources/gigaom-report-sql-transactional-processing-price-performance/` including how they configured storage.

The key point to make here is that you need to match the right VM size to meet your storage needs as VM sizes have limits on number of data disks and total IOPS across all disks. Then provision the data disks you need for database and transaction log files within that total IOPS.

Performance Monitoring

Since SQL Server is deployed inside a virtual machine, you should use all the normal techniques available to you to monitor performance including SQL tools such as Dynamic Management Views (DMVs) and operating system tools such as Windows Performance Monitor or Linux tools.

Having said that, Azure Monitor provides integrated performance metrics for virtual machines including SQL Server performance counters (for Windows only).

Earlier in this chapter, I showed you during the deployment process from the Azure Portal in the "Management" section an option called **Enabled detailed monitoring** and **OS guest diagnostics**. Using these options will enable abilities to use the Azure Monitor system to look at various metrics about the performance of the guest VM. In addition, you can configure the ability to integrate basic SQL Server performance metrics into this system.

Azure Metrics

I showed earlier in this chapter in the Monitoring Pane of the Overview page of the VM basic metrics you can see visually for things like CPU, Network, and I/O. From the Resource Menu, you can click Metrics to see a different view of this information such as in Figure 3-24.

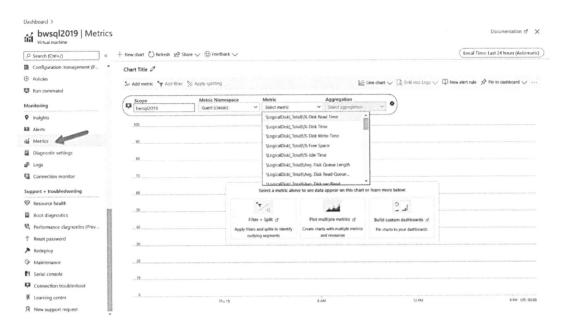

Figure 3-24. *Azure metrics for a virtual machine*

Think of Azure metrics like your Windows Performance Monitor for the VM that automatically has a history of 14 days.

You can use the Diagnostic Settings option in the Resource Menu to add in SQL Server metrics to this metric collection. By selecting Diagnostic Settings and then selecting the option for Configure performance counters, you can check the option for SQL Server and click Save. It will take a few minutes to save these diagnostic settings.

Tip   Notice on the Diagnostic Settings screen many other options to collect other data like event logs.

Once these are saved, you can go back and look at common SQL Server performance metrics as seen in Figure 3-25.

Figure 3-25. *Using Azure Metrics for SQL Server*

Logs

Another way to look at metrics over time is to use the Logs option from the Resource Menu. Azure metrics are stored in Azure Monitor Logs. You can use the *Kusto* Query Language (KQL) to view this data. After selecting Logs from the Resource Menu, see an example query by choosing **Chart CPU usage trends** and click Run. You should see a chart like Figure 3-26.

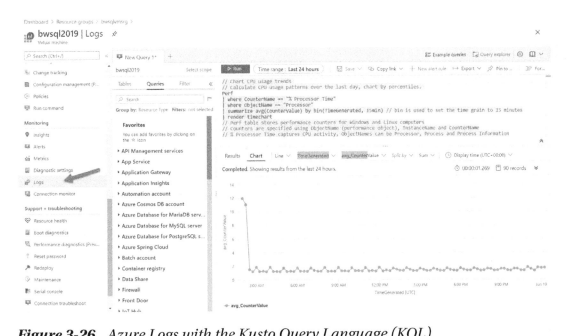

Figure 3-26. *Azure Logs with the Kusto Query Language (KQL)*

I will show you how to use Kusto in later chapters in this book for Azure SQL Database. For now, you can learn more about Kusto at `https://docs.microsoft.com/en-us/azure/data-explorer/kusto/concepts/`.

Insights

When you selected **Enabled detailed monitoring** and chose a Log Analytics workspace during deployment, Azure Monitor started collecting metrics in a Log Analytics workspace. By choosing the Insights option from the Resource Menu, you can look at another visualization of these metrics. A Log Analytics workspace will keep metrics for 93 days of history. You can see an example of these metrics in Figure 3-27.

Figure 3-27. *Insights for Azure Virtual Machine using Log Analytics*

You can go even farther using a concept called Workbooks which you can read more about `https://docs.microsoft.com/en-us/azure/azure-monitor/insights/vminsights-workbooks`.

Networking

When I deployed the Azure virtual machine earlier in this chapter, several types of network resources were created in the resource group, including a virtual network, network interface, public IP address, and network security group.

The public IP address is important as it allows you to use tools like Remote Desktop to connect to the virtual machine. The network interface is the interconnection between the VM and the virtual network. The network security group (NSG) provides an Access Control List (ACL) for rules to allow or deny network traffic to the VM. You can read the complete picture of networks and Azure virtual machines at `https://docs.microsoft.com/en-us/azure/virtual-machines/windows/network-overview#network-security-groups`.

Previously I connected to the virtual machine using the Remote Desktop Client (RDP) which used the public IP address and access to the RDP port (3389). There could be other methods you want to use to connect to the virtual machine.

I earlier recommend against enabled the SQL Server port 1433 to be open to the public Internet. However, that is the only method for you to connect a SQL Server client application or tool (like SSMS) the SQL Server instance in the Azure Virtual Machine unless you run the application or tool in a computer that is connected to the virtual network of the VM. One method to do this is to deploy the application or another VM in Azure and join the same Azure virtual network (a simple way to do this for another Azure VM is deploy it in the same resource group). You can also deploy in another Azure virtual network and set up a configuration called Virtual Network Peering which you can read about at https://docs.microsoft.com/en-us/azure/virtual-network/virtual-network-peering-overview.

Finally, you may find yourself wanting to connect on-premises resources such as applications or other computer or virtual machines to the virtual network for the Azure VM. You can read more about the details of setting up a configuration like this at https://docs.microsoft.com/en-us/azure/architecture/reference-architectures/hybrid-networking/.

Tip   A great resource to learn everything you need to know about Azure Virtual Networks can be found at https://docs.microsoft.com/en-us/azure/virtual-network/.

HADR

No matter where you deploy SQL Server, almost everyone wants high availability at some level and the ability to execute when necessary disaster recovery techniques. Azure provides methods to deliver several choices for HADR.

Azure Storage

In the example in this chapter where I showed you how to deploy SQL Server in Azure Virtual Machine, I used *data disks* based on Premium managed disks from Azure storage. By default, managed disks have built-in redundancy called **Locally Redundant Storage (LRS)**. LRS maintains three copies of data within the data center region. You can read more about Azure Storage redundancy at `https://docs.microsoft.com/en-us/azure/storage/common/storage-redundancy`.

Backups

Since you are running SQL Server in the Azure infrastructure, you will no doubt want to store backups of SQL Server database and transaction logs within Azure. You could store your backups using T-SQL to a separate data disk using managed disks. However, another option is to store your backups to Azure Storage accounts using the *backup to URL* capability of SQL Server. You can read more about SQL Server Backup to URL at `https://docs.microsoft.com/en-us/sql/relational-databases/backup-restore/sql-server-backup-to-url?view=sql-server-ver15`. One advantage of using URL backups is you can configure your Azure Storage account to use a higher level of availability called **geo-redundant storage (GRS)**. View the Service-Level Agreement (SLA) for Azure Storage accounts at `https://azure.microsoft.com/en-us/support/legal/sla/storage/v1_5/`.

Another option is to integrate backups for SQL Server with the **Azure Backup** service. Azure Backup offers a streaming-based service to back up SQL Server to Azure Storage. Azure Backups involve a VM extension that will use the Virtual Device Interface (VDI) APIs with SQL Server for backups. Read more about using Azure Backup with SQL Server at `https://docs.microsoft.com/en-us/azure/backup/backup-azure-sql-database`.

The final option for backups in Azure uses **file snapshot backups**. File snapshot backups can be extremely fast. They require storing SQL Server data files directly to an Azure storage account vs. a managed disk. You can read more about SQL Server file snapshot backups in Azure at `https://docs.microsoft.com/en-us/sql/relational-databases/backup-restore/file-snapshot-backups-for-database-files-in-azure?view=sql-server-ver15`.

Always On Failover Cluster Instance

A failover cluster instance (FCI) provides high availability for SQL Server through shared storage. Since this is a virtual machine, using an FCI will be very much like a normal SQL Server. However, one of the key aspects to FCI is shared storage. Azure provides a concept called a *premium file share* which can be used for this purpose. Mine Tokus has a very nice blog post you can read about using premium file shares at `https://azure.microsoft.com/en-us/blog/leverage-azure-premium-file-shares-for-high-availability-of-data/`. In addition, you can read a complete list of instructions for the process of configuring an FCI with premium file shares at `https://docs.microsoft.com/en-us/azure/azure-sql/virtual-machines/windows/failover-cluster-instance-premium-file-share-manually-configure`. These instructions also include steps to configure an *Azure load balancer* for the IP address of the FCI.

Always On Availability Groups

Always On Availability Groups (AG) increase your high availability RPO and RTO using replicas. You can read through the process of setting up an AG in Azure at `https://docs.microsoft.com/en-us/azure/azure-sql/virtual-machines/windows/availability-group-manually-configure-tutorial`. I will tell you up front this is a fairly complex process but uses Azure storage for each replica and an Azure load balancer to support the AG listener. However, if you need the capabilities of SQL AG based on your RPO and RTO needs, it can be worth it to get this deployed and configured correctly.

The **az sql vm** CLI provides option to help you set up an AG with the SQL Resource Provider. In addition, we have built ARM templates to help automate the process of deploying and configuring an AG in Azure. You can read more at `https://azure.microsoft.com/en-us/blog/automate-always-on-availability-group-deployments-with-sql-virtual-machine-resource-provider/`. You can also directly access templates at `https://docs.microsoft.com/en-us/azure/azure-sql/virtual-machines/windows/availability-group-quickstart-template-configure`.

One other scenario to consider is to set up a secondary replica for an AG in Azure from an on-premises AG primary replica. You can get more guidance on how to set this up at `https://docs.microsoft.com/en-us/azure/virtual-machines/windows/sqlclassic/virtual-machines-windows-classic-sql-onprem-availability`.

Go Further with Azure Availability

Azure virtual machine is part of the Azure infrastructure that provides for availability during unplanned and planned events. For example, if an unplanned hardware problem occurs, Azure can use live migration technologies to fail over your azure virtual machine to a healthy host. Azure also may update the underlying hosts of your virtual machine which may or may not require a reboot. You can read more about unplanned and planned downtime for Azure virtual machines at `https://docs.microsoft.com/en-us/azure/virtual-machines/windows/manage-availability#understand-vm-reboots---maintenance-vs-downtime`.

Azure offers more options to go further with high availability for Azure virtual machines:

1. **Availability Set** – Spreads your VMs across multiple fault and update domains in the same datacenter. Basically, this makes sure your VMs are spread across different racks and switches. The SLA is 99.95%.

2. **Availability Zone** – Think of this as spreading an availability set across data centers within a region. The SLA is 99.99% but can cost more.

Unfortunately, you need to make this choice when you deploy. You can change it later, but you must migrate your VM to do it.

These choices only make sense if you plan to use an HADR solution for SQL Server like AGs, FCI, DB Mirroring, Replication, Log Shipping, and so on.

SQL Server and Linux Availability

SQL Server on Linux supports Always On Failover Cluster Instance and Availability Groups functionality through the database engine. Automatic failover capabilities are often supported through Linux packages like Pacemaker. In order to properly ensure high availability with Pacemaker and Azure virtual machine, you may need to consider using a Linux distribution like Red Hat Enterprise Linux (RHEL). Azure has integrated concepts like STONITH with Azure virtual machine with RHEL. Learn more how to configure an AG with SQL Server on RHEL and Azure virtual machine at `https://docs.microsoft.com/en-us/azure/azure-sql/virtual-machines/linux/rhel-high-availability-stonith-tutorial`.

Summary

You have learned in this chapter how to deploy and configure SQL Server with Azure virtual machine looking at many different options as part of deployment. You have also learned unique aspects of security, performance, and HADR related to SQL Server and Azure VM.

Azure VM provides a great infrastructure for running SQL Server. Mine Tokus summed it up when I was talking to her about SQL Server and Azure VM. "Our customers love the agility and elasticity Azure VMs. It is amazing that cores and memory available to SQL Server can be increased only with a VM restart exactly when the workload demands; no need to plan for hardware purchases months away. Azure VM has price performance advantages of running SQL Server on Azure. For example, Azure Storage offers high performance and high capacity reads which is critical for SQL Server performance for free. Considering the close collaboration between SQL Server, Azure Compute, and Azure Storage engineering teams, Azure will stay as the best hosting platform for SQL Server in the future."

Now that you have studied SQL Server on Azure VM, it is time to show you how to deploy and configure Azure SQL Database and Managed Instance.

CHAPTER 4

Deploying Azure SQL

Deploying an Azure SQL Managed Instance or Database is a different but similar experience than deploying SQL Server on Azure Virtual Machine. The experience is the same because you can use the Azure portal and CLI. The difference is that Azure is managing the virtual machine and infrastructure, so several of the options you pick for a virtual machine you do not have to worry about.

In this chapter, you will learn the options and process to deploy and connect to an Azure SQL Managed Instance and Database. You will also learn the options to migrate existing databases into Azure SQL. In addition, you will learn some implementation details of the architecture used to host Azure SQL Managed Instances and Databases.

You have the option to follow along the examples in this chapter. You will need the following to complete these examples:

- An Azure subscription.

- A minimum of Contributor role access to the Azure subscription. You can read more about Azure built-in roles at `https://docs.microsoft.com/en-us/azure/role-based-access-control/built-in-roles`.

- Access to the Azure Portal (web or Windows application).

- Installation of the **az** CLI (see `https://docs.microsoft.com/en-us/cli/azure/install-azure-cli?view=azure-cli-latest` for more details). You can also use the Azure Cloud Shell instead since az is already installed. You can read more about the Azure Cloud Shell at `https://azure.microsoft.com/en-us/features/cloud-shell/`.

© Bob Ward 2021
B. Ward, *Azure SQL Revealed*, https://doi.org/10.1007/978-1-4842-5931-3_4

- You will run some T-SQL in this chapter, so install a tool like SQL Server Management Studio (SSMS) at `https://docs.microsoft.com/en-us/sql/ssms/download-sql-server-management-studio-ssms?view=sql-server-ver15`. You can also use Azure Data Studio at `https://docs.microsoft.com/en-us/sql/azure-data-studio/download-azure-data-studio?view=sql-server-ver15`.

- For migration scenarios, you will need to download the Data Migration Assistant (DMA) tool from `https://docs.microsoft.com/en-us/sql/dma/dma-overview` and have access to a SQL Server instance.

Pre-deployment Planning

Before you jump into deploying an Azure SQL Database or Managed Instance, I recommend you spend some time doing some pre-deployment planning. Reviewing your choices and making a few informed decisions will save you time and money.

New Deployment or Migration

One of the first decisions to make which may be easy is whether you plan to migrate an existing database or instance or deploy a new database or instance. The process of deploying will be the same, but migrating implies you need to assess your current SQL Server instance, database, or other database environment before you deploy. Your assessment will give you guidance on what type of deployment choice you need to make based on your current requirements. You must decide what possible changes must be made to your application, schema, scripts, or other aspects to your current deployment with SQL Server or other database platforms. You also must consider how to migrate your actual data into the new deployment. This chapter will include sections specifically geared around what consideration and tools you can use to migrate to Azure SQL Managed Instance and Database. Here are two great resources for you to consider as you think about migration:

- Azure Migration Program – `https://azure.microsoft.com/en-us/migration/migration-program/`

- The Microsoft Data Migration Guide – `https://datamigration.microsoft.com/`

Making Deployment Choices

Whether you are migrating or creating a new deployment, you have several choices to make that is worth the time to plan out. Chapter 2 of this book is invaluable to go back and read as it describes choices and differences between Azure SQL Managed Instance and Azure SQL Database.

Having said that, let us quickly review some important choices at a high level that can affect your decision-making:

- If you need SQL Server instance features like SQL Server Agent, Database Mail, and cross-database queries, Managed Instance is the choice you need to make.

- If your database size is > 8TB, your only choice as of the time of writing this book is Azure SQL Database Hyperscale.

Past these two choices, either Azure SQL Managed Instance or Database likely meets your needs. However, as I called out in Chapter 2 of the book, there can be advantages in using Azure SQL Database because Microsoft will manage both the infrastructure and the SQL Server instance to let you focus on the database. Furthermore, Azure SQL Database can offer you more options such as Serverless compute and Automated Tuning for indexes.

The options you will pick as you deploy a Managed Instance or Database will look like the following as seen in Figure 4-1.

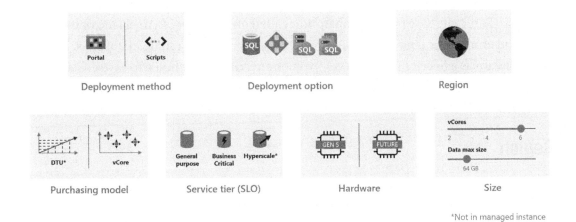

Figure 4-1. *Deployment choices for Azure SQL*

Deployment Method

You can deploy an Azure Managed Instance using the Azure Portal or through a CLI with the az utility, PowerShell, or even REST APIs (az rest can be used if you do not want to write code).

If you are just trying out Azure SQL or doing a proof of concept, you can easily use the Azure Portal. However, for a repeatable process to deploy (imagine if you needed to for some reason redeploy at any time), a script using a CLI is a better option. Remember you also can use Azure templates to help automate deployments. You can read more about using Azure templates for Azure SQL at `https://docs.microsoft.com/en-us/azure/azure-sql/database/arm-templates-content-guide?tabs=single-database`.

Another option for developers to automate deployment is with Azure DevOps and Pipelines. I really like this blog post by my colleague at Microsoft Arvind Shyamsundar on DevOps and Azure SQL at `https://devblogs.microsoft.com/azure-sql/devops-for-azure-sql/`.

Deployment Option

I discussed earlier whether you will consider Azure SQL Managed Instance or Database. Within each of these options are a choice of using a *pool*. Azure SQL Managed Instance offers a *Managed Instance Pool* which could be a better fit for a smaller, cost-effective Managed Instance. Deployment times are also much faster with pools. You can read more about Managed Instance Pools at `https://docs.microsoft.com/en-us/azure/azure-sql/managed-instance/instance-pools-overview`.

Azure SQL Database provides an option called an *elastic pool*. An elastic pool can be a good choice if you plan to use Azure SQL Database to host many databases. ISVs and Software as a Service (SaaS) developers often look at this choice to save costs and manage databases more efficiently. You can read more about elastic pools at `https://docs.microsoft.com/en-us/azure/azure-sql/database/elastic-pool-overview`.

Region

Choosing a specific Azure region can be important just as I described in Chapter 3 on virtual machines. You need to make sure your deployment options are available in your Azure region choice. A full list of Azure products by region can be found at `https://azure.microsoft.com/en-us/global-infrastructure/services/`.

You may have certain compliance and security requirements which also dictate what region you choose.

You may be implementing specific HADR options like Availability Zones, Geo-replication, or Auto-Failover Groups and have specific regions in mind to make those deployments successful.

If you need to move an Azure SQL Managed Instance or database to another region, read a checklist in our documentation at `https://docs.microsoft.com/en-us/azure/azure-sql/database/move-resources-across-regions`.

Azure SQL Database is a "Ring 0" service which means it gets deployed in every region as a default service. Managed Instance is not exactly at that status yet, but it is generally available in all regions.

In addition, you need to consider where your application will be hosted and latency requirements between where the application will be hosted and your Azure SQL deployment. Consider performance and proximity to other services. I was chatting with my colleague Anna Thomas on this topic. She said, "…but I feel that it's not just where the application is – where are the users? Where should the application be? If you have geo-replication or auto-failover groups, how do you build a globally available solution?"

Purchasing Model

For Azure SQL Database only, you will need to choose a *Purchasing model*. The choices are DTU or vCore. I explained these models and the history behind them in Chapters 1 and 2 of the book. While the DTU model may be a valid choice for you, I recommend the vCore model.

If you select the DTU model and want to move to the vCore model at a later date, consult the documentation at `https://docs.microsoft.com/en-us/azure/azure-sql/database/migrate-dtu-to-vcore`.

Service Tier (SLO)

If Azure SQL Managed Instance is your deployment option, then you will need to select a *Service Tier* of General Purpose (GP) or Business Critical (BC). A SLO stands for Service Level Objective and is the combination of choices of Purchasing Model, Service Tier, and Hardware. I described these service tier options in Chapter 2 of the book. While resource limits and performance may differ, one of the primary differences with these tiers is how Availability works which you will learn more about in Chapter 8 of the book. One notable difference for Business Critical is that it supports In-Memory OLTP capabilities. A comparison between GP and BC for Managed Instance can be found at `https://docs.microsoft.com/en-us/azure/azure-sql/database/service-tiers-general-purpose-business-critical`.

Tip   You will see later in this chapter that the time it takes to deploy for Managed Instance can be lengthy. Changing between GP and BC is possible but could result in significant downtime.

If Azure SQL Database is your deployment option, then you also have the choice of General Purpose (GP) vs. Business Critical (BC) service tiers. In addition, you have the choice of *Hyperscale*. If you choose General Purpose, you also have the choice of *Provisioned* vs. *Serverless*. This is also called a *computer model or tier*. I covered all these options in Chapter 2 of the book.

GP vs. BC is a similar choice as with Azure SQL Managed Instance. Read the same documentation page at `https://docs.microsoft.com/en-us/azure/azure-sql/database/service-tiers-general-purpose-business-critical` for a comparison. Hyperscale is your best choice for very large databases and has some attractive capabilities for scaling, replicas, and restore performance. You can read more about Hyperscale at `https://docs.microsoft.com/en-us/azure/azure-sql/database/service-tier-hyperscale`. Serverless is a unique option we have created for autoscale and scenarios where your database may always not be utilized. It provides a new cost-effective way to deploy and use an Azure SQL Database. Read more about Serverless at `https://docs.microsoft.com/en-us/azure/azure-sql/database/serverless-tier-overview`.

Switching between GP and BC for Azure SQL Database is typically significantly faster than with Managed Instance. You can also switch between Serverless and Provisioned easily. However, Hyperscale is the one option you cannot switch back once you choose it without completing migrating your database to the new deployment option.

Hardware

Even though for Azure SQL we abstract you from the infrastructure and virtualization used for the deployment, we provide options for a *hardware generation*.

We are constantly looking to take advantage of new hardware supplied within the Azure infrastructure so these choices may be new by the time you are reading this book.

As of summer of 2020, the only hardware generation choices aside from the default Gen5 generation are with Azure SQL Database. The Fsv2-series is available in certain regions for General Purpose. This hardware option provides more CPU performance per vCore than Gen5. The M-series option for Business Critical offers more memory and vCores. Keep track of the latest on hardware generations at `https://docs.microsoft.com/en-us/azure/azure-sql/database/service-tiers-vcore?tabs=azure-portal#hardware-generations`.

Note   You might see some evidence of Gen4 hardware as you use Azure SQL. This hardware generation is being phased out, so focus on Gen5 or newer hardware generations.

Sizes

Once you have figured these options, you have choices on size. The DTU model for Azure SQL Database has a DTU number you can choose (and a data size). For the vCore purchasing you model, you have both number of vCores and database size to select. There are a few differences on how these options work depending on your other choices. I will describe these differences as I walk you through the deployment process in the rest of this chapter.

Price

Just like with Azure Virtual Machine, take advantage of the Azure Pricing Calculator to plug in some of these choices to get an idea of your costs. This includes using Azure Hybrid Benefit. You can find the pricing calculator for Azure SQL Managed Instance at `https://azure.microsoft.com/en-ca/pricing/details/azure-sql/sql-managed-instance/single/` and Azure SQL Database at `https://azure.microsoft.com/en-us/pricing/calculator/?service=sql-database`. Figure 4-2 shows an example of the pricing calculator for Azure SQL Database.

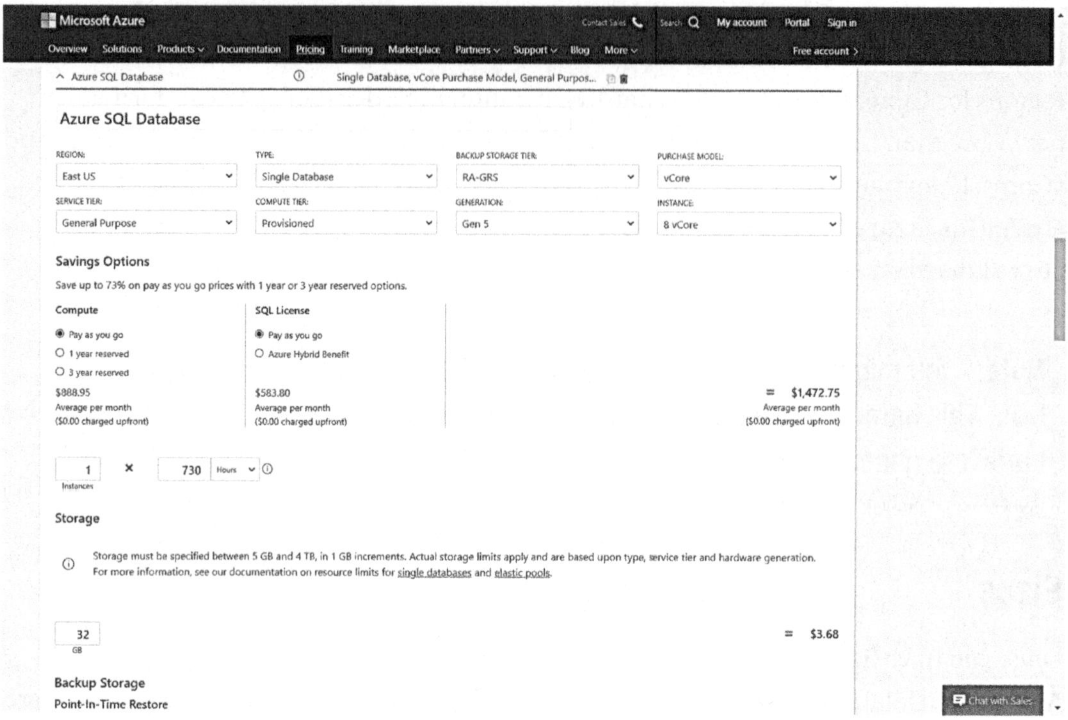

Figure 4-2. *The pricing calculator for Azure SQL Database*

Consider Resource Limits

Your choices from deployment options, service tier, and sizes can affect your resource limits. These are the following resource limits to consider as you make these choices. I call these out because these may not be obvious as you deploy through the Azure Portal:

- Max Memory

- Max Log Size

- Log Rate Governance

- IOPS and I/O latency

- Max size of Tempdb

- Max concurrent workers

- Backup Retention

I will discuss more about Log Rate Governance and IOPS and I/O latency in Chapter 7 of this book. For now, keep these concepts in mind as they can affect performance of applications such as those that are heavy transaction log users.

To see the specific limits for Azure SQL Managed Instance, please see these very well-documented tables at `https://docs.microsoft.com/en-us/azure/sql-database/sql-database-managed-instance-resource-limits`.

To see the specific limits for Azure SQL Database, please see the table at `https://docs.microsoft.com/en-us/azure/sql-database/sql-database-vcore-resource-limits-single-databases`.

You should also know that you have overall Azure SQL limits per subscription per region. You can view what these limits are at `https://docs.microsoft.com/en-us/azure/sql-database/sql-database-managed-instance-resource-limits#regional-resource-limitations` and `https://docs.microsoft.com/en-us/azure/sql-database/sql-database-resource-limits-database-server#maximum-resource-limits`.

It is possible to make a request to Microsoft increase your subscription limits. This is called a *quota increase request*. Read more at `https://docs.microsoft.com/en-us/azure/sql-database/quota-increase-request`.

Deploying Azure SQL Managed Instance

Similar to the process I documented in Chapter 3 for a virtual machine, deploying an Azure SQL Managed Instance through the Azure Portal starts by using the Azure SQL option from the Azure Marketplace (I showed you this view in Figure 3-1).

Using the three Azure SQL choices, you would select SQL Managed Instance and single instance and then click **Create**.

Note   At the time of writing this book, an instance pool can only be created through PowerShell. I will talk more about Instance Pools in the section titled "Implementation Details." You can read more about Instance Pools at `https://docs.microsoft.com/en-us/azure/azure-sql/managed-instance/instance-pools-overview`.

Like the experience of deploying a virtual machine, you will have options but not the same options. You can see in Figure 4-3 you will have options for *Basics*, *Networking*, *Additional settings*, and *Tags*. Basics is the only required set of fields, while the others are optional.

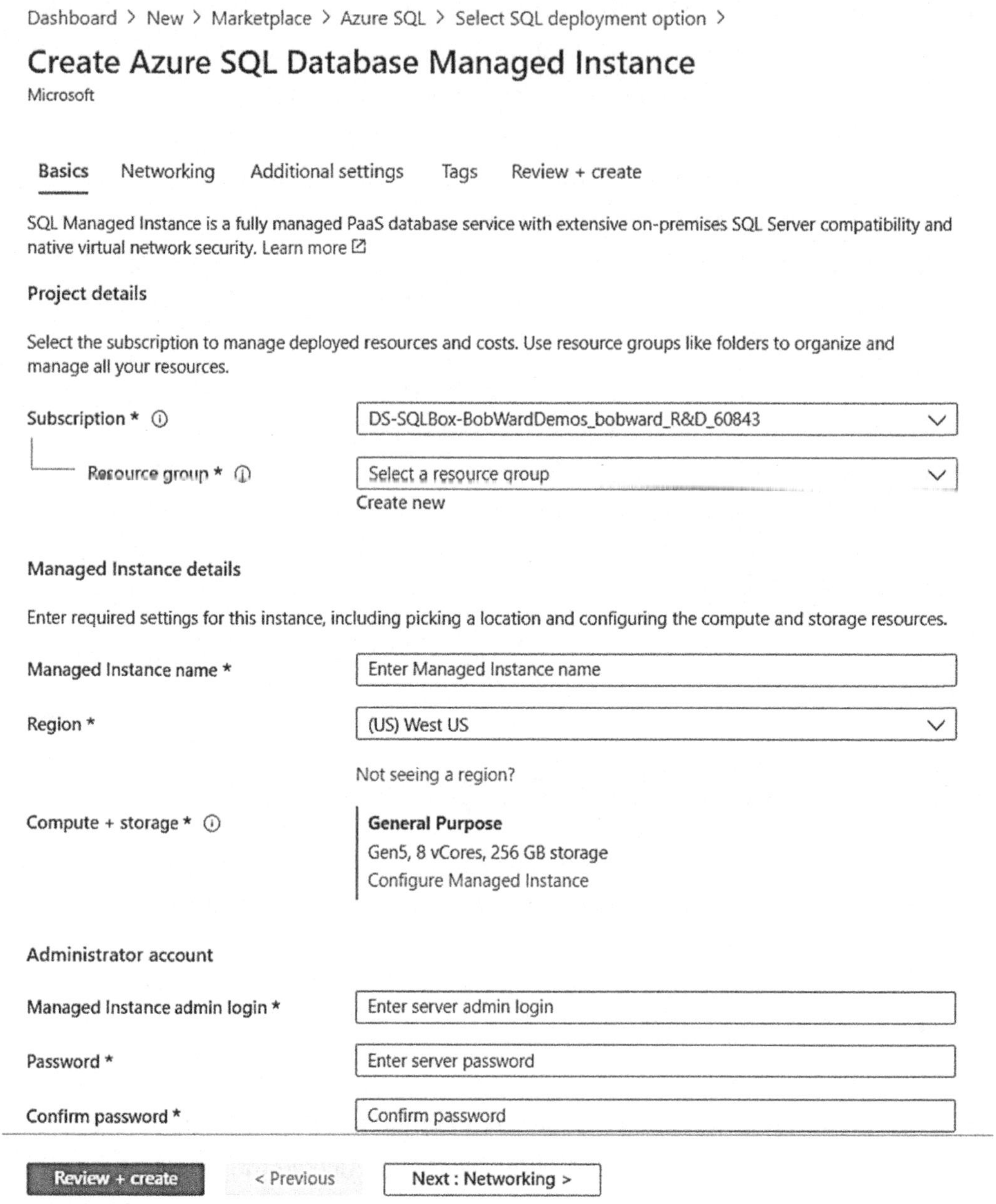

Dashboard > New > Marketplace > Azure SQL > Select SQL deployment option >

Create Azure SQL Database Managed Instance
Microsoft

Basics   Networking   Additional settings   Tags   Review + create

SQL Managed Instance is a fully managed PaaS database service with extensive on-premises SQL Server compatibility and native virtual network security. Learn more ⌕

Project details

Select the subscription to manage deployed resources and costs. Use resource groups like folders to organize and manage all your resources.

Subscription * ⓘ	DS-SQLBox-BobWardDemos_bobward_R&D_60843 ⌄
⌐ Resource group * ⓘ	Select a resource group ⌄
	Create new

Managed Instance details

Enter required settings for this instance, including picking a location and configuring the compute and storage resources.

Managed Instance name *	Enter Managed Instance name
Region *	(US) West US ⌄
	Not seeing a region?
Compute + storage * ⓘ	**General Purpose** Gen5, 8 vCores, 256 GB storage Configure Managed Instance

Administrator account

Managed Instance admin login *	Enter server admin login
Password *	Enter server password
Confirm password *	Confirm password

[Review + create]   < Previous   [Next : Networking >]

Figure 4-3. *The initial Azure SQL Managed Instance screen in the portal*

Deployment and Options

Let us walk through each screen with deployment options of a Managed Instance and then deploy it through the Azure Portal.

Basics

Figure 4-4 shows the fields you complete on the Basics screen, including choosing Subscription, Resource group, Region, Managed Instance name (this becomes part of the server name and @@SERVERNAME of the instance), and Administrator account and password.

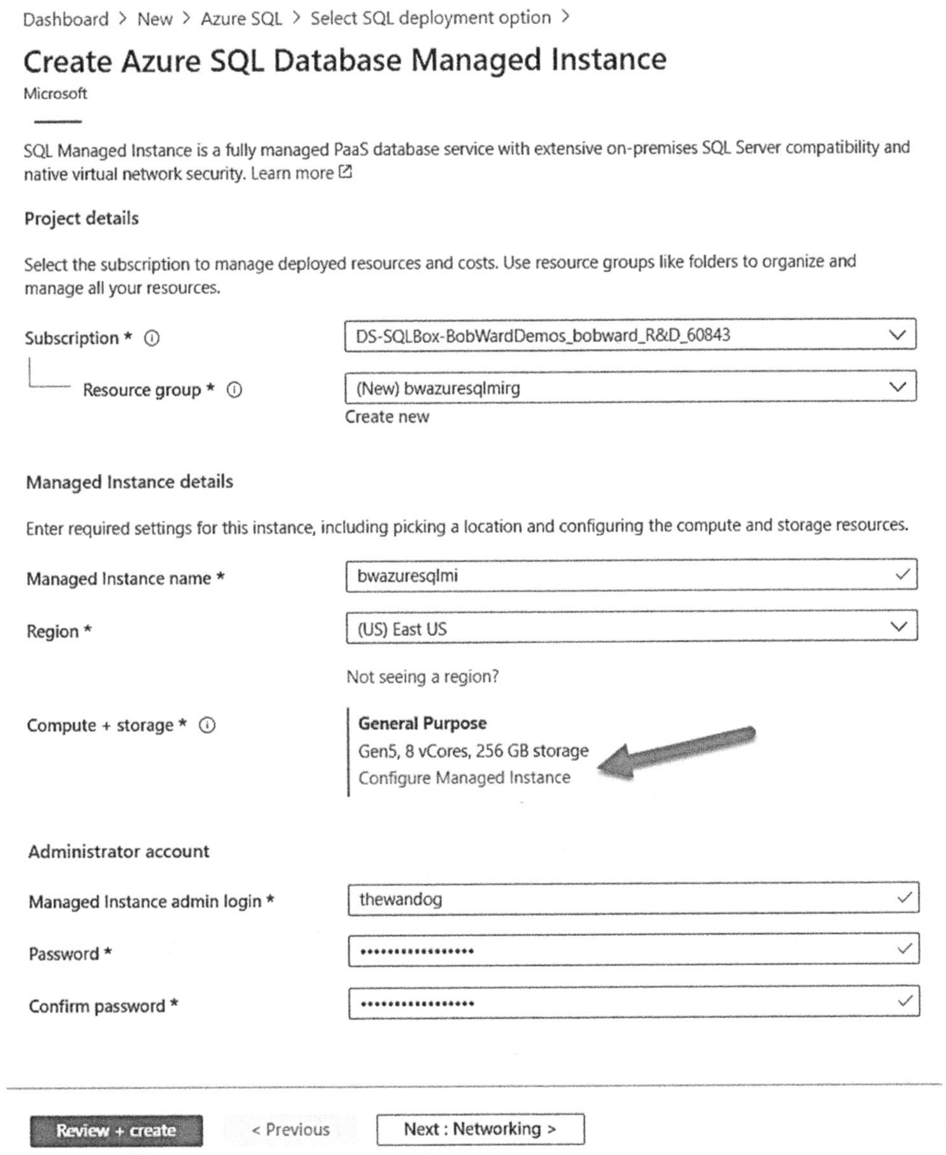

Dashboard > New > Azure SQL > Select SQL deployment option >

Create Azure SQL Database Managed Instance

Microsoft

SQL Managed Instance is a fully managed PaaS database service with extensive on-premises SQL Server compatibility and native virtual network security. Learn more ☐

Project details

Select the subscription to manage deployed resources and costs. Use resource groups like folders to organize and manage all your resources.

Subscription * ⓘ	DS-SQLBox-BobWardDemos_bobward_R&D_60843 ∨
Resource group * ⓘ	(New) bwazuresqlmirg ∨
	Create new

Managed Instance details

Enter required settings for this instance, including picking a location and configuring the compute and storage resources.

Managed Instance name *	bwazuresqlmi ✓
Region *	(US) East US ∨
	Not seeing a region?
Compute + storage * ⓘ	**General Purpose** Gen5, 8 vCores, 256 GB storage Configure Managed Instance

Administrator account

Managed Instance admin login *	thewandog ✓
Password *	•••••••••••••••• ✓
Confirm password *	•••••••••••••••• ✓

[Review + create]   [< Previous]   [Next : Networking >]

Figure 4-4. *Filling out the basics for an Azure SQL Managed Instance deployment*

The Administrator account becomes a SQL Server login assigned to the sysadmin role.

Notice in the middle is an option called **Compute + storage**. This is where you will choose Service Tier and Size (vCores + Storage). Notice for me the default is General Purpose with 8 vCores and 256Gb max storage. Click **Configure Managed Instance** to see what your options are which should look like Figure 4-5.

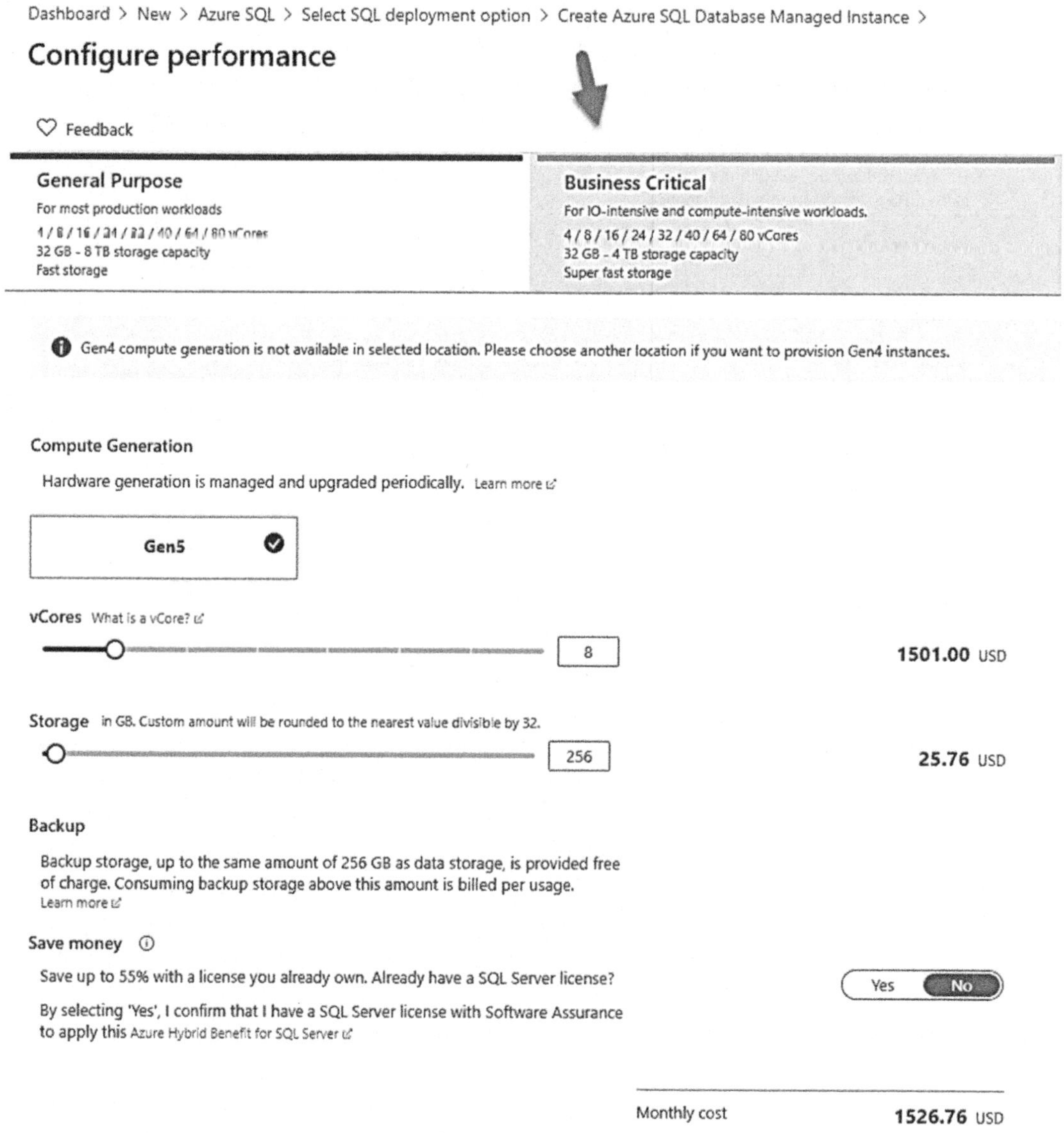

Figure 4-5. *Azure SQL Managed Instance Service Tier options*

At the top of this screen, you can see that you can choose General Purpose (GP) or Business Critical (BC), and some of the resource limits and performance expectations are listed with each. From pre-deployment planning, remember there are other significant reasons to choose BC including

- Access to the In-memory OLTP feature

- Higher availability because BC uses a local storage and replica architecture

Below this are *slider bars* to choose the desired number of vCores and Maximum Storage. As you use each slider, the expected costs are updated to the right. vCores are only allowed in the increments shown on the screen. Managed Instance today supports up to 80 vCores for both GP and BC. 4 vCores is the minimum choice (Instance Pools support 2 vCore deployments).

The maximum storage value is called the *maximum instance size* and is the maximum size allowed for **all** database and transaction log files associated with databases for the managed instance. You should think of this like the maximum of a storage drive for your databases. The maximum storage size is different depending on your vCore choice and choice of GP and BC:

- 4 vCores have a max storage limit of 2TB for GP and 1TB for BC.

- Any other vCore choice past this supports up to 8TB for GP and 4TB for BC.

Note   I discussed the architecture of Business Critical deployments in Chapter 2 of the book and will elaborate more on this architecture in Chapter 8. The reason for the lower limit of storage for BC is the fact that databases are stored on local SSD drives which have lower capacity than using Azure Storage.

Tempdb max sizes are dependent on vCore selections but are counted toward the overall maximum storage limit. In fact, all databases including system databases count toward the overall max instance storage size.

You can run the following query after you deploy your managed instance to see how much space your databases are taking up in relation to the max storage for the instance:

```
select top 1 used_storage_gb = storage_space_used_mb/1024,
    max_storage_size_gb = reserved_storage_mb/1024
from sys.server_resource_stats order by start_time desc
```

You also have a choice to save money using your existing SQL Server licenses with Azure Hybrid Benefit (AHB).

There is also a statement about backup storage and costs on this page. I will discuss more about Backups and Managed Instance in Chapter 8 of the book. Click **Apply** after you make any changes (Apply is only enabled if you change the defaults. You can click the X to get back to the Basics screen). For my example, I will leave the choice at 8 vCores and 256Gb of max storage.

Tip   Hitting Apply will not deploy the Managed Instance yet but take your time to get your choices here as close to correct as possible. Why? You can change them later, but Managed Instance changes to tiers and sizes can be a long operation. Instance pools will not require as much time.

Networking

Click **Next: Networking** > to review your networking choices. Your screen should look like Figure 4-6.

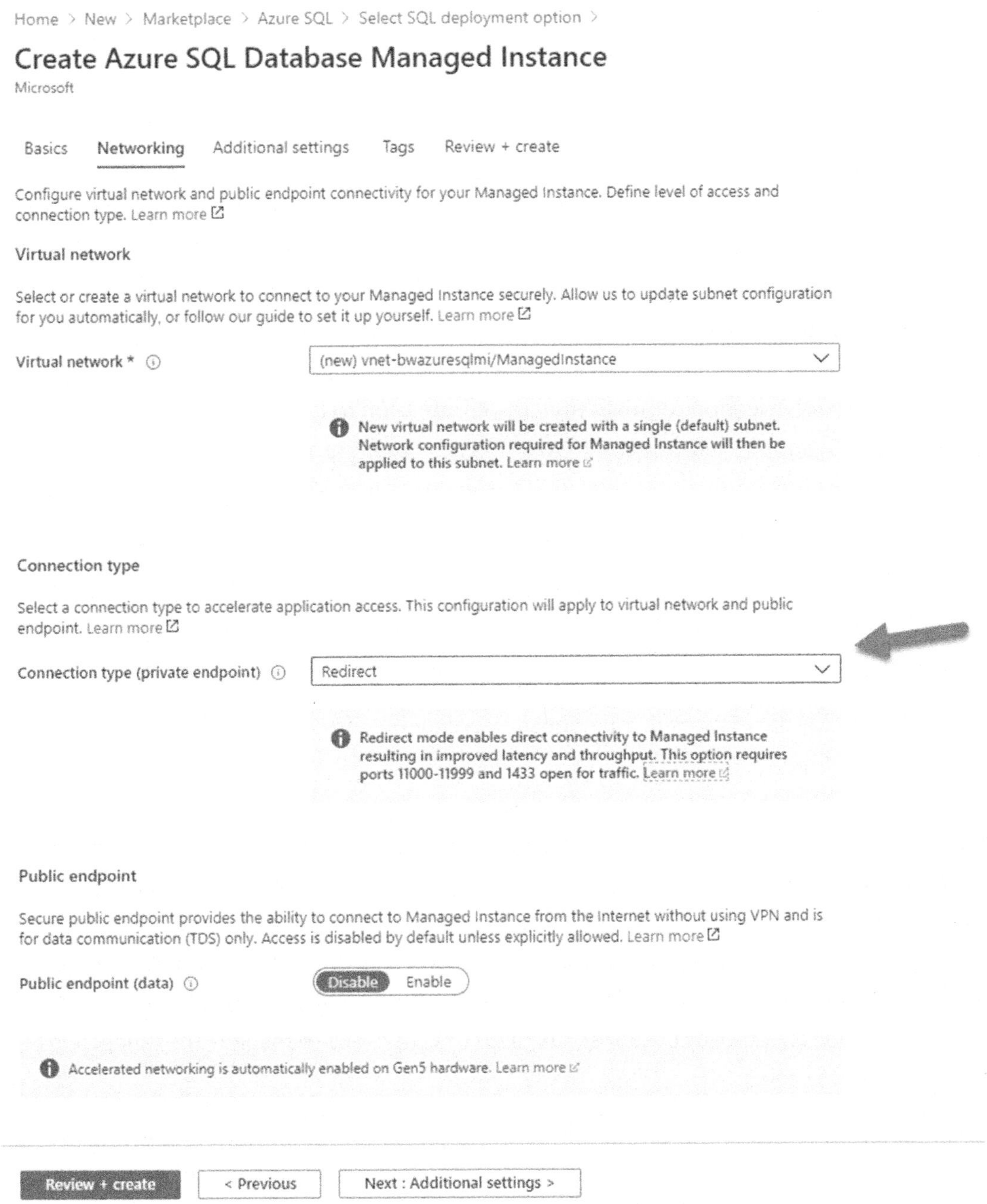

Home > New > Marketplace > Azure SQL > Select SQL deployment option >

Create Azure SQL Database Managed Instance
Microsoft

Basics   **Networking**   Additional settings   Tags   Review + create

Configure virtual network and public endpoint connectivity for your Managed Instance. Define level of access and connection type. Learn more ☑

Virtual network

Select or create a virtual network to connect to your Managed Instance securely. Allow us to update subnet configuration for you automatically, or follow our guide to set it up yourself. Learn more ☑

Virtual network * ⓘ   (new) vnet-bwazuresqlmi/ManagedInstance   ∨

> ⓘ New virtual network will be created with a single (default) subnet. Network configuration required for Managed Instance will then be applied to this subnet. Learn more ☑

Connection type

Select a connection type to accelerate application access. This configuration will apply to virtual network and public endpoint. Learn more ☑

Connection type (private endpoint) ⓘ   Redirect   ∨

> ⓘ Redirect mode enables direct connectivity to Managed Instance resulting in improved latency and throughput. This option requires ports 11000-11999 and 1433 open for traffic. Learn more ☑

Public endpoint

Secure public endpoint provides the ability to connect to Managed Instance from the Internet without using VPN and is for data communication (TDS) only. Access is disabled by default unless explicitly allowed. Learn more ☑

Public endpoint (data) ⓘ   (**Disable** Enable)

> ⓘ Accelerated networking is automatically enabled on Gen5 hardware. Learn more ☑

[Review + create]   [< Previous]   [Next : Additional settings >]

Figure 4-6. *Azure SQL Managed Instance Networking options*

Virtual Network

You can see at the top of the screen that a new virtual network will be created to host the Azure SQL Managed Instance. One of the advantages of Managed Instance is that it is deployed in a private virtual network. You could deploy your own Azure Virtual Network first (you can use the Azure portal or CLI) and select that virtual network on this deployment screen. If you choose to use your own virtual network, you must configure it a specific way which you can read at `https://docs.microsoft.com/en-us/azure/azure-sql/managed-instance/vnet-existing-add-subnet`.

Connection Type

Notice on my screen I have chosen a connection type of *Redirect*. The default is *proxy*. A proxy connection requires that any connection to the Managed Instance by a tool or application (a connection to the TDS port 1433) must always go through a *gateway*. A redirect connection type uses the gateway to find the direct virtual private IP address of the node containing the Managed Instance. All subsequent traffic flows directly to the node. You can read more about these connection types at `https://docs.microsoft.com/en-us/azure/azure-sql/managed-instance/connection-types-overview`. Proxy can be more secure, but redirect can be faster. The virtual network and included subnet will have all the appropriate Network Security Group (NSG) rules applied for these types if you choose to create the virtual network as part of this deployment step.

Public Endpoint

You have the option to enable TDS traffic on a public endpoint. The public endpoint will be enabled on port 3342 (and get redirected in the virtual network to the node instance port 1433). While I do not recommend using this option, it is one of the quickest ways to get connected to a Managed Instance. There could be other scenarios where you want to enable this. You can read more about the public endpoint for Managed Instance at `https://docs.microsoft.com/en-us/azure/azure-sql/managed-instance/public-endpoint-overview`.

Notice that Accelerated networking is automatically enabled for the Managed Instance.

Additional Settings

Click **Next: Additional settings** > to enable a few additional options for the deployment as seen in Figure 4-7.

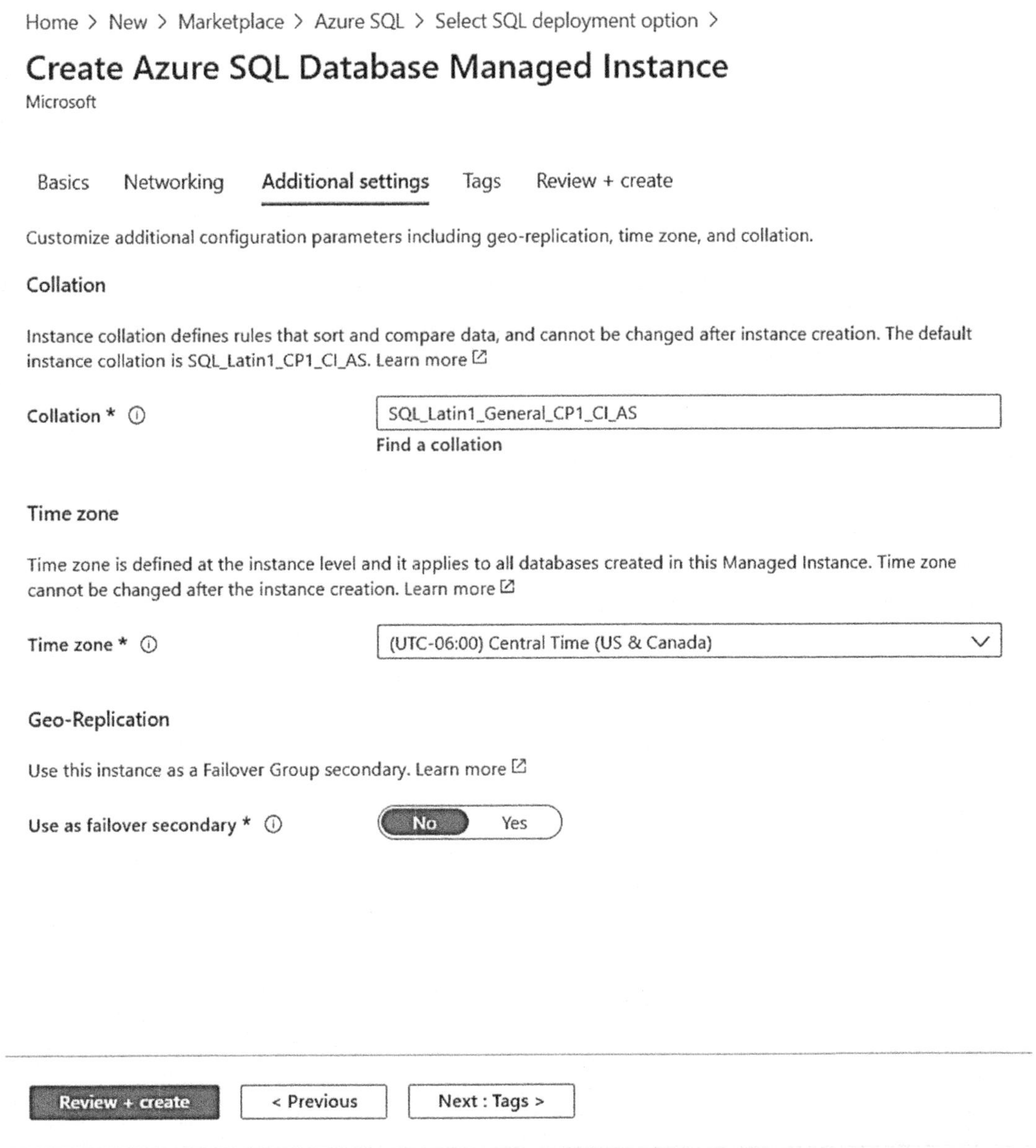

Home > New > Marketplace > Azure SQL > Select SQL deployment option >

Create Azure SQL Database Managed Instance
Microsoft

Basics   Networking   **Additional settings**   Tags   Review + create

Customize additional configuration parameters including geo-replication, time zone, and collation.

Collation

Instance collation defines rules that sort and compare data, and cannot be changed after instance creation. The default instance collation is SQL_Latin1_CP1_CI_AS. Learn more ⬚

Collation * ⓘ | SQL_Latin1_General_CP1_CI_AS |
                                   Find a collation

Time zone

Time zone is defined at the instance level and it applies to all databases created in this Managed Instance. Time zone cannot be changed after the instance creation. Learn more ⬚

Time zone * ⓘ | (UTC-06:00) Central Time (US & Canada)   ⌄ |

Geo-Replication

Use this instance as a Failover Group secondary. Learn more ⬚

Use as failover secondary * ⓘ   (**No**   Yes)

[Review + create]   [< Previous]   [Next : Tags >]

Figure 4-7. *Additional settings for Managed Instance*

The **Collation** here is like setting a collation for a SQL Server. It is important to know that you cannot change the instance collation after it is supplied here.

Note   You can set and change database collations on Managed Instance after deployment.

The **Time zone** is the recognized time zone by the SQL Server engine on the Managed Instance node. I have changed this to my local time zone, but it can be UTC or whatever time zone you want to choose. You cannot change this after deployment.

The Managed Instance can be part of a **failover group** which we will talk more about in Chapter 8 of the book. You will use that option when you review those topics later. For now, leave it to the default of No.

Tags

Click **Next: Tags** > to define a tag like how I described in Chapter 3 with Azure Virtual Machines. I will use a Name = Environment and Value = Development with a SQL managed instance resource.

Deploy!

Click **Next: Review + create** > to view the final screen before deploying as seen in Figure 4-8.

Figure 4-8. *The validation screen for Managed Instance before deploy*

Like Figure 3-16 for Azure Virtual Machine, this screen shows estimated costs, Terms of use, Privacy Policy, a review of all the options you have chosen, and the option to download an Azure template that describes these deployment options. Notice the important warning at the top of the screen on the time it takes to deploy. So, click **Create** to deploy, leave this screen open to see the progress, and read on to the next section about deploying with a CLI and then some architecture and implementation details you might find interesting why the deployment runs. This section will explain a bit why the deployment can take so long.

Deploying with a CLI

An Azure Managed Instance can be deployed with command-line interfaces (CLI) through the **az sql mi** (`https://docs.microsoft.com/en-us/cli/azure/sql/mi?view=azure-cli-latest`) command interfaces or through **New-AzSQLInstance** PowerShell cmdlet (`https://docs.microsoft.com/en-us/powershell/module/az.sql/New-AzSqlInstance`).

I went down the path to build an example with az sql mi and found that I needed to run several az CLI commands to create the virtual network, subnet, and all associated settings. Therefore, I only recommend you use the az sql mi CLI with *Azure templates*. An example template can be found at `https://docs.microsoft.com/en-us/azure/azure-sql/managed-instance/create-template-quickstart?tabs=azure-cli`.

PowerShell requires you to set up the virtual network and other context before executing New-AzSQLInstance. There is a good tutorial on using PowerShell at `https://docs.microsoft.com/en-us/azure/azure-sql/managed-instance/scripts/create-configure-managed-instance-powershell`.

Implementation Details

Note   These implementation details may change over time as we change and improve the service. I offer up some of these details so you can understand how we build, manage, and run the service.

Azure SQL Managed Instance is deployed on nodes (virtual machines) powered by Azure Service Fabric in a concept called a *ring* or *virtual cluster*. A virtual cluster is a dedicated set of isolated virtual machines that run in a virtual network subnet. Using a dedicated ring or cluster gives Managed Instance the isolation and private connection that was lacking for years from Azure SQL Database (which you will see has also been resolved).

When you deploy your first managed instance in a new virtual network (subnet) as I did in my example, you are in fact deploying an entire virtual cluster. This explains why the initial deployment can take so long to complete. You can deploy other managed instances in the *same virtual network subnet*, and the deployment is much faster.

A managed instance is a full SQL Server engine database instance deployed in a dedicated virtual machine in the virtual cluster. Microsoft will decide how to deploy these virtual machines on various nodes of the cluster. It is possible that a node may have one virtual machine with an instance or multiple virtual machines. As per the promise of Platform as a Service (PaaS), Microsoft abstracts you from those details. Your interface with the Managed Instance is through either standard SQL Server interfaces such as T-SQL or Azure interfaces such as the portal, CLI, or REST API. You will never directly access the underlying virtual machines.

This architecture explains also why certain management operations such as scaling vCores can also take a long period of time as some of these operations can require a deployment of a new virtual cluster with either attaching files from Azure Storage or reseeding a replica.

I described some of the architecture of General Purpose (GP) vs. Business Critical (BC) tiers in Chapter 2 of the book. I will describe them further in Chapter 8 of the book. Either of these service tiers uses the same virtual cluster architecture just with different storage and HA implementations.

Resource limits for a Managed Instance such as memory limits, max storage size, and others are enforced through several mechanisms. For example, memory limits are enforced with Windows Job Objects (and you cannot configure "max server memory"). You can read more about *Windows Job Objects* at `https://docs.microsoft.com/en-us/windows/win32/procthread/job-objects`. Storage capacity (or max size) is enforced by The File Server Resource Manager (FSRM) which you can read more about at `https://docs.microsoft.com/en-us/windows-server/storage/fsrm/fsrm-overview`.

A *Managed Instance pool deployment* can be far faster because an instance pool can be a set of SQL Server instances running in the same virtual machine. Isolation and resource limits are applied using Windows Job Objects. Figure 4-9 represents a visual comparing managed instance and pools. This figure comes from the documentation at `https://docs.microsoft.com/en-us/azure/azure-sql/managed-instance/instance-pools-overview#architecture`.

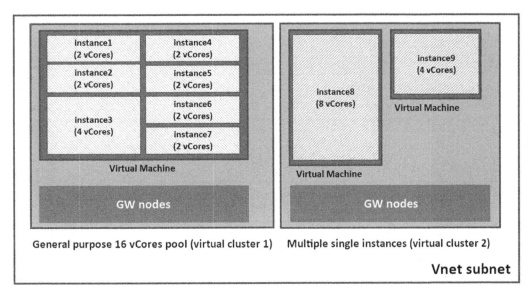

Figure 4-9. *The Managed Instance and pool architecture*

Connecting and Verifying Deployment

Once your deployment is complete, you can view the details of the deployment using the Activity Log like an Azure Virtual Machine as seen in Figure 4-10.

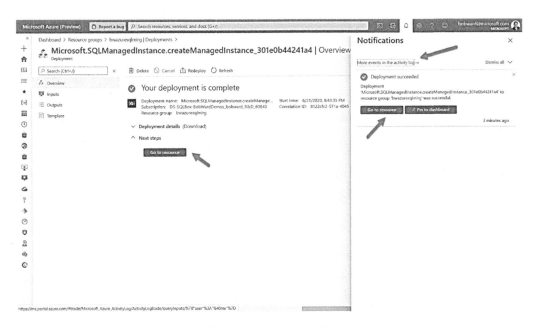

Figure 4-10. *Deployment complete for Managed Instance*

If you select More events in the activity log, you will see a screen like in Figure 4-11.

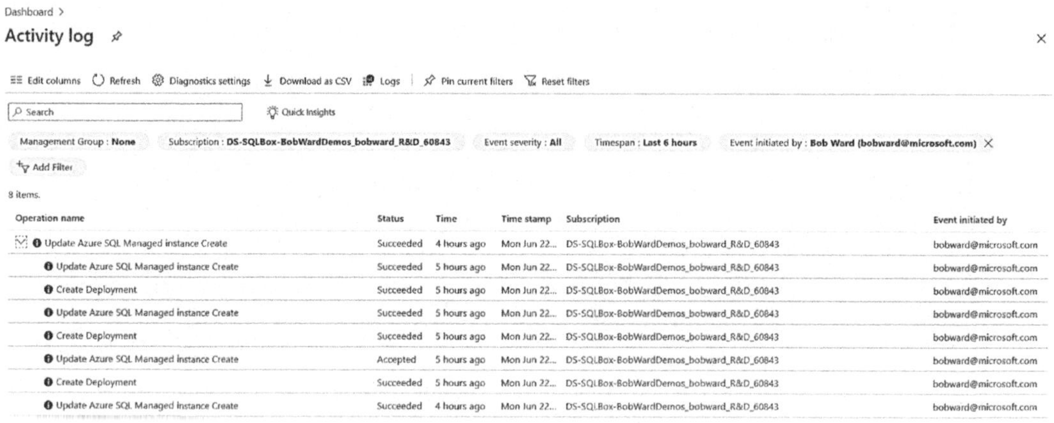

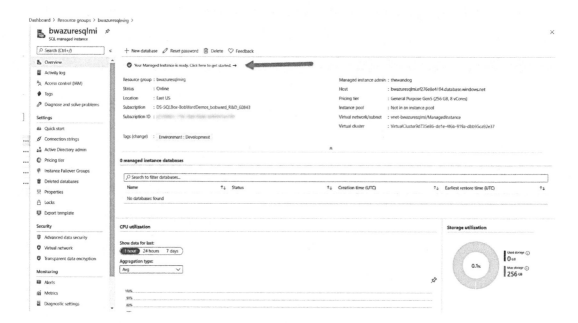

Figure 4-11. *The activity log for the deployment for Managed Instance*

If you click **Go to Resource**, you will see a screen like in Figure 4-12.

Figure 4-12. *The Overview screen for Azure SQL Managed Instance*

One of the first steps you will want to do at this point is try and connect to the new instance and verify the deployment. I like to verify my SQL Server installations with a set of simple T-SQL queries, but I will show you other navigation details as well.

Connect to a Managed Instance

You can see at the top of Figure 4-12 guidance to get started for a Managed Instance. If you click this message, you will see choices like the following in Figure 4-13.

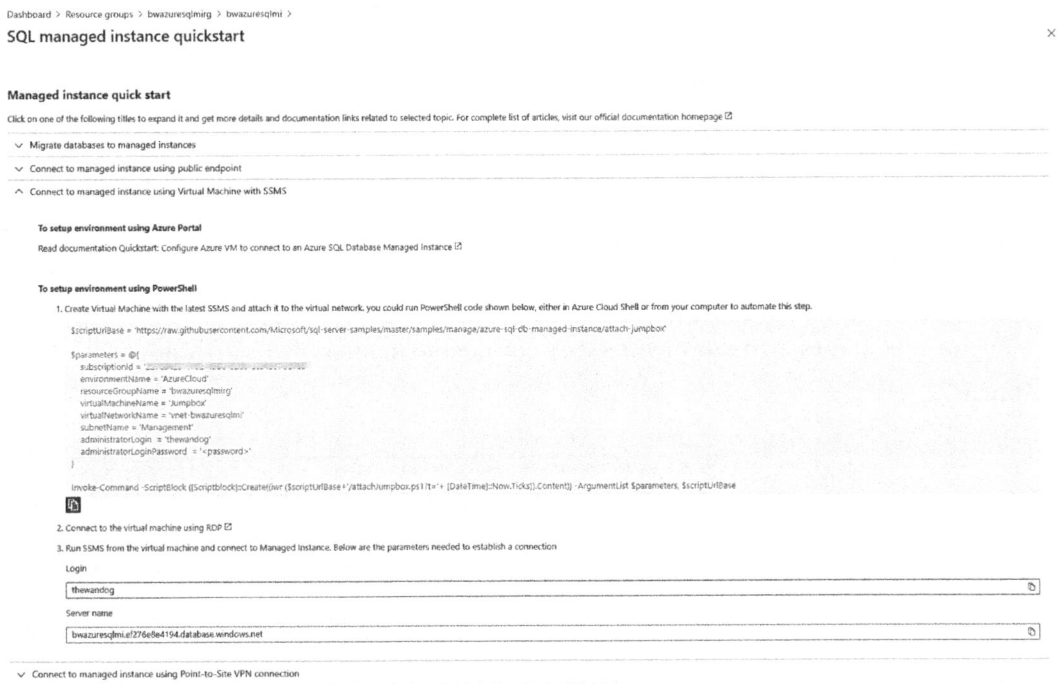

Figure 4-13. *Connecting to Azure SQL Managed Instance with a VM*

The list on this screen points to guidance on how to perform various tasks for a newly deployed Azure SQL Managed Instance. Since I did not enable the Public endpoint for the deployed Managed Instance, I have expanded the option to connect through a Virtual Machine.

I will follow these steps by first using the provided PowerShell script and executing it from the Azure Cloud shell. I used the copy button , edited the script, to provide an admin password, and then pasted the script into an Azure Cloud Shell.

This virtual machine is deployed in the same virtual network as the Azure SQL Managed Instance. Therefore, you can RDP into this virtual machine and then use tools like SSMS (which is already installed in this VM) to connect to the Managed Instance. The screen shows you the DNS name to use to connect with SSMS (in my case, the server name to connect to is bwazuresqlmi.ef276e8e4194.database.windows.net).

Tip   You can navigate to the newly created virtual machine by finding the Resource Group of the Managed Instance (which is bwazuresqlmirg in my example). The new VM is called **Jumpbox**. Navigate to the overview screen for this VM and select Connect and use the RDP file with a Remote Desktop Client. Once you use RDP to log in to the Windows Server, use SSMS to connect to the Managed Instance name with the SQL admin login and password you used during deployment.

The concept of using a virtual machine to connect to SQL Server for a Managed Instance is called a *jumpbox*. Jumpbox is the actual name of the VM created by the script provided as an example by Microsoft (but can be any name).

Figure 4-14 shows an example of SSMS connected to an Azure SQL Managed Instance.

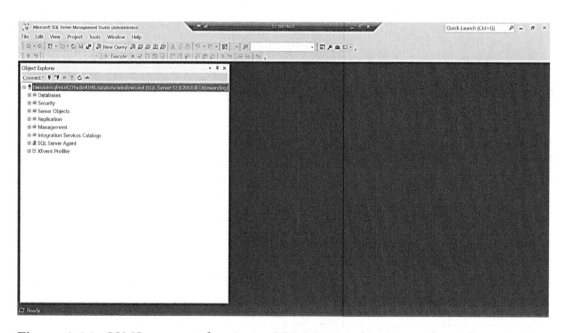

Figure 4-14. *SSMS connected to Azure SQL Managed Instance through a jumpbox*

If you want to connect from on-premises, you would need to either enable the public endpoint or connect your network to the Azure virtual network created.

Verify the Deployment

Notice that Object Explorer in SSMS looks almost identical to a SQL Server except for the Fully Qualified Domain Name (FQDN) for the server name.

To verify an installation of SQL Server, I often use a few techniques including running queries against system catalog views and DMVs and look at the ERRORLOG.

Examining the ERRORLOG

You do not have access to the filesystem for the virtual machine hosting the Managed Instance. To look at the ERRORLOG, we will need a tool like SSMS or T-SQL.

You can use Object Explorer in SSMS to view the ERRORLOG, but I prefer just T-SQL so can I execute `sp_readerrorlog` to look at the current ERRORLOG file. I must warn you that we dump all types of extra information in the ERRORLOG for a Managed Instance (yes even more than a SQL Server). My colleague Dimitri Furman wrote a blog post with some sample code to filter down the ERRORLOG for a Managed Instance. You can view this at `https://techcommunity.microsoft.com/t5/datacat/azure-sql-db-managed-instance-sp-readmierrorlog/ba-p/305506`.

There are a few key messages I look at startup in the ERRORLOG and found these in my Managed Instance:

```
SQL Server detected 1 sockets with 4 cores per socket and 8 logical
processors per socket, 8 total logical processors; using 8 logical
processors based on SQL Server licensing. This is an informational message;
no user action is required.
SQL Server is starting at normal priority base (=7). This is an
informational message only. No user action is required.
Detected 44645 MB of RAM. This is an informational message; no user action
is required.
```

I can see that eight logical processors were detected which is what I expect given I deployed an 8 vCore instance.

The memory detected is how much memory the SQL Server engine detects from the host or VM. You will see in several places in the book how Azure will use Windows Job Objects to limit the memory visible to SQL Server to enforce resource limits per service tier and vCores. You will find for this Managed Instance the job object will not allow SQL Server to access all the memory as shown here in the ERRORLOG. In fact, you should never rely on what the ERRORLOG shows but instead on the DMV sys.dm_os_job_object which I will show you how to use in the next section.

Verification Queries

Whenever I install a SQL Server, I typically use a few T-SQL queries as a *sanity check*. Let us look these and the results from the Managed Instance compared to SQL Server (I will not show the complete results of every query):

```
SELECT @@version
```

```
Microsoft SQL Azure (RTM) - 12.0.2000.8   May 15 2020 00:47:08   Copyright
(C) 2019 Microsoft Corporation
```

I explained in Chapter 1 of the book in describing the history of Azure SQL why v12 was a monumental moment for the service. Since that time, we have not changed the major version of 12.

Basically, the major version of Azure SQL Managed Instance has no meaning. It does not line up with any major version of SQL Server since Azure SQL Managed Instance is *versionless*. I will discuss more the concept of versionless in Chapter 5 of the book. Just know that Microsoft strives to keep instances and databases of Azure SQL up to date with all the right changes and fixes, so you do not worry about applying updates:

```
SELECT database_id, name, compatibility_level FROM sys.databases
```

database_id	name	compatibility_level
1	master	150
2	tempdb	150
3	model	150
4	msdb	150

This looks normal (I have not created any user databases), except the mssqlsystemresource database is not listed as with SQL Server (it does exist as you can see it in the ERRORLOG). Notice the compatibility level is set to 150 which is the latest dbcompat level of SQL Server 2019:

```
SELECT name, object_id, type_desc FROM sys.objects
```

The results from this query are what you would normally think from a master database on a SQL Server with system tables at the top of the list. About 113 rows returned from this query in master which is very close to a SQL Server:

```
SELECT * FROM sys.dm_os_schedulers
```

Since we have deployed an 8 vCore Managed Instance, I would expect eight VISIBLE ONLINE schedulers which is the case. I also expect to see a few HIDDEN ONLINE schedulers which are there in the result of this query:

```
SELECT * FROM sys.dm_os_sys_info
```

This is a DMV that provides system information about SQL Server. I can see from the output of this DMV the number of CPUs detected, amount of memory detected, the target (max server memory), and total memory used by the engine and the actual worker thread max (1640 for 8 vCores), and that the conventional memory model is not used. I will talk more about locked pages in Chapter 5 of the book:

```
SELECT * FROM sys.dm_os_process_memory
```

This DMV shows OS-related memory information including whether locked or large pages are used (they are not for Azure SQL Managed Instance or Database). I normally just use this as a sanity check that enough memory is available for SQL Server in a VM or server:

```
SELECT * FROM sys.dm_exec_requests
```

This is one of the most common DMVs in the world to check the state of what is running on a SQL Server. I run this just to make sure all the normal background processes are running including LAZ WRITER, RECOVERY WRITER, LOCK MONITOR, and so on and that I can see active queries:

```
SELECT SERVERPROPERTY('EngineEdition')
```

Per the documentation at `https://docs.microsoft.com/en-us/sql/t-sql/functions/serverproperty-transact-sql`, the value of 8 is for a Managed Instance.

There are also two new DMVs specific to Azure not found in SQL Server:

```
SELECT * FROM sys.dm_user_db_resource_governance
```

This DMV is really intended to show you resource limits for a specific Azure SQL Database, but it also works for Managed Instance (you will see a row for all databases including system databases except for tempdb). You can view limits like memory, max storage, log rates, and so on. You can read the documentation for this DMV at `https://docs.microsoft.com/en-us/sql/relational-databases/system-dynamic-management-views/sys-dm-user-db-resource-governor-azure-sql-database?view=azuresqldb-current`. Note that the docs say this is mostly for internal use, which means it might change in the future:

> **Note**   There is an undocumented DMV called **sys.dm_instance_resource_ governance** which shows resource limits at the instance level.

```
SELECT * FROM sys.dm_os_job_object
```

This is a DMV specific to Azure (although I tested it and it works for a SQL Server, but you can't rely on the results there because it is not applicable) that shows resource limits Azure applies to a Managed Instance using Windows Job Objects. The specific column I look at is **memory_limit_mb** which shows me the true amount of memory the Managed Instance has access to. I talked about Windows Job Objects in the preceding section "Implementation Details."

You may be asking at this point what is so special about Managed Instance, since from the perspective of using a tool like SSMS, it feels like a SQL Server running in an Azure Virtual Machine. This is the point of a Managed Instance. We want you to have the feel of a SQL Server instance, but not worry about the details you might have to consider with a virtual machine. And since Azure SQL Managed Instance (MI) is a PaaS service, you will see the benefits of using MI, especially when it comes to a versionless SQL Server, predictable performance, and built-in high availability and disaster recovery.

Migrating to Azure SQL Managed Instance

As part of deploying an Azure SQL Managed Instance, you may be migrating existing databases. The process to migrate should include assessment and planning, the actual migration, application changes, and post-migration optimization.

Let us look at each of these aspects to the migration process.

Assessment and Planning

An assessment for migration includes analyzing any problems that might occur for your migration depending on what the source of your migration and your preferred Managed Instance deployment option. This is when you use the details I described with pre-deployment planning earlier in this chapter.

Most users migrating to Azure SQL Managed Instance are coming from an existing SQL Server installation. However, it is possible to migrate from other data platforms including Oracle. Check out this blog post on how to migrate from Oracle to Azure SQL Managed Instance, `https://techcommunity.microsoft.com/t5/microsoft-data-migration/migrate-your-oracle-database-to-azure-sql-database-managed/ba-p/368750`.

The key to getting an entire migration project started is to use **Azure Migrate** at `https://azure.microsoft.com/en-us/services/azure-migrate/`. From there, you can start an Azure Migrate project and use the Data Migration Assistant (DMA) tool (`https://docs.microsoft.com/en-us/sql/dma/dma-overview`) and Data Migration Service (DMS) (`https://azure.microsoft.com/en-us/services/database-migration/`).

I could show you a ton of details here and walk you through an example. But I have something better. My colleague Anna Thomas developed an entire workshop complete with slides and exercises at `https://github.com/microsoft/sqlworkshops-sqlg2c/tree/master/sqlgroundtocloud` (Modules 4 and 5). Anna walks you through everything to see how DMA and DMS work to perform an assessment and migration. You have the choice to migrate all the databases for the instance or one or more databases incrementally.

Note   Two important things you should consider as you migrate are in the documentation, and I want to highlight them here.

When you are migrating a database protected by Transparent Data Encryption to a managed instance using native restore option, the corresponding certificate from the on-premises or Azure VM SQL Server needs to be migrated before database restore.

Restore of system databases is not supported. **To migrate instance-level objects** (stored in master or msdb databases), we recommend to script them out and run T-SQL scripts on the destination instance.

One last important point: consider using a database compatibility level that matches your current SQL Server installation and then move later to the latest compat level. Learn more about dbcompat at `https://aka.ms/dbcompat`.

Migration

To perform an actual migration of an existing SQL Server instance (the entire instance or just a database), Azure SQL Managed Instance provides a great capability to make this faster and better: the ability to restore a database from a backup of SQL Server.

This allows you to perform an *offline* migration (restore a full database backup) while the application is down and then connect back again to the Managed Instance when the restore finishes.

The Database Migration Service (DMS) specifically allows for an online migration using technology based on SQL Server Log Shipping to restore a full backup and then a series of log backups until you are ready for the migration cutover. Anna's workshop goes through both options.

In addition, you can watch me on the Microsoft Mechanics channel at `https://youtu.be/P_4EaqVR5PI` and go through the entire migration process including a demo of migration to a Managed Instance. One of the aspects of using DMA I love is the SKU recommendation PowerShell script. This script analyzes your current SQL Server workload to guide you on Azure SQL Managed Instance deployment choices. Read more at `https://docs.microsoft.com/en-us/sql/dma/dma-sku-recommend-sql-db?view=sql-server-ver15`.

Note   Even though I am the person interviewed for this video and demo, the real heroes behind the scenes are the migration team, including folks like Venkata Raj Pochiraju and Sreraman Narasimhan.

Application Changes

One of the best stories for migration is the minimal changes required by your application after migrating to Managed Instance. The most basic change for you to make is the connection string to use the new server name. You may also have to change the authentication method (SQL Authentication or Azure Active Directory). But other than that, provided you are using all the features supported by Managed Instance, these may be the only changes you need to get your application up and running.

Post Migration

After you have migrated your database(s) and made the necessary application changes, you may want to make some configuration changes or adjustments for security, performance, and availability.

Here is the good news. The rest of the book is devoted to these topics, so you have the resources you need to make any changes to go bigger with Azure.

Deploying an Azure SQL Database

Deploying an Azure SQL Database is both different and like Azure SQL Managed Instance. The experience is similar as you will use the Azure Portal or CLI (or even T-SQL) to deploy a database but different since you are...well deploying a database, not an instance of SQL Server. Since you are deploying just a database, you get more options as I have described in this book, including Serverless and Hyperscale.

The basic process to deploy Azure SQL Database is

- Decide to deploy a single database or elastic pool.

- Choose a Resource Group and Region.

- Choose an existing or new logical database server.

- Choose your purchasing model, compute model, service tier, and size.

- Optionally supply other configuration choices.

- Deploy it!

Deployment and Options

To get started, I will use the **Azure SQL** screen to deploy by searching for Azure SQL in the marketplace. With a screen like in Figure 4-15, I can choose to deploy a Single database, Elastic pool, or Database server. I will show you how to deploy a Single database which will allow me to also deploy a Database server (and I will describe what and why you need a Database server).

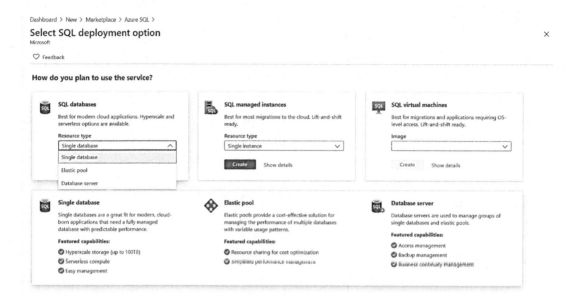

Figure 4-15. *Using Azure SQL to choose to deploy an Azure SQL Database*

Basics

If you choose Single database, you are presented with a Basics screen like Azure SQL Managed Instance as seen in Figure 4-16.

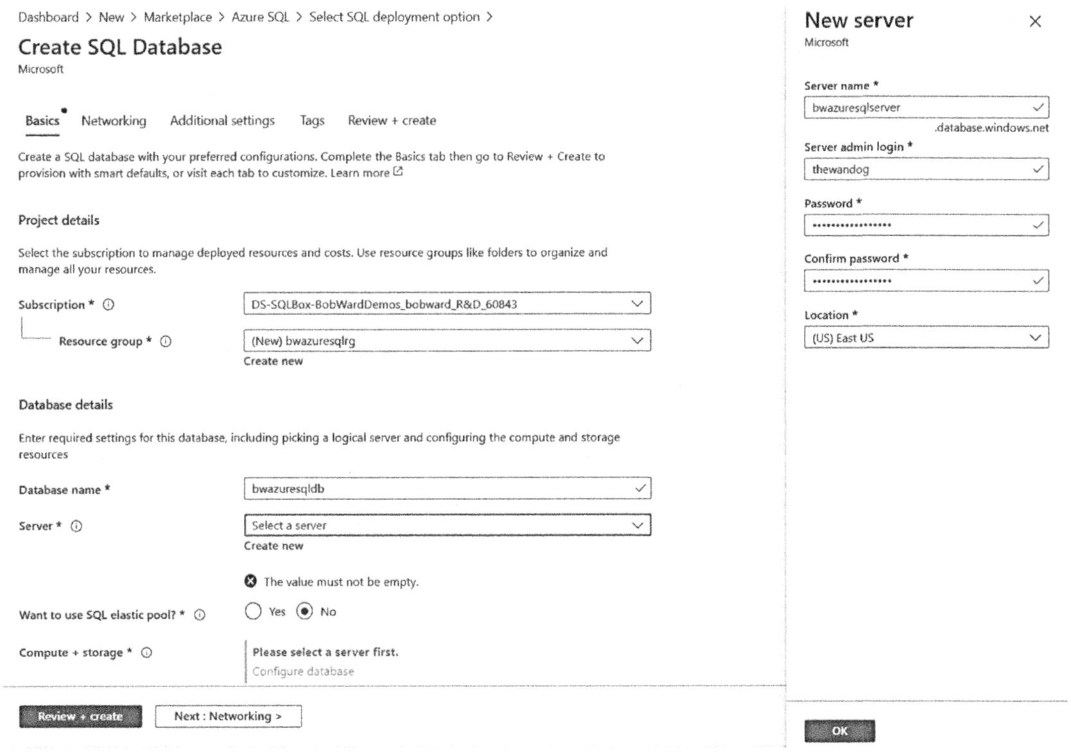

Figure 4-16. *Defining a Database server as part of Azure SQL deployment*

You can see from my screen that I have already created a new Resource Group, defined a Database name, and chose to create a new Database server. You may be wondering why you need a Database server when the promise of Azure SQL Database is "you own the database; Azure will manage everything else."

A **Database server**, also known as a *logical server,* is a collection of metadata stored in the Azure infrastructure used to organize one or more Azure SQL databases. It is not a single SQL Server instance on a physical server. A Database server contains a **logical master database** just like a true SQL Server instance. Notice the region is associated with the logical server, not the database. Any database created for the logical server will be hosted in the region of the server. All connectivity and networking will be associated with the logical server. In fact, you could create a logical server first, connect to that server, and use T-SQL CREATE DATABASE to create Azure SQL databases. The login and password you supply for the logical server becomes a login in the logical master database which is a server-level principal who is effectively a *server admin* for all databases. In Modules 6 and 7, I will show you how to integrate Azure Active Directory (AAD) for an admin login.

Once you click **OK** for the logical server (it will be created as part of the deployment), you can choose if you want to make this part of an elastic pool and select your options for purchasing model, service tier, and size. I will not spend a lot of time in the book discussing the details of how to create and manage an elastic pool. I recommend you use this documentation to learn and go further with using elastic pools, `https://docs.microsoft.com/en-us/azure/azure-sql/database/elastic-pool-overview`.

Figure 4-17 shows an example of selecting **Configure database** to see your deployment options.

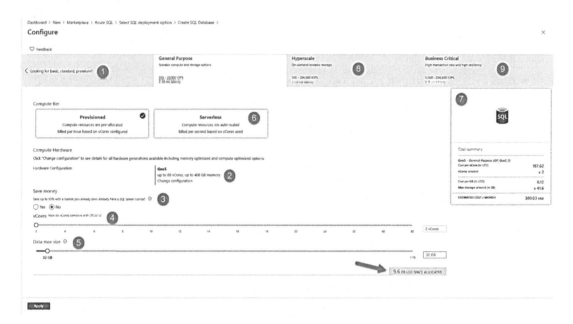

Figure 4-17. *Azure SQL purchasing, compute, service tier, and size options*

Let us look at the various options on this screen, what they mean, and how they affect your deployment:

1. The default *purchasing model* is vCore. You can select on this screen the ability to choose the DTU purchase model. While I will not cover details about deploying the DTU model, you can read about this option at `https://docs.microsoft.com/en-us/azure/azure-sql/database/service-tiers-dtu`.

2. The default *hardware generation* for the vCore model is Gen5. As I described in pre-deployment planning, choosing Change configuration allows you to pick other hardware generations such as Fsv2- and M-series.

3. Just like a Managed Instance, you can choose to apply your existing SQL Server license with Azure Hybrid Benefit (AHB).

4. Just like a Managed Instance, you have a slider bar to choose the number of vCores for your deployment. You will notice that for Azure SQL Database, you have more granular choices for vCores.

5. Just like a Managed Instance, you have a slider bar for Data max size. The more vCores you choose, the larger the max size. This max size is the maximum size of the single database file hosting your database. Notice below the size is a number for LOG SPACE ALLOCATED. You are given for free a maximum transaction log size that is 30% over your data max size.

Note   If you are worried this may not be enough, we continuously back up the transaction log and have Accelerated Database Recovery enabled by default (which means a long active transaction does not hold up log truncation). As much as I tried, I never ran out of log space in my testing with Azure SQL Database.

---

6. Provisioned is the default *Compute model*. For the General Purpose service tier, you have the choice of the *Serverless* model. I will show you Serverless options in the section titled "Deploying Serverless" later in this chapter.

7. As you make choices, the portal will show you estimated costs per month broken out by costs for vCores and storage.

8. Besides General Purpose, you also have the choice to deploy a Hyperscale service tier. I will show you the process of deploying Hyperscale in the following section titled "Deploying Hyperscale."

9. You also have the choice to choose the Business Critical service tier. I will show you the process of deploying a Business Critical database in the following section titled "Deploying Business Critical."

I know there are many choices which is one of the benefits of Azure SQL Database but does require some thinking for your requirements. Thankfully, changing these options or resizing your Azure SQL Database is flexible and fast (the exception is Hyperscale).

I will leave the default of General Purpose, 2 vCore, 32Gb max data size and click **Apply**.

Networking

Click **Next: Networking** > to see your choices for connectivity and network security as seen in Figure 4-18.

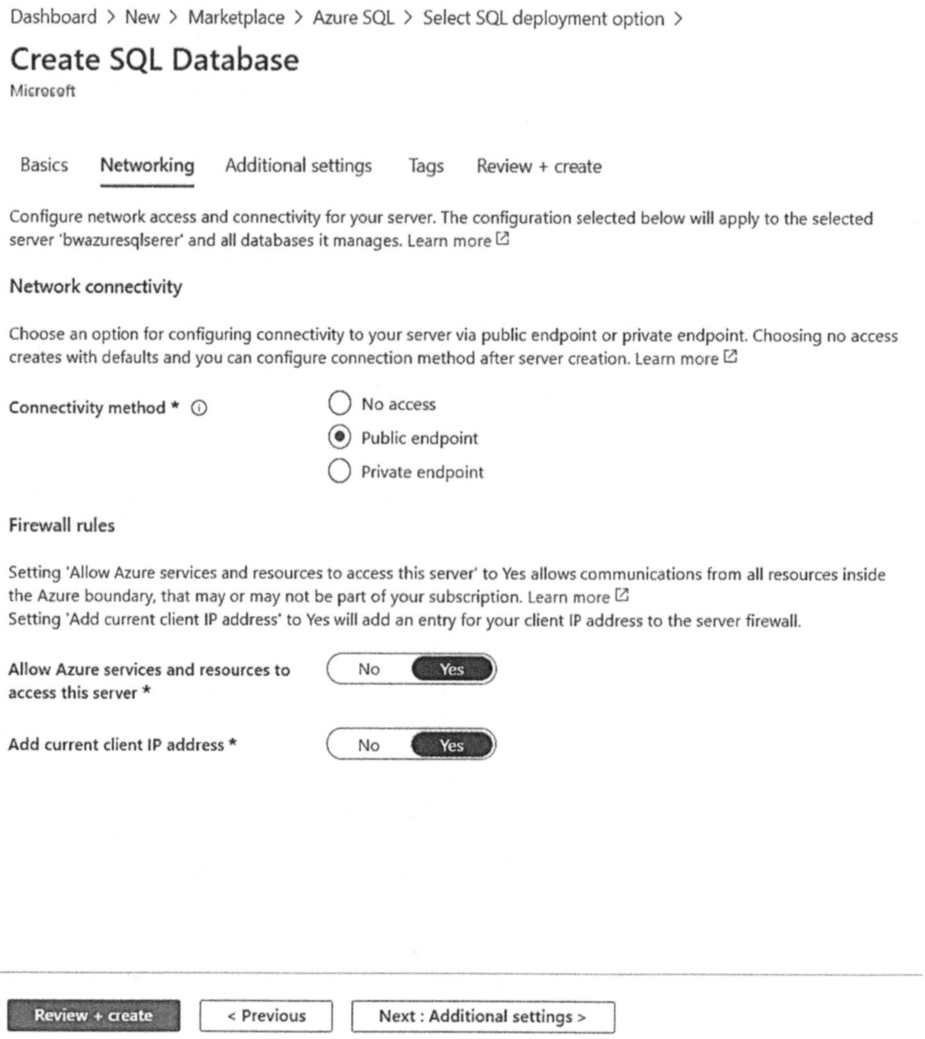

Dashboard > New > Marketplace > Azure SQL > Select SQL deployment option >

Create SQL Database
Microsoft

| Basics | **Networking** | Additional settings | Tags | Review + create |

Configure network access and connectivity for your server. The configuration selected below will apply to the selected server 'bwazuresqlserer' and all databases it manages. Learn more

Network connectivity

Choose an option for configuring connectivity to your server via public endpoint or private endpoint. Choosing no access creates with defaults and you can configure connection method after server creation. Learn more

Connectivity method * ⓘ

○ No access
◉ Public endpoint
○ Private endpoint

Firewall rules

Setting 'Allow Azure services and resources to access this server' to Yes allows communications from all resources inside the Azure boundary, that may or may not be part of your subscription. Learn more
Setting 'Add current client IP address' to Yes will add an entry for your client IP address to the server firewall.

Allow Azure services and resources to access this server *   No **Yes**

Add current client IP address *   No **Yes**

Review + create   < Previous   Next : Additional settings >

Figure 4-18. Networking choices when deploying an Azure SQL Database

Unlike Azure SQL Managed Instance, Azure SQL Database is not part of a virtual network. You have three choices during deployment:

No access – Deploy the database, but do not allow any connectivity until you are ready to make your choice.

Public endpoint – Expose connectivity of the logical server and/or database to the public within Azure or to the Internet (or both).

Private endpoint – This is a new addition to Azure SQL Database to make it very secure. This allows you to deny public access to your server and/or database and only allows private connectivity within defined virtual networks in and outside of Azure.

For now, I will select Public endpoint and set **Allow Azure services and resources access this server** to Yes and **Add current client IP address** to Yes. This allows me to deploy an Azure Virtual Machine and connect to this database or to connect with SQL client tools on the client computer where I am currently deploying the browser. My client IP address will be added to a *firewall rule* to connect to the logical server associated with this database. I will show you how to tighten up the security of this model in Chapters 6 and 7 of the book.

Additional Settings

Click **Next: Additional settings >** to see more options for the deployment. Figure 4-19 shows these additional options.

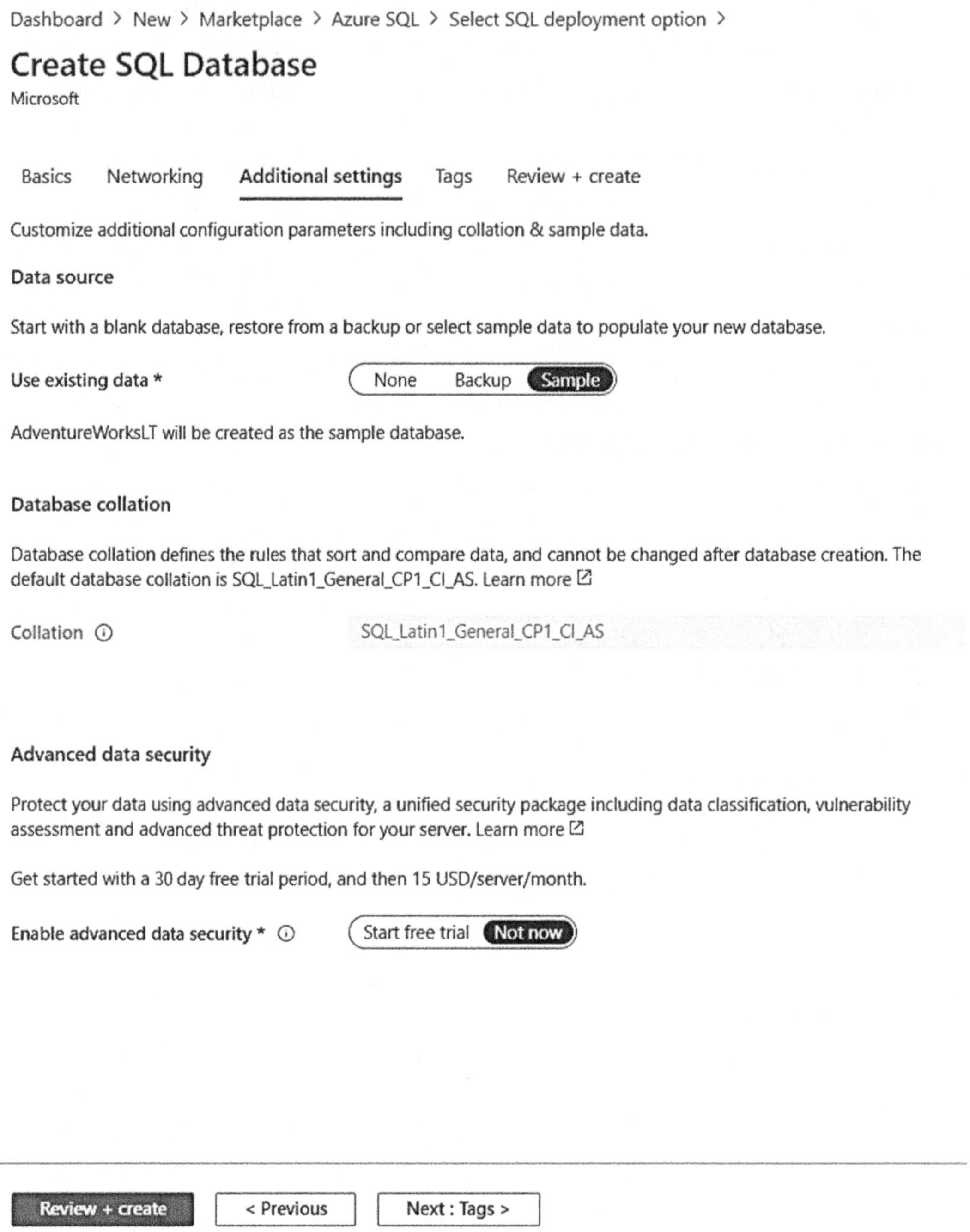

Dashboard > New > Marketplace > Azure SQL > Select SQL deployment option >

Create SQL Database
Microsoft

Basics   Networking   **Additional settings**   Tags   Review + create

Customize additional configuration parameters including collation & sample data.

Data source

Start with a blank database, restore from a backup or select sample data to populate your new database.

Use existing data *   (None   Backup   **Sample**)

AdventureWorksLT will be created as the sample database.

Database collation

Database collation defines the rules that sort and compare data, and cannot be changed after database creation. The default database collation is SQL_Latin1_General_CP1_CI_AS. Learn more ☑

Collation ⓘ   SQL_Latin1_General_CP1_CI_AS

Advanced data security

Protect your data using advanced data security, a unified security package including data classification, vulnerability assessment and advanced threat protection for your server. Learn more ☑

Get started with a 30 day free trial period, and then 15 USD/server/month.

Enable advanced data security * ⓘ   (Start free trial   **Not now**)

[Review + create]   [< Previous]   [Next : Tags >]

Figure 4-19. *Additional settings for the deployment of Azure SQL Database*

Your first choice is to either create a blank database or create a database based on a backup of a geo-replicated Azure SQL Database or from the sample AdventureWorksLT (LT stands for light). You can learn more about how to restore from a geo-replicated backup at https://docs.microsoft.com/en-us/azure/azure-sql/database/recovery-using-backups#geo-restore. I will choose the sample AdventureWorksLT database because I want to show some demonstrations of other capabilities using that database later in the book.

Your next choice is *Database collation*. Since I chose a sample database, the collation is already decided. For a new blank database, it is important to choose this during deployment because you cannot change it later.

The final choice is to enable *Advanced Data Security*. I will not enable this for now and show you more about this capability in Chapters 6 and 7 of the book.

Tags

Click **Next: Tags >** to define a tag for the deployment. Just like with Azure Virtual Machine and Managed Instance, I will use a Name = Environment and Value = Development. In this case, I will leave the resources selected for both SQL Database and SQL database server.

Note   After you deploy, you can now search for Tags for your description and see all your resources that are "for development purposes."

Deploy It!

Click **Next: Review + create >** to see the final validation screen as seen in Figure 4-20.

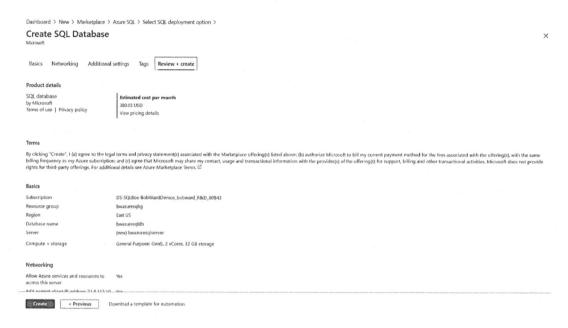

Figure 4-20. *Final screen before deployment of Azure SQL Database*

Just like with Managed Instance, you can see estimated costs, Terms of Use, privacy policy, a review of your choices, and the ability to download an Azure template.

Click **Create** to see the deployment take off. Just like with Managed Instance, if you do not leave this screen, you will see a progress of your deployment in both the Notifications area of the portal and on your main screen.

There is no warning of time to deploy like with Managed Instance, because in most cases, the deployment should finish quickly. In my example, the deployment only took a matter of minutes as shown in Figure 4-21.

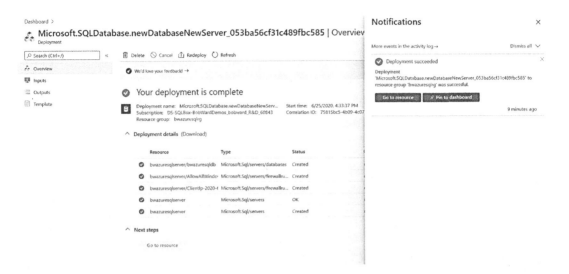

Figure 4-21. *A completed deployment of Azure SQL Database*

Tip   I have found that I can connect to the logical server and use the database being deployed even before I get signaled the deployment is complete.

Just like a Managed Instance deployment, you can click More events in the activity log to see the sequence of deploying all resources.

Click Go to resource to see the Overview screen on the database like Figure 4-22.

Figure 4-22. *The Overview screen of an Azure SQL Database*

Just like with a Virtual Machine and Managed Instance, the portal shows a Resource Menu, Command Bar, Working Pane, and Monitoring Pane. While this looks like other Azure resources, most of this information is specific to Azure SQL Database. We will use many of these options throughout the rest of the chapter as you explore security, performance, availability, and other features.

Let us see the experience of deploying an Azure SQL Database Business Critical, Hyperscale, and Serverless database on the *same logical server*. In the Working Pane, click the Server Name.

This is the Overview screen for the Database Server as seen in Figure 4-23.

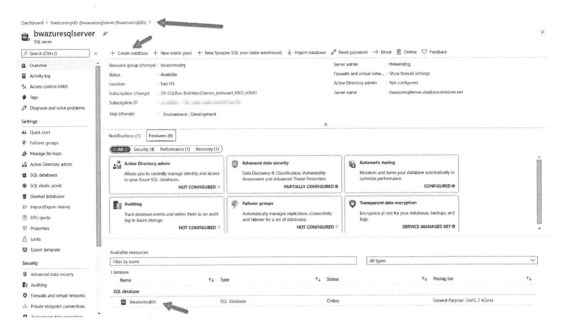

Figure 4-23. *Overview of an Azure SQL Database Server*

Notice at the bottom the database we just deployed. I also want to stop and point out a key feature of the portal called *breadcrumbs*. You were brought to the overview screen of the database server by selecting it from the overview screen of the database. The breadcrumbs "show you where you came from" and allow you to *navigate* to a specific resource in the portal.

Click **Create database** from the command bar.

Note   The following sections for Business Critical, Serverless, and Hyperscale require costs if you leave these deployments active. You can choose to go through and deploy these or just follow along.

Deploying Business Critical

Notice now you are brought to a Basics screen to create a new database, but the resource group and server are already selected. Click configure database and choose the Business Critical service tier. Notice some new choices as seen in Figure 4-24.

Figure 4-24. *Azure SQL Business Critical service tier choices*

You still choose the number of vCores and Data max size. But you also choose whether this database will enable read scale-out and zone redundancy. I will discuss these high availability capabilities in Chapters 10 and 11 of the book. For now, I will leave Read scale-out Enabled (you should; it is free) and select Yes for zone redundancy.

Click **Apply** and put in a database name. I will use a new name and call it **bwazuresqldbbc**. Instead of making additional choices, I will choose **Review + create** and then **Create**.

Note   You could make other choices here including setting up a Private endpoint for your database different than the choice made for the first database on the server.

Once this deployment is complete (it should be fast), you can click **Go to resource** and see you now have a Business Critical database deployed. Click the **Server name** again and repeat the process to create a new database.

Deploying Serverless

Like the Business Critical Scenario, click **configure database**. Then select Serverless as seen in Figure 4-25 with new choices.

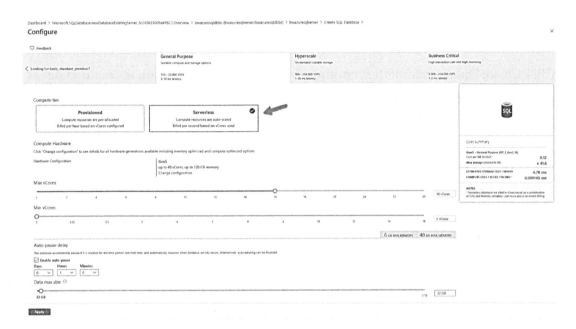

Figure 4-25. *Serverless compute options*

Instead of a slider to choose vCores, I can choose a min and max vCore. Serverless will *autoscale* based on the CPU needs of my workload. Notice the values for min and max memory. This means that for my Serverless database I can use a maximum of 48Gb, but when my usage is idle, my memory may be trimmed down to as low as 6Gb. Think of this like max and min server memory configuration values for SQL Server. The difference is that our Azure services will trim memory (almost like external memory pressure) if usage is idle.

So, what defines idle? That is the choice for Auto-pause delay. If there is no usage for 1 hour, the compute for this database will be *paused* and memory resources reclaimed. Drill more into Serverless at https://docs.microsoft.com/en-us/azure/azure-sql/database/serverless-tier-overview.

Click Apply and put in a database name. I used **bwazuresqldbserverless**. Click **Review + create**. Notice on the validation screen the costs is listed as per second which is one of the great stories of saving costs with Serverless. Click **Create** and wait for the deployment to finish. When the deployment is finished, click **Go to resource**. Notice in the Monitoring Pane metrics for Compute utilization vs. App CPU billed. This helps you track billing per second of compute usage for a Serverless database.

Click the Server name again so you can create a Hyperscale database.

Deploying Hyperscale

Click Create Database from the command bar to see the screen again to create a new database on the same logical server. Click configure database and select the Hyperscale option as seen in Figure 4-26.

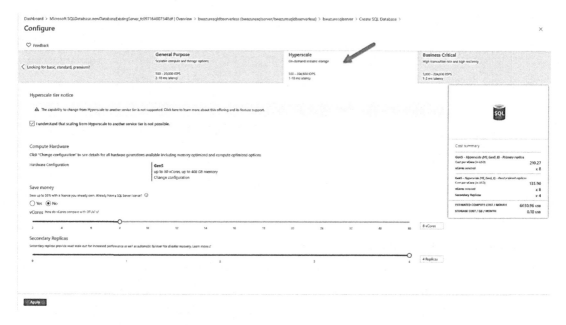

Figure 4-26. *Hyperscale deployment options*

The first thing you may notice about this screen is that you must select the option that you understand that by choosing Hyperscale you cannot change the service tier (to General Purpose or Business Critical) once you deploy.

The slider for vCores looks just like General Purpose and Business Critical. But notice there is no Data max size. Hyperscale is theoretically limitless (although today we limit you to a 100TB database but a large transaction log). When you deploy a Hyperscale database, we create an initial size of ~40Gb and then just grow as you need space.

Hyperscale offers a unique choice for number of replicas. You will learn in Chapter 8 of this book about how Hyperscale provides unique availability. Allowing you to specify up to four replicas which can be used for read scale is one of them.

I will choose 8 vCores and four Secondary Replicas. Click Apply, put in a database name (I will use **bwazuresqldbhyper**), and click **Review + create**. I will click **Create** to start the deployment.

Once the deployment is complete, you can click **Go to resource** to bring up the Overview page of the database. If you select Server name, you can see now you have four databases spanning all the service and compute tiers as seen in Figure 4-27.

Available resources

Filter by name		All types			∨

4 databases

Name	↑↓	Type	↑↓	Status	↑↓	Pricing tier	↑↓
SQL database							
bwazuresqdbhyper		SQL database		Online		Hyperscale: Gen5, 8 vCores	
bwazuresqldb		SQL database		Online		General Purpose: Gen5, 2 vCores	
bwazuresqldbbc		SQL database		Online		Business Critical: Gen5, 2 vCores	
bwazuresqldbserverless		SQL database		Paused		General Purpose: Serverless, Gen5, 16 vCores	

Figure 4-27. *Available databases from an Azure logical server*

Notice that my Serverless database is already paused because quite frankly I had paused for an hour before I deployed the Hyperscale database. Before we try to connect to these databases, let us explore more how to deploy with CLI tools and some implementation details of Azure SQL Database.

Deploying with a CLI

An Azure SQL Database can be deployed with command-line interfaces (CLI) through the **az sql db** (`https://docs.microsoft.com/en-us/cli/azure/sql/db?view=azure-cli-latest`) command interfaces or through **New-AzSQLDatabase** PowerShell cmdlet (`https://docs.microsoft.com/en-us/powershell/module/az.sql/New-AzSqlDatabase`).

Unlike Managed Instance, it is easier to use the az CLI for Azure SQL Database without an Azure template because I only have to create the logical server and then I can create the database (I don't have to create a virtual network and all the components first).

Here is an example of using az sql db to create a single database for a General Purpose, 2 vCore database:

```
az group create –name bwazuresqlrg2 -l eastus
az sql server create --location eastus --resource-group bwazuresqlrg2
--name bwazuresqlserver2 -u thewandog -p '<password>' --enable-public-
network true
az sql db create --resource-group bwazuresqlrg2 --server bwazuresqlserver2
--name bwazuresqldb2 --edition GeneralPurpose --family Gen5 --capacity 2
--sample-name AdventureWorksLT
```

> **Note**   The only option that cannot be done with the az CLI for database that I could in the portal is to set Allow Azure services to Yes and set the current Client IP address for a firewall rule. You can easily configure this after the deployment or use an Azure template.

PowerShell does give you all the options you need to deploy as with the portal. There is a good tutorial on using PowerShell at https://docs.microsoft.com/en-us/azure/azure-sql/database/scripts/create-and-configure-database-powershell?toc=/powershell/module/toc.json.

An Azure template is still a great idea to use and in fact is the best option to automate deployment of many databases. Read about how to use Azure templates and Azure SQL Database at https://docs.microsoft.com/en-us/azure/azure-sql/database/single-database-create-arm-template-quickstart.

Implementation Details

> **Note**   These implementation details may change over time as we change and improve the service. I offer up some of these details so you can understand how we build, manage, and run the service.

In Chapter 1 of this book, I covered the incredible history of how we have built an architecture to power millions of databases for Azure SQL Database. Let me give you a few more details about how we implement Azure SQL Database behind the scenes.

Note   As I interviewed many people in the Microsoft engineering team behind the scenes about Azure SQL Database even as I write this chapter, we are looking into how to make our implementation more efficient. Therefore, it is possible even some of these details could be a bit outdated by the time you read this chapter. That is the *speed of the cloud* and an author's nightmare!

Dedicated Rings and Instances

Unlike Managed Instance, we pre-deploy rings dedicated to hosting Azure SQL Databases. With only a few exceptions, each database is hosted by a dedicated SQL Server instance (exceptions being "subcore" DTU options and elastic pools). This allows us to provide better isolation for a customer and keep the "just worry about the database" model while opening some instance-level surface area (e.g., DMVs and columnstore indexes). We may provision these instances on the same VM or node, but those details are abstracted from you, provided we keep to our SLA agreement and objectives for performance.

All the rings and instances are powered and managed using **Azure Service Fabric**. This is the same service fabric software that you can build your own microservices. The Azure Service Fabric architecture is well documented at `https://docs.microsoft.com/en-us/azure/service-fabric/service-fabric-architecture`.

The Logical Server

As I stated earlier in this chapter, a database or logical server is just a metadata concept. We provide an interface to a server and a master database. But, when you query various aspects of the master database, we may be pulling data from other stores or files within the service to show you the information. There is a good description of why you need a logical server for even one database at `https://docs.microsoft.com/en-us/azure/azure-sql/database/logical-servers`.

Storage, Compute, and Gateways

You will see in Chapter 8 for Availability more details on the architecture behind the scenes on how we implement High Availability (HA) for General Purpose, Business Critical, and Hyperscale service tiers. We achieve certain HA capabilities by either using Azure Storage or local storage with technologies like Always On Availability Groups.

In each of these cases, one of the key components for connectivity is a *gateway*. Gateways are nodes that basically route traffic to nodes hosting SQL Server databases. I mentioned the use of redirect vs. proxy connection types with a Managed Instance earlier in the chapter. The same concept will apply with an Azure SQL Database. Gateways are critical to connectivity in that they provide abstractions to an application for connectivity no matter where the node for the database lives which you will learn more about in Chapter 6 on Security and Chapter 8 on Availability.

Serverless

Serverless compute models involve several interesting technologies we implement within the standard deployment of a SQL Server. Many of these details are described in our documentation at `https://docs.microsoft.com/en-us/azure/azure-sql/database/serverless-tier-overview`.

Since storage and compute are separated for a Serverless deployment, *pausing* a database is not that difficult since no application is connected. We just need to keep around enough state information that when a new login is made, we can connect the database to an instance and "warm up" the application.

Autoscaling is more interesting. We need to scale up or down the database CPU resources without application disruption. And if we can scale on a node that can meet the new scaling demand, there is no disruption. However, if we cannot meet that demand, we may need to use an Azure Load Balance to keep the application connected if possible until a new node is found to meet demand, but there can be a disconnection when the new node is brought up.

Memory management is also different in that we must deploy memory policies to reclaim memory for the SQL Server instance when CPU or cache utilization is low. Think of this concept as though we are signaling SQL Server there is external memory pressure and lowering the target for memory. Autoscaling and Memory Management for Serverless is described more at `https://docs.microsoft.com/en-us/azure/azure-sql/database/serverless-tier-overview#autoscaling`.

Hyperscale

Hyperscale is a unique implementation for a database within the same architecture of databases (dedicated rings and nodes) implemented much differently than General Purpose or Business Critical service tiers.

A hyperscale deployment involves a series of nodes for compute, logging, and caching combined with Azure Storage. I talked about this architecture in Chapter 1 of the book, but it is worth showing you again as seen in Figure 4-28 (which is directly from the documentation at `https://docs.microsoft.com/en-us/azure/azure-sql/database/service-tier-hyperscale#distributed-functions-architecture`).

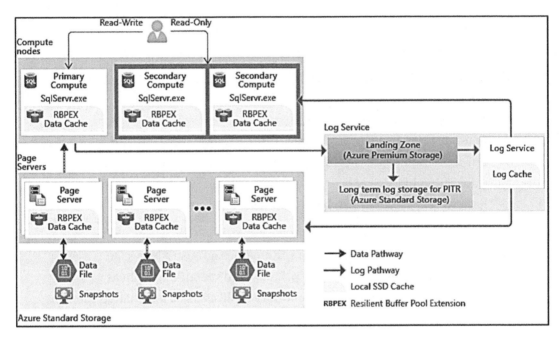

Figure 4-28. *The Hyperscale architecture*

I will show you more of the working parts of this architecture in Chapter 8 of this book, but let me stop and call out a few key components:

- Separate of compute and storage

  Just like General Purpose, we store database files on Azure storage. But notice here we use Azure Standard Storage. Speed to access the database files is not as important because of the caching system.

- The *caching* system

  We use a combination of page servers (actual nodes that host database pages) and buffer pool caches (think SSD drives that extend the buffer pool) on page servers and compute nodes.

- Log Service

  For Hyperscale, any logged changes are still in a log cache on the primary compute node. However, when log changes must be flushed to disk (a commit), these I/O requests are *redirected* to another node where a component called the Log Service runs (this is also called Xlog). The Log Service is responsible for ensuring changes are stored locally (called the *Landing Zone*) and are refreshed to the caching system, secondary replicas, and eventually to Azure storage.

- Decoupled Replicas

  In a way Hyperscale provides you the best of both the General Purpose and Business Critical tiers. The actual database and transaction log files are stored in Azure Storage (which has its own redundancy), but we also have replicas for extremely fast high availability.

  However, the secondary replica system does not use Always On Availability Groups. In fact, the primary and secondary replicas are not aware of each other. Secondary replicas use a log change methodology but are fed changes from the Log Service. Commits on the primary replica can proceed once the Log Service has hardened the changes not sending to a replica.

  High availability is even allowed with no secondary replicas. How? If the primary node has an issue, we can deploy a new primary replica on a new node and use page servers or even the database files on Azure Storage because it is decoupled. Having said this, RTO is much faster with the presence of secondary replicas. The secondary replica system (because you can have four of these) provides the best read-scale option for Azure SQL Database.

- *Hyperfast* Backup and Restore

  Because most of the data access comes from the caching system, reading database pages from the database files is rare with a *warm* system. This allows us to use snapshot backups for database files.

Snapshot backups are extremely fast since we just copy the files to another storage location. And the other amazing story is Restore. Restoring a database snapshot is crazy fast!

My colleague Kevin Farlee has an excellent video describing the Hyperscale architecture including the great story of restore at `https://youtu.be/Z9AFnKI7sfI`.

Resource Governance

To meet the SLA requirements for Azure SQL Database, we must put some resource limits on the usage of the database. I have described some of these limits in this chapter. Behind the scenes, we use these technologies to enforce these limits:

SQL Server Resource Governor

Azure SQL Managed Instance allows for user-defined workload groups and pools. Azure SQL Database uses Resource Governor behind the scenes to enforce certain limits. Moving to a dedicated SQL Server instance was a key driver in allowing us to use Resource Governor.

Engine enhancements

The engine has been enhanced in Azure to detect the generation of a certain size and rate of transaction log records and govern the application if necessary. The primary signal this governance is happening is seeing a wait type of LOG_RATE_ GOVERNOR. You can read more about log rate governance at `https://docs. microsoft.com/en-us/azure/azure-sql/database/resource-limits-logical- server#transaction-log-rate-governance`.

Windows Job Objects

I have mentioned this technology before in this chapter. Windows Job Objects allow us to control resource usage on the SQL Server engine process to ensure we properly enforce resource limits like memory.

File Source Resource Manager (FSRM)

FSRM provides a mechanism so we can properly enforce storage maximum sizes outside of what we control through SQL Server file size limits.

We have created a great blog post talking about how we enforce resource limits using these technologies and why we use them at `https://azure.microsoft.com/en-us/ blog/resource-governance-in-azure-sql-database/`.

Connecting and Verifying Deployment

Once you deploy an Azure SQL Databases, you are likely going to want to quickly connect and verify aspects of the deployment.

Connecting to Azure SQL Database

Earlier in this chapter, I deployed my logical server and Azure SQL Database allowing public endpoint access with options to access through Azure services and with a firewall rule for the client IP address where I deployed through the portal. I will show you how to connect using both techniques.

Because I used the option Allow Azure services and resources to access this server when I deployed the logical server for the database, I can use an Azure Virtual Machine or even sqlcmd from the Azure Cloud Shell to connect to this server and database.

To connect with Azure Cloud shell, you need to find the name of the logical server for the deployment. There are many ways to do this through the portal. You can simply look at your resource groups or resources from the home of the portal and find the server **bwazuresqlserver** (or your name).

Figure 4-29 shows the Working pane of the server with the Server name to use when connecting with a SQL Server tool or application.

Figure 4-29. *Find the Server name to connect*

Notice I clicked next to the server name to copy the Fully Qualified Domain Name (FQDN) to the clipboard. You will find the FQDN is a combination of the logical server name and .database.windows.net.

Note   Azure SQL Database also supports the concept of a DNS alias which you can read about at `https://docs.microsoft.com/en-us/azure/azure-sql/database/dns-alias-overview`.

I can now bring up the Azure Cloud Shell (you can use the home page of the portal, but I like to use `https://shell.azure.com`).

Since sqlcmd is installed with the cloud shell, I can use a syntax like Figure 4-30.

Figure 4-30. *Using sqlcmd from the Azure Cloud Shell*

I also configured the logical server for a firewall rule for the IP address of the computer when I was using the Azure Portal. In the working pane of the logical server, I can select **Show firewall settings** to see the following information. Figure 4-31 shows this firewall setting along with other network options.

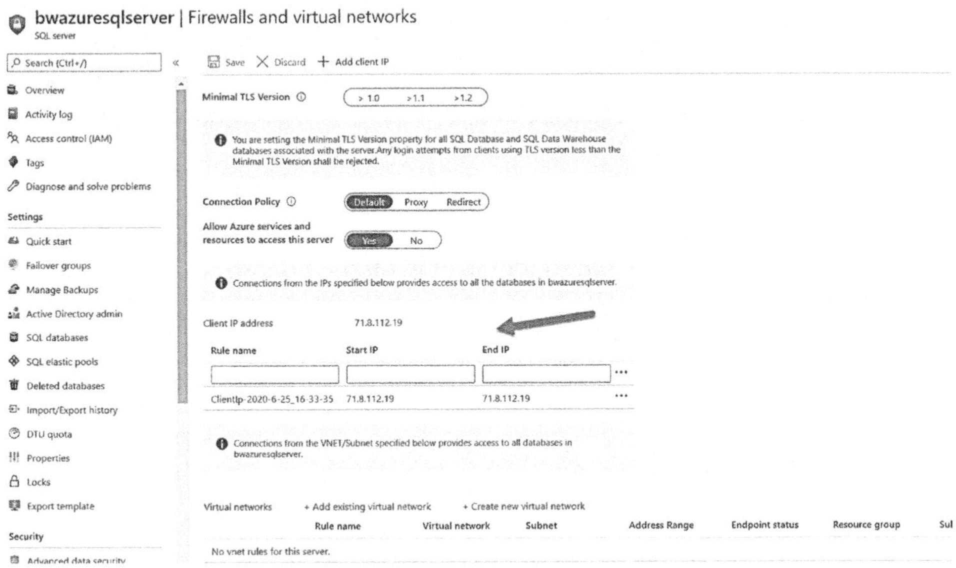

Figure 4-31. *Configure firewall rules for Azure SQL Database*

A firewall rule is very much like a firewall rule you would configure in Windows Server or Linux. If you have used SQL Server before you know that by default, we do not open the firewall rules in the OS for port 1433 by default. The firewall rule earlier is opening access to the gateway for this logical server for this specific IP address. Firewall rules can be specified at the logical server or database level. You can read more about firewall rules for Azure SQL Database at `https://docs.microsoft.com/en-us/azure/azure-sql/database/firewall-configure`.

Since my client IP address is in the firewall rule, I can use a tool like SQL Server Management Studio to connect to the logical server as seen in Figure 4-32.

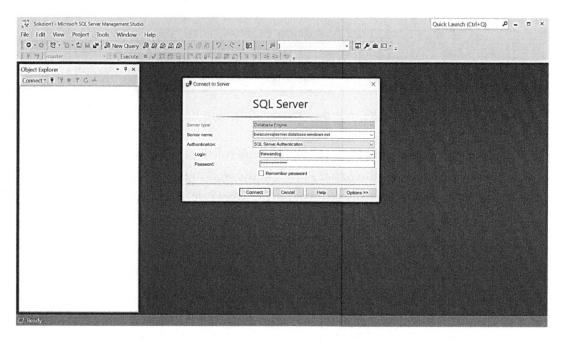

Figure 4-32. *Connecting to Azure SQL Database with SSMS*

Once I hit Connect, I get the familiar Object Explorer, and expanding the list of databases, I see all the databases I have deployed in this chapter. I can right-click the server, select New Query, and try to switch database context to one of my databases as seen in Figure 4-33.

Figure 4-33. *Trying to switch database context for Azure SQL Database*

You can first see some differences for Object Explorer (OE) including the color of the icon (Azure blue) for the server name. Notice also there are not as many choices in OE as there are with SQL Server or Managed Instance (because this is not a full SQL Server instance).

When I connected with SSMS specifying no options, I was put in the context of the logical master for the logical server. I tried to change database context with the familiar T-SQL USE statement, but if fails. Why?

If you think about T-SQL USE on a SQL Server, the engine switches context to a database stored on the instance. For an Azure SQL Database logical server, the databases are on separate SQL Server instances that can be spread across various rings in the Azure region. The USE statement is not built to redirect connections to different server.

Therefore, for SSMS, you can either specify the database to connect to before you hit the Connect button (use the Options button) or switch database context using the drop-down box (which does change the connection context).

In Chapter 5 of the book, I will show you how to configure the connection type for the Azure SQL Database to use redirect instead of proxy. In Chapter 6 of the book, I will show you how to make the connection to the database more secure.

Verifying Deployment

While you can use the Activity Log to verify the deployment of the database, there is no method to see the ERRORLOG behind the SQL Server instance. Therefore, you can use several T-SQL queries to examine the deployment:

Note   Even though there are some queries that make sense to run in the context of the logical master, I ran these queries in the context of my database bwazuresqldb.

```
SELECT @@version
```

```
Microsoft SQL Azure (RTM) - 12.0.2000.8   May 15 2020 00:47:08   Copyright
(C) 2019 Microsoft Corporation
```

This is the exact same result as with Azure SQL Managed Instance indicating a versionless SQL Server:

```
SELECT database_id, name, compatibility_level FROM sys.databases
```

database_id	name	compatibility_level
1	master	150
5	bwazuresqldb	150

You will always see master and only your database from the context of a user database. But note that this is still the logical master, not the physical master on the SQL Server instance hosting the database:

```
SELECT name, object_id, type_desc FROM sys.objects
```

Since this database was built on the sample AdventureWorksLT, I have ~204 rows from this catalog view including system tables:

```
SELECT * FROM sys.dm_os_schedulers
```

This is one of the DMVs we can expose since we are running on a dedicated SQL Server instance. I deployed a 2 vCore General Purpose database so as I would expect I get two ONLINE schedulers:

```
SELECT * FROM sys.dm_os_sys_info
```

Just like with a Managed Instance, I can use this to look at CPU and memory information for the database deployment. Keep in mind though that true limits must be observed with other DMVs as described as follows:

Note   I used **sys.dm_os_process_memory** with Managed Instance, but that is not supported with Azure SQL Database.

```
SELECT * FROM sys.dm_exec_requests
```

This is one of the most common DMVs in the world to check the state of what is running on a SQL Server. I run this just to make sure all the normal background processes are running, including LAZ WRITER, RECOVERY WRITER, LOCK MONITOR, and so on.

Here is the interesting twist on this DMV for Azure SQL Database. This will show you requests for the instance for your database, not requests for other databases on your logical server (because they are deployed on other instances):

```
SELECT SERVERPROPERTY('EngineEdition')
```

Per the documentation at https://docs.microsoft.com/en-us/sql/t-sql/ functions/serverproperty-transact-sql, the value of 5 is a SQL Database.

There are also two new DMVs specific to Azure not found in SQL Server:

```
SELECT * FROM sys.dm_user_db_resource_governance
```

This DMV is really intended to show you resource limits for a specific Azure SQL Database. You can view limits like memory, max storage, log rates, and so on. You can read the documentation for this DMV at https://docs.microsoft.com/en-us/ sql/relational-databases/system-dynamic-management-views/sys-dm-user-db-resource-governor-azure-sql-database?view=azuresqldb-current. Note that the docs say this is mostly for internal use, which means it might change in the future:

```
SELECT * FROM sys.dm_os_job_object
```

This is a DMV specific to Azure (although I tested it and it works for a SQL Server, but you can't rely on the results there because it is not applicable) that shows resource limits Azure applies to the Database using Windows Job Objects. The specific column I look at is **memory_limit_mb** which shows me the true amount of memory the database has access to. I talked about Windows Job Objects in the section "Implementation Details."

Note   I do not recommend you rely on any results of running these queries in the context of the logical master. Even though you might see results, they do not mean anything since the logical master is not a true physical master database. There are a few queries that make sense to run in the logical master which you will see later in the book.

Migrating to Azure SQL Database

Migrating to Azure SQL Database involves the same process as with a Managed Instance of assessment and planning, migration, application changes, and post migration.

While the steps are the same, you will find several differences that are important:

- Azure SQL Database has more restrictions on features, so you may find your assessment is going to find more problems you need to take care before migrating. An example is a feature like Service Broker which is supported in Managed Instance but not in Azure SQL Database.

- Let me give you a simple example. When I first tried to migrate the example WideWorldImporters (`https://github.com/Microsoft/sql-server-samples/releases/tag/wide-world-importers-v1.0`) to Azure SQL Database, I ran into a bunch of problems because certain features used in the sample didn't work in Azure SQL Database. Therefore, I needed to use the Standard WideWorldImporters found at `https://github.com/Microsoft/sql-server-samples/releases/download/wide-world-importers-v1.0/WideWorldImporters-Standard.bacpac`.

- Migrating to Azure SQL Database involves migrating your schema (all your definitions) first and then the data. You can use DMS and DMA to do this. Read more about how to do this at `https://docs.microsoft.com/en-us/azure/dms/tutorial-sql-server-to-azure-sql`. Like Managed Instance, consider using a database compatibility level that matches your current SQL Server installation and then move later to the latest compat level. Learn more about dbcompat at `https://aka.ms/dbcompat`.

- You can also load your data into Azure SQL Database using SSIS packages, Azure Data Factor, bcp, or a BACPAC file. Remember that minimal logging for bulk import is not supported in Azure SQL Database.

- Even though the Microsoft Mechanics video I did on migration focuses demonstrations more on Azure Managed Instance, it is still worth watching for tips on migration to Azure SQL Database. Watch the video at `https://youtu.be/P_4EaqVR5PI`. One of the aspects of using DMA I love is the SKU recommendation PowerShell script. This script analyzes your current SQL Server workload to guide you on Azure SQL Database deployment choices. Read more at `https://docs.microsoft.com/en-us/sql/dma/dma-sku-recommend-sql-db?view=sql-server-ver15`.

Like Managed Instance, the application needs to change the connection string and possibly authentication method. Depending on what T-SQL features and language constructs are used, further application changes may be needed. The DMA tool does a good job of finding these based on database compatibility. To be more thorough, please look over this documentation for T-SQL differences at `https://docs.microsoft.com/en-us/azure/azure-sql/database/transact-sql-tsql-differences-sql-server`.

Use the rest of the chapters in the book to guide you on any post-migration changes you need to make to fully take advantage of security, performance, and availability in Azure.

Summary

In this chapter, you learned how to go through a pre-deployment exercise to make the best choices possible to deploy Azure SQL Managed Instance or Database. You learned the details of deployment for both a Managed Instance and Database along with some interesting implementation details.

You learned how to connect and run verification queries against a Managed Instance and Database deployment. You also learn migration techniques and tools to migrate an existing SQL Server to Azure SQL Managed Instance and Database.

Now that you have deployed, learn more in the next chapter about how to make configuration choices and compare these choices to configuring a SQL Server instance or database.

CHAPTER 5

Configuring Azure SQL

Now that you have deployed your Azure SQL Managed Instance or Database, there could be some configuration changes you may want to make before or after moving into production.

In this chapter, we will explore configuration options for Azure SQL Managed Instance and Database as it compares to configuration options for SQL Server. I will discuss some of the configuration choices for SQL Server that are restricted for Azure SQL and why. I will also spend time toward the end of the chapter explaining space management, various techniques to load data, and why Azure SQL is referred to as versionless.

You can try out some of the methods I describe in the chapter. I will use the existing deployment I did in Chapter 4 of the book when discussing configuration choices and restrictions. For you to try out any of the techniques or commands I use in this chapter, you will need

- An Azure subscription.

- A minimum of Contributor role access to the Azure subscription. You can read more about Azure built-in roles at `https://docs.microsoft.com/en-us/azure/role-based-access-control/built-in-roles`.

- Access to the Azure Portal (web or Windows application).

- A deployment of an Azure SQL Managed Instance and/or an Azure SQL Database.

- Installation of the **az** CLI (see `https://docs.microsoft.com/en-us/cli/azure/install-azure-cli?view=azure-cli-latest` for more details). You can also use the Azure Cloud Shell instead since az is already installed. You can read more about the Azure Cloud Shell at `https://azure.microsoft.com/en-us/features/cloud-shell/`.

© Bob Ward 2021
B. Ward, *Azure SQL Revealed*, https://doi.org/10.1007/978-1-4842-5931-3_5

- You will run some T-SQL in this chapter, so install a tool like SQL Server Management Studio (SSMS) at `https://docs.microsoft.com/en-us/sql/ssms/download-sql-server-management-studio-ssms?view=sql-server-ver15`. You can also use Azure Data Studio at `https://docs.microsoft.com/en-us/sql/azure-data-studio/download-azure-data-studio?view=sql-server-ver15`.

Configuring Azure SQL Managed Instance

There are several options you can choose from to configure the instance of a SQL Server. Let us look at a few of these compared to configuring an Azure SQL Managed Instance.

sp_configure

One of the ways to configure SQL Server at the instance level is with the system procedure **sp_configure**. This stored procedure is supported to use with Azure SQL Managed Instance with these exceptions:

- Any configuration value that requires a server restart is not supported (since we do not offer an interface for you to restart the instance). For example, if you try to change the **scan for startup procs** configuration option, you will get an error:

```
Msg 5869
Changes to server configuration option scan for startup procs are
not supported in SQL Database Managed Instances
```

- Advanced configuration values are supported.

- Some options are not supported because we do not allow that level of configuration or are enforced in a different manner through resource limits. For example, if I try to change the **max server memory** value, I get the following error:

```
Msg 5870
Changes to server configuration option max server memory (MB) are
not supported in SQL Database Managed Instances
```

Trace Flags

Azure SQL Managed Instance sets a predetermined set of global trace flags ON which you can see with **DBCC TRACESTATUS** (there are some 26 trace flags set as of the time of the writing of this book).

Some trace flags we set which you cannot turn off, such as trace flag 1800 (which is used for disk sector size alignments), and some you can turn off and on. To see a list of trace flags you can turn on and off, please see `https://docs.microsoft.com/en-us/sql/t-sql/database-console-commands/dbcc-traceon-transact-sql?view=sql-server-ver15#remarks`.

For a complete list of all trace flags so you can understand the meaning of any of these trace flags, please see the documentation at `https://docs.microsoft.com/en-us/sql/t-sql/database-console-commands/dbcc-traceon-trace-flags-transact-sql?view=sql-server-ver15#trace-flags`.

Session-level trace flags are not supported.

Note   We have been striving for some time to eliminate the need for trace flags, but clearly some are still needed. The addition of commands like ALTER DATABASE SCOPED CONFIGURATION are examples of configuration methods to use instead of trace flags.

Tempdb

Tempdb size or number of files is not configurable with Azure SQL Managed Instance directly with T-SQL.

Note   This is something we are looking to allow in the future.

The number of tempdb files is fixed at 12 no matter what deployment option you choose for a Managed Instance.

The size of tempdb is configurable by changing your deployment option or size. For a General Purpose deployment, you get 24Gb per vCore but limited to a max of ~2TB. For a Business Critical deployment, you are limited by the maximum storage size of the instance. The transaction log is capped at 120Gb, but since Accelerated Database Recovery is ON by default and we regularly back up the transaction log, I do not foresee a problem with you running out of space.

Master and Model

Like SQL Server, you can configure the size of the master database and even add objects to it (but that is usually not recommended on SQL Server anyway).

The same concept applies to model. You can configure the model database size so that new databases will take on that size. Furthermore, you can add objects to model which will be picked up by new user databases.

Configuring Edition

You can use the SQL Server setup program (or mssql-conf with Linux) to change the edition of SQL Server (e.g., Standard to Enterprise).

For Azure SQL Managed Instance, you can change the deployment service tier (General Purpose or Business Critical) or size (vCores or max storage) using the Azure Portal or CLI interfaces such as **az sql mi update** or PowerShell **Set-AzSqlInstance**.

Note   As I have mentioned to this point in the book, deploying or changing the deployment for a Managed Instance can be a time-consuming operation.

Networking Configuration

Once you have deployed a Managed Instance, you may need to make some adjustments to the network configuration for the instance. As seen in Figure 5-1, you can select **Virtual Network** from the Azure Portal Resource Menu to change several network options.

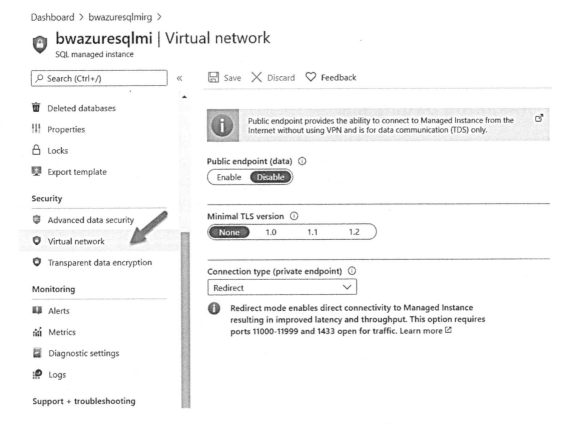

Figure 5-1. *Configuring network options for a Managed Instance*

This screen offers choices to enable the Public Endpoint (which I left disabled during deploy) and change the Connection Type to Proxy (which is the default, but I chose Redirect during deployment).

In addition, there is another option that was not offered during deployment which is the **TLS version**. Transport Layer Security (TLS) is a protocol for encrypting connections and is supported by SQL Server and Azure SQL. TLS 1.2 is the minimal supported version recommended today as it includes fixes for some vulnerabilities found in previous versions. However, be careful with this setting as it could break an application not using that TLS version. You can read more about minimal TLS version at https://docs.microsoft.com/en-us/azure/azure-sql/database/connectivity-settings#minimal-tls-version.

Networking options for Managed Instance can also be configured using **az sql mi update** and PowerShell **Set-AzSqlInstance**.

You can read about all possible other options to configure for a Managed Instance by looking at the az sql mi update documentation at `https://docs.microsoft.com/en-us/cli/azure/sql/mi?view=azure-cli-latest#az-sql-mi-update`.

Configuring Databases

Once you deploy an Azure SQL Managed Instance, you can now add databases or configure existing databases using the Azure Portal, tools like SSMS, or the T-SQL CREATE DATABASE or ALTER DATABASE statements.

The CREATE DATABASE T-SQL syntax is very simple since you do not specify files or any WITH options. For example, for the Managed Instance I deployed, I can run the following T-SQL statement to create a new database:

```
CREATE DATABASE gocowboys;
```

The new database will take on the properties of the model database just like SQL Server. The one difference is that we automatically create a memory-optimized filegroup called XTP, which you can see if you query the **sys.filegroups** catalog view. We create XTP filegroup even if you are using the General Purpose service tier which does not support In-Memory OLTP. This makes it easier to support this feature if you move to Business Critical.

This database will also take on the properties set by Model and is like SQL Server, except for two key options that are on by default: **query store** and **accelerated database recovery**.

Once a database is created, you can use the ALTER DATABASE statement to make various changes to options or to add/remove files and filegroups. One of the nifty things we have done with the T-SQL documentation is to allow you to choose a product to see the exact syntax support for statements like ALTER DATABASE. Figure 5-2 shows the documentation reference for ALTER DATABASE (which is at `https://docs.microsoft.com/en-us/sql/t-sql/statements/alter-database-transact-sql?view=azuresqldb-mi-current`) after I selected Managed Instance.

ALTER DATABASE (Transact-SQL)

06/10/2020 • 34 minutes to read • 🔵 👤 🟤 🟢 ⚫ +13

Modifies certain configuration options of a database.

This article provides the syntax, arguments, remarks, permissions, and examples for whichever SQL product you choose.

For more information about the syntax conventions, see Transact-SQL Syntax Conventions.

Click a product!

In the following row, click whichever product name you are interested in. The click displays different content here on this webpage, appropriate for whichever product you click.

| SQL Server | SQL Database single database/elastic pool | * SQL Database managed instance * | Azure Synapse Analytics | Analytics Platform System (PDW) |

Is this page helpful?

👍 Yes 👎 No

In this article

Click a product!

Overview: Azure SQL Database managed instance

Syntax

Arguments

Remarks

Viewing Database Information

Permissions

Examples

See also

Overview: Azure SQL Database managed instance

In Azure SQL Database managed instance, use this statement to set database options.

Because of its length, the ALTER DATABASE syntax is separated into the multiple articles.

Figure 5-2. *ALTER DATABASE reference for Managed Instance*

Most of the SET options you normally see for SQL Server are available for Managed Instance. One notable exception is ACCELERATED_DATABASE_RECOVERY. We turn on this option by default for your database and do not allow you to disable it. Why? It is important for this option to be on for us to meet SLA requirements and ensure you do not have issues with running out of transaction log space.

One of the key options for a database is *database compatibility level,* and Managed Instance supports setting the "dbcompat" with ALTER DATABASE. Compat levels 90 through 150 are currently supported for Managed Instance databases. Read more about dbcompat at `https://aka.ms/dbcompat`.

I asked my colleague Joe Sack more about the use of dbcompat with Azure SQL. He told me, "150 is the current default and means you will have support for features like Intelligent Query Processing out-of-the-gate. Customer can shift down to lower levels if they choose. We will never force a customer to the latest dbcompat level for existing databases. New databases will use the latest default and then customers can change per their needs."

209

> **Note** If you restore a backup from an existing SQL Server database to Managed Instance, we will retain the dbcompat level of that database when it is was backed up.

Even though you do not have to worry about physical file placement, you do have the ability to add database files and change file sizes up to the maximum instance storage limit. You can also create filegroups. A good example of why you might want to increase the number of files or size is to improve I/O performance. My colleague Jovan Popovic has a very nice blog post describing how to do this at `https://medium.com/azure-sqldb-managed-instance/increasing-data-files-might-improve-performance-on-general-purpose-managed-instance-tier-6e90bad2ae4b`.

> **Note** SQL Server Managed Studio (SSMS) also supports changing database options and file options as you can with SQL Server.

It is also important to know that the ALTER DATABASE SCOPED CONFIGURATION T-SQL statement is supported for Azure SQL Managed Instance just like SQL Server. You can read more at `https://docs.microsoft.com/en-us/sql/t-sql/statements/alter-database-scoped-configuration-transact-sql?view=sql-server-ver15`.

Configuring Azure SQL Database

Since deploying an Azure SQL Database is effectively creating a database, you may want to configure some settings about the database from the deployment. You may also want to perform some configuration on the logical server associated with the database including creating a new database on the logical server.

Creating New Databases

The T-SQL CREATE DATABASE statement is supported when connected to a logical server (in any database context). You can view the full syntax of CREATE DATABASE for Azure SQL Database at `https://docs.microsoft.com/en-us/sql/t-sql/statements/create-database-transact-sql?view=azuresqldb-current`.

Note   Remember that creating a database for Azure SQL Database with CREATE DATABASE is a deployment. For SQL Server, we create new files and add metadata to the master database. For Azure SQL Database, we are building a new deployment (i.e., a dedicated instance for the database) to host the database and storing information in our control plan (e.g., gateways). This means the CREATE DATABASE is an asynchronous operation but can be tracked with the DMV **sys.dm_operation_status**. You must query this DMV from the logical master, and we retain history for 1 hour.

You will notice that you only have two options when creating a new database: collation and deployment options. Deployment options allow you to choose a purchasing model, service tier, compute model, and size.

If you remember in Chapter 4, I deployed several databases using different options for the deployment. Using the logical server bwazuresqlserver I used in the Chapter 4 examples, I can create a new Business Critical, 4 vCore database with the following T-SQL syntax:

```
CREATE DATABASE bwazuresqldbbc2
(EDITION = 'BusinessCritical', MAXSIZE = 1000 GB, SERVICE_OBJECTIVE =
'BC_GEN5_4');
```

The preceding documentation reference shows all the possible options you can use for EDITION and SERVICE_OBJECTIVE. In this case, the EDITION is used to decide a DTU model, General Purpose, Business Critical, or Hyperscale. The SERVICE_OBJECTIVE is used to select options like Serverless, hardware generation, and number of vCores.

The CREATE DATABASE statement for Azure SQL Database also supports the AS COPY OF option to create a database as a copy of another database even from another logical server.

Any database that is created has the following options turned on by default:

- SNAPSHOT_ISOLATION_STATE

- READ_COMMITTED_SNAPSHOT

- FULL RECOVERY

- CHECKSUM

- TDE

- QUERY_STORE

- ACCELERATED_DATABASE_RECOVERY

One option you may not notice is set on if you examine **sys.databases** is *stale page detection*. Stale page detection assists Azure SQL Database to find possible data integrity problems due to I/O problems in the infrastructure. I will discuss more data integrity checks provided by Azure SQL in Chapter 8 of the book.

Altering Databases

For any database that is created, you can use the T-SQL ALTER DATABASE statement to modify certain SET options. You can use this documentation reference to see what options you can turn on and off at `https://docs.microsoft.com/en-us/sql/t-sql/statements/alter-database-transact-sql-set-options?view=azuresqldb-current`. You do not have the ability to change any properties of the files behind this database. To change the maximum size of the database, you would use the MAXSIZE parameter. You can also change the EDITION or SERVICE_OBJECTIVE with ALTER DATABASE or the Azure Portal. Any execution of ALTER DATABASE is also asynchronous and can be tracked with **sys.dm_operation_status**.

One of the key options for a database is *database compatibility level*, and Azure SQL Database supports setting the "dbcompat" with ALTER DATABASE. Compat levels 90 through 150 are currently supported for Azure SQL Database. Read more about dbcompat at `https://aka.ms/dbcompat`.

It is also important to know that the ALTER DATABASE SCOPED CONFIGURATION T-SQL statement is supported for Azure SQL Database just like SQL Server. You can read more at `https://docs.microsoft.com/en-us/sql/t-sql/statements/alter-database-scoped-configuration-transact-sql?view=sql-server-ver15`.

The **az sql db** CLI also supports the ability to change options about the deployment of the database as documented at `https://docs.microsoft.com/en-us/cli/azure/sql/db?view=azure-cli-latest#az-sql-db-update`. PowerShell also provides the **Set-AzSQLDatabase** which is documented at `https://docs.microsoft.com/en-us/powershell/module/az.sql/Set-AzSqlDatabase?view=azps-4.3.0`.

And of course the Azure Portal supports changing several options about the database deployment from the Resource Menu, Command Bar, and Working Pane. I will show you examples of these configuration options in other chapters of the book.

Network Configuration

When we deployed an Azure SQL Database in Chapter 4 of the book, we were able to specify a few networking options for the logical server, including public endpoint access, allowing azure services, and firewall rules.

There are a few other networking options you may want to configure for the logical server or database as seen in Figure 5-3.

Two of the network options that were not available when you deployed the database and logical server are Minimal TLS Version and Connection Policy.

Minimal TLS Version is exactly like the TLS requirements as I described earlier in this chapter for a Managed Instance.

Figure 5-3. *Networking options for a logical server*

Connection Policy is like the Connection type for a Managed Instance: Proxy or Redirect. Notice here for Azure SQL Database there is the choice of Default. Default uses a policy to use a Proxy connection type if the connection originates outside of Azure while Redirect if the connection is within Azure.

The Redirect connection policy can be much faster for application latency because the Gateway is used to redirect traffic to the direct node for the Azure SQL Database. My colleague Anna Thomas has a nice example to how much faster Redirect can be over Proxy at `https://github.com/microsoft/sqlworkshops-azuresqlworkshop/tree/master/azuresqlworkshop/02-DeployAndConfigure`. This example uses a notebook with Azure Data Studio. Learn more how to use notebooks with Azure Data Studio at `https://docs.microsoft.com/en-us/sql/azure-data-studio/notebooks-guidance`.

There are other network options on this screen such as virtual networks. I will describe more about how to use other networking options in Chapters 6 and 7 of the book.

Configuration Restrictions

While there are several options to configure an Azure SQL Managed Instance and Database, I thought it is important to call out some of the configuration options you can make for SQL Server both at the instance and database level *but are restricted* in Azure SQL. When possible, I will call out why certain options are restricted or are not needed in a PaaS environment.

Azure SQL Managed Instance Restrictions

Many of the configuration choices at a SQL Server level are done using the SQL Server Configuration Manager (Windows) or mssql-conf (Linux), T-SQL, or tools like SSMS. Since I have worked with SQL Server for many years, I thought it would be interesting for you to know what options exist in these tools and interfaces and why they are restricted for Azure SQL Managed Instance and Databases.

Start and Stop Services

You are not allowed to stop your Managed Instance (therefore, you cannot start it). Your Managed Instance is always running. There are no configuration options allowed that require a restart, so effectively there is no reason for you to have to restart the SQL Server instance. Since every deployment option for Managed Instance supports High Availability, a failover will occur if necessary due to an unforeseen event or maintenance.

Since you are abstracted from the SQL Server instance for Azure SQL Database, there is also no interface to restart the instance.

Note   You will learn in Chapters 10 and 11 of the book how to manually fail over an Azure SQL Database using the PowerShell command **Invoke-AzSqlDatabaseFailover**.

Instant File Initialization

There is no interface for you to enable Instant File Initialization (IFI) which you can read about at https://docs.microsoft.com/en-us/sql/relational-databases/databases/database-instant-file-initialization?view=sql-server-ver15. However, there are two important points on why I do not think this is a big factor:

- IFI is not supported or used when the database has Transparent Data Encryption (TDE) enabled. TDE is enabled by default for databases for Azure SQL Managed Instance and Database.

- I did some testing for "autogrow" scenarios and could never cause any major performance bottlenecks.

Locked Pages

There is no interface to enable Locked Pages (or Large Pages) as with SQL Server. We have not seen many issues with working set trim issues that would require the need to enable this.

Having said that, we are investigating for the future whether we should enable this by default behind the scenes for Azure SQL.

FILESTREAM and Availability Groups

SQL Server Configuration Manager allows you to enable the FILESTREAM and Always On Availability Group features. FILESTREAM is not supported in Azure SQL. Always On Availability Groups (AG) are used behind the scenes for Business Critical service tiers, but you cannot set up or configure an AG on your own.

Server Collation

You can set the collation for the SQL Server instance during deployment of a Managed Instance but cannot change it after that. You can set collations for databases or columns in tables like SQL Server.

Azure SQL Database allows you to specify a database collation during deployment, but you cannot change it later. You can also define collations at the column level.

Startup Parameters

SQL Server Configuration Manager allows you to set certain startup parameters for the SQL Server engine as documented at `https://docs.microsoft.com/en-us/sql/database-engine/configure-windows/database-engine-service-startup-options?view=sql-server-ver15`. None of these options are exposed to modify for Azure SQL. In my experience, most of these options are used for certain "edge" scenarios that you won't need or can't use (like starting SQL Server in single user mode).

ERRORLOG Configuration

SSMS allows you to configure the number of ERRORLOG files and maximum size. These options are not supported to configure for Azure SQL Managed Instance because it requires a restart of the instance. Furthermore, while it might be nice to have more than the default of six ERRORLOG files, the maximum size of the ERRORLOG value is generally used to control disk space, but that is not a concern with Managed Instance.

Note   The system procedure sp_cycle_errorlog is supported on Managed Instance. However, ERRORLOG files are stored on the local node, so they are not saved on a failover.

Error Reporting and Customer Feedback

SQL Server provides a way to configure error reporting and customer feedback as documented at `https://docs.microsoft.com/en-us/sql/sql-server/usage-and-diagnostic-data-configuration-for-sql-server?view=sql-server-ver15`. This configuration is not possible for Azure SQL but does not apply.

> **Note**   We do use telemetry to improve Azure SQL. Take a look at this article where one of our partner architects, Conor Cunningham, explains in more detail: `https://redmondmag.com/articles/2018/02/14/qa-lead-sql-architect-part-1.aspx`.

If you have any concerns about what information about your deployment is collected or used by Microsoft, I recommend you read over privacy and other legal documents at `https://azure.microsoft.com/en-us/support/legal/`.

ALTER SERVER CONFIGURATION

ALTER SERVER CONFIGURATION was introduced several releases ago with SQL Server as a new way to configure the instance vs. sp_configure.

ALTER SERVER CONFIGURATION is not supported with Azure SQL, but there are no options where it makes sense to configure an instance for Azure SQL given most of these options are done automatically or do not apply.

"Mixed Mode" Security

Because a SQL login is required to deploy Azure SQL Managed Instance and Database, Mixed Mode Security is enabled and cannot be configured.

> **Note**   We are investigating in the future whether we would support an Azure Active Directory only concept for Azure SQL, thereby offering an option to not support SQL Authentication.

Logon Auditing

The SQL Server engine for years has supported the ability to track successful, failed, both (and none) login attempts. This tracking is written to the ERRORLOG and is configured typically through SSMS. While for Managed Instance the options exist to configure this tracking of logins, they do not take effect because it requires a restart of SQL Server. Failed login, which is the default, is tracked in the ERRORLOG.

You can perform your own audit of logins with Extended Events or SQL Audit for Azure SQL. I will show you more about auditing for Azure SQL in Chapters 6 and 7 of the book.

Server Proxy Account

SSMS supports the configuration of a Server proxy account for the system procedure **xp_cmdshell**. This configuration is not supported for Managed Instance since xp_cmdshell is not supported for Azure SQL Managed Instance or Database.

Database Restrictions

Many of the common options to configure a database through ALTER DATABASE are allowed for Managed Instance just like SQL Server. One notable exception is that you cannot disable ACCELERATE_DATABASE_RECOVERY. That is because we rely on ADR technology to ensure the promised SLA for availability.

Azure SQL Database Restrictions

All the restrictions listed in the previous section for Managed Instance also apply to Azure SQL Database.

A few other notable restrictions you may have guessed since Azure SQL Database does not expose a full SQL Server instance are as follows:

- sp_configure is not supported.

- DBCC TRACEON is not supported. In fact, if you run this command, it fails with Msg 2571 (i.e., no permissions).

- You can use DBCC TRACESTATUS to see what trace flags we enable even if you cannot turn them on or off (the list is pretty much the same as is used with Managed Instance).

ACCELERATED_DATABASE_RECOVERY is also enabled by default and cannot be disabled.

Azure SQL Space Management

One other topic related to Azure SQL configuration is space management. While we have abstracted the physical placement of database and transaction log files for both Azure SQL Managed Instance and Database, *sizes* are still a factor you must manage and consider. Because Azure SQL Managed Instance and Database provide different deployment surface areas, space management can be different between each option.

Azure SQL Managed Instance Space Management

As I have described in Chapter 4 for deployment, the maximum size for data for a Managed Instance is the overall size for all database storage. Your choice of vCores and options like Business Critical affect the maximum storage size for the instance.

You can configure files for databases including size and number of files. As I mentioned earlier in this chapter, changing the size and number of files can potentially improve I/O performance for the General Purpose service tier (which uses Azure Storage). You can read more about this technique at `https://medium.com/azure-sqldb-managed-instance/increasing-data-files-might-improve-performance-on-general-purpose-managed-instance-tier-6e90bad2ae4b`.

With SQL Server, when a database file has a limit on size, you may encounter Msg 1105 to indicate you have run out of space. This error could occur if you also run out of disk space on the filesystem hosting your database. For a Managed Instance, you can also encounter Msg 1105 if you have run out of space on the maximum size of your database. However, since we enforce maximum storage limits for all databases, you may also encounter an error before you run out of space in your database like this:

```
Msg 1133
The managed instance has reached its storage limit. The storage usage for
the managed instance cannot exceed (%d) MBs.
```

To be clear what this means, it is possible for you to hit this error before hitting the maximum size of an individual database because collectively you have hit the limit for all databases (including system databases).

Azure SQL Database Space Management

Azure SQL Database manages space differently than Managed Instance. The maximum size as specified during deployment is the *possible* maximum size of a single database file.

If you deploy an Azure SQL Database, the maximum size is typically reflected in the **max_size** column of **sys.database_files** for a single data file. However, for larger maximum database size values (e.g., 1TB), we may not set the max_size to that value but grow as data is added to the eventual max_size.

If you run out of space in the database, you will get a quota error instead of the traditional 1105 error like this:

```
Msg 40544, Level 17, State 2, Line 12
The database '<database>' has reached its size quota. Partition or delete
data, drop indexes, or consult the documentation for possible resolutions.
```

The transaction log is handled differently. While your subscription is charged for the maximum database size, you get 30% above this size for free for your transaction log. Do not use the max_size in sys.database_files for the maximum size of the transaction log. It does not accurately reflect the quota. In all my testing, I never ran out of transaction log space due to two factors:

- We regularly and often back up the transaction log (remember we use full recovery).

- We have Accelerated Database Recovery (ADR) enabled by default and you cannot disable it. With ADR, the log can be truncated even in the presence of active transactions.

The one exception to space management for Azure SQL Database is the Hyperscale service tier. A Hyperscale database has a 100TB limit, but theoretically, we believe it could be unlimited. When you deploy a Hyperscale database, we create multiple database files that total around 40Gb. Then as you add data, we automatically grow the database. The transaction log has a limit of 1TB, but we back up the log regularly and rely also on ADR so I do not think you will run out of space.

Loading Data

Whether you deployed a new Managed Instance or Database or migrated from an existing instance or database, you inevitably will want to load data. Just like a SQL Server installation, you have several tools and options to load data. In addition, you have new services available to you in Azure.

Keep These in Mind

Just like a SQL Server, you may need **additional resources** when importing large amounts of data. For Azure SQL Managed Instance or Database, keep in mind any additional vCore or size requirements for importing data. I have described how long scaling can take for Managed Instance, so keep this mind as you deploy.

Several of the data loading techniques involve loading a *file*. While you can always use these techniques to load files from on-premises environment, any tool or command run in the Azure infrastructure should be done using Azure Storage or Azure Files. Some of your data may not be *cloud born*, so consider using tools like **AzCopy** to load your files into Azure Storage or Azure Files. You can read more about AzCopy at `https://docs.microsoft.com/en-us/azure/storage/common/storage-use-azcopy-files`. If your files are very large, take a look at our documentation on guidance and tools at `https://docs.microsoft.com/en-us/azure/storage/common/storage-solution-large-dataset-moderate-high-network`.

I have mentioned already in the book that Azure SQL Managed Instance and Database both use the FULL recovery model, and this cannot be changed (we need this to meet SLA requirements). This means that **minimal logging is not supported** for bulk operations (except for tempdb). Therefore, you should ensure you use certain techniques like *batch sizes*. A batch for bulk import is a defined unit of transaction. So a batch size of 10000 means 10000 rows are imported for a transaction. Typically, using large batch sizes can improve bulk performance and should be used for Azure SQL. However, you should also keep in mind that if you use too large of a batch size, you might be throttled by *Log Rate Governance*. You can read more about log rate governance at `https://docs.microsoft.com/en-us/azure/azure-sql/database/resource-limits-logical-server#transaction-log-rate-governance`. If you intended target for data is columnstore, you should consider directly importing into a clustered columnstore index. You can read more about data loading guidance for columnstore at https://docs.microsoft.com/en-us/sql/relational-databases/indexes/columnstore-indexes-data-loading-guidance?view=sql-server-ver15.

Azure does charge on certain type of network traffic called **inbound** and **outbound**. Any inbound traffic (e.g., bulk import data from your on-premises environment into Azure) is free.

Outbound traffic can be charged if that traffic travels between Azure regions. So if you bulk import from an Azure Virtual Machine or Azure Data Factory Service from one region into an Azure SQL Database in another region, there could be outbound network charges. You can read more at https://azure.microsoft.com/en-us/pricing/details/bandwidth/.

Note   Some network connectivity options may vary these charges. Read more at https://azure.microsoft.com/en-us/pricing/details/virtual-network/.

---

bcp

The bulk copy program (bcp) is perhaps the oldest and most popular tool in the history of SQL Server to export and import data. The bcp program runs on Windows, Linux, and macOS computers. You can get all the latest information about bcp at https://docs.microsoft.com/en-us/sql/tools/bcp-utility.

Since bcp is a program that reads a file and *bulk imports* data into a SQL Server or Azure SQL, you must run the bcp program on a computer that can access the file and connect to Azure SQL. That could be on a computer on-premises or Azure Virtual Machine. In any of these scenarios, you can use bcp against a file that is hosted on your on-premises environment, local to the Azure Virtual Machine storage (which may be data disks in Azure Storage), or in Azure Storage. Since bcp does not support a direct path to Azure Storage (i.e., URL), you can use Azure Files.

One other option is to use bcp from the Azure Cloud Shell. bcp in the Azure Cloud Shell runs in the Azure infrastructure (think of it like running in a temporary VM), so provided you have network connectivity set up correctly, you can bulk import into Azure SQL Managed Instance or Database. The only provision here is that the cloud shell cannot join a virtual network, so you would have to set up a public endpoint access.

The Azure Cloud Shell supports persistence of files through a concept called a *clouddrive* which you can read more about at `https://docs.microsoft.com/en-us/azure/cloud-shell/persisting-shell-storage#clouddrive-commands`. So you can copy files into your clouddrive and then use bcp to import the file into Azure SQL.

bcp uses *Bulk APIs* behind the scenes so you can also write applications that use the Bulk APIs. Here is an example of Bulk APIs with ODBC at `https://docs.microsoft.com/en-us/sql/relational-databases/native-client-odbc-extensions-bulk-copy-functions/sql-server-driver-extensions-bulk-copy-functions?view=sql-server-ver15`.

BULK INSERT and OPENROWSET

The T-SQL BULK INSERT and OPENROWSET (using the BULK option) statements support bulk import of data from a file. One nice advantage of these commands is that they run in the context of the SQL Server engine.

For SQL Server, it is common to copy a file to drive or network share that the computer hosting SQL Server can access. Then you use BULK INSERT to reference that file to import. The problem is that for Azure SQL Managed Instance and Database, you do not have access to the underlying node file system. Therefore, BULK INSERT and OPENROWSET statements have been enhanced to support Azure Blob Storage (even from an on-premises SQL Server).

Here is how this works. You create an EXTERNAL DATA SOURCE (like Polybase) to reference an Azure Storage account. The BULK INSERT and OPENROWSET statements have been enhanced to support a DATA_SOURCE parameter.

Now you can connect directly to your Azure SQL Managed Instance or Database with your favorite SQL tool (remember it could be sqlcmd in the Azure Cloud shell) and bulk import data having the SQL Server engine do the work.

Here is an example syntax on how to do this with BULK INSERT from the documentation at `https://docs.microsoft.com/en-us/sql/t-sql/statements/bulk-insert-transact-sql?view=sql-server-ver15#f-importing-data-from-a-file-in-azure-blob-storage`. This requires you first create an Azure Storage account and container:

```
CREATE MASTER KEY ENCRYPTION BY PASSWORD = 'YourStrongPassword1';
GO
--> Optional - a DATABASE SCOPED CREDENTIAL is not required because the
blob is configured for public (anonymous) access!
CREATE DATABASE SCOPED CREDENTIAL MyAzureBlobStorageCredential
 WITH IDENTITY = 'SHARED ACCESS SIGNATURE',
 SECRET = '******srt=sco&sp=rwac&se=2017-02-01T00:55:34Z&st=2016-12-
 29T16:55:34Z***************';

 -- NOTE: Make sure that you don't have a leading ? in SAS token, and
 -- that you have at least read permission on the object that should be
 loaded srt=o&sp=r, and
 -- that expiration period is valid (all dates are in UTC time)

CREATE EXTERNAL DATA SOURCE MyAzureBlobStorage
WITH ( TYPE = BLOB_STORAGE,
        LOCATION = 'https://***************.blob.core.windows.net/
        invoices'
        , CREDENTIAL= MyAzureBlobStorageCredential --> CREDENTIAL is not
        required if a blob is configured for public (anonymous) access!
);

BULK INSERT Sales.Invoices
FROM 'inv-2017-12-08.csv'
WITH (DATA_SOURCE = 'MyAzureBlobStorage');
```

SQL Server Integration Services (SSIS)

SSIS packages are one of the most popular methods today for Extract Transform and Load (ETL) applications with SQL Server.

Azure SQL Managed Instance and Database can always be targets for data loading with SSIS packages no matter where you run the SSIS package with the SSIS runtime. This means you can build SSIS packages and run them on-premises in your data center or in Azure Virtual Machine. Here is a simple tutorial on how to use SSIS to load data into Azure SQL Database: https://docs.microsoft.com/en-us/sql/integration-services/load-data-to-sql-database-with-ssis.

There are other methods to execute an SSIS package in Azure SQL itself (which you could use to have packages that import data into Azure SQL Managed Instance or Database).

Azure SSIS

There is no specific service called *Azure SSIS*, but I have coined this term to refer to services in Azure to host and execute SSIS packages. There are two components to make Azure SSIS a reality:

- **Azure SSIS Integration Runtime (SSIS IR)**

  Azure Data Factor (ADF) is a service in Azure that provides ETL capabilities. ADF supports an *Integration runtime* compute environment. One of the choices for an integration runtime environment is SSIS. Effectively, ADF will host compute nodes that allow you to run SSIS packages. This compute environment can also be connected to a virtual network paving the way for connectivity to Azure SQL resources. The steps to deploy SSIS IR can be found at `https://docs.microsoft.com/en-us/azure/data-factory/create-azure-ssis-integration-runtime`.

- **SSIS Catalog Database (SSISDB) in Azure**

  Although not required to use SSIS IR, you can host the catalog database for SSIS called *SSISDB* in Azure SQL Database or Managed Instance. This way, you can execute packages that are stored in Azure SQL Database or Managed Instance, leaving all your ETL packages, managed, and execution in the cloud. These packages can access any data source a normal SSIS package could including on-premises. Think of this as a way of executing everything in Azure and *pulling* data from on-premises. The easiest method to create the SSISDB catalog in Azure SQL is to provision it when deploying SSIS IR. You will need to have already deployed an Azure SQL Database Logical Server or Managed Instance to deploy the SSISDB in Azure. Check out this tutorial at `https://docs.microsoft.com/en-us/azure/data-factory/tutorial-deploy-ssis-packages-azure`.

Once you have deployed SSIS IR and SSISDB for Azure, you basically have a compute structure to run packages and a catalog to host them (without you having to provision your own VM).

Note   You still can execute packages stored in a file system such as Azure Files.

You now have the option to execute these packages using several methods:

- Execute packages with **SQL Server Data Tools (SSDT)**. Learn more at `https://docs.microsoft.com/en-us/azure/data-factory/how-to-invoke-ssis-package-ssdt`.

- Execute packages using SQL Server Agent on a Managed Instance. Learn more at `https://docs.microsoft.com/en-us/azure/data-factory/how-to-invoke-ssis-package-managed-instance-agent`.

- Execute packages with the Azure enabled version of dtexec called **AzureDTExec** (Windows only). Learn more at `https://docs.microsoft.com/en-us/azure/data-factory/how-to-invoke-ssis-package-azure-enabled-dtexec`.

- Execute an **Execute SSIS Package activity** as part of an Azure Data Factory (ADF) pipeline. Learn more at `https://docs.microsoft.com/en-us/azure/data-factory/how-to-invoke-ssis-package-ssis-activity`. You can also use ADF to run a stored procedure activity. Read more at `https://docs.microsoft.com/en-us/azure/data-factory/how-to-invoke-ssis-package-stored-procedure-activity`.

Using SSIS IR and SSISDB in Azure could be a book in itself! To find out more details about other options including migrating existing SSIS packages to Azure, read the following documentation at `https://docs.microsoft.com/en-us/sql/integration-services/lift-shift/ssis-azure-lift-shift-ssis-packages-overview`.

BACPAC

A BACPAC file (.bacpac extension) is a file that includes schema and data for a database. You can use a BACPAC file generated through tools like SSMS, SqlPackage, or PowerShell to import into Azure SQL. The import process in this case *creates a full database* with the schema and data in the file. You can store your BACPAC file in Azure Storage or in a local file depending on what tool and where you are importing the data.

Azure SQL Database supports importing to a new database using the Azure Portal (the BACPAC file would be in Azure Storage), the SqlPackage tools, SSMS, or PowerShell. Figure 5-4 shows the option from the command bar of a logical server to import a database with a BACPAC file.

***Figure 5-4.** Importing a database from the Azure Portal*

For Azure SQL Managed Instance, you can use SSMS or SqlPackage.

To read more about using BACPAC files to import a new database in Azure SQL, consult our docs at `https://docs.microsoft.com/en-us/azure/azure-sql/database/database-import`.

Database Copy

Azure SQL Database supports the ability to create a new database by making a transactional consistent copy from another deployed database. You can use the Azure Portal, PowerShell, az cli, or the T-SQL CREATE DATABASE statement. One nice aspect to this capability is that you can copy a database to a different logical server. The portal also allows you to configure the deployment option for the target database.

Figure 5-5 shows that the copy database capability can be accessed from the command bar in the Azure Portal from the context of an existing database.

Figure 5-5. *Copying a database using the Azure Portal*

You can read more about how to copy a database for Azure SQL Database at `https://docs.microsoft.com/en-us/azure/azure-sql/database/database-copy`.

Note   The copy option may not be available for Hyperscale databases in the Azure portal but is supported through T-SQL.

RESTORE to Managed Instance

Since Azure SQL Managed Instance is a full SQL Server instance with almost all surface area including T-SQL available to you, you can perform a *native* restore of a SQL Server backup to the instance.

This means you can back up a database from a SQL Server, copy the backup file to Azure Storage, and then restore the database using the RESTORE DATABASE statement to the Azure Managed Instance.

At this time, only a full database backup can be restored. There is a key difference in RESTORE with Managed Instance from SQL Server. A RESTORE is an asynchronous operation. You can drop the connection and the restore option is done in the background. You can use the DMVs **sys.dm_operation_status** to check on the deployment.

To learn more about how to use RESTORE with Azure SQL Managed Instance, check out the documentation at `https://docs.microsoft.com/en-us/sql/t-sql/ statements/restore-statements-transact-sql?view=azuresqldb-mi-current`.

Note   You cannot restore the other direction. In other words, you cannot back up a database from Managed Instance (which is supported) and restore it on a SQL Server on-premises. This is due to the nature of versionless Azure SQL.

Spark Connector

Spark is a technology that can often be used for ETL operations. Microsoft supports a Spark connector that allows you to export and import data to and from Azure SQL Database and Managed Instance. It supports bulk operations that can be very fast and even use Azure Active Directory Authentication.

Anywhere you can run Spark and connect to Azure SQL, you can use this connector. Learn more at `https://docs.microsoft.com/en-us/azure/azure-sql/database/ spark-connector`. Get examples on GitHub at `https://github.com/microsoft/sql- spark-connector`.

Azure Data Factory (ADF)

Azure Data Factor (ADF) is a cloud service built for data integration. You can build *pipelines* to orchestrate data integration activities much like SSIS. ADF can be as simple or complex as you want or need. You can see a simple example of using ADF to copy data from Azure Blob storage to Azure SQL Database at `https://docs.microsoft.com/en- us/azure/data-factory/tutorial-copy-data-portal`.

While ADF uses compute integration runtime environments for execution, you should think of ADF as *PaaS service for data integration* (it includes an SLA). The ADF team likes to think of their service as **Code-free ETL as a Service**.

If you do not have a lot of investment in SSIS packages already and need to perform ETL or just data movement operations in Azure on a consistent basis, I highly encourage you to consider ADF. Start by reading the introduction at https://docs.microsoft.com/en-us/azure/data-factory/introduction.

Like SSIS, ADF supports a rich set of data sources (called data stores). Check out the complete list at https://docs.microsoft.com/en-us/azure/data-factory/concepts-pipelines-activities#data-movement-activities.

SQL Data Sync

SQL Data Sync is a cloud service that lets you synchronize data between sources even bidirectionally. SQL Data Sync was in preview at the time of the writing of this book.

One possible scenario is to synchronize data and changes between a SQL Server on-premises and Azure SQL Database.

Note   SQL Data Sync does not currently support Azure SQL Managed Instance.

Learn more about how to set up and use SQL Data Sync at https://docs.microsoft.com/en-us/azure/azure-sql/database/sql-data-sync-data-sql-server-sql-database.

Replication Subscriber

SQL Transaction replication is a proven technology with SQL Server to synchronize changes between a publisher and a subscriber.

While Azure SQL Managed Instance supports the ability to set up and create a replication topology in Azure, Azure SQL Database can also be a subscriber to a SQL Server publisher on-premises, in Azure Virtual Machine, or from Managed Instance (which is one way to move a database between Azure SQL Managed Instance and Database).

You could therefore set up an Azure SQL Database as a subscriber and perform a *semi-online migration* from SQL Server. Replicate data from your on-premises SQL Server and then stop replication when you are ready to switch to your Azure SQL Database. Both snapshot and transaction replication are supported. Learn more at https://docs.microsoft.com/en-us/azure/azure-sql/database/replication-to-sql-database.

Updating Azure SQL

I have mentioned in this book that Azure SQL Managed Instance and Azure SQL Database are *versionless*. Versionless means that we do not release major versions of SQL Server in Azure SQL and then let you adopt them. We are continuously updating the software that powers Azure SQL to give you the latest updates and enhancements. **You are completely unburdened from keeping up and updating both the Operating System and SQL Server**.

Maintenance of Azure SQL

But what exactly does the latest updates mean in comparison to SQL Server. For SQL Server (as of SQL Server 2017), we release major versions, Cumulative Updates (CU), and General Distribution Releases (GDR). Customers download and apply the updates they would like to use.

When we release a new major version, for example, SQL Server 2019, it includes new features and capabilities, but it also includes a series of bug fixes that includes fixes from all CU and GDR builds from the previous major release, plus a set of fixes we believe makes sense to include in the major release.

For bug fixes (and some minor enhancements that are not necessarily features), we are constantly keeping these fixes up to date in our main branch of the source code. These changes are pushed into Azure SQL on a frequent basis and often available earlier to our customers vs. having to wait for a CU, GDR, or even major version release. This is a major advantage in running in Azure. We are constantly testing these fixes and changes, but effectively, you are getting a constant flow of bug fixes only found in a major version release.

We do not document or publish how often we roll out updates to SQL Server and other components that power Azure SQL. The process of rolling these updates is called a *train*. A train contains updates to all the components that support Azure SQL including OS, SQL Server, Service Fabric components, and other software we use to power Azure SQL. We do not roll out trains to every Azure Region at one time. Rather, these trains roll out across regions. If we detect any issue in rolling out a train in an early phase, we can easily roll it back. Since every Azure SQL deployment has built-in availability, when we update nodes and instances, we can fail over the deployment and ensure your data is available per the SLA agreement associated with your deployment. Concepts like Availability Zones also help provide further availability. I will discuss more about Availability Zones in Chapters 10 and 11 of the book. Resource Health options in the Azure Portal or through REST APIs can provide you information about whether a failover occurred because of *deployments*. Deployments are planned maintenance events that affect availability.

Note   It is possible the timing of a Cumulative Update for SQL Server may result in a fix landing in a CU before it rolls out in a train for Azure SQL. Unless the fix in the CU has a regression, that fix will make it eventually in a deployment train.

At the time of the writing of this book, we are working on plans to provide better notification and control of maintenance events.

Note   If we have a major impacting customer problem, we may notify a specific customer that their deployment may be affected so we can correct their problem.

Part of the improvements we are working on will provide advance maintenance notification to customers so they can plan for these events. Furthermore, we are also investigating the ability for customers to select a custom schedule for a maintenance event.

Our work in the cloud often generates innovation. One very cool capability we have rolled out to reduce the number of scenarios where maintenance of Azure SQL requires a restart of SQL Server (and therefore a failover) is called **hot patching**. You can read more how hot patching improves availability in Azure SQL in this blog post by my colleague Hans Olav Norheim at https://azure.microsoft.com/en-us/blog/hot-patching-sql-server-engine-in-azure-sql-database/.

New Features and Capabilities in Azure SQL

In general over the last few years, we have tried to adopt a *cloud-first mentality* for SQL Server. We build a new capability and roll it out in Azure SQL first through a private (limited customers and usually requires a sign-up) and public preview (not fully Generally Available but customers can try it out) program. Eventually, this capability goes into General Availability (GA).

Then based on the timing of a new major version of SQL Server, that capability is included in that major version. A great example of this is Intelligent Query Processing (IQP) which you can read about at `https://docs.microsoft.com/en-us/sql/relational-databases/performance/intelligent-query-processing`. We rolled out IQP for Azure SQL customers before it was released in SQL Server 2019. You can use this website to read about and subscribe to a RSS feed for new enhancements for Azure SQL Managed Instance and Database: `https://azure.microsoft.com/en-us/updates/?product=sql-database`. You can also use this documentation page to track new features that come in preview: `https://docs.microsoft.com/en-us/azure/azure-sql/database/doc-changes-updates-release-notes`.

Do not forget about the use of database compatibility to control the enablement of some functionality like Intelligent Query Processing. See more at `https://aka.ms/dbcompat`.

Finally, as much as we try to ensure that all new capabilities are first in Azure SQL, in some cases, this is not possible. In most cases, this is because the functionality involves access to external resources and can be complex to ensure it is secure in Azure SQL. For SQL Server 2019, a great example of this is Polybase. However, we try our best to catch up quickly. **Machine Learning Services**, which involves the ability to run R and Python code, is now in Preview for Azure SQL Managed Instance. You can learn more at `https://azure.microsoft.com/en-us/updates/machine-learning-on-azure-sql-managed-instance-limited-preview-available/`.

Summary

In this chapter, you learned the various method, capabilities, techniques, and restrictions for configuring Azure SQL Managed Instance and Database after you deploy. You learned both configuration options specific to Azure SQL and ones for the database engine and databases using familiar techniques like T-SQL.

You also learned some interesting aspects to Space Management which can be important as you manage database in Azure SQL.

In this chapter, we covered the various methods to load data from both on-premises and in Azure to Azure SQL.

Finally, you learned the details of how Azure SQL is updated and why it is referred to as a versionless database.

Now that you have learned how to deploy and configure Azure SQL, it is time to jump into the first category of the *meat and potatoes* of Azure SQL, security. In the next chapter, we will cover the capabilities of security for Azure SQL as it compares to SQL Server.

CHAPTER 6

Securing Azure SQL

Now that you have deployed and configured your Azure SQL Managed Instance or Database, you will want to ensure you have done all the right things to fully secure your Azure SQL deployment. Azure SQL has all the capabilities that come with SQL Server for security plus more.

My colleague Anna Hoffman asked me why I keep calling security, performance, and availability the *meat and potatoes* of SQL Server and Azure SQL. I can't take credit. This phrase comes from my longtime colleague, the famous Conor Cunningham. Conor and I have together presented several demos at the PASS Summit keynote. One time I was thinking of doing some pretty leading edge demos, and Conor stopped me and said, "Bob, that is nice, but our customers expect you and I to showcase the core innovation of the engine. Things like security, performance, and availability. You know, the meat and potatoes of SQL Server." The phrase has stuck ever since.

Note   For those who don't know the phrase, it is one we use in Texas to mean something fundamental or core. A basic meal consists of meat and potatoes. Not a problem for me since I love both.

So in this chapter, we will explore all the capabilities and tasks you normally use to secure a SQL Server and compare it with Azure SQL. You will also learn about unique capabilities and methods you will use to secure your Azure SQL Managed Instance and Database deployments.

This chapter (and the next two) will have many more examples than you have seen so far in the book. I will use the deployments I did in Chapter 4 of the book when discussing security. For you to try out any of the techniques or commands I use in this chapter, you will need

235

© Bob Ward 2021
B. Ward, *Azure SQL Revealed*, https://doi.org/10.1007/978-1-4842-5931-3_6

- An Azure subscription.

- A minimum of Contributor role access to the Azure subscription. You can read more about Azure built-in roles at `https://docs.microsoft.com/en-us/azure/role-based-access-control/built-in-roles`.

- Access to the Azure Portal (web or Windows application).

- A deployment of an Azure SQL Managed Instance and/or an Azure SQL Database as I did in Chapter 4.

- To connect to Managed Instance, you will need a *jumpbox* or virtual machine in Azure to connect. I showed you how to do this in Chapter 4 of the book. One simple way to do this is to create a new Azure Virtual Machine and deploy it to the same virtual network as the Managed Instance (you will use a different subnet than the Managed Instance).

- To connect to Azure SQL Database, you can use your on-premises client using firewall rules, but this chapter also shows you how to connect using a private endpoint in a virtual network, so you will need an Azure Virtual Machine. For my example, I will use the virtual machine I created in Chapter 3 of the book, called **bwsql2019**.

- Installation of the **az** CLI (see `https://docs.microsoft.com/en-us/cli/azure/install-azure-cli?view=azure-cli-latest` for more details). You can also use the Azure Cloud Shell instead since az is already installed. You can read more about the Azure Cloud Shell at `https://azure.microsoft.com/en-us/features/cloud-shell/`.

- You will run some T-SQL in this chapter, so install a tool like SQL Server Management Studio (SSMS) at `https://docs.microsoft.com/en-us/sql/ssms/download-sql-server-management-studio-ssms?view=sql-server-ver15`. You can also use Azure Data Studio at `https://docs.microsoft.com/en-us/sql/azure-data-studio/download-azure-data-studio?view=sql-server-ver15`. I installed both SSMS and ADS in the bwsql2019 Azure Virtual Machine.

Security Capabilities and Tasks

As I studied Azure SQL and compared this to my own knowledge of SQL Server security, I found out that Azure SQL Managed Instance and Azure SQL Database have just about all the capabilities for security as SQL Server. And the tasks you use to secure an Azure SQL deployment will feel a lot like SQL Server.

Before we dig into some of the details, let's review a few of these important capabilities and tasks.

Security Capabilities

This list doesn't represent all the capabilities because as I've mentioned already that many fundamental security capabilities in SQL Server are available in Azure SQL. However, it is worth mentioning a few capabilities to ensure you know what is possible. We will dive into more details and see examples later in the chapter.

Active Directory Authentication

You have seen in this book during deployment that you provide an admin SQL Server login and password for authentication. With SQL Server, you are used to using Windows Authentication, also known as Integrated Security, using protocols like Kerberos for a more secure solution.

Since the platform for Azure SQL is abstracted, you don't have access to set up domain authentication services and Kerberos with Windows Server. SQL Server on Linux provides Kerberos authentication using Active Directory, but that technique still uses a domain-joined system with a Window Server.

Azure Active Directory (AAD) to the rescue! AAD provides domain services and Kerberos authentication for Azure services like Azure SQL. You will see later in this chapter how to set up an AAD admin for Azure SQL and add logins and users based on AAD.

Azure RBAC and Locks

Azure Role-Based Access Control (RBAC) provides an authorization system for Azure SQL resources for operations like deployment. You will learn more about Azure RBAC and Azure SQL in the section later in this chapter "Authentication and Access."

Auditing

Auditing actions and operations against SQL Server has been available through the SQL Server Audit capability for several releases. Azure SQL provides SQL Server Audit capabilities and goes further using technologies like Log Analytics. You will learn in this chapter how to configure and use audits.

Data Encryption

SQL Server provides various methods to encrypt data and connections, including TLS, column level encryption, Transparent Data Encryption (TDE), and Always Encrypted. Azure SQL supports all these encryption methods and techniques which use services like Azure Key Vault for maximum control of keys. Azure SQL enables TDE by default for newly created databases.

Dynamic Data Masking

Dynamic Data Masking can protect the view of sensitive data to granted users shifting the logic to the database from the application. Dynamic Data Masking is supported with Azure SQL through the same T-SQL statements as SQL Server but also provides visual aids through the Azure portal.

Advanced Data Security

Azure SQL provides new capabilities to help you classify, analyze, and protect your data assets through **Data Classification**, **Vulnerability Assessments**, and **Advanced Threat Protection**. This suite of services is known as **Advanced Data Security**. Some of this functionality exists in SQL Server, but Azure SQL provides even more capabilities and visual aids through the Azure portal.

Security Tasks

The tasks to secure Azure SQL are very similar to SQL Server, but some of these tasks require specific work to integrate with the Azure infrastructure. You will learn how to use the security capabilities of Azure SQL on how to accomplish these tasks in this chapter.

Set Up and Configure Network Security

With SQL Server, you sometimes must deal with OS firewalls, but generally, your assets are protected within your data center. For Azure, you need to consider how to secure your network connectivity either with firewall or virtual networks.

Set Up and Configure Authentication and Authorization

For SQL Server, you are used to establishing logins and users for certain roles and then granting access to databases and objects. For Azure SQL, this process will be very familiar with some differences for Azure SQL Database.

Set Up and Configure Data Protection

You want your data protected, so you will learn in this chapter how to set up encryption for connections and data. You will also learn how to configure and use Dynamic Data Masking.

Monitor Security

Auditing can be a key aspect to ensuring your deployment is protected. You will learn in this chapter how to configure and monitor audits for access to your Azure SQL assets.

Go Bigger with Advanced Data Security

You will learn in this chapter how to take advantage of Data Classification, Vulnerability Assessments, and Advanced Threat Protection.

Network Security

Most administrators who install SQL Server use a private network within a company infrastructure. Firewalls block incoming traffic within this network. In addition, Operating Systems provide firewalls to protect ports for applications like SQL Server. In fact, if you have installed SQL Server before, you know that by default the firewall for port 1433 is blocked for both Windows and Linux. You generally must take action to add an exception for this port for remote connectivity to SQL Server.

Azure SQL is no different except that you have options to allow connectivity to the SQL Server instance behind the scenes as a public endpoint on the Internet or private within a virtual network.

I will admit to you as you review the information in this section of the chapter that you should absolutely consult networking experts in your organization to configure Azure SQL Managed Instance or Database for the requirements you need.

Azure SQL Managed Instance Network Security

As you saw in Chapter 4 to deploy Azure SQL Managed Instance, a virtual network and private connectivity are baked into the Managed Instance experience (although you can expose a public endpoint).

Since you use a virtual network, you will have choices to connect from a resource in the same virtual network as the Managed Instance (using a different subnet) or to connect with another virtual network that is connected to the Managed Instance Virtual Network.

Figure 6-1 shows an example of possible connectivity to a Managed Instance.

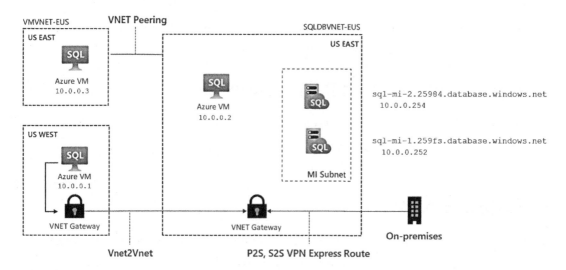

Figure 6-1. *Network security to Azure SQL Managed Instance*

Based on this figure, the Azure VM with a Private IP address of 10.0.0.2 is very much like the *jumpbox* VM I deployed in Chapter 4. Let's say though that you want to connect to one of these Managed Instances from another virtual network or on-premises.

VNet Peering allows you to connect from a resource in one virtual network that is peered to another. In the preceding figure, the Azure VM with the Private IP address of 10.0.0.3 is an example. Check out this blog post for instructions to connect to a Managed Instance with VNet peering: `https://techcommunity.microsoft.com/t5/azure-database-support-blog/connect-to-azure-sql-database-managed-instance-with-virtual/ba-p/369077`. You can read more about virtual network peering at `https://docs.microsoft.com/en-us/azure/virtual-network/virtual-network-peering-overview`. Virtual network peering can occur within a region or across regions.

If you would like to connect to the Managed Instance from on-premises, you will need to use an **Azure Virtual Network Gateway**. There are several options to connect your on-premises environment with a virtual network gateway: Point-to-Site (P2S), Site-to-Site (S2S), and ExpressRoute. ExpressRoute is by far the fastest (but the most expensive) way to connect with a gateway. You can learn about all of these gateway options at `https://docs.microsoft.com/en-us/azure/vpn-gateway/vpn-gateway-about-vpngateways`. As I've said earlier in this chapter, if networking is not your area of expertise (it is not mine), then I would consult networking engineers in your organization on the best option.

Our documentation also provides an overview of your networking options for a Managed Instance at `https://docs.microsoft.com/en-us/azure/azure-sql/managed-instance/connect-application-instance`. Here is an important point made in the documentation if you have connectivity issues:

If you've established an on-premises to Azure connection successfully and you can't establish a connection to SQL Managed Instance, check if your firewall has an open outbound connection on SQL port 1433 as well as the 11000–11999 range of ports for redirection.

The documentation also has a tutorial to set a P2S connections from your on-premises network to a Managed Instance at `https://docs.microsoft.com/en-us/azure/azure-sql/managed-instance/point-to-site-p2s-configure`.

A virtual network gateway can also be used to connect an existing virtual network in Azure instead of using VNet Peering. If you are running inside Azure, VNet Peering is probably your choice because everything is private and network latency is typically faster. However, there may be some reasons why you need a *VNet2VNet* gateway scenario. Here is a great resource to compare both options: `https://azure.microsoft.com/en-us/blog/vnet-peering-and-vpn-gateways/`.

It is important to know that besides the SQL Server endpoint (the standard TCP port to connect and run queries), an Azure SQL Managed Instance has a *Management endpoint*. Since a Managed Instance is deployed in its own virtual cluster, various services outside the cluster but within Azure (such as deployment within Resource Manager) must be able to access the cluster. That access is through the Management endpoint. The Management endpoint is a public endpoint protected by firewalls. This means when you use the portal or CLIs to manage the Manage Instance (e.g., scaling operations), you are connecting to this endpoint. Read more about how the Management endpoint is protected at `https://docs.microsoft.com/en-us/azure/azure-sql/managed-instance/connectivity-architecture-overview#management-endpoint`.

A few last points on network security for Managed Instance are as follows:

- You can enable a public endpoint for an Azure SQL Managed Instance. If you decide to do this, the endpoint is on port 3342, not 1433. Additionally, you can use Network Security Group (NSG) rules to effectively set up a firewall on the port. Read more at `https://docs.microsoft.com/en-us/azure/azure-sql/managed-instance/public-endpoint-configure`.

- I showed during deployment in Chapter 4 the connection type of Proxy vs. Redirect. Even though the SQL Server endpoint is in a private virtual network, technically a Proxy connection is more secure because all traffic is routed through a *Gateway*. With a redirect connection, the connection is first made to the Gateway, and then all subsequent traffic goes directly to the Managed Instance node. Redirect can be much faster, and since a private endpoint is being used, I recommend this option. Any use of a public endpoint always uses proxy connection. You can learn more about these policies at `https://docs.microsoft.com/en-us/azure/azure-sql/database/connectivity-architecture#connection-policy`.

There is no exercise or example here for Managed Instance network security since I already showed you how to connect to Azure SQL Managed Instance with a *jumpbox* VM in Chapter 4 of the book.

Azure SQL Database Network Security

Network security for Azure SQL Database (any deployment option) is a bit different than Managed Instance because when you deploy a database, we do not have a dedicated private virtual cluster. Rather, all database deployments share virtual clusters (rings) in Azure regions. Remember that when I talk about these network security options, they apply to the logical server for all databases. The only exception to this rule is that you can configure firewall rules specific to a database different than the logical server.

This doesn't mean you can't be protected and have a private endpoint to your database deployment as you will see in this section of the chapter.

Using the Public Endpoint

In Chapter 4 for deployment, I showed you some of the connection options for a database deployment:

- **Allow access to Azure services** – This option allows any Azure resource (e.g., VM, Application, or Cloud shell) to access the public endpoint for the database deployment.

- **Firewall rules** – This option allows you to create specific firewall rules for client computers outside of Azure. I used this technique in Chapter 4 to connect to the logical server I deployed with my laptop and SQL Server Management Studio (SSMS).

Figure 6-2 shows a network connectivity diagram of how both Azure resource and on-premises computers can be connected to the logical server with a public endpoint.

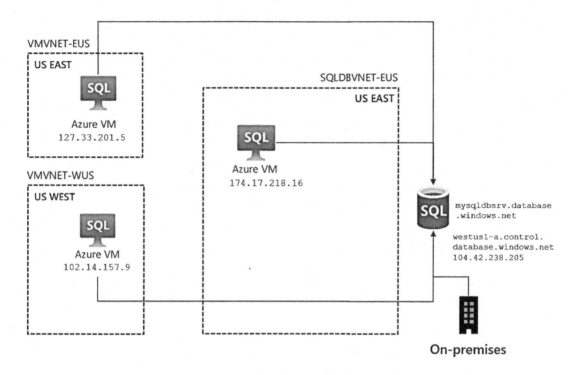

Figure 6-2. *Connecting to a logical server with a public endpoint*

You can see in this figure Azure VM resources that are connected through the Allow access to Azure services and on-premises computers connecting through a firewall rule. Notice the IP addresses of the Azure Virtual Machines are using their public IP address because even they are using a public endpoint connection within Azure.

Note   To be clear, you could use Allow access to Azure services and turn OFF all other firewall rules. While this is not a private endpoint scenario, it does prevent any connection unless it comes *within* Azure to connect to the logical server.

Notice in this figure the name of the logical server is mysqldbsrv.database.windows. net (this is from an example that is not the logical server I used). That is the name of the logical server, but how does the public endpoint get resolved on the Internet? Notice underneath this name in the figure is a public IP address and a network name of westus1-a.control.database.windows.net. This name is part of the DNS name of the node for the gateways when connecting to the logical server.

Since Allow access to Azure services is enabled, let's use the Azure Virtual Machine I created in Chapter 3, **bwsql2019**, to examine connectivity properties to the logical server.

I used RDP to connect into the virtual machine (I noted earlier in the chapter I installed SSMS and Azure Data Studio in the VM). I then connected using SSMS to the Azure Logical Server just like I showed you in Figure 4-32. **dm_exec_connections** is a DMV for SQL Server that can provide key information about connections to the server. Therefore, I ran the following T-SQL statement from SSMS:

```
SELECT client_net_address FROM sys.dm_exec_connections
WHERE session_id = @@SPID;
```

And the returned result is the following:

```
52.188.149.54
```

This IP address is the *Public IP address* of the Azure Virtual Machine, bwsql2019. This proves that the VM is connecting to the logical server over a public endpoint. However, the VM has access (without allowing the connection through a firewall) because I used the option **Allow access to Azure services**.

Another interesting way to look at the public endpoint aspect to Azure SQL Database is to examine the DNS infrastructure of the logical server. You can use the **nslookup** command to do this (nslookup is available by default on Windows and Linux operating systems. See more at `https://docs.microsoft.com/en-us/windows-server/administration/windows-commands/nslookup`).

From my Azure Virtual Machine, I then ran nslookup from PowerShell like the following:

```
nslookup bwazuresqlserver.database.windows.net
```

I received the following results:

```
Server:  UnKnown
Address:  168.63.129.16

Non-authoritative answer:
Name:    cr5.eastus1-a.control.database.windows.net
Address:  40.78.225.32
Aliases:  bwazuresqlserver.database.windows.net
          dataslice6.eastus.database.windows.net
          dataslice6eastus.trafficmanager.net
```

The top result is IP Address 168.63.129.16. It turns out this address is a special virtual IP address used for Azure communications, so within Azure your address will always say this (see more information at `https://docs.microsoft.com/en-us/azure/virtual-network/what-is-ip-address-168-63-129-16`).

The results at the bottom show the DNS hierarchy of the logical server, which includes a DNS server within the *control ring* (gateways) of Azure.

Also note that a ping is blocked, but it shows how a public endpoint is attempted to be accessed:

```
ping bwazuresqlserver.database.windows.net
```

```
Pinging cr5.eastus1-a.control.database.windows.net [40.78.225.32] with 32
bytes of data:
Request timed out.
```

There is a third option to secure the connectivity to access the logical server. Let's say you want to turn off Allow access to Azure services but don't want to have to use a fixed IP address for a firewall rule. You can use a **virtual network service endpoint** to allow only specific Azure sources in a virtual network (which could include on-premises connections) to connect to the logical server. This is still a public endpoint connection but strictly limited to resources from a specific Azure Virtual Network. Read more about how to use a virtual network service endpoint at `https://docs.microsoft.com/en-us/azure/azure-sql/database/vnet-service-endpoint-rule-overview`.

Let's use different technique to tighten up the security of the network connectivity to the Azure logical server.

Using Private Link

Let's say you do not want to allow any public endpoint access to your Azure SQL Databases regardless whether connections come from within or outside of Azure. The Azure team has created a concept called **private link** to allow PaaS services like Azure SQL Database to restrict access only through a private endpoint. You can read an overview about Private Link at `https://docs.microsoft.com/en-us/azure/private-link/private-link-overview`.

Let's look at new variation of Figure 6-2 using private link. Figure 6-3 shows how private link provides a private endpoint for Azure SQL Database.

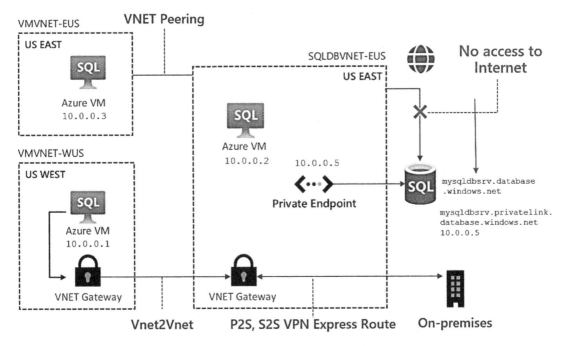

Figure 6-3. *Private link with Azure SQL Database*

Private link will expose a private endpoint in an existing Azure virtual network. Notice in this diagram the DNS name for the logical server is no longer in a public DNS hierarchy.

Let's see how to implement a private link connection using the existing deployment of Azure SQL Database from Chapter 4 and the Azure portal.

The first step is to disable public endpoint access to the logical server. From my logical server (mine is called **bwazuresqlserver**), I'll select Firewalls and virtual networks from the Azure Portal Resource menu. Then I'll turn Deny public network access to Yes and set Allow Azure services to No as seen in Figure 6-4.

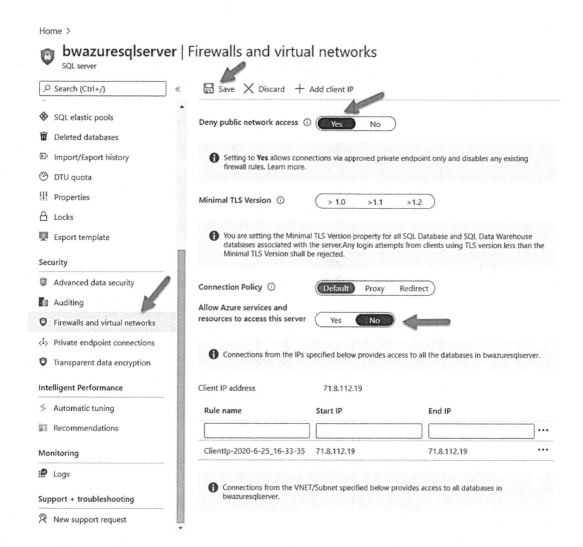

Figure 6-4. *Turning off public endpoint for Azure SQL Database*

I'll select **Save** to commit these changes. This change should be effective in a manner of seconds. I then verified I could not connect with SSMS in my Azure Virtual Machine as I did previously in this chapter. Figure 6-5 shows the error I get when trying to connect with SSMS.

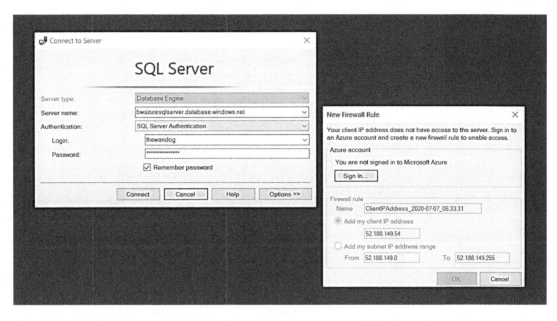

Figure 6-5. *Connection error with no access to Azure SQL Database*

This error is a detection that the client has no access but can add a firewall rule to get connected. However, there is another way.

I need to create a private link and associate this with my Azure SQL Database logical server and the virtual network of my Azure Virtual Machine.

Using the Azure portal home page, I added a resource and searched for the word Private Link. I picked Private link and selected Create private endpoint. You may be then presented with a screen that is called the Private Link Center. Select the option Create private endpoint as seen in Figure 6-6.

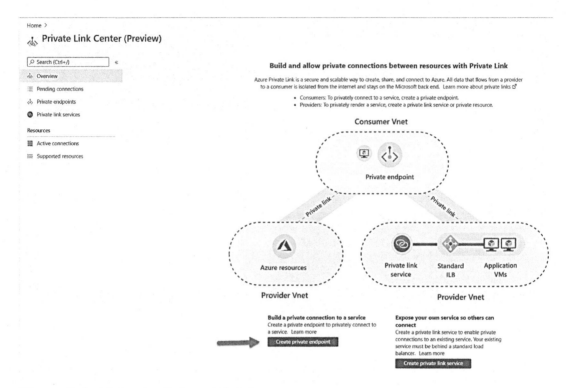

Figure 6-6. *Using the Private Link Center*

Like other Azure resources, you will now go through a series of screens starting with **Basics** to fill out information about the resource to deploy it.

Figure 6-7 shows how I will use Basics to place the private endpoint in the same resource group as my Azure SQL Database, give it a name, and place it in the same region as the virtual network of my Azure Virtual Machine.

Note   The private endpoint must be in the same region as the Azure Virtual Network you choose. Remember the endpoint now becomes a resource in that VNet. However, your client connection could be in another virtual network using VNet Peering or VNet Gateways as seen in Figure 6-3.

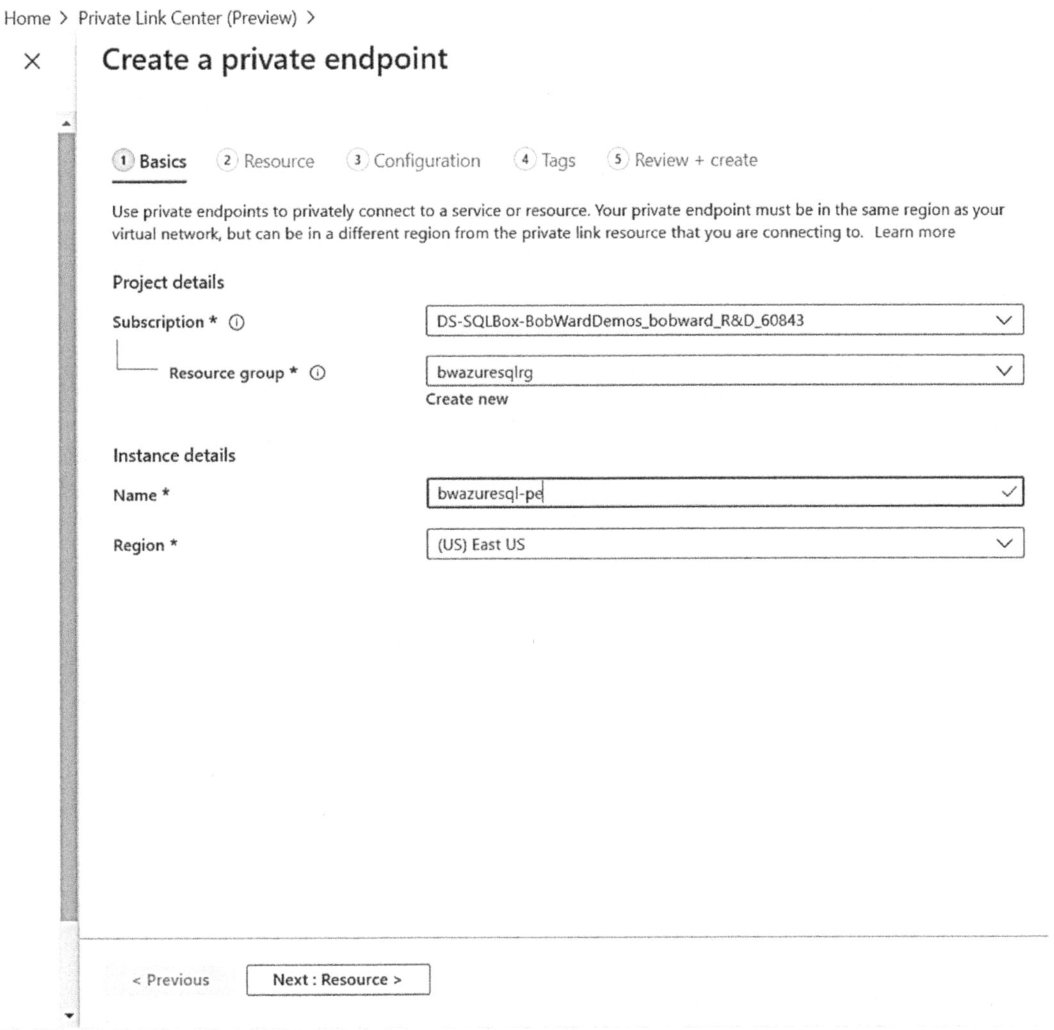

Home > Private Link Center (Preview) >

×   ## Create a private endpoint

① **Basics**   ② Resource   ③ Configuration   ④ Tags   ⑤ Review + create

Use private endpoints to privately connect to a service or resource. Your private endpoint must be in the same region as your virtual network, but can be in a different region from the private link resource that you are connecting to. Learn more

Project details

Subscription * ⓘ

| DS-SQLBox-BobWardDemos_bobward_R&D_60843 | ∨ |

Resource group * ⓘ

| bwazuresqlrg | ∨ |
Create new

Instance details

Name *

| bwazuresql-pe | ✓ |

Region *

| (US) East US | ∨ |

< Previous   Next : Resource >

Figure 6-7. Basics for creating a private endpoint

Click **Next: Resource >**. Now you need to associate the private endpoint with the Azure SQL Database logical server. Figure 6-8 shows these choices.

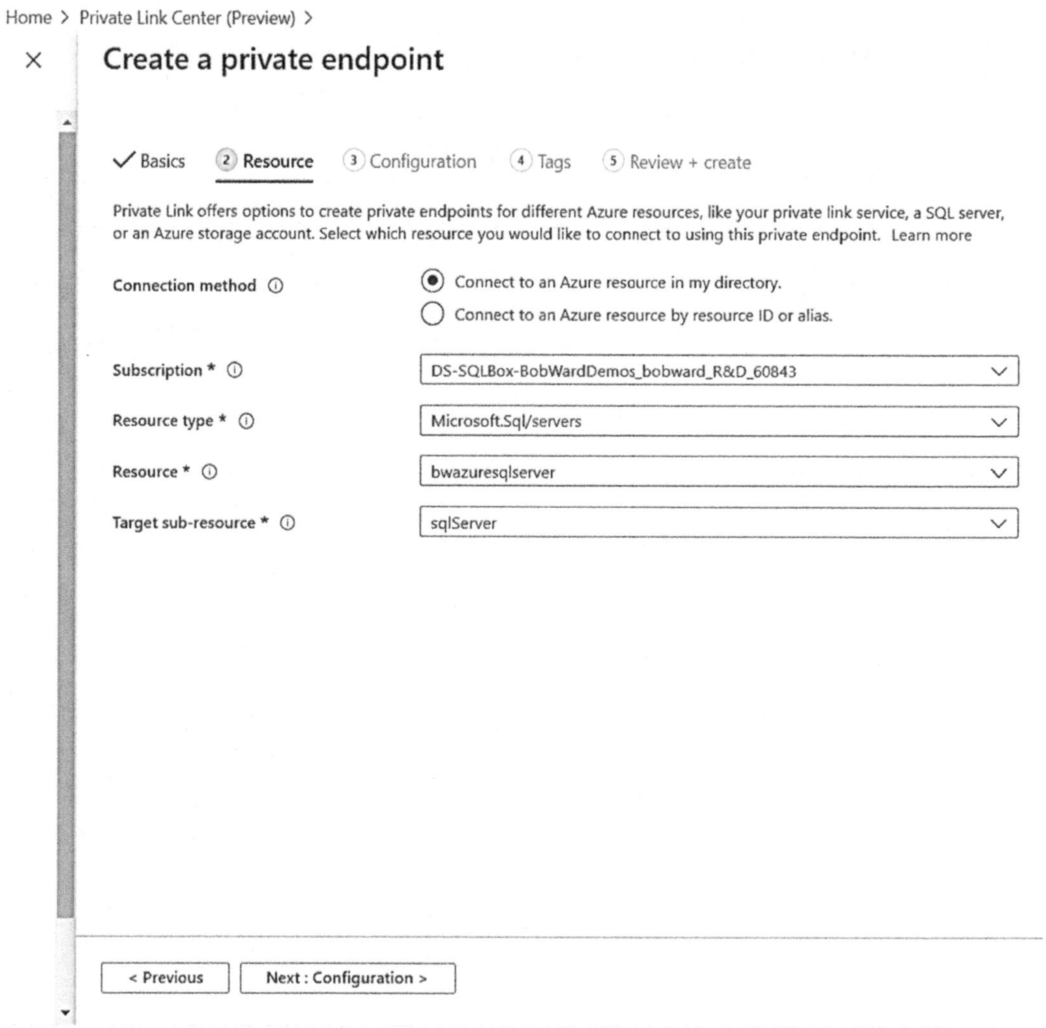

Home > Private Link Center (Preview) >

×   **Create a private endpoint**

✓ Basics   ② **Resource**   ③ Configuration   ④ Tags   ⑤ Review + create

Private Link offers options to create private endpoints for different Azure resources, like your private link service, a SQL server, or an Azure storage account. Select which resource you would like to connect to using this private endpoint. Learn more

Connection method ⓘ   ⦿ Connect to an Azure resource in my directory.
                             ○ Connect to an Azure resource by resource ID or alias.

Subscription * ⓘ   DS-SQLBox-BobWardDemos_bobward_R&D_60843   ⌄

Resource type * ⓘ   Microsoft.Sql/servers   ⌄

Resource * ⓘ   bwazuresqlserver   ⌄

Target sub-resource * ⓘ   sqlServer   ⌄

[< Previous] [Next : Configuration >]

Figure 6-8. *Associating the private endpoint with Azure SQL Database*

Click **Next: Configuration** > to associate this with the virtual network of the Azure
Virtual Machine as seen in Figure 6-9.

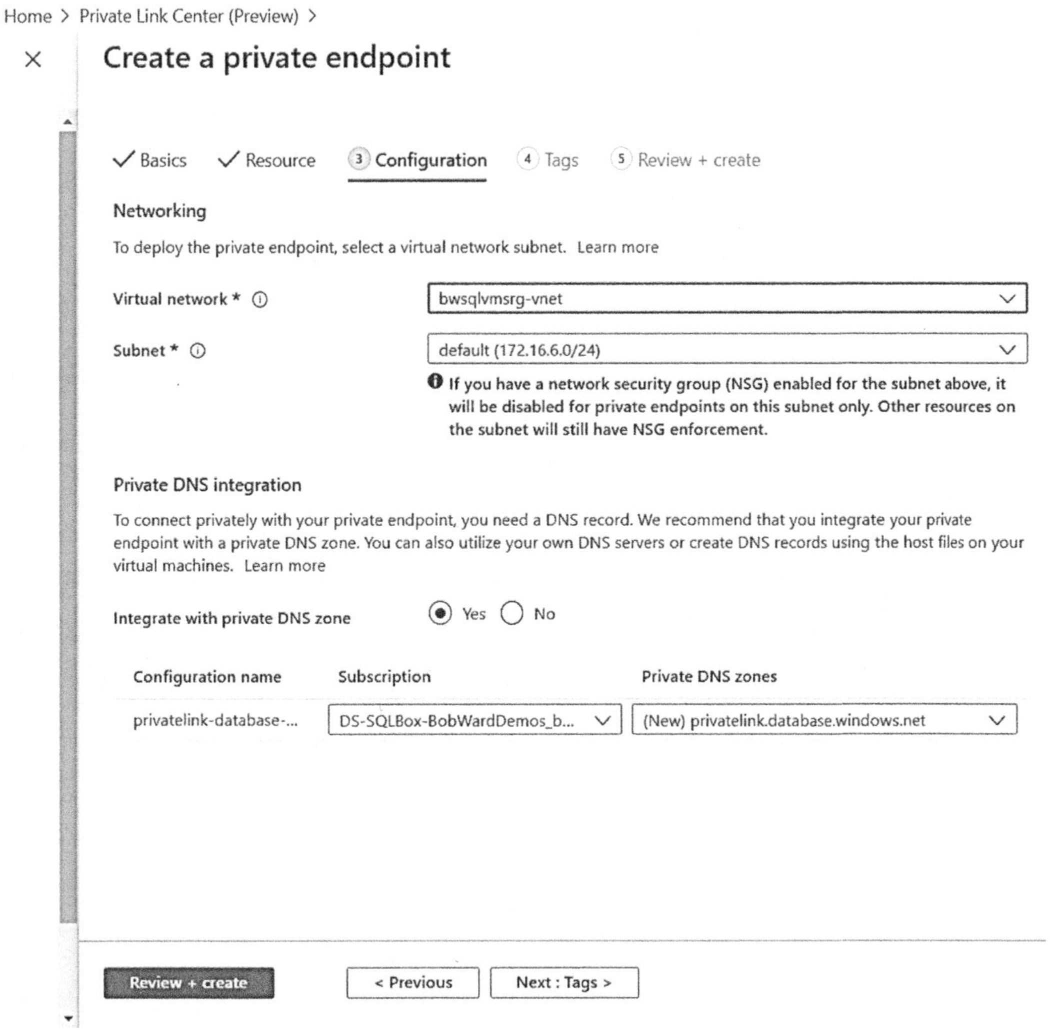

Figure 6-9. *Configuring a private endpoint for Azure SQL Database*

Note   I found the virtual network of my Azure Virtual Machine on the Working Pane of the Overview of the virtual machine **bwsql2019**.

Leave the default for the DNS zone information. I decided to not put a tag on this source so just clicked **Review + create** and then **Create**. The deployment for the private endpoint took only a few minutes to complete.

After the deployment if I navigate to the Private endpoint resource, it looked like Figure 6-10.

Figure 6-10. *Deployed private endpoint*

Take note of the Private IP on this screen of 172.16.6.5. This address is a Private IP for the private endpoint within the IP range for the virtual network **bwsqlvmsrg-vnet**.

You can now navigate to the Azure SQL Database logical server and select Private endpoint connections from the Resource Menu to see the linked private endpoint connection like Figure 6-11.

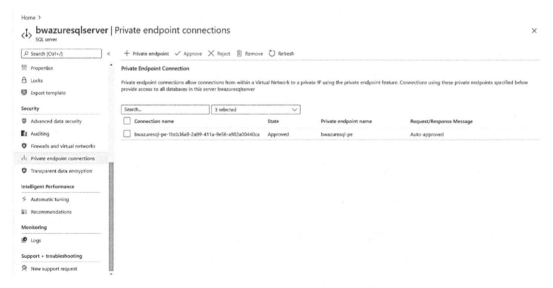

Figure 6-11. *A private endpoint connection for Azure SQL Database*

You can see the private endpoint in my case was "auto-approved," but you can use an approval process to approve a private endpoint to be associated with an Azure SQL Database. Read more at https://docs.microsoft.com/en-us/azure/private-link/private-endpoint-overview#access-to-a-private-link-resource-using-approval-workflow.

Now I'll go back to my Azure VM bwsql2019 and try to connect again with SSMS. My connection now works. If I run the following T-SQL statement

```
SELECT client_net_address FROM sys.dm_exec_connections
WHERE session_id = @@SPID;
```

the result is this:

```
172.16.6.4
```

This is the private IP address of the Azure Virtual Machine bwsql2019. Let's try to ping the logical server this time:

```
ping bwazuresqlserver.database.windows.net
```

```
Pinging bwazuresqlserver.privatelink.database.windows.net [172.16.6.5] with
32 bytes of data:
Request timed out.
```

Notice the private IP address of the server and the new DNS name which is not in the public hierarchy.

Also note the output for nslookup:

```
nslookup bwazuresqlserver.database.windows.net
```

```
Server:   UnKnown
Address:  168.63.129.16

Non-authoritative answer:
Name:     bwazuresqlserver.privatelink.database.windows.net
Address:  172.16.6.5
Aliases:  bwazuresqlserver.database.windows.net
```

Read more in our documentation at using Azure Private Link for Azure SQL Database at https://docs.microsoft.com/en-us/azure/azure-sql/database/private-endpoint-overview. For anyone wanting to integrate their on-premises environment, pay special attention to this documentation page: `https://docs.microsoft.com/en-us/azure/azure-sql/database/private-endpoint-overview#connecting-from-an-on-premises-environment-over-vpn`.

Tip   Private link connections for Azure SQL Database currently only support Proxy connection types. We had left the Connection Policy for our Azure SQL Database as Default, so if a connection uses Private Link which is inside of Azure, it will not use Redirect but Proxy.

Technically, Private Link is even more secure than the virtual network configuration of Managed Instance which is why we are even looking to enable this functionality for Managed Instance in the future.

Go further with your knowledge of Azure SQL and Network Security by watching videos from Anna Hoffman and Rohit Nayak as part of the Data Exposed Channel at `www.youtube.com/playlist?list=PL3EZ3A8mHhOxtbf4Cr2yR4-xsUtELwPjw`.

Authentication and Access

You have now successfully deployed an Azure SQL Managed Instance and Database(s) and connected using a secure network architecture. When you deployed both Azure SQL services, you specified an *admin*, which is a SQL login and password. The next steps are to set up and configure other logins and users just like you would a SQL Server deployment. I call this process setting up *Authentication*. Then you will want to grant access to users to the objects they need based on the requirements of your application and business.

Before we talk about the details of authentication and access for Azure SQL, let's review first the authentication and access for Azure SQL resources outside of SQL but in the Azure infrastructure called Azure Role-Based Access Control (RBAC).

Azure Role-Based Access Control (RBAC)

I've mentioned the concept of Azure RBAC in previous chapters in the book. Today when you deploy SQL Server on Windows or Linux, you must have certain rights and privileges to install SQL Server. For example, on Windows, most use local administrator accounts when installing SQL Server.

At this point in the book, I've listed in several chapters the requirements to deploy Azure SQL such as the *Contributor role*. An Azure account user that is part of the Contributor role has the permissions to manage everything, except grant access to resources to other accounts (that access is reserved for members of the Owner or User Access Administrator roles).

Therefore, if you are assigned the Contributor role for your Azure subscription, you should have the rights to deploy Azure SQL Managed Instances and Databases.

It is possible you want to set up a system for your organization so that some Azure users have rights to deploy or manage Azure SQL Managed Instances and Databases but not access the resources. Think of an administrator that only deploys or manages resources but doesn't have access to the underlying SQL Server.

Azure provides the following built-in roles for these purposes:

SQL DB Contributor

Members of this role can deploy and manage Azure SQL databases but not access them.

SQL Server Contributor

Members of this role can deploy and manage Azure SQL logical servers and databases but not access them.

SQL Security Manager

Members of this role can manage security policies of Azure SQL logical servers and databases but not access them.

SQL Managed Instance Contributor

Members of this role can deploy and manage Azure SQL Managed Instances but not access them.

You can read more about Azure built-in roles at `https://docs.microsoft.com/en-us/azure/role-based-access-control/built-in-roles`. You can learn more about role definitions at `https://docs.microsoft.com/en-us/azure/role-based-access-control/role-definitions`.

Authentication for Azure SQL Managed Instance

When you deploy SQL Server on Windows, the default authentication *mode* is Windows only. This means only Windows users can log in to SQL Server. **Mixed mode security** allows both SQL and Windows logins (Linux requires mixed mode). Azure SQL Managed Instance forces Mixed Mode security and you cannot change this.

When you deploy an Azure SQL Managed Instance, you specify an **Administrator Account** as I showed you in Figure 4-4. This account will be created as a SQL login for the SQL Server instance and added as a member of the sysadmin role. The sa login is disabled by default, but you can enable and use it (but I don't recommend it).

With this sysadmin login, you can add other SQL logins, assign them to roles (even sysadmin) just like SQL Server. You can also create users in database and map them to logins just like SQL Server.

Note   You cannot change the admin once you deploy. You can reset the password for the admin through the Azure portal, az CLI, or PowerShell.

You can even create a contained database which supports containers users just like SQL Server. You can read more about contained database users at `https://docs. microsoft.com/en-us/sql/relational-databases/security/contained-database-users-making-your-database-portable`.

Azure Active Directory Authentication

Since you don't have access to the underlying Windows Operating System of the VMs, you cannot join domains and set up Windows Authentication. Therefore, we provide the ability for you to add **Azure Active Directory logins** to your Managed Instance.

When you use Windows or domain authentication with SQL Server, you are using behind-the-scenes Active Directory Domain Services. SQL Server on Linux even supports this concept. Azure provides the same type of service through Azure Active Directory Services (AADS).

The first step in using Azure Active Directory authentication for a Managed Instance is to provision an administrator for the Managed Instance from an Azure Active Directory user. To use AAD with Managed Instance, you first need to create an AAD domain. You can read the process for setting this up at `https://docs.microsoft.com/ en-us/azure/active-directory-domain-services`. It is possible when you sign into the Azure Portal, you are already part of an AAD for your organization. For me, that is the case at Microsoft.

To set up an AAD admin for a Managed Instance, you must have "Administrator" rights for your AAD to grant read permissions. I don't have these at Microsoft. The documentation shows the process to configure this AAD admin at https://docs.microsoft.com/en-us/azure/azure-sql/database/authentication-aad-configure?tabs=azure-powershell#provision-azure-ad-admin-sql-managed-instance. This covers both the portal and CLI options to configure an AAD admin for Managed Instance.

The new AAD admin will become a member of the sysadmin server role for the Managed Instance. Now you can use the T-SQL CREATE LOGIN statement to create new logins based on AAD users. The FROM EXTERNAL PROVIDER clause provides this capability. The documentation shows an example of this syntax at https://docs.microsoft.com/en-us/sql/t-sql/statements/create-login-transact-sql?view=azuresqldb-mi-current like the following T-SQL statement:

```
CREATE LOGIN [bob@contoso.com] FROM EXTERNAL PROVIDER;
```

Note   If you look at the logins for a Managed Instance, you will notice two logins that are created by default for any Managed Instance: WASDRGTenantMonitoringRO and xtsuser (which is actually disabled). These logins are part of the internal role Microsoft creates for DevOps purposes. These roles only have CONNECT and VIEW SERVER STATE permissions, don't have access to your data, and have no ability to make any modifications.

You can read more about authentication and access for Azure SQL Managed Instance at https://docs.microsoft.com/en-us/azure/azure-sql/database/logins-create-manage.

Authentication for Azure SQL Database

When I showed you how to deploy an Azure SQL Database in Chapter 4 of the book, I supplied a **Server admin login**. I used this login to connect to the logical server using SQL Authentication. Just like Managed Instance, mixed mode security is forced for the logical server. This admin account is a *server-level principal* for the logical server and is mapped as **dbo** in all databases.

Note   You cannot change the admin once you deploy. You can reset the password for the admin through the Azure portal, az CLI, or PowerShell.

If you would like to create other logins who have admin capabilities (but not full server admin), you use the CREATE LOGIN statement to create standard SQL logins for the logical server in the context of the logical master database. You can then create a user in context of the logical master database and assign this user to two special roles for Azure SQL Database using ALTER ROLE:

dbmanager – Users assigned to this role can create and manage databases and will be mapped to the dbo of that database, so has full database owner permissions.

loginmanager – Users assigned to this role can create new logins in the context of the logical master but are not mapped to the dbo role of databases.

You can now use the standard process as with SQL Server to create SQL logins and map them to users in any database they need access. You can assign users to roles and even create new roles just like SQL Server.

Note   One complexity with using logins is that when you choose a failover option like geo-replication, you must create the login on the secondary server manually.

Using Contained Users

You can also create contained database users that don't require a login. This concept has been around a while with SQL Server using contained databases. Azure SQL Database is in a way a contained database. Contained users are also called **user accounts**.

The CREATE USER T-SQL statement supports contained users using the WITH PASSWORD clause. One advantage of a contained user is that the information is stored in the database and therefore replicated as part of a geo-replication failover deployment.

I'll show you an example of how to connect and use a contained user in the next section.

Azure Active Directory Authentication

Like Managed Instance, Azure SQL Database supports Azure Active Directory (AAD) Authentication. Like using Windows authentication for SQL Server, AAD authentication can be the most secure and best method to use with Azure SQL Database. You can create an AAD server admin (in addition to the SQL server admin you create during deployment) for the logical server. You can then create contained users based on an AAD account. You can even create users based on AAD groups.

Let's explore using the logical server and databases I deployed in Chapter 4 how to set up an AAD admin, how to connect with the admin, and how to create and connect with AAD contained users.

I love how the documentation at `https://docs.microsoft.com/en-us/azure/azure-sql/database/authentication-aad-overview` lists out the steps to use AAD with Azure SQL Database:

- Create and populate Azure AD.

- Create an Azure Active Directory administrator.

- Create contained database users in your database mapped to Azure AD identities.

- Connect to your database by using Azure AD identities.

Microsoft has already created and populated an Azure AD and associated it with my subscription. So I'll now create an Azure AD administrator.

I'm going to navigate to my logical server called **bwazuresqlserver** and select **Active Directory admin** from the Resource Menu, select **Set admin**, and search for my name in the AD as seen in Figure 6-12.

Figure 6-12. *Creating an AAD admin for Azure SQL Database*

I then click **Save**, and within a few seconds, the AAD admin is created.

Now let's try to connect with SSMS using the Azure VM bwsql2019 that is now set up with Private Link. Connecting with SSMS shows options you may not be familiar with as seen in Figure 6-13.

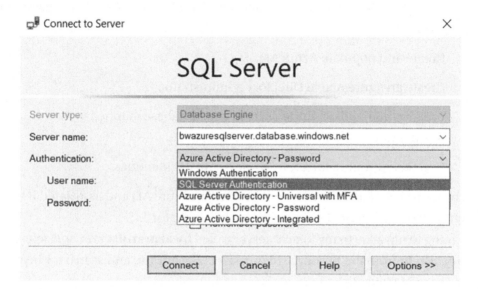

Figure 6-13. *AAD options when connecting with SSMS*

Let's look at each of these options:

AAD – Universal with MFA

Log in with your AAD account but require multi-factor authentication (MFA). MFA is a secure method used for many secure connection purposes including websites, and AAD for Azure SQL Database supports this. Learn more at `https://docs.microsoft.com/en-us/azure/azure-sql/database/authentication-mfa-ssms-overview`.

AAD – Integrated

This option is like Windows Authentication when you are logged into a client computer using your AAD credentials. Windows 10 offers this type of capability. Learn more about a seamless AAD experience at `https://docs.microsoft.com/en-us/azure/active-directory/hybrid/how-to-connect-sso`.

AAD – Password

Use this method if you are using a client where your computer is not domain joined. You can put in your full AAD account with password.

At Microsoft, we have a policy where we must use MFA, so I'll use that method to connect. In my VM when I choose this method, I get a dialog box to complete the MFA process.

The AAD admin is going to look a big strange to the average SQL Server user since it technically is not a login in the logical master. It is a user where the type is **EXTERNAL**.

You can see this by running these T-SQL statements in the context of the logical master connected as the AAD admin:

```
SELECT name, type_desc, authentication_type_desc
FROM sys.database_principals WHERE name = 'bobward@microsoft.com';
GO
SELECT suser_name();
GO
```

The results look like the following:

name	type_desc	authentication_type_desc
bobward@microsoft.com	EXTERNAL_GROUP	EXTERNAL

and

```
bobward@microsoft.com
```

EXTERNAL_GROUP is a type for an AAD user or group. And EXTERNAL for authentication_type is reserved for an AAD connection.

If you run a query in the context of a user database like the one I created called **bwazuresqldb**, you can run these queries to see the "login" connected or the server principal and the user of the database which is mapped to dbo (and is the owner of the database):

```
SELECT suser_name()
GO
SELECT user_name()
GO
```

The results are

```
bobward@microsoft.com
```

and

```
dbo
```

Note   SELECT user_name( ) in logical master would have yielded your AAD login since you are added as a user in the logical master.

PowerShell supports creating an AAD admin using the **Set-AzSqlServerActiveDirec toryAdministrator** cmdlet, and az CLI supports **az sql server ad-admin create**.

Connected as the AAD admin to this user database, I could then create a contained user based on another AAD account like this (this is hypothetical account in the Microsoft AAD):

```
CREATE USER [thereisonlyonebuckwoody@microsoft.com] FROM EXTERNAL PROVIDER;
GO
```

I will then give this user access to read data by adding them to the db_datareader role:

```
ALTER ROLE db_datareader ADD MEMBER [thereisonlyonebuckwoody@microsoft.com];
GO
```

You can also create AAD contained users based on the display name of a security group in AAD or with an AAD token. Learn more how to do this at https:// docs.microsoft.com/en-us/azure/azure-sql/database/authentication-aad- configure?tabs=azure-cli#create-contained-users-mapped-to-azure-ad- identities.

You might want to connect with AAD to Azure SQL Database other than just with SSMS. Here are some tips:

- Learn how to connect with an application at https:// docs.microsoft.com/en-us/azure/azure-sql/database/ authentication-aad-configure?tabs=azure-cli#using-an- azure-ad-identity-to-connect-from-a-client-application.

- The popular **sqlcmd** utility supports the **-G** parameter to connect with AAD.

- The new popular tool Azure Data Studio supports AAD authentication with MFA. Figure 6-14 shows an example where I connected with AAD to my Azure SQL Database.

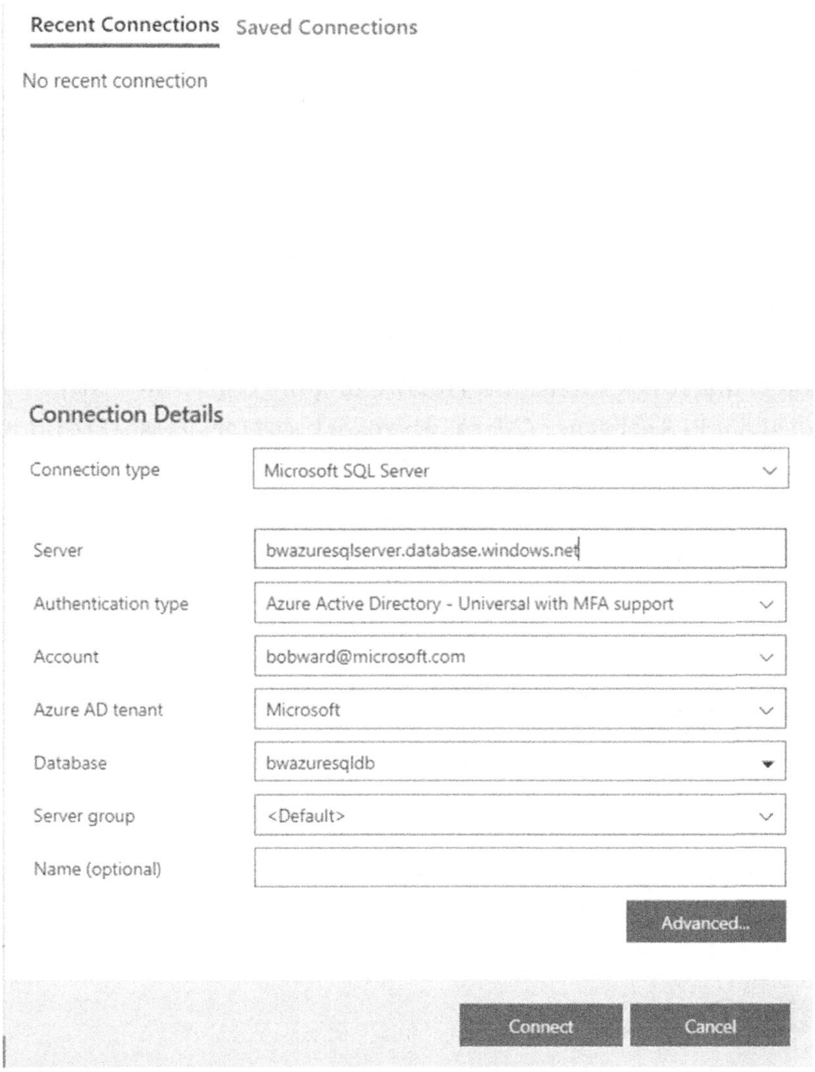

Recent Connections   Saved Connections

No recent connection

Connection Details

Connection type   Microsoft SQL Server   ∨

Server   bwazuresqlserver.database.windows.net

Authentication type   Azure Active Directory - Universal with MFA support   ∨

Account   bobward@microsoft.com   ∨

Azure AD tenant   Microsoft   ∨

Database   bwazuresqldb   ▼

Server group   <Default>   ∨

Name (optional)

                                                                    Advanced...

                                          Connect   Cancel

Figure 6-14. *Using AAD with Azure Data Studio*

Check out our documentation for more information about the trust architecture and limitations using AAD users and groups: `https://docs.microsoft.com/en-us/azure/azure-sql/database/authentication-aad-overview`. Also, read about how to configure a conditional access policy with AAD at `https://docs.microsoft.com/en-us/azure/azure-sql/database/conditional-access-configure#configure-conditional-access`.

Set Up and Configure Access

Now that you have created logins and users, what do you do now? You do what you do
for SQL Server. You grant access and permissions to objects within your database to
meet your application requirements.

This could involve creating schemas, roles, and grant or revoking specific
permissions. To get a primer on permissions for SQL Server, refer to the docs at `https://
docs.microsoft.com/en-us/sql/relational-databases/security/permissions-
database-engine?view=sql-server-ver15`.

Don't forget that row-level security (RLS) is supported in Azure SQL just like SQL
Server. Read about RLS at `https://docs.microsoft.com/en-us/sql/relational-
databases/security/row-level-security?view=sql-server-ver15`.

You can read more about authentication and access for Azure SQL Database at
`https://docs.microsoft.com/en-us/azure/azure-sql/database/logins-create-
manage`.

Protecting Your Data

Ensuring you have set up proper authorization to connect and access data is just the
first step. You need to protect your data for all aspects of your deployment, including
connections, data at rest, data end to end, and ensuring only the right people can view
important data. Azure SQL has all the capabilities to protect data just like SQL Server.

Encrypting Connections

Like SQL Server, Azure SQL supports encryption of connections through the Transparent
Layer Security (TLS) protocol (you can read about TLS at `https://en.wikipedia.org/
wiki/Transport_Layer_Security`).

By default, Azure SQL Managed Instance enforces encryption for connections. Tools
and applications should enable an encrypted connection for a Managed Instance to
avoid client/server negotiation. In addition, you can force a minimal TLS version for a
client connection. The latest TLS version, 1.2, fixes some known security vulnerability,
so you may consider requiring this version. You can set the minimal version through the

Azure portal, through PowerShell (**Set-AzInstance**) or az cli (**az sql mi update**). You can read more about TLS and Managed Instance at `https://docs.microsoft.com/en-us/azure/azure-sql/managed-instance/minimal-tls-version-configure`.

Azure SQL Database forces encrypted connections whether the client or application enables it. You can verify this by examining the **encrypt_option** column for **sys.dm_exec_connections** and seeing it will always be a value of TRUE for any user TCP connection. Azure SQL Database also offers enforcement of a minimal TLS version (1.0, 1.1, and 1.2) through the Azure portal, PowerShell (**Set-AzSqlServer**), and az cli (**az sql server update**). You can read more at `https://docs.microsoft.com/en-us/azure/azure-sql/database/connectivity-settings#minimal-tls-version`.

Tip   Because Azure SQL Database forces an encrypted connection, a best practice is to enable this for your client tool or application. This speeds up connection time since the server must negotiate with the client to set the encryption if not set by the client.

Transparent Data Encryption (TDE)

Transparent Data Encryption (TDE) is an *encryption at rest* technology that has been in use with SQL Server for many releases. The concept is that the SQL Server engine will encrypt and decrypt data to the files for the database as data is written and read from disk. This way, the data in the file is encrypted to protect any *offline* attempt to access the files of the database. Azure SQL Managed Instance and Database enable this option **by default**.

You might wonder why you would need this encryption option since you or anyone doesn't have access to files in the underlying virtual machines of Azure SQL. Enabling TDE by default is just another mechanism in Azure's commitment to a *defense-in-depth* methodology to protect your data. Many use TDE with SQL Server deployments in their own data center to protect from an unexpected intrusion to access database files outside the engine. The same holds true for Azure even though the Azure ecosystem has many protection mechanisms in place for data centers.

For Azure SQL Managed Instance, TDE is on by default for the instance, which means all databases created for the instance are enabled by TDE. You cannot disable this option for the instance, but you can individually disable TDE through ALTER DATABASE or tools like SSMS. One option you do have for a Managed Instance is to control what keys are used for encryption for TDE. By default, Azure SQL Managed Instance uses a service-managed key, which means Azure SQL manages a certificate for the key (rotates the key and protects it with a root key within Azure).

Azure SQL Database also supports configuring TDE for databases with ALTER DATABASE (ENCRYPTION option) but also allows you to enable and disable TDE through the Azure portal, PowerShell (**Set-AzSqlDatabaseTransparentDataEncry ption**), and az cli (**az sql db tde set**). The default key management is also a service-managed key at the logical server level.

Bring Your Own Key (BYOK)

SQL Server provides a method to use an Extensible Key Management (EKM) provider to protect the Database Encryption Key (DEK) used to encrypt data with TDE. One of the EKM providers allowed is Azure Key Vault. This allows keys used for encryption to be stored outside of SQL Server.

Azure SQL provides a similar mechanism affectionately called *Bring Your Own Key* (BYOK). You may also see this referred to as *Customer-managed key*. The mechanism to use Azure Key Vault for BYOK is referred to as a **TDE protector**. Azure Key Vault is a service in Azure to help you centrally store and manage secrets and keys. As stated in the introductory documentation for Azure Key Vault at `https://docs.microsoft.com/ en-us/azure/key-vault/general/overview`, Azure Key Vault is "Secrets and keys are safeguarded by Azure, using industry-standard algorithms, key lengths, and hardware security modules (HSMs). The HSMs used are Federal Information Processing Standards (FIPS) 140-2 Level 2 validated."

Authorization to create a key vault and create and manage keys is done through Azure Active Directory. Azure Key Vault keys are set at the instance or logical server level and apply to all databases in the instance or logical server. I like the diagram in this blog post at `https://azure.microsoft.com/en-us/blog/announcing-transparent-data- encryption-tde-with-customer-managed-keys-for-managed-instance/` to show how Azure Key Vault BYOK works as seen in Figure 6-15.

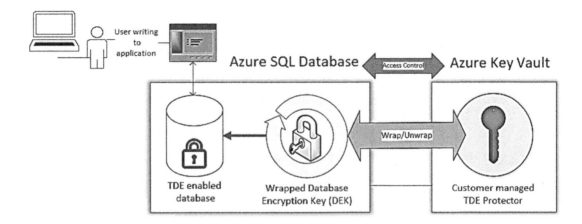

Figure 6-15. *Using Azure Key Vault for BYOK with TDE*

I used my Azure subscription to create a new Azure Key Vault and added a key to the vault (see a tutorial at `https://docs.microsoft.com/en-us/azure/key-vault/general/quick-create-portal`). I then navigated to the logical server I created called **bwazuresqlserver**, selected Transparent data encryption from the Resource Menu, and selected Customer-managed key as seen in Figure 6-16.

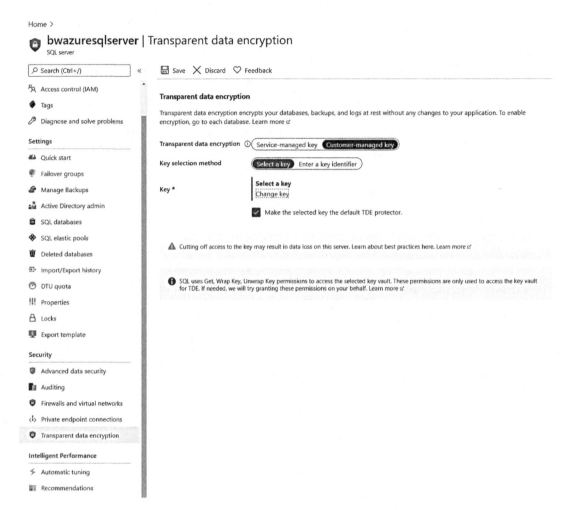

Figure 6-16. *Changing to a customer-managed key for TDE*

I then selected Change key and picked my key vault and key as seen in Figure 6-17.

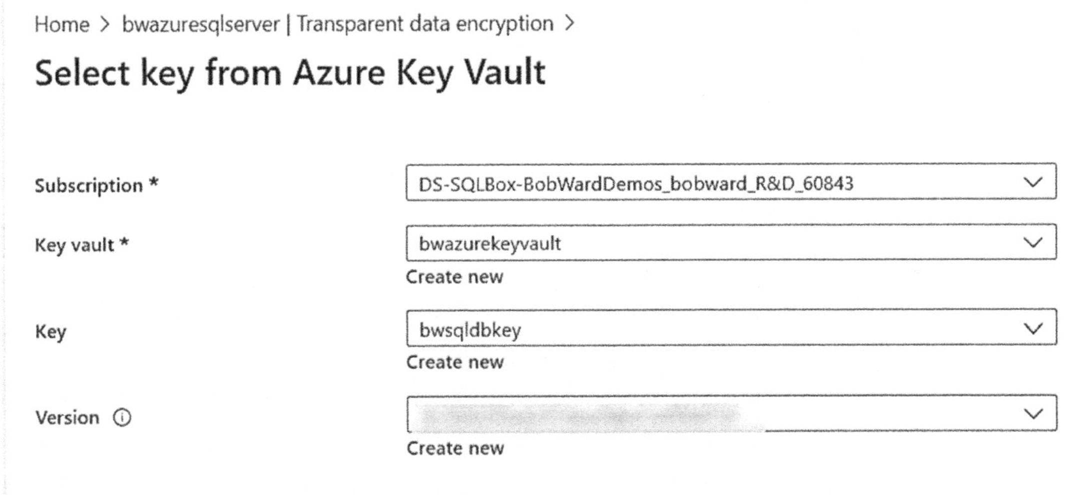

Home > bwazuresqlserver | Transparent data encryption >

Select key from Azure Key Vault

Subscription *	DS-SQLBox-BobWardDemos_bobward_R&D_60843 ∨

Key vault *	bwazurekeyvault ∨

Create new

Key	bwsqldbkey ∨

Create new

Version ⓘ	∨

Create new

Figure 6-17. *Choosing a key from Azure Key Vault*

I chose Select and then Save on the next screen. Within a few seconds, my key is now enabled as the TDE protector.

This seems easy enough, but there are several tasks and considerations when you use BYOK with Azure SQL:

- COPY_ONLY backups for Managed Instance are only supported when you use BYOK (because you have the keys to restore). Learn more about COPY_ONLY backups at https://docs.microsoft.com/ en-us/sql/relational-databases/backup-restore/copy-only- backups-sql-server.

- Your key vault and Azure SQL deployment must belong to the same Azure Active Directory tenant.

- Like any scenario where you manage keys, you should back them up regularly. Learn more about Azure Key Vault backups at https:// docs.microsoft.com/en-us/azure/key-vault/general/backup.

- There are considerations for BYOK with high availability. Read more at https://docs.microsoft.com/en-us/azure/ azure-sql/database/transparent-data-encryption-byok- overview?view=sql-server-ver15#high-availability-with- customer-managed-tde.

When using BYOK with Azure SQL, I highly recommend you read thoroughly our documentation at `https://docs.microsoft.com/en-us/azure/azure-sql/database/transparent-data-encryption-byok-overview`.

Always Encrypted

Always Encrypted is a technology based on work from Microsoft research used to provide end-to-end encryption for SQL applications. It was introduced in SQL Server 2016 and has all the same capabilities in Azure SQL. Just like with SQL Server, keys for Always Encrypted can be stored in Azure Key Vault. Read the entire story about how Always Encrypted works and how to set it up at `https://docs.microsoft.com/en-us/sql/relational-databases/security/encryption/always-encrypted-database-engine`.

The one exception in capabilities at the time of the writing of this book is secure enclaves. Secure enclaves extend the capabilities of Always Encrypted but is currently not available for Azure SQL Managed Instance or Database. You can read more about secure enclaves with Always Encrypted at `https://docs.microsoft.com/en-us/sql/relational-databases/security/encryption/always-encrypted-enclaves`.

Dynamic Data Masking (DDM)

One other method to protect your data is to control which users have access to view *sensitive* data. Many applications provide this type of protection by *masking* data in the display layers of their program. For example, a web application may display a phone number as XXX-XXX for some users and the full phone number for others. The problem with this approach is that the application must be modified if any rule changes on the masks used or which users can see data or masked data.

SQL Server provides a method to control masking of data at the database layer instead of the application. Then *any* application or tool would only see data based on masking rules defined with T-SQL. This feature is called Dynamic Data Masking (DDM) and was introduced in SQL Server 2016. You can read the full documentation of DDM at `https://docs.microsoft.com/en-us/sql/relational-databases/security/dynamic-data-masking`.

Azure SQL supports DDM through T-SQL statements as referenced in the documentation. In addition, Azure SQL Database allows you to manage masks and permissions through the Azure portal as seen in Figure 6-18.

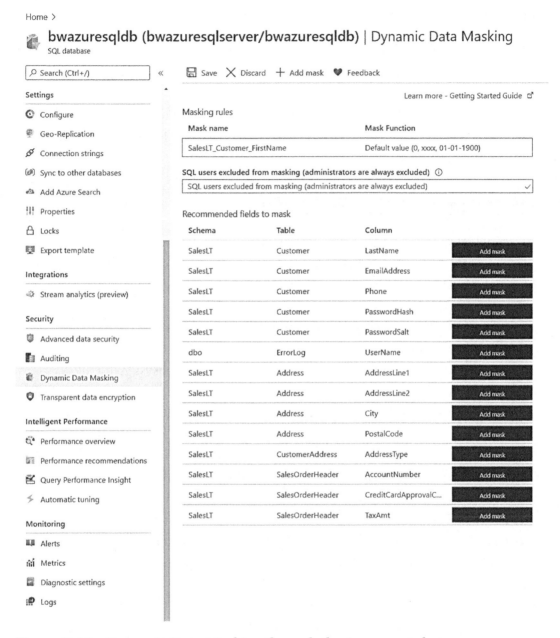

***Figure 6-18.** Dynamic Data Masking through the Azure portal*

You can see using the Azure portal will provide recommendations on columns to mask based on the column names (e.g., LastName or EmailAddress).

Monitoring Security

After you have configured security for authentication, access, and data protection, you will most likely want to monitor all activity against your Azure SQL Managed Instance and Database deployments.

Monitoring typically means auditing activity against your deployment. You can audit activities against your deployment within the Azure ecosystem (or outside of SQL) and activity within Azure SQL.

Monitoring the Azure Ecosystem

When you deploy and manage SQL Server on Windows and Linux, the operating system provides several different methods to audit activity outside of SQL Server. You may have other methods within your data center to audit this type of activity.

The Azure ecosystem provides this same type of audit capabilities. You may have seen in Chapter 4 after deploying Azure SQL Managed Instance and Database the **Activity Log** for these types of activities.

The Activity Log is a *platform log* supported by the Azure ecosystem for all subscriptions. In fact, the activity log is a record of all events for your Azure subscription and includes events specific to Azure SQL Managed Instance and Database. Basically, any operation you perform against an Azure SQL resource that is *outside* of SQL Server is recorded in the Activity Log. I've used the Windows Event Log for many years, and I like to think of the Activity Log as the Event log of Azure.

The Azure portal provides an excellent way to view activity log entries specific to an Azure resource. For example, if I navigate to my logical server **bwazuresqlserver** in the Azure portal, select Activity log from the Resource menu, and then change the timeframe to Last week I see entries like in Figure 6-19.

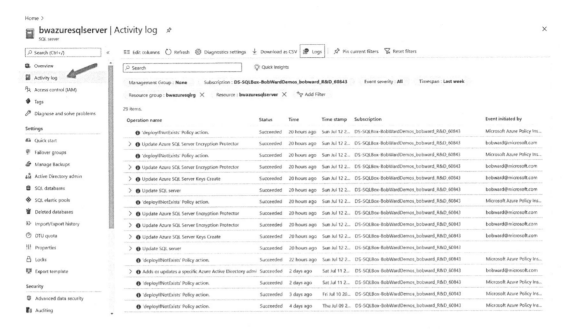

Figure 6-19. *The activity log for Azure SQL Database logical server*

You can see at the top of this screen filters automatically set to the logical server, but at this point, you can adjust these to any resource in your subscription (or for all events in your subscription). You also have options here to download the log as .csv file. You can review activity log entries through the portal, through PowerShell (**Get-AzLog**), az CLI (**az monitor activity-log**), or even REST (`https://docs.microsoft.com/en-us/ rest/api/monitor/`). If you look at the column **Event initiated by**, you can see that some events are logged based on an operation from the Azure infrastructure and some based on actions by a user. If you look at the Operation name, you can tell from some entries what the activity is all about. For example, **Update Azure SQL Server Encryption Protector** was an action when I enabled TDE BYOK for the server and a good example of an operation outside the scope of SQL. The operation **"deployifNotExists" Policy action** are Azure Policy compliance checks. It is common to see these coupled with operations against an Azure resource. Read more at `https://docs.microsoft.com/en-us/azure/ governance/policy/concepts/effects`.

By default, Azure activity log entries are kept for 90 days (and the roll over). If you want to keep activity log entries longer than this, you can create a Log Analytics workspace. A Log Analytics workspace also gives you more capabilities to query and visualize activity log entries. On this screen, there is an option at the top for

Diagnostic settings. This allows you to create a Log Analytics workspace and add activity log entries to it. You also have the option to send activity log entries to Event Hub for streaming. To read more about using the Activity Log in general, go to `https://docs.` `microsoft.com/en-us/azure/azure-monitor/platform/activity-log`.

Auditing Azure SQL Managed Instance

Since Azure SQL Managed Instance is very much like a full SQL Server instance, many of the familiar tools and features for auditing are available to you.

Tracking Logins

Since I can remember, almost every SQL Server version tracks failed logins in the ERRORLOG of SQL Server. A failed login looks like this in the ERRORLOG for a Managed Instance:

```
Error: 18456, Severity: 14, State: 7.
Login failed for user 'sa'. Reason: An error occurred while evaluating the
password. [CLIENT: 10.1.0.4]
```

SQL Server provides the ability to turn off this tracking or also track successful logins. That capability is not available for a Managed Instance (even though SSMS gives you the appearance it is allowed) because it requires a restart of SQL Server which you don't have access to do.

Since Azure SQL Managed Instance gives you full access to Extended Events, there are events you can use to track logins, including **process_login_finish**, **login_event**, and **login**. Extended Events for Azure SQL Managed Instance supports all events, actions, and targets. File targets must use Azure Blob Storage since you don't have access to the underlying OS file system.

SQL Server Audit

SQL Server Audit is a capability that has been in SQL Server in several releases to audit and track instance and database activity. SQL Server Audit is fully supported with Azure SQL Managed Instance with a few exceptions:

- Audit files are stored in Azure Blob Storage. Read more how to do this at `https://docs.microsoft.com/en-us/azure/azure-sql/managed-instance/auditing-configure#set-up-auditing-for-your-server-to-azure-storage`.

- The option to shut down SQL Server on an audit failure is not supported (but continue and fail options are supported).

If you have never used SQL Server Audit, look through the documentation at `https://docs.microsoft.com/en-us/sql/relational-databases/security/auditing/sql-server-audit-database-engine`.

SQL Server Audit produces files to track activity based on the Extended Event format (SQL Server Audit uses Extended Event sessions behind the scenes). Azure SQL Managed Instance also allows you to produce audit events to Azure Monitor Logs and Event Hub. The option TO EXTERNAL MONITOR has been added to the CREATE SERVER AUDIT T-SQL statement.

See an example of how to configure SQL Server Audit to Azure logs or Event Hub at `https://docs.microsoft.com/en-us/azure/azure-sql/managed-instance/auditing-configure#set-up-auditing-for-your-server-to-event-hubs-or-azure-monitor-logs`.

Auditing Azure SQL Database

Auditing activity for Azure SQL Database is provided through metrics in Dynamic Management Views (DMVs) and Azure Metrics. In addition, the SQL Server Audit capability is exposed as a feature called SQL Database auditing.

Tracking Connections

Azure SQL Database provides a DMV called **sys.event_log** that can be queried *in the context of the logical master database* of the logical server. This DMV shows information collected in 5-minute aggregate intervals for connectivity metrics. This DMV doesn't track individual successful or failed connection but rather connectivity metrics across all databases (including the logical master) for the logical server.

Examples of what you can view for this DMV include

- Number of successful connections

- Number of failed connections due to invalid login name

- Number of failed connections due to blocked firewall rule

While this information is stored across all databases, you can use Azure Metrics and Logs to capture aggregate numbers for failed connections, connections blocked by firewall rules, and successful connections.

Figure 6-20 shows how I've added the number of successful connections over the last 30 days (in 6-hour measures) to an Azure Metric chart for one of my Azure SQL databases.

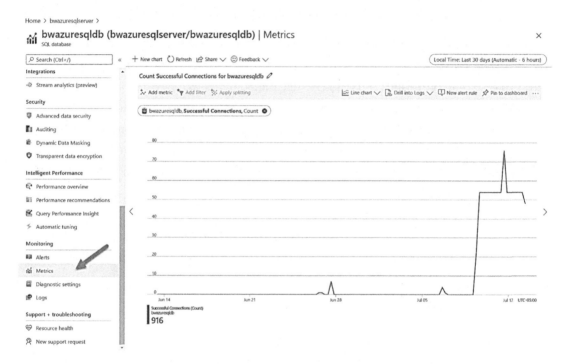

Figure 6-20. *Tracking successful connections with Azure Metrics*

SQL Database Auditing

Since you don't have access to the underlying SQL Server instance for an Azure SQL Database, you don't have access to use the T-SQL statement CREATE SERVER AUDIT to use SQL Server Audit capabilities.

Therefore, we have created interfaces *outside* of Azure SQL Database to audit database and logical server activities. We call this **SQL Database auditing**. Read the complete documentation at https://docs.microsoft.com/en-us/azure/azure-sql/database/auditing-overview. SQL Database Auditing can be enabled through the Azure portal, PowerShell (**Set-AzSqlDatabaseAudit** and **Set-AzSqlServerAudit**), az cli (**az sql db audit-policy**), and REST APIs (https://docs.microsoft.com/en-us/rest/api/sql/database%20auditing%20settings/createorupdate).

You can direct SQL Database auditing to an Azure storage account, a Log Analytics workspace, or Event Hub for streaming.

Let's look at an example of creating an audit for the logical server and direct the audit to a Storage Account **and** Log Analytics workspace (and explain why you might want to you one vs. the other or both). Auditing the logical server will audit all activities for all databases.

Note   You could also create a separate audit specific to each database, but when you audit a logical server, all activities for all databases go into that audit as well.

I started the process by navigating to my logical server **bwazuresqlserver**, selected Auditing from the Resource menu, turned on Auditing, and checked Storage Account and Log Analytics as seen in Figure 6-21.

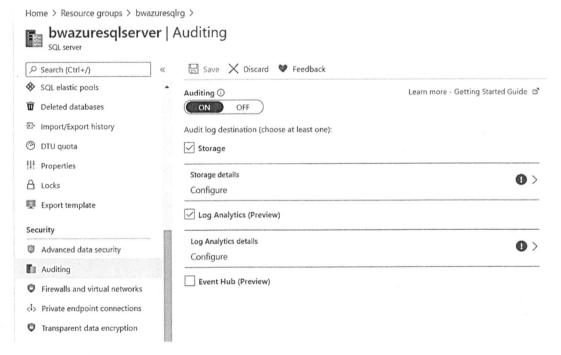

Figure 6-21. *Configuring auditing for Azure SQL Database*

To have the audits started, I need to configure the Azure Storage details and Log Analytics details.

I selected **Configure** from **Storage details** and was presented with this screen as seen in Figure 6-22 (0 days means unlimited).

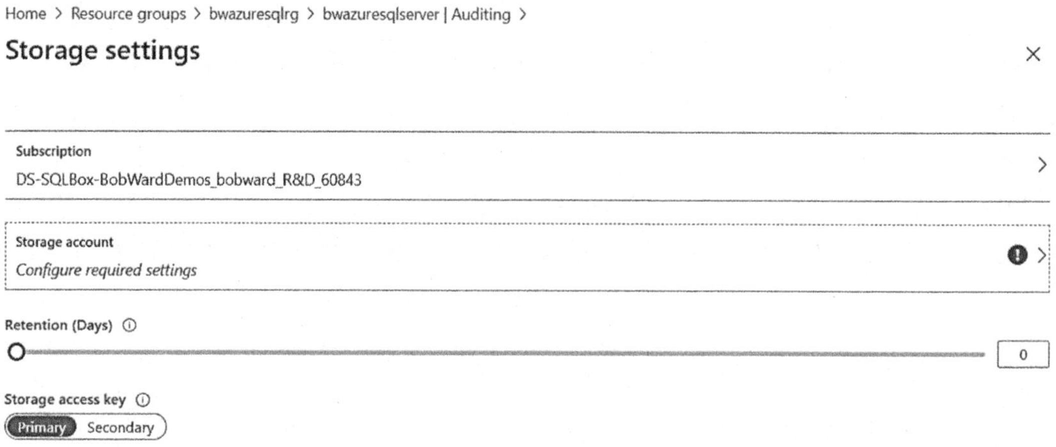

Home > Resource groups > bwazuresqlrg > bwazuresqlserver | Auditing >

Storage settings   ×

Subscription
DS-SQLBox-BobWardDemos_bobward_R&D_60843   >

Storage account
Configure required settings   ❗ >

Retention (Days) ⓘ

○━━━ [0]

Storage access key ⓘ
(**Primary** Secondary)

Figure 6-22. Configuring storage details for auditing for Azure SQL Database

Since I don't have a storage account, I selected Configure required settings and was presented with a list of storage accounts for my subscription. I chose to create a new storage account with this screen as seen in Figure 6-23.

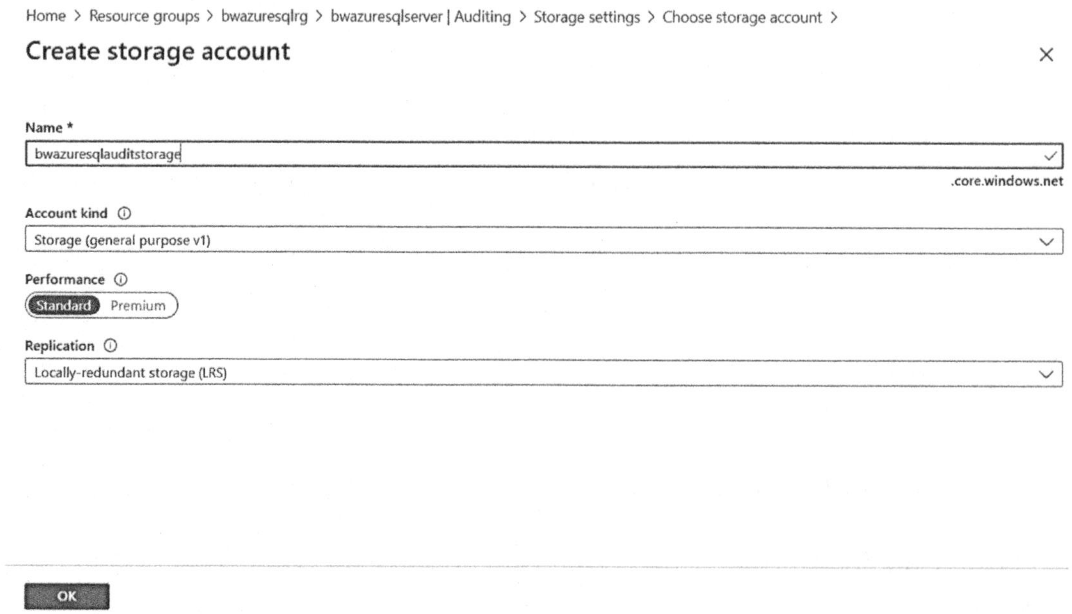

Home > Resource groups > bwazuresqlrg > bwazuresqlserver | Auditing > Storage settings > Choose storage account >

Create storage account   ×

Name *
[bwazuresqlauditstorage   ✓]
.core.windows.net

Account kind ⓘ
[Storage (general purpose v1)   ⌄]

Performance ⓘ
(**Standard** Premium)

Replication ⓘ
[Locally-redundant storage (LRS)   ⌄]

[**OK**]

Figure 6-23. Creating a new storage account for auditing for Azure SQL Database

I selected OK. The account took less than a minute to create, and now I was brought to the screen to configure Log Analytic details. I was presented with a list of existing Log Analytic workspaces, but I chose Create New Workspace and was presented with a screen like in Figure 6-24 to create the new workspace.

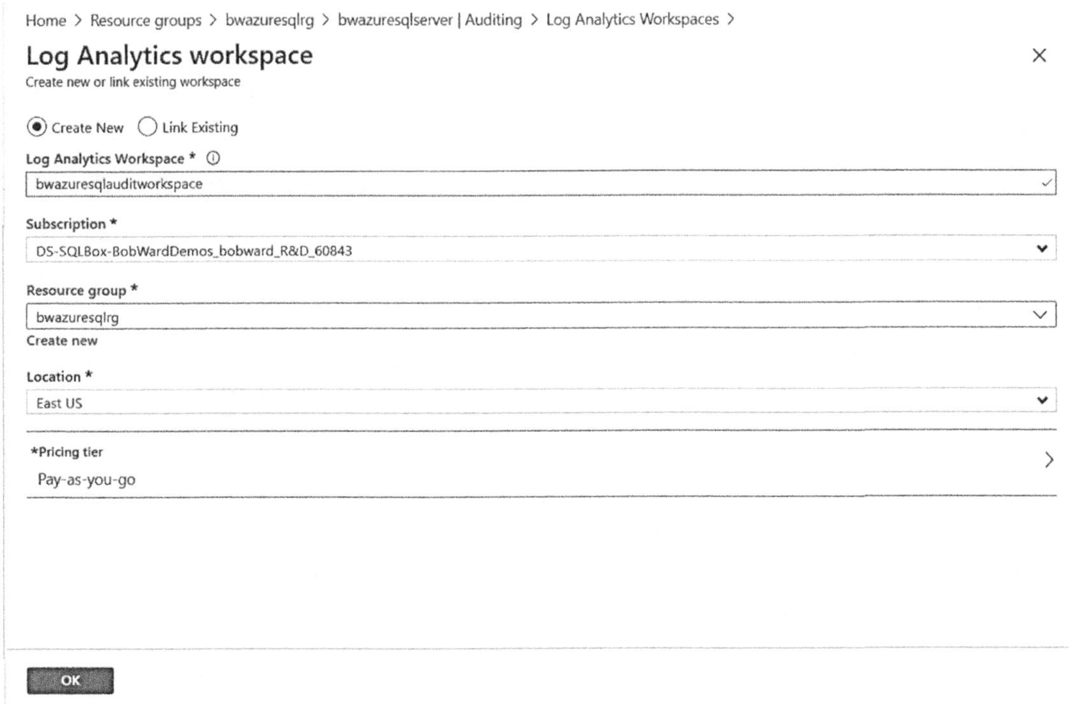

Figure 6-24. *Creating a Log Analytics workspace for auditing for Azure SQL Database*

I then clicked **Save** to save the audit configuration for Storage and Log Analytics. Once this was successful, the user interface looks odd here since it is tempting to hit Save again. Don't do that or hit the X in the right-hand corner! Just select Overview in the Resource menu of the logical server.

SQL Server Audit has a concept called an action group which defines what activities are audited. SQL Database auditing has by default the following action groups enabled:

- BATCH_COMPLETED_GROUP – Audit all successful SQL statements.

- SUCCESSFUL_DATABASE_AUTHENTICATION_GROUP – Audit a successful login to a database.

- FAILED_DATABASE_AUTHENTICATION_GROUP – Audit a failed connection to a database.

All the possible action groups to use can be found at `https://docs.microsoft.com/en-us/sql/relational-databases/security/auditing/sql-server-audit-action-groups-and-actions`. You can use the PowerShell cmdlet **Set-AzSqlDatabaseAudit** to enable other action groups.

With SQL Server, you typically can view an audit through SSMS or using the system function **sys.fn_get_audit_file**. It turns out you can do the same thing for each database as part of the logical server. Let's look at two different ways to view this audit data using the Azure portal.

I'll navigate to my database called **bwazuresqldb**, select Auditing in the Resource Menu, and View audit logs from the command bar as seen in Figure 6-25.

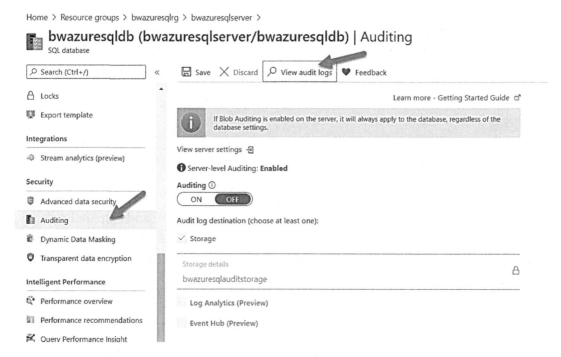

Figure 6-25. *Selecting an audit for an Azure SQL Database*

Notice on this screen Auditing is off for the database, but the information message above it says it is enabled for the server. This means auditing is also enabled for this database.

If I select View audit logs, I get a screen like in Figure 6-26.

Home > Resource groups > bwazuresqlrg > bwazuresqlserver > bwazuresqldb (bwazuresqlserver/bwazuresqldb) | Auditing >

Audit records   ×

⟳ Refresh   ▼ Filter   Log Analytics   View dashboard

ⓘ Click here to learn more about methods for viewing & analyzing audit records.

Audit source ⓘ
(Server audit   Database audit)

Showing audit records up to Mon, 13 Jul 2020 21:14:21 UTC.

Run in Query Editor ⓘ

Event time (UTC)	Principal name	Event type	Action status
7/13/2020 9:13:14 PM	thewandog	DATABASE AUTHENTICATION SUCCEEDED	Succeeded
7/13/2020 9:10:04 PM	bobward@microsoft.com	DATABASE AUTHENTICATION SUCCEEDED	Succeeded
7/13/2020 9:10:04 PM	bobward@microsoft.com	BATCH COMPLETED	Succeeded
7/13/2020 9:06:34 PM	thewandog	DATABASE AUTHENTICATION SUCCEEDED	Succeeded

Figure 6-26. *Viewing audit for Azure SQL Database*

First notice the Audit source is Server audit. This just means the source for auditing this database is from the overall server vs. just the database. You will also notice a list of audit records. These are audit records from the Azure storage option I selected earlier. Notice the option to **Run in Query Editor**. I mentioned in Chapter 2 in the book the Query Editor and said "we would not use this in the book," but there is an opportunity to peek at it. When you select this option, you will be prompted to log in to the server. You will then see a screen like Figure 6-27 after you hit the Run button.

Figure 6-27. *Using the Query Editor to view audit data*

Notice a query is automatically populated to use sys.fn_get_audit_file to read from the Azure storage account I configured for auditing and is the same result as the Audit records in the previous screen. I now will use the breadcrumbs at the top of the screen to go back to the Audit Records and view audit data for the database (I'll get prompted to discard my changes).

Let's click **View dashboard** from the command bar to see a unique way to view audit data from the Log Analytics workspace. Figure 6-28 shows a dashboard with a graph for *Azure SQL – Security Insights.*

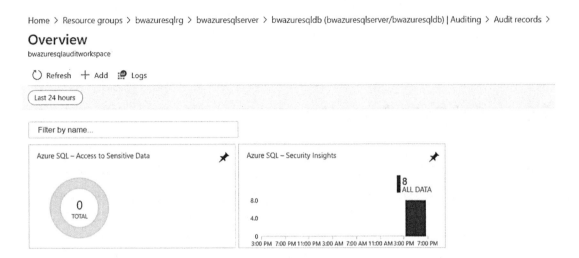

Figure 6-28. *Log Analytics dashboard for auditing for Azure SQL Database*

After I select the Azure SQL – Security Insights chart, I'm presented with a series of dashboards related to audit data for the Azure SQL Database as seen in Figure 6-29 (there is a scrollback to see more charts).

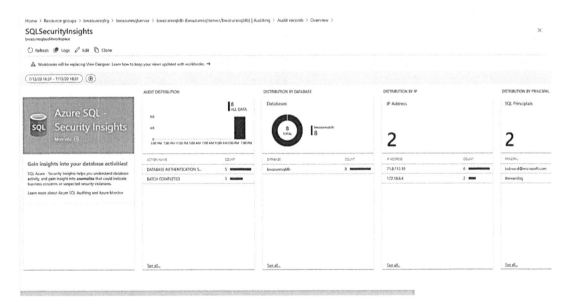

Figure 6-29. *Azure SQL – Security Insights dashboards*

I'll leave these audits active as they might help when looking at certain scenarios later in the book. Use the breadcrumbs to navigate back to the Overview of the logical server.

Advanced Data Security

Now that you have seen how to authenticate, protect your data, and audit activities to monitor security, let me show you some capabilities to go further with security with Azure SQL. We call this suite of capabilities **Advanced Data Security (ADS)**. At any point, you can read our documentation covering ADS at `https://docs.microsoft.com/en-us/azure/azure-sql/database/advanced-data-security`.

Advanced Data Security is managed and works the same with Azure SQL Managed Instance and Database. I'll use my Azure SQL Database for examples in the rest of this section of the chapter.

To use any of the features for Advanced Data Security, I'll need to enable this from the Azure portal since I did not enable ADS during deployment back in Chapter 4. Advanced Data Security is enabled at the logical server level for Azure SQL Database. I'll navigate to my logical server, **bwazuresqlserver**, select Advanced Data Security from the Resource menu, and then select a few options from the screen as seen in Figure 6-30.

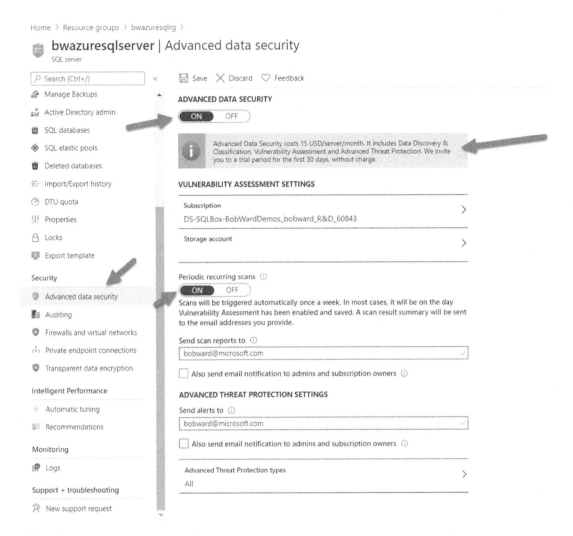

Figure 6-30. *Configuring Advanced Data Security*

There are a few things worth pointing out here on this screen. I turned Periodic recurring scans to ON. This means Vulnerability scans are done on a scheduled basis. I also added an email account to send the scanned results. I also added an email address to send Advanced Threat Protection alerts. Also notice that Advanced Data Security does not come for free included with your costs for the database. There is a trial period of no charge, but then after that, there is a small charge each month for using these services. Before saving, I selected the Storage Account for auditing **bwazuresqlauditstorage** to hold the Vulnerability results.

Notice on this screen you can configure different Advanced Threat Protection (ATP) types to track which include SQL injection, Brute Force, and others (or just use the default of All). You will learn more about ATP types later in this chapter.

Once you have configured Advanced Data Security for the logical server, you can use the Azure portal and other methods to manage and view the results for each database. Let's use the portal to see how each of the pieces of Advanced Data Security works. The first path is to select ADS from the portal from the context of a specific database as seen in Figure 6-31.

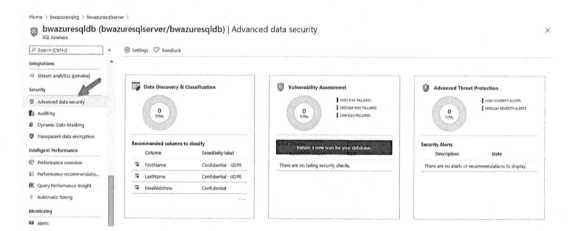

Figure 6-31. *Advanced Data Security for Azure SQL Database*

Data Classification

You may be in a situation where you need to classify and label columns for tables in your database and then audit access to these columns. One possible scenario where you need to do this is for compliance with certain regulations such as General Data Protection Regulation (GDPR).

Azure SQL and SQL Server provide a capability to label and classify your columns through T-SQL statements like ADD SENSITIVITY CLASSIFICATION. You can use T-SQL against SQL Server, Azure SQL Managed Instance, and Database. You can see how to use T-SQL for Data Classification in a workshop I built for SQL Server 2019 at `https://github.com/microsoft/sqlworkshops-sql2019workshop/blob/master/sql2019workshop/03_Security.md`.

In addition, PowerShell cmdlets exist to work with data classification for Azure SQL. See **Set-AzSqlDatabaseSensitivityClassification** and Set-**AzSqlInstanceDatabaseSensitivity** as examples. az CLI also provides interfaces for data classification such as **az sql db classification**.

Let's see how to manage Data Classifications from the Azure portal. Using the navigation from Figure 6-31, select Data Discover & Classification. You can see in Figure 6-32 a dashboard of existing classifications (which is empty) and recommendations to classify columns.

Figure 6-32. *Data Classification for Azure SQL Database*

If you click the recommendations, you will see a list of recommendations for **Information types** and **Sensitivity labels** for columns in your database as seen in Figure 6-33.

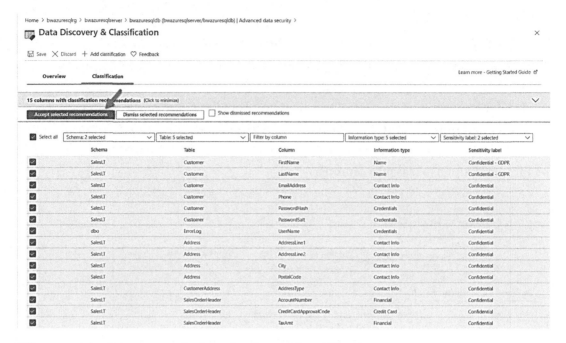

Figure 6-33. *Recommendations for Data Classification*

These recommendations for types and labels are based on the name of the columns. If you select Accept selected recommendations and then Save, you can select Overview to see a new chart of classifications as seen in Figure 6-34.

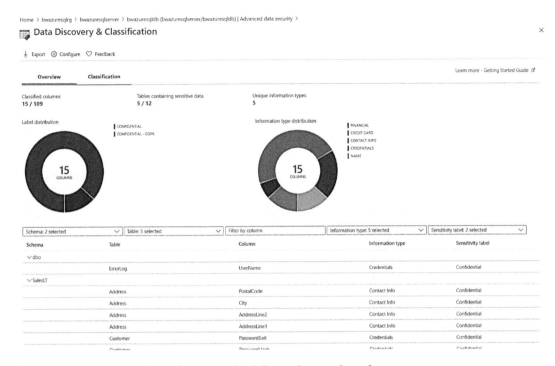

Figure 6-34. *Data classification dashboard populated*

You have several options to manage classifications at this point. If you select Classification, you can add a classification through the portal. As a developer, you can query the **sys.sensitivity_classifications** catalog view to see classification definitions. You can also use PowerShell to view classification definitions with **Get-AzSqlDatabaseS ensitivityClassification** and even recommendations with **Get-AzSqlDatabaseSensitivit yRecommendation.** Similar interfaces exist for Azure SQL Managed Instance.

If you select **Configure** as seen in Figure 6-34, you can add your own Information Types and Sensitivity Labels that can now appear as options to choose for other classifications in the portal. This is called **SQL Information Protection** policies and is only available with certain permissions in your Active Directory. Because this is considered an information protection policy for the Azure tenant, you must have administrative privileges, which I don't at Microsoft (another example of separation of duties for a corporation). You can read more about information protection policies at `https://docs.microsoft.com/en-us/azure/security-center/security-center-info-protection-policy`.

Note   When you add classifications, you can add your own information types and labels for a new column through the portal, T-SQL, and PowerShell. However, they won't show up as options to choose from a list of information types and labels unless you use information policies.

Once you have classified columns for your tables, you will likely want to audit who has accessed these columns. Since we configured auditing previously in this chapter, we should be able to see this access.

I'll use my Azure VM **bwsql2019** with SSMS to connect (with my AAD account) to the logical server and the context of the **bwazuresqldb** database. I then will use Object Explorer to find the **SalesLT.Customer** table, right-click the icon for the table, and use the Select Top 1000 rows option.

Now if I navigate back to the **bwazureqsldb** database in the Azure portal and select Auditing from the Resource menu and View audit logs from the command bar, I see a screen like Figure 6-35.

Figure 6-35. *Audit records from SQL Database Audit*

I can see there is a BATCH COMPLETED event. If I click this, I can see the query that was run for the Object Explorer option and I see SENSITIVITY INFORMATION was audited as part of the query like Figure 6-36.

Figure 6-36. *An audit record showing sensitivity information access*

If I now use breadcrumbs to get back to Audit Records, I can choose View Dashboard. You will now see like in Figure 6-37 a populated graph showing Access to Sensitive Data.

Figure 6-37. *Log analytics dashboard showing access to sensitive data*

You can click this graph to drill into the details. I can now drill into several dashboards showing more access to sensitive data like Figure 6-38.

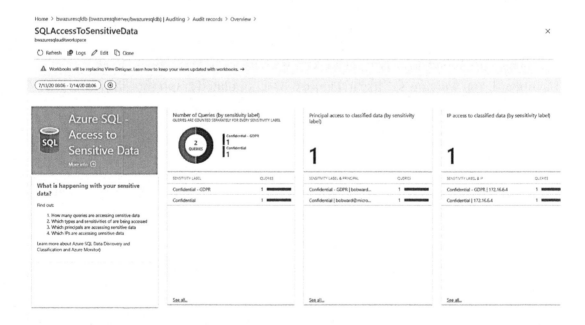

Figure 6-38. *Access to sensitive data audit dashboard*

Note   Data classification functionality is included in SSMS and works against SQL Server 2019 and Managed Instance (but not Azure SQL Database). This functionality existed in SQL Server 2017 but used a different approach. If SSMS is pointed to a SQL Server 2019 or Managed Instance, it uses T-SQL interfaces. Any modifications to Data Classification through SSMS will show up in the Azure portal for Managed Instance and likewise in SSMS.

For a complete review of Data Classification, look through the documentation at `https://docs.microsoft.com/en-us/azure/azure-sql/database/data-discovery-and-classification-overview`.

You can now use the breadcrumbs at the top to navigate back to the overview of your database.

Vulnerability Assessment

Another aspect to securing your data is to proactively monitor and check for any known security vulnerabilities. But what are known vulnerabilities? Azure SQL has a knowledge base of rules we have built (based on an industry standard from `www.cisecurity.org/cis-benchmarks/`) to scan your Azure SQL Manage Instances and Databases for configurations that might be considered vulnerable. I like to think of a vulnerability assessment like a virus checker which uses a *scan* method to look for possible issues.

The best way to see what I mean by this is to see it in action. Let's navigate back to the database **bwazuresqldb** and select Advanced Data Security from the Resource menu. This shows the Advanced Data Security dashboard for Data Classification, Vulnerability Assessment, and Advanced Threat Protection. Click the Vulnerability Assessment dashboard. You should see results like Figure 6-39.

Figure 6-39. *A scanned vulnerability assessment for Azure SQL Database*

From the command bar, you can initiate a scan on-demand (remember when we configured Advanced Data Security, we set up for periodic scans which is once a week) or click Scan if you don't see results immediately. A scan is very lightweight, typically only takes a few seconds, and is completely a read-only operation. You can also from the command bar export results to a .csv file and go back and look at the history of previous scans.

You can see in the results of the scan that we categorize **Findings** as High Risk, Medium, and Low Risk. You can also see there is an option to look at **Passed** results, which are checks we make that we determine are *good* on your deployment (at least for this scan).

Let's look at one of these rules that have fired to see how you can use Vulnerability Assessments in an effective way.

First, click the High Risk rule that describes a scenario for firewall rules. You can see from Figure 6-40 a description of the condition detected to fire this rule and the possible impact to security.

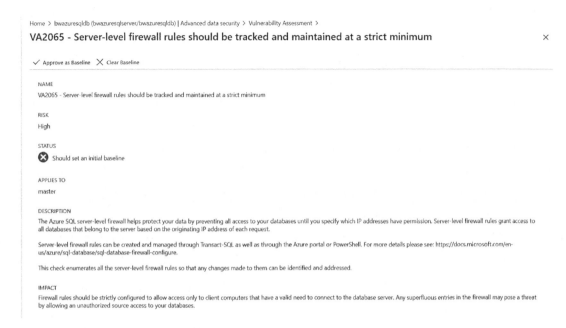

Figure 6-40. *A high risk vulnerability detected for Azure SQL Database*

If you scroll down, you can find out how we detected this condition and how you can remediate it as seen in Figure 6-41.

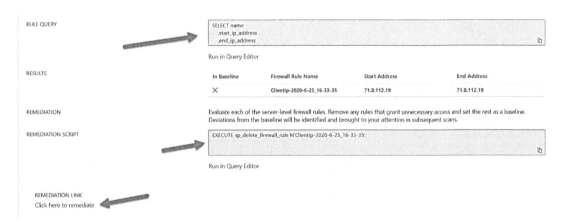

Figure 6-41. *Details of high risk rule from Vulnerability Assessment*

This page shows you the query we use to detect the rule and remediation steps both with T-SQL and a link that will allow you to change this in the Azure portal. Once you make the remediation, the fired rule will move to the Passed category. Since we have private link configured for this logical server, it may make sense to remove this firewall rule. If you later added the firewall back after a scan, the subsequent scan would pick it back up again.

Note   The existence of a firewall rule doesn't mean you will be open to widespread hacking. As I've started earlier in this chapter, it is not the most secure way to allow connections to your server.

Let's say you are OK with the firewall rule and don't want any scans to flag this as a high-risk problem. You can use the option on the command bar for the rule to **Approve as Baseline**. When you do that, this rule will never fire unless you clear the baseline. You can apply a baseline to any rule that is fired.

When I configured Advanced Data Security, I also set up my email account to send details of any scheduled scans. Figure 6-42 shows an example of the body of an email I received showing a summary of scans across all databases for my logical server.

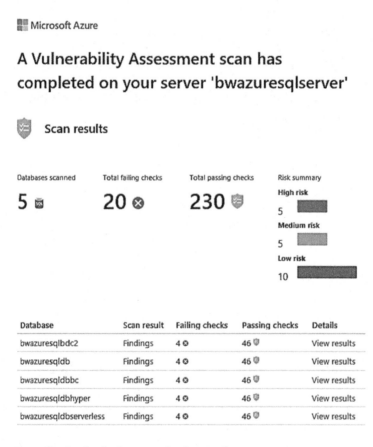

Figure 6-42. *Email of schedule scan for logical server*

You can also use PowerShell (e.g., **Get-AzSqlDatabaseVulnerabilityAssessment ScanRecord**) to show and manage Vulnerability Assessments.

Note   SSMS provides a feature to run a Vulnerability Assessment. It works against both Managed Instances and Database and has similar rules, but the tool is not integrated or tied into Azure portal or PowerShell.

You can learn more about Vulnerability Assessments at `https://docs.microsoft.com/en-us/azure/azure-sql/database/sql-vulnerability-assessment`.

Advanced Threat Protection (ATP)

The last component of Advanced Data Security is **Advanced Threat Protection** (ATP). I mentioned the history behind ATP in Chapter 1 of the book. ATP is a service run in Azure that is designed to detect potential harmful attacks, access, or exploits to Managed Instance or Database.

ATP uses Extended Events and Machine Learning technology to detect and alert you to certain types of suspicious activities. An example of a suspicious activity is code designed for a *SQL injection*. You can read all the various rules and alerts detected by ATP at `https://docs.microsoft.com/en-us/azure/security-center/alerts-reference#alerts-sql-db-and-warehouse`.

While we don't document the details of how we detect all rules, I can show you how to simulate a SQL injection using SSMS to see an alert fire.

Using my Azure VM **bwsql2019** with SSMS, I'll create a new query connection using SSMS but used the Additional Connection Parameters of SSMS (from the Options button) to put in this string:

```
Application Name=webappname
```

I also used the Connect to database to connect to the **bwazuresqldb** database. In the query editor window, I put in this query and executed it:

```
SELECT * FROM SalesLT.Customer WHERE CustomerID like '' or 1 = 1 --' and
family = 'test1';
```

Note   We filter out SSMS as an application because no one sends in injections from a tool like SSMS. Therefore, I used a different application name to simulate a real application sending a query that looks like it could be a SQL injection attack.

Within a matter of seconds, the Advanced Data Security dashboard showed a Security Alert. I selected Advanced Threat Protection and saw a chart like Figure 6-43.

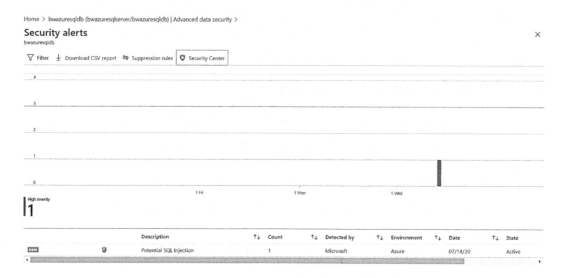

Figure 6-43. *A SQL injection detected by Advanced Threat Protection*

SQL injection is an interesting security topic and we have documentation at https://docs.microsoft.com/en-us/sql/relational-databases/security/sql-injection to explain it and why the query pattern I used was detected as an injection.

Just like a Vulnerability Scan, I received an email after this alert showed up on my dashboard for the threat. The email body looks like Figure 6-44.

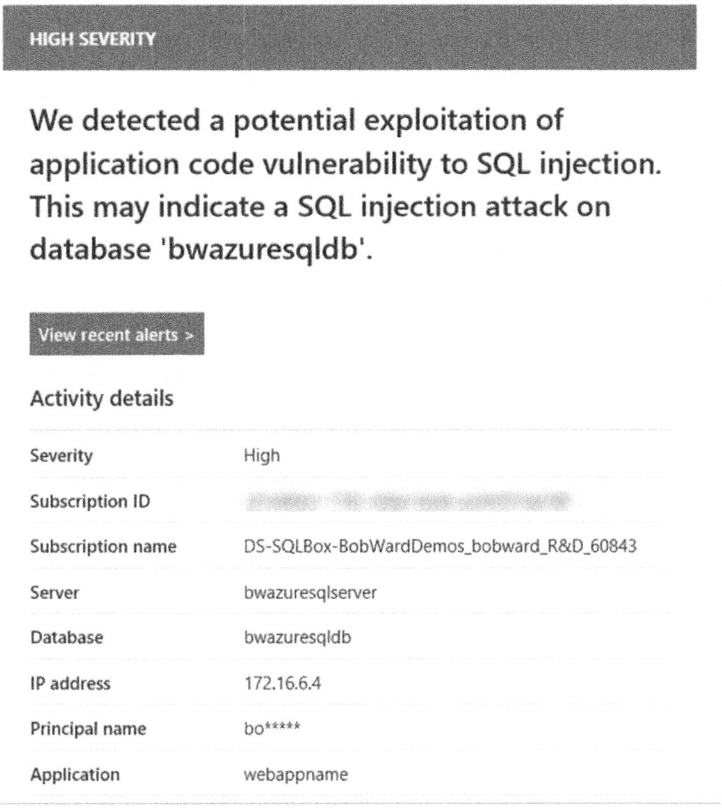

HIGH SEVERITY

We detected a potential exploitation of application code vulnerability to SQL injection. This may indicate a SQL injection attack on database 'bwazuresqldb'.

View recent alerts >

Activity details

Severity	High
Subscription ID	
Subscription name	DS-SQLBox-BobWardDemos_bobward_R&D_60843
Server	bwazuresqlserver
Database	bwazuresqldb
IP address	172.16.6.4
Principal name	bo*****
Application	webappname

Figure 6-44. Email for security alert from Advanced Threat Protection

You can see on the dashboard screen you have an option to download a report as a .csv file or create rules to suppress certain types of alerts.

ATP also has interfaces for PowerShell (e.g., **Set-AzSqlDatabaseThreatDetection Policy**) and az CLI (e.g., **az sql db threat-policy**).

Advanced Threat Protection (ATP) is one of the signature capabilities that is unique to Azure. ATP works for Managed Instance and Azure SQL Database and at the time of the writing of this book was in preview for Azure Virtual Machine.

Azure Security Center

Among the benefits of deploying your resources in Azure are services that work across all your resources. **Azure Security Center** (ASC) is a security management system that works within the Azure ecosystem across all your Azure assets. You can read the full story of the Azure Security Center at `https://docs.microsoft.com/en-us/azure/security-center/`.

Every Azure subscription gets the Free tier of the Azure Security Center which covers resources like Virtual Machines. You can pay a monthly subscription fee for the Standard tier. The standard tier will include integration into assets like Azure SQL and more. You can compare the features of Free vs. Standard tier at `https://azure.microsoft.com/en-us/pricing/details/security-center/`.

There are a few ways you can access ASC with Azure SQL. One is from an icon on your home page of your Azure portal. The other way you saw in Figure 6-43 is Advanced Threat Protection at the command bar.

If you select Security Center from there, you will be brought to an overview screen like in Figure 6-45 for Policy & compliance, Security hygiene, and Threat protection across **all** Azure resources in your subscription.

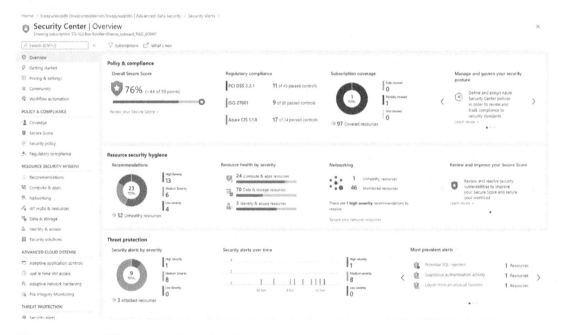

Figure 6-45. *The Azure Security Center*

You can see in the Threat protection section information about threats detected by ATP for Azure SQL. The Azure Security Center is truly one of the most innovative services in Azure and is well worth your time and investment to use across all your Azure resources.

Summary

In this chapter, you learned how Azure SQL security is just like SQL Server in many ways. You learned how to secure your network and authenticate logins and users including with Azure Active Directory. You learned how to protect your data with various encryption techniques. You learned all the audit capabilities you can use outside and in Azure SQL. Furthermore, you learned to go further with the cloud using Advanced Data Security.

I believe Azure SQL Security has the capabilities for any enterprise. Security is something baked into our engineering teams. As Andrea Wolter, Senior Program Manager in our security team, tells it, "Trust is the most fundamental design principle for Azure SQL. From early design on, every feature is scrutinized by security reviews and on an ongoing regular basis. And this is more than plainly implementing the Security Development Lifecycle (SDL). We continuously test our services and infrastructure in so-called wargame exercises and the results are shared with the teams to keep improving our security posture against potential attack vectors even before they could get used."

You have learned in this book that the speed of the cloud helps us innovate and adapt quickly. Security is always part of that innovation. According to Joachim Hammer, Principal Group PM Manager for Security, "We continue to invest in a three-pronged approach to ensure Azure SQL meets the most stringent security requirements as well as regulatory compliances in the industry. These areas include State-of-the-art, built-in Security Controls, Trust and Compliance, and Threat detection and assessment."

In the next section, we will explore and dive deep into the second major aspect to the core of Azure SQL: performance.

CHAPTER 7

Monitoring and Tuning Performance for Azure SQL

You now have seen how to secure your Azure SQL deployment. Another aspect to ensure you have the best possible database for your application is understanding how to monitor and tune performance. If you know SQL Server, here is some good news. The engine that powers Azure SQL is the same one for SQL Server! This means that just about any performance capability you need exists for Azure SQL. It also means that many of the same tasks and skills you use for SQL Server apply to Azure SQL. In this chapter, we will explore all the capabilities and tasks you normally use to monitor and tune performance for a SQL Server and compare it with Azure SQL.

This chapter will contain examples for you to try out and use as you read along. For you to try out any of the techniques, commands, or examples I use in this chapter, you will need

- An Azure subscription.

- A minimum of Contributor role access to the Azure subscription. You can read more about Azure built-in roles at `https://docs.microsoft.com/en-us/azure/role-based-access-control/built-in-roles`.

- Access to the Azure Portal (web or Windows application).

- A deployment of an Azure SQL Managed Instance and/or an Azure SQL Database as I did in Chapter 4. The Azure SQL Database I deployed uses the AdventureWorks sample which will be required to use some of the examples.

© Bob Ward 2021
B. Ward, *Azure SQL Revealed*, https://doi.org/10.1007/978-1-4842-5931-3_7

- To connect to Managed Instance, you will need a *jumpbox* or virtual machine in Azure to connect. I showed you how to do this in Chapter 4 of the book. One simple way to do this is to create a new Azure Virtual Machine and deploy it to the same virtual network as the Managed Instance (you will use a different subnet than the Managed Instance).

- To connect to Azure SQL Database, I'm going to use the Azure VM I deployed in Chapter 3, called **bwsql2019**, and configured for a private endpoint in Chapter 6 (you could use another method as long as you can connect to the Azure SQL Database).

- Installation of the **az** CLI (see `https://docs.microsoft.com/en-us/cli/azure/install-azure-cli?view=azure-cli-latest` for more details). You can also use the Azure Cloud Shell instead since az is already installed. You can read more about the Azure Cloud Shell at `https://azure.microsoft.com/en-us/features/cloud-shell/`.

- You will run some T-SQL in this chapter, so install a tool like SQL Server Management Studio (SSMS) at `https://docs.microsoft.com/en-us/sql/ssms/download-sql-server-management-studio-ssms?view=sql-server-ver15`. You can also use Azure Data Studio at `https://docs.microsoft.com/en-us/sql/azure-data-studio/download-azure-data-studio?view=sql-server-ver15`. I installed both SSMS and ADS in the bwsql2019 Azure Virtual Machine.

- For this chapter, I have script files you can use for several of the examples. You can find these scripts in the **ch7_performance** folder for the source files included for the book. I will also use the very popular tool ostress.exe for exercises in this chapter which comes with the RML Utilities. You can download RML from `www.microsoft.com/en-us/download/details.aspx?id=4511`. Make sure to put the folder where RML gets installed in your system path (which is by default C:\Program Files\Microsoft Corporation\RMLUtils).

Performance Capabilities

Since the engine that powers Azure SQL is the same as SQL Server, just about any performance capability is available to you. Having said that, I feel it is important to cover a few important areas that are similar and different that can affect your ability to ensure maximum performance for your Azure SQL deployment. This includes maximum capacities, indexes, In-Memory OLTP, Partitions, SQL Server 2019 performance enhancements, and new Azure SQL Intelligent performance capabilities.

Max Capacities

When you choose a platform to install SQL Server, you typically *size* the resources you need. In many cases, you plot out the maximum capacities you will need for resources such as CPU, memory, and disk space. You may also ensure you have the correct performance capabilities for I/O with regard to IOPS and latency.

In Chapters 4 and 5 of the book, I showed you all the options to choose, deploy, and configure your Azure SQL Managed Instance and Azure SQL Database deployments. To ensure you have the performance, you need keep these capacities in mind with Azure SQL:

- Azure SQL Managed Instance can support *up to* 80 vCores, ~400Gb of memory, and a maximum storage of 8TB. The Business Critical tier is limited to 4TB because that is the current maximum size we can store on the local SSD drives of the nodes that host Managed Instance.

- Azure SQL Database can support up to 128 vCores, ~4TB Memory, and a 4TB database using the M-Series.

- The Hyperscale deployment option for Azure SQL Database can support up to 100TB database and unlimited transaction log space.

- Your decision on deployment options such as number of vCores greatly affects other resource capacities whether it is a Managed Instance or Database deployment. For example, the number of vCores for a General Purpose Azure SQL Database affects the maximum memory, maximum database size, maximum transaction log size, and maximum log rate, among others.

Let's stop here to help you get oriented. How can you see a chart or table to figure out the limits for all these choices?

For a Managed Instance, go to this documentation page: `https://docs.microsoft.com/en-us/azure/azure-sql/managed-instance/resource-limits#service-tier-characteristics`.

Figure 7-1 shows an example of the table that describes the resource limits (this may be hard to read, but I wanted to squeeze as much as I could in a screenshot).

Feature	General Purpose	Business Critical
Number of vCores*	Gen4: 8, 16, 24 Gen5: 4, 8, 16, 24, 32, 40, 64, 80	Gen4: 8, 16, 24 Gen5: 4, 8, 16, 24, 32, 40, 64, 80 *Same number of vCores is dedicated for read-only queries.
Max memory	Gen4: 56 GB - 168 GB (7GB/vCore) Gen5: 20.4 GB - 408 GB (5.1GB/vCore) Add more vCores to get more memory.	Gen4: 56 GB - 168 GB (7GB/vCore) Gen5: 20.4 GB - 408 GB (5.1GB/vCore) for read-write queries + additional 20.4 GB - 408 GB (5.1GB/vCore) for read-only queries. Add more vCores to get more memory.
Max instance storage size (reserved)	- 2 TB for 4 vCores (Gen5 only) - 8 TB for other sizes	Gen4: 1 TB Gen5: - 1 TB for 4, 8, 16 vCores - 2 TB for 24 vCores - 4 TB for 32, 40, 64, 80 vCores
Max database size	Up to currently available instance size (max 2 TB - 8 TB depending on the number of vCores).	Up to currently available instance size (max 1 TB - 4 TB depending on the number of vCores).
Max tempDB size	Limited to 24 GB/vCore (96 - 1,920 GB) and currently available instance storage size. Add more vCores to get more TempDB space. Log file size is limited to 120 GB.	Up to currently available instance storage size.
Max number of databases per instance	100, unless the instance storage size limit has been reached.	100, unless the instance storage size limit has been reached.
Max number of database files per instance	Up to 280, unless the instance storage size or Azure Premium Disk storage allocation space limit has been reached.	32,767 files per database, unless the instance storage size limit has been reached.
Max data file size	Limited to currently available instance storage size (max 2 TB - 8 TB) and Azure Premium Disk storage allocation space.	Limited to currently available instance storage size (up to 1 TB - 4 TB).
Max log file size	Limited to 2 TB and currently available instance storage size.	Limited to 2 TB and currently available instance storage size.
Data/Log IOPS (approximate)	Up to 30-40 K IOPS per instance*, 500 - 7500 per file *Increase file size to get more IOPS	10 K - 200 K (2500 IOPS/vCore) Add more vCores to get better IO performance.
Log write throughput limit (per instance)	3 MB/s per vCore Max 22 MB/s	4 MB/s per vCore Max 48 MB/s
Data throughput (approximate)	100 - 250 MB/s per file *Increase the file size to get better IO performance	Not limited.
Storage IO latency (approximate)	5-10 ms	1-2 ms
In-memory OLTP	Not supported	Available, size depends on number of vCore
Max sessions	30000	30000

Figure 7-1. *Resource capacities and limits for Azure SQL Managed Instance*

What about Azure SQL Database? You can view a table for capacities and limits based on vCores at `https://docs.microsoft.com/en-us/azure/azure-sql/database/resource-limits-vcore-single-databases` like in Figure 7-2.

General purpose - serverless compute - Gen5

The serverless compute tier is currently available on Gen5 hardware only.

Gen5 compute generation (part 1)

Compute size (service objective)	GP_S_Gen5_1	GP_S_Gen5_2	GP_S_Gen5_4	GP_S_Gen5_6	GP_S_Gen5_8
Compute generation	Gen5	Gen5	Gen5	Gen5	Gen5
Min-max vCores	0.5-1	0.5-2	0.5-4	0.75-6	1.0-8
Min-max memory (GB)	2.02-3	2.05-6	2.10-12	2.25-18	3.00-24
Min-max auto-pause delay (minutes)	60-10080	60-10080	60-10080	60-10080	60-10080
Columnstore support	Yes	Yes	Yes	Yes	Yes
In-memory OLTP storage (GB)	N/A	N/A	N/A	N/A	N/A
Max data size (GB)	512	1024	1024	1024	1536
Max log size (GB)	154	307	307	307	461
TempDB max data size (GB)	32	64	128	192	256
Storage type	Remote SSD	Remote SSD	Remote SSD	Remote SSD	Remote SSD
IO latency (approximate)	5-7 ms (write) 5-10 ms (read)	5-7 ms (write) 5-10 ms (read)	5-7 ms (write) 5-10 ms (read)	5-7 ms (write) 5-10 ms (read)	5-7 ms (write) 5-10 ms (read)
Max data IOPS *	320	640	1280	1920	2560
Max log rate (MBps)	3.8	7.5	15	22.5	30
Max concurrent workers (requests)	75	150	300	450	600
Max concurrent sessions	30,000	30,000	30,000	30,000	30,000
Number of replicas	1	1	1	1	1
Multi-AZ	N/A	N/A	N/A	N/A	N/A

Is this page helpful?
👍 Yes 👎 No

In this article

General purpose - serverless compute - Gen5
Hyperscale - provisioned compute - Gen4
Hyperscale - provisioned compute - Gen5
General purpose - provisioned compute - Gen4
General purpose - provisioned compute - Gen5
General purpose - provisioned compute - Fsv2-series
Business critical - provisioned compute - Gen4
Business critical - provisioned compute - Gen5
Business critical - provisioned compute - M-series
Next steps

Figure 7-2. *Resource capacities and limits for Azure SQL Database*

The default table is the first choice which is a Serverless compute tier. You can see on the right-hand side of this figure you can choose different deployment options to see what the capacity and limits for different options. Bookmark these documentation links. I use them all the time. It is possible these limits will change over time as we evolve the capabilities of Azure SQL services.

Keep in mind that some limits like memory are enforced by Windows Job Objects. I mentioned this implementation in Chapter 4 of the book. Use the DMV **sys.dm_os_job_object** to see the true limits for memory and other resources for your deployment.

> **Tip**   I'm a developer at heart, so I wanted a way to find out these capacities and
> limits without looking at a table. The best method I could find is REST APIs. An
> example is in our documentation at `https://docs.microsoft.com/en-us/`
> `rest/api/sql/capabilities/listbylocation`. Once you deploy, you get to
> see your resource limits with DMVs like **sys.dm_user_db_resource_governance**.

What if you make the wrong choice and need more capacity? The good news is that
you can make changes for Azure SQL Managed Instance and Database to get more (or
less) without any database migration required. You will see an example of this later in
this chapter. Just remember that a change for Managed Instance can take a significant
amount of time.

> **Note**   There are two exceptions to this statement about migration. First, you
> cannot switch between Azure SQL Database and Azure SQL Managed Instance.
> Second, if you deploy or switch to the Hyperscale service tier, you cannot switch
> back.

Indexes

Anyone who works with SQL Server knows that without proper indexes, it is difficult to
obtain the query performance you need.

Every type of index option you can use in SQL Server is available to you with Azure
SQL, including clustered, non-clustered, online, and resumable indexes. You can read
an index primer at `https://docs.microsoft.com/en-us/sql/relational-databases/`
`indexes/clustered-and-nonclustered-indexes-described?view=sql-server-ver15`
and details on online indexes at `https://docs.microsoft.com/en-us/sql/relational-`
`databases/indexes/perform-index-operations-online`. Resumable online indexes
are a recent capability. You can read more at `https://azure.microsoft.com/en-us/`
`blog/modernize-index-maintenance-with-resumable-online-index-rebuild/`.

Columnstore indexes are nothing short of amazing. I continue to see customers
who just don't take advantage of this capability. Columnstore index can accelerate read
query performance by 100x for the right workload. Columnstore indexes are supported
in every deployment option you choose with Azure SQL. One myth about columnstore is

that it is *only* an in-memory technology. The truth is that columnstore indexes perform best when they fit in memory and use compression so more will fit in your memory limits. However, a columnstore index does not have to all fit in memory. To get a start on columnstore indexes, see the documentation at `https://docs.microsoft.com/en-us/sql/relational-databases/indexes/columnstore-indexes-overview`.

In-Memory OLTP

In SQL Server 2014 (and greatly enhanced in SQL Server 2016), we introduced a revolutionary capability for high-speed transactions called In-Memory OLTP (code name Hekaton). In-Memory OLTP is available for Azure SQL Managed Instance and Databases if you choose the Business Critical service tier.

Memory-optimized tables are the mechanism to use In-Memory OLTP. Memory-optimized tables are truly *in-memory* as they must completely fit in memory. The memory available for store memory-optimized tables is a subset of the memory limits of your Business Critical service tier. The number of vCores for your deployment determines what percentage of memory is available for memory-optimized tables.

Note   Memory-optimized tables require a memory-optimized filegroup. Azure SQL creates this filegroup for any databases even if it is not a Business Critical (BC) service tier. This way, if you move to BC, the filegroup is set up for memory-optimized tables.

New to In-Memory OLTP? Start with our documentation at `https://docs.microsoft.com/en-us/sql/relational-databases/in-memory-oltp/overview-and-usage-scenarios`.

Partitions

Partitions are often used with SQL Server for tables with many rows to improve performance by sub-dividing data by a column in the table. Consider these points for partitions and Azure SQL:

- Partitions are supported for Azure SQL Database and Managed Instance.

- You can only use filegroups with partitions with Azure SQL Managed Instance (remember, Azure SQL Database only has a primary partition, while Managed Instance supported user-defined filegroups).

Need a primer for partitions? Start with this documentation page: `https://docs.microsoft.com/en-us/sql/relational-databases/partitions/partitioned-tables-and-indexes?view=sql-server-ver15`.

Note   There are some interesting partitioning techniques with Azure SQL Database not associated with SQL partitions you may want to look at as a developer. Read more at `https://docs.microsoft.com/en-us/azure/architecture/best-practices/data-partitioning-strategies#partitioning-azure-sql-database`.

SQL Server 2019 Enhancements

SQL Server 2019 was a monumental release including several new capabilities. Performance was an area of major investment for SQL Server 2019. Because Azure SQL is *versionless*, almost all the performance enhancements for SQL Server 2019 are part of Azure SQL including built-in engine features like **Intelligent Query Processing**. The one exception is Tempdb Metadata Optimization. We first built this feature in SQL Server 2019 and have yet to integrate this into Azure SQL. But rest assured, we are working on either baking this into Azure SQL as a default or providing an option to enable it.

Note   It is important to know that some "hidden gem" capabilities like merry-go-round scans and buffer pool ramp-up are all used behind the scenes for all editions of Azure SQL.

Intelligent Performance

Over the past few releases of SQL Server, we have been striving to provide built-in capabilities to enhance performance without you making application changes. Our goal is to use data and automation to make smart decision to make your queries run faster.

We call this *Intelligent Performance*. These capabilities exist in Azure SQL, but we go further in the cloud. We use the power of the cloud to offer even more. You learn more details about Intelligent Performance for Azure SQL in the final section of this chapter.

Configuring and Maintaining for Performance

In Chapter 5 of this book, I described many of the options to configure an Azure SQL Managed Instance and Database. There are some configuration options that can affect performance worth diving deeper into. This includes the Tempdb database, configuring database options, files and filegroups, max degree of parallelism, and Resource Governor. In addition, it is worth reviewing the various tasks you would go through to maintain indexes and statistics for database for Azure SQL as compared to SQL Server.

Tempdb

The Tempdb database is an important shared resource used by applications. Ensuring the right configuration of tempdb can affect your ability to deliver consistent performance. Tempdb is used the same with Azure SQL like SQL Server, but your ability to configure tempdb is different, including placement of files, the number and size of files, tempdb size, and tempdb configuration options.

In Azure SQL, Tempdb files are always automatically stored on local SSD drives, so I/O performance shouldn't be an issue.

SQL Server professionals often use more than one database file to partition allocations for tempdb tables. For Azure SQL Database, the number of files is scaled with the number of vCores (e.g., 2 vCores = 4 files, etc.) with a max of 16. The number of files is not configurable through T-SQL against tempdb but by *changing the deployment option*. The maximum size of the tempdb database is scaled per number of vCores.

You get 12 files with Azure SQL Managed Instance independent of vCores, and you cannot change this number. We are looking in the future to allow configuration of the number of files for Azure SQL Managed Instance.

Tempdb database option MIXED_PAGE_ALLOCATION is set to OFF and AUTOGROW_ALL_FILES is set to ON. This cannot be configured, but they are the recommended defaults as with SQL Server.

Currently, the Tempdb Metadata Optimization feature in SQL Server 2019, which can alleviate heavy latch contention, is not available in Azure SQL but is planned for the future.

Database Configuration

As I described in Chapter 5, just about every database configuration option is available to you with Azure SQL as it is with SQL Server through ALTER DATABASE and ALTER DATABASE SCOPED configuration. Consult the documentation at `https://docs.microsoft.com/en-us/sql/t-sql/statements/alter-database-transact-sql` and `https://docs.microsoft.com/en-us/sql/t-sql/statements/alter-database-scoped-configuration-transact-sql`. You will see later in this chapter there are new options specific to Azure SQL from ALTER DATABASE.

For performance, one database option that is not available to change is the *recovery model* of the database. The default is full recovery and cannot be modified. This ensures your database can meet Azure service-level agreements (SLAs). Therefore, minimal logging for bulk operations is not supported. Minimal logging for bulk operations is supported for tempdb.

Files and Filegroups

SQL Server professionals often use files and filegroups to improve I/O performance through physical file placement. Azure SQL does not allow users to place files on specific disk systems. However, Azure SQL has resource commitments for I/O performance with regard to rates, IOPS, and latencies, so abstracting the user from physical file placement can be a benefit.

Azure SQL Database only has one database file (Hyperscale may have several), and the size is configured through Azure interfaces. There is no functionality to create additional files, but again you don't need to worry about this given IOPS and I/O latency commitments.

Note   Hyperscale has a unique architecture and may create one or more files upon initial deployment depending on your vCore choice. For example, for an 8 vCore deployment, I've seen Hyperscale create multiple files totaling 40Gb. This implementation may change, and you shouldn't rely on it. Hyperscale simply creates the files and size it needs to meet your requirements.

Azure SQL Managed Instance supports adding database files and configuring sizes but not physical placement of files. The number of files and file sizes for Azure SQL Managed Instance can be used to improve I/O performance. I will discuss more of the details on how this works later in this chapter. In addition, user-defined filegroups are supported for Azure SQL Managed Instance for manageability purposes such as use with partitions and using commands like DBCC CHECKFILEGROUP.

Max Degree of Parallelism

Max degree of parallelism (MAXDOP), which can affect the performance of individual queries, works the same in the engine for Azure SQL as SQL Server. The ability to configure MAXDOP may be important to delivering consistent performance in Azure SQL. You can configure MAXDOP in Azure SQL like SQL Server using the following techniques:

- ALTER DATABASE SCOPED CONFIGURATION to configure MAXDOP is supported for Azure SQL.

- sp_configure for "max degree of parallelism" is supported for Managed Instance.

- MAXDOP query hints are fully supported.

- Configuring MAXDOP with Resource Governor is supported for Managed Instance.

Read more about MAXDOP at https://docs.microsoft.com/en-us/sql/database-engine/configure-windows/configure-the-max-degree-of-parallelism-server-configuration-option?view=sql-server-ver15.

Resource Governor

Resource Governor is a feature in SQL Server that can be used to control resource usage for workloads through I/O, CPU, and memory. While Resource Governor is used behind the scenes for Azure SQL Database, it is only supported for Azure SQL Managed Instance for user-defined workload groups and pools. If you would like to use Resource Governor in Azure SQL Managed Instance, consult our documentation at https://docs.microsoft.com/en-us/sql/relational-databases/resource-governor/resource-governor.

Maintaining Indexes

Unfortunately, indexes for SQL don't just maintain themselves, and they do occasionally need maintenance. In fairness, index maintenance (specifically rebuild or reorganization) does not have a single answer. I've seen many customers perform too often a rebuild or reorganization when it is not necessary. Likewise, there can be many times where these operations can help performance. You might consider looking at our documentation on index fragmentation as one reason why index maintenance can make sense: `https://docs.microsoft.com/en-us/sql/relational-databases/indexes/reorganize-and-rebuild-indexes`.

Note   I'm not telling the complete truth. For Azure SQL, there is a solution here that can help with decisions on building or dropping indexes. But I won't get too far ahead. The tale of that story is at the end of the chapter.

Indexes for SQL Server occasionally need to be reorganized and sometimes rebuilt. Azure SQL supports all the options you have for SQL Server to reorganize and rebuild indexes including online and resumable indexes.

Online and resumable index operations can be extremely important to maintain maximum application availability. Read all about these capabilities at `https://docs.microsoft.com/en-us/sql/relational-databases/indexes/guidelines-for-online-index-operations`.

Maintaining Statistics

Correct statistics can be the lifeblood for query performance. SQL Server offers options to automatically keep statistics up to date based on database modification, and Azure SQL supports all those options. Our documentation has a very detailed explanation on how statistics are used for query performance at `https://docs.microsoft.com/en-us/sql/relational-databases/statistics/statistics`.

One interesting aspect to automatic statistics updates is a database scoped configuration we specifically introduced for Azure SQL to help improve application availability. You can read about this in great detail from a blog post by my colleague Dimitri Furman at `https://techcommunity.microsoft.com/t5/azure-sql-database/improving-concurrency-of-asynchronous-statistics-update/ba-p/1441687`.

Monitoring and Troubleshooting Performance

If you want to ensure you have the best performance for a SQL application, you need to learn how to monitor and troubleshoot performance scenarios. Azure SQL comes with the performance tools and capabilities of SQL Server to help you with this task. This includes tools from the Azure ecosystem as well as capabilities built into the SQL Server engine that powers Azure SQL.

In this part of the chapter of the book, you will learn not just monitoring capabilities but how to apply them to performance scenarios for Azure SQL including examples.

Monitoring Tools and Capabilities

Are you used to using Dynamic Management Views (DMV) and Extended Events? Azure SQL has what you need. Do you need to debug query plans? Azure SQL has all the capabilities of SQL Server including Lightweight Query Profiling and *showplan* details.

Query Store has become the bedrock for performance tuning, and it is on by default in Azure SQL. The Azure portal includes visualizations, such as Query Performance Insight, to view Query Store data without needing tools like SSMS.

All this lines up to be a formidable set of tools and capabilities to help you monitor and troubleshoot performance for Azure SQL.

We want to invest more to make Azure SQL monitoring the best experience as possible. According to Alain Dormehl, Senior Program Manager for Azure SQL, "Our continued investment into infrastructure and new features on the platform will continue to drive the expectations from our customers for deep insights. On a daily basis we gather a huge amount of telemetry data and our teams will continue to innovate in how we present this data to customers, so that it adds value, but also to build smarter, more innovative features for monitoring, alerting, and automating."

Azure Monitor

Azure Monitor is part of the Azure ecosystem, and Azure SQL is integrated to support Azure Metrics, Alerts, and Logs. Azure Monitor data can be visualized in the Azure Portal or accessed by applications through Azure Event Hub or APIs. An example of why Azure Monitor is important is accessing resource usage metrics for Azure SQL outside of SQL Server tools much like Windows Performance Monitor. Read more about how to use

Azure Monitor with Azure SQL in the Azure portal at `https://docs.microsoft.com/en-us/azure/azure-sql/database/monitor-tune-overview#monitoring-and-tuning-capabilities-in-the-azure-portal`.

Dynamic Management Views (DMV)

Azure SQL provides the same DMV infrastructure as with SQL Server with a few differences. DMVs are a crucial aspect to performance monitoring since you can view key SQL Server performance data using standard T-SQL queries. Information such as active queries, resource usage, query plans, and resource wait types are available with DMVs. Learn more details about DMVs with Azure SQL later in this chapter.

Extended Events (XEvent)

Azure SQL provides the same Extended Events infrastructure as with SQL Server. Extended Events is a method to trace key events of execution within SQL Server that powers Azure SQL. For performance, extended events allow you to trace the execution of individual queries. Learn more details about Extended Events with Azure SQL later in this chapter.

Lightweight Query Profiling

Lightweight Query Profiling is a capability to examine the query plan and running state of an active query. This is a key feature to debug query performance for long-running statements as they are running. This capability cuts down the time for you to solve performance problems vs. using tools like Extended Events to trace query performance. Lightweight Query Profiling is accessed through DMVs and is on by default for Azure SQL just like SQL Server 2019. Read more about Lightweight Query Profiling at `https://docs.microsoft.com/en-us/sql/relational-databases/performance/query-profiling-infrastructure?view=sql-server-ver15#lwp`.

Query Plan Debugging

In some situations, you may need additional details about query performance for an individual T-SQL statement. T-SQL SET statements such as SHOWPLAN and STATISTICS can provide these details and are fully supported for Azure SQL as they are for SQL Server. A good example of using SET statements for query plan debugging can be found at `https://docs.microsoft.com/en-us/sql/t-sql/statements/set-statistics-profile-transact-sql`. In addition, looking at plans in a graphical or XML format is always helpful and completely works for Azure SQL. Learn more at `https://docs.microsoft.com/en-us/sql/relational-databases/performance/display-the-estimated-execution-plan?view=sql-server-ver15`.

Query Store

Query Store is a historical record of performance execution for queries stored in the user database. Query Store is on by default for Azure SQL and is used to provide capabilities such as Automatic Plan Correction and Automatic Tuning. SQL Server Management Studio (SSMS) reports for Query Store are available for Azure SQL. These reports can be used to find top resource consuming queries including query plan differences and top wait types to look at resource wait scenarios. I will show you an example of using the Query Store in this chapter with Azure SQL. If you have never seen or used Query Store, start reading at `https://docs.microsoft.com/en-us/sql/relational-databases/performance/monitoring-performance-by-using-the-query-store`.

Performance Visualization in Azure Portal

For Azure SQL Database, we have integrated Query Store performance information into the Azure Portal through visualizations. This way, you can see some of the same information for Query Store as you would with a client tool like SSMS by using the Azure Portal with an option called **Query Performance Insight**. I'll show you an example of using these visuals in the portal later in the chapter. For now to get started using it, check out our documentation at `https://docs.microsoft.com/en-us/azure/azure-sql/database/query-performance-insight-use`.

Dive into DMVs and Extended Events

Dynamic Management Views (DMV) and Extended Events (XEvent) have been the *bedrock* of diagnostics including performance monitoring and troubleshooting for SQL Server for many years. I can truthfully tell you that DMV and XEvent technology all started with the brains of folks like Slava Oks and Conor Cunningham so many years ago. Many on the engineering team have worked, molded, and shaped these technologies, but I remember being there from the beginning with Slava and my colleague for many years Robert Dorr working on these technologies when we were in Microsoft support together. DMVs and XEvent are very important technologies to support performance monitoring and troubleshooting for Azure SQL because Azure SQL is powered by the SQL Server engine and the SQL Server engine powers Azure SQL Managed Instance and Database.

Let's dive a bit deeper into what DMV and XEvent capabilities are the same and new for Azure SQL vs. SQL Server.

DMVs Deep Dive

Let's dive deeper into DMV for Azure SQL vs. SQL Server across Azure SQL Managed Instance and Database.

Azure SQL Managed Instance

All DMVs for SQL Server are available for Managed Instance. Key DMVs like **sys. dm_exec_requests** and **sys.dm_os_wait_stats** are commonly used to examine query performance.

One DMV is specific to Azure called **sys.server_resource_stats** and shows historical resource usage for the Managed Instance. This is an important DMV to see resource usage since you do not have direct access to OS tools like Performance Monitor. You can learn more about sys.server_resource_stats at `https://docs.microsoft.com/en-us/ sql/relational-databases/system-catalog-views/sys-server-resource-stats- azure-sql-database?view=azuresqldb-current`.

Azure SQL Database

Most of the common DMVs you need for performance including **sys.dm_exec_ requests** and **sys.dm_os_wait_stats** are available. It is important to know that these DMVs only provide information specific to the database and not across all databases for a logical server.

sys.dm_db_resource_stats is a DMV specific to Azure SQL Database and can be used to view a history of resource usage for the database. Use this DMV similar to how you would use sys.server_resource_stats for a Managed Instance. I will show you how to use this DMV in an example later in this chapter. For now, you can read more at `https://docs.microsoft.com/en-us/sql/relational-databases/ system-dynamic-management-views/sys-dm-db-resource-stats-azure-sql- database?view=azuresqldb-current`.

sys.elastic_pool_resource_stats is similar to sys.dm_db_resource_stats but can be used to view resource usage for elastic pool databases.

DMVs You Will Need

There are a few DMVs worth calling out you will need to solve certain performance scenarios for Azure SQL:

sys.dm_io_virtual_file_stats is important for Azure SQL since you don't have direct access to operating system metrics for I/O performance per file.

sys.dm_os_performance_counters is available for both Azure SQL Database and Managed Instance to see SQL Server common performance metrics. This can be used to view SQL Server Performance Counter information that is typically available in Windows Performance Monitor.

sys.dm_instance_resource_governance can be used to view resource limits for a Managed Instance. You can view this information to see what your expected resource limits should be without using the Azure portal.

sys.dm_user_db_resource_governance can be used to see common resource limits per the deployment option, service tier, and size for your Azure SQL Database deployment. You can view this information to see what your expected resource limits should be without using the Azure portal. I'll show you an example of looking at this DMV in an example. For now, you can read more at `https://docs.microsoft.com/en-us/sql/relational-databases/system-dynamic-management-views/sys-dm-user-db-resource-governor-azure-sql-database?view=azuresqldb-current`.

DMVs for Deep Troubleshooting

These DMVs provide deeper insight into resource limits and resource governance for Azure SQL. They are not meant to be used for common scenarios but might be helpful when looking deep into complex performance problems:

- **sys.dm_user_db_resource_governance_internal (Managed Instance only)**

- **sys.dm_resource_governor_resource_pools_history_ex**

- **sys.dm_resource_governor_workload_groups_history_ex**

Geek out with these DMVs. The last two DMVs provide historical information across time (right now about 30 minutes). Be warned when using these DMVs. We kind of built these for our internal purposes to debug issues with Azure to look at problems like background activity vs. user load. So don't be surprised if we change these to suit our needs to ensure we provide a great database service.

XEvent at Your Service

Extended Events (XEvent) was introduced as the new tracing mechanism for SQL Server in SQL Server 2005 to replace SQL Trace. XEvent today supports some 1800+ trace points in the SQL Server engine. XEvent powers other capabilities including SQL Audit and Advanced Threat Protection (ATP).

Extended Events for Azure SQL Managed Instance

Extended Events can be used for Azure SQL Managed Instance just like SQL Server by creating sessions and using events, actions, and targets. Keep these important points in mind when creating extended event sessions:

- All events, targets, and actions are supported.

- File targets are supported with Azure Blob Storage since you don't have access to the underlying operating system disks.

- Some specific events are added for Managed Instance to trace events specific to the management and execution of the instance.

You can use SSMS or T-SQL to create and start sessions. You can use SSMS to view extended event session target data or the system function **sys.fn_xe_file_target_ read_file**.

Let's peek at how XEvent is used behind the scenes in Managed Instance to power Advanced Threat Protection (ATP). I had disabled Advanced Data Security from my Managed Instance and then enabled it again using the portal and techniques I described in Chapter 6 of the book. I then used my *jumpbox* (my Azure VM I showed you how to deploy in Chapter 4 of the book) to bring up SSMS and look at XEvent sessions in Object Explorer. Figure 7-3 shows the definition of a new session that shows up when you enable Advanced Data Security.

Figure 7-3. *XEvent session to help track queries for Advanced Threat Protection (ATP)*

Warning   You are the administrator of this SQL Server and have permissions to delete that XEvent session. If you do this, you will effectively disable us from serving you ATP needs. To get the XEvent session back, disable and enable Advanced Data Security from the portal. This session for ATP is part of the solution we use internally. Don't rely on its definition or output as we may change this in the future.

There is another XEvent session defined which is used for availability purposes called TPS_TdService_session_control. You can look at the event definition but don't rely on this. We use this internally and may change it in the future. You will also notice the system_health session and AlwaysOn_health session which are normally with any SQL Server. I'll take more about system_health in Chapter 8 of the book. AlwaysOn_health is not started and not used for a Managed Instance.

Extended Events for Azure SQL Database

Extended Events can be used for Azure SQL Database just like SQL Server by creating sessions and using events, actions, and targets. Keep these important points in mind when creating extended event sessions:

- Most commonly used Events and Actions are supported. For example, the fundamental event sql_batch_completed is available to you. Azure SQL Database offers ~400 events vs. SQL Server (and Managed Instance) which has around 1800. Use the DMV **sys.dm_xe_objects** to find out all objects available to you.

- File, ring_buffer, and counter targets are supported.

- File targets are supported with Azure Blob Storage since you don't
  have access to the underlying operating system disks. Here is a
  blog from the Azure Support team for a step-by-step process to set
  up Azure Blob Storage as a file target: `https://techcommunity.`
  `microsoft.com/t5/azure-database-support-blog/extended-`
  `events-capture-step-by-step-walkthrough/ba-p/369013.`

You can use SSMS or T-SQL to create and start sessions. You can use SSMS to view extended event session target data or the system function **sys.fn_xe_file_target_read_file**.

Note   The ability with SSMS to View Live Data is not available for Azure SQL Database.

It is important to know that any extended events fired for your sessions are specific to your database and not across the logical server. Therefore, we have a new set of catalog views such as **sys.database_event_sessions** (definitions) and DMVs such as **sys.dm_xe_database_sessions** (active sessions).

Take a look through our documentation for a complete list of differences for XEvent between Azure SQL Database and SQL Server: `https://docs.microsoft.com/en-us/` `azure/azure-sql/database/xevent-db-diff-from-svr`.

Performance Scenarios

In a galaxy, far, far away when I was in Microsoft Support, my longtime friend Keith Elmore was considered our expert on performance troubleshooting. As we trained other support engineers, Keith came up with an idea that most SQL performance problems could be categorized as either **Running** or **Waiting**.

Note   Keith's work led to a report called the Performance Dashboard reports. That report is now part of the Standard Reports for SQL Server Management Studio. Unfortunately, the report relies on some DMVs which are not exposed for Azure SQL Database. However, the reports will work for Managed Instance.

One way to look at this concept is with Figure 7-4.

It is just SQL: Running or waiting

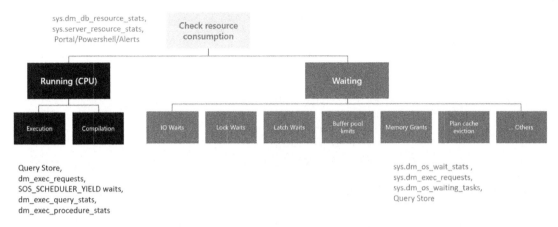

Figure 7-4. *The Running vs. Waiting for SQL performance*

Let's take a look at more of the details of this figure from the perspective of performance scenarios.

Note   As you look at DMVs in this section, remember that for Azure SQL Database you are only looking at results for a specific database not across all databases for the logical server.

Running vs. Waiting

Running or waiting scenarios can often be determined by looking at overall resource usage. For a standard SQL Server deployment, you might use tools such as Performance Monitor in Windows or top in Linux. For Azure SQL, you can use the following methods:

Azure Portal/PowerShell/Alerts

Azure Monitor has integrated metrics to view resource usage for Azure SQL. You can also set up alerts to look for resource usage conditions such as high CPU percent. Since we have integrated some Azure SQL performance data with Azure Monitor, having alerts is a huge advantage to snapping into the ecosystem. Read more about how to set up alerts with Azure Metrics at `https://docs.microsoft.com/en-us/azure/azure-monitor/platform/alerts-metric`.

Figure 7-5 shows an example of an alert on high CPU for my database sent to my phone from Azure Metrics.

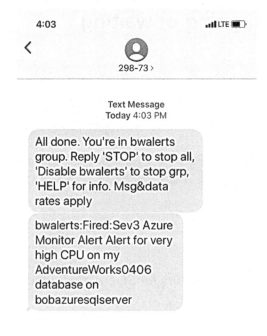

Figure 7-5. *Azure Metric alerts sent via SMS text*

sys.dm_db_resource_stats

For Azure SQL Database, you can look at this DMV to see CPU, memory, and I/O resource usage for the database deployment. This DMV takes a snapshot of this data every 15 seconds. The reference for all columns in this DMV can be found at `https://docs.microsoft.com/en-us/sql/relational-databases/system-dynamic-management-views/sys-dm-db-resource-stats-azure-sql-database?view=azuresqldb-current`. I'll use this DMV in an example later in this section.

Note   A DMV called **sys.resource_stats** works within the logical master to review resource stats for up to 14 days across all Azure databases associated with the logical server. Learn more at `https://docs.microsoft.com/en-us/sql/relational-databases/system-catalog-views/sys-resource-stats-azure-sql-database?view=azuresqldb-current`.

---

sys.server_resource_stats

This DMV behaves just like sys.dm_db_resource_stats, but it used to see resource usage for the Managed Instance for CPU, memory, and I/O. This DMV also takes a snapshot every 15 seconds. You can find the complete reference for this DMV at `https://docs.microsoft.com/en-us/sql/relational-databases/system-catalog-views/sys-server-resource-stats-azure-sql-database?view=azuresqldb-current`.

Running

If you have determined the problem is high CPU utilization, this is called a *running scenario*. A running scenario can involve queries that consume resources through compilation or execution. Further analysis to determine a solution can be done by using these tools:

Query Store

Query Store was introduced with SQL Server 2016 and has been one of the most game-hanging capabilities for performance analysis. Use the Top Consuming Resource reports in SSMS, Query Store catalog views, or Query Performance Insight in the Azure Portal (Azure SQL Database only) to find which queries are consuming the most CPU resources. Need a primer for Query Store? Start with our documentation at `https://docs.microsoft.com/en-us/sql/relational-databases/performance/monitoring-performance-by-using-the-query-store`.

sys.dm_exec_requests

This DMV has become perhaps the most popular DMV to use for SQL Server in history. This DMV displays a snapshot of all current active requests, which could be a T-SQL query or background task. Use this DMV in Azure SQL to get a snapshot of the state of active queries. Look for queries with a state of RUNNABLE and a wait type of SOS_SCHEDULER_YIELD to see if you have enough CPU capacity. Get the complete reference for this DMV at `https://docs.microsoft.com/en-us/sql/relational-databases/system-dynamic-management-views/sys-dm-exec-requests-transact-sql`.

sys.dm_exec_query_stats

This DMV can be used much like Query Store to find top resource consuming queries but only is available for query plans that are cached where Query Store provides a persistent historical record of performance. This DMV also allows you to find the query plan for a cached query. Get the complete reference at https://docs.microsoft.com/en-us/sql/relational-databases/system-dynamic-management-views/sys-dm-exec-query-stats-transact-sql.

Since Query Store is not yet available for readable secondaries, this DMV could be useful for those scenarios.

sys.dm_exec_procedure_stats

This DMV provides information much like sys.dm_exec_query_stats, except the performance information can be viewed at the stored procedure level. Get the complete reference at https://docs.microsoft.com/en-us/sql/relational-databases/system-dynamic-management-views/sys-dm-exec-procedure-stats-transact-sql.

Once you determine what query or queries are consuming the most resources, you may have to examine whether you have enough CPU resources for your workload or debug query plans with tools like Lightweight Query Profiling, SET statements, Query Store, or Extended Events tracing.

Waiting

If your problem doesn't appear to be a high CPU resource usage, it could be the performance problem involves waiting on a resource. Scenarios involving waiting on resources are as follows:

I/O Waits – This includes wait types such as PAGEIOLATCH latches (wait on database I/O) and WRITELOG (wait on transaction log I/O).

Lock Waits – These waits show up as standard "blocking" problems.

Latch Waits – This includes PAGELATCH ("hot" page) or even just LATCH (concurrency on an internal structure).

Buffer Pool limits – If you run out of Buffer Pool, you might run into unexpected PAGEIOLATCH waits.

Memory Grants – A high number of concurrent queries that need memory grants or large grants (could be from overestimation) could result in RESOURCE_SEMAPHORE waits.

Plan Cache Eviction - If you don't have enough plan cache and plans get evicted, this could lead to higher compile times (which could result in higher CPU) or RUNNABLE status with SOS_SCHEDULER_YIELD because there is not enough CPU capacity to handle compiles. You also might see waiting on locks for schema to compile queries.

To perform analysis on waiting scenarios, you typically look at the following tools:

sys.dm_os_wait_stats

Use this DMV to see what the top wait types for the database or instance are. This can guide you on what action to take next depending on the top wait types. Remember that for Azure SQL Database these are just waits for the database, not across all databases on the logical server. You can view the complete reference at https://docs.microsoft. com/en-us/sql/relational-databases/system-dynamic-management-views/sys-dm-os-wait-stats-transact-sql.

Note   There is a DMV specific to Azure SQL Database called **sys.dm_db_wait_ stats** (it also works with Managed Instance, but I don't recommend using it given you are looking at the instance) which only shows waits specific for the database. You might find this useful, but sys.dm_os_wait_stats will show all waits for the dedicated instance hosting your Azure SQL Database.

---

sys.dm_exec_requests

Use this DMV to find specific wait types for active queries to see what resource they are waiting on. This could be a standard blocking scenario waiting on locks from other users.

sys.dm_os_waiting_tasks

Queries that use parallelism use multiple tasks for a given query so you may need to use this DMV to find wait types for a given task for a specific query.

Query Store

Query Store provides reports and catalog views that show an aggregation of the top waits for query plan execution. The catalog view to see waits in Query Store is called **sys. query_store_wait_stats** which you can read more about at https://docs.microsoft. com/en-us/sql/relational-databases/system-catalog-views/sys-query-store-wait-stats-transact-sql. It is important to know that a **wait of CPU** is equivalent to a **running** problem.

Tip   Extended Events can be used for any running or waiting scenarios but requires you to set up an extended events session to trace queries and can be considered a *heavier* method to debug a performance problem.

Let's look at an example of a performance scenario to show how to use tools and capabilities I've discussed in this section to identify a performance scenario. I'll use the following resources for this exercise:

- The logical server **bwazuresqlserver** as well as the database **bwazuresqldb**. This database was deployed as a General Purpose 2 vCore database.

- The Azure VM called **bwsql2019**. I left my security settings from Chapter 6 so this VM has access to the logical server and database.

- I'll use SQL Server Management Studio (SSMS) to run some queries and look at Query Store Reports.

Tip   If you connect with SSMS to an Azure SQL Database logical server and with SSMS choose a specific database, Object Explorer will only show you the logical master and your database. If you connect to the logical master with a server admin account, Object Explorer will show you all databases.

- I'll use the Azure portal to view Azure Metrics and look at logs.

- For this chapter, I have script files you can use for several of the examples. You can find scripts for this example (and the next one) in the **ch7_performance\monitor_and_scale** folder for the source files included for the book. I will also use the very popular tool ostress. exe for exercises in this chapter which comes with the RML Utilities. You can download RML from `www.microsoft.com/en-us/download/details.aspx?id=4511`. Make sure to put the folder where RML gets installed in your system path (which is by default C:\Program Files\ Microsoft Corporation\RMLUtils).

Let's go through an example in a step-by-step fashion:

Note   In some of these examples, you may see a different database name than I deployed. I've run these exact examples with different database names so you might see some different context in figures in this chapter.

---

1. Set up to monitor Azure SQL Database with a DMV query.

Tip   To open a script file in the context of a database in SSMS, click the database in Object Explorer and then use the File/Open menu in SSMS.

Launch SQL Server Management Studio (SSMS) and load a query in the context of the database to monitor the Dynamic Management View (DMV) **sys.dm_exec_requests** from the script **dmexecrequests.sql** which looks like this:

```
SELECT er.session_id, er.status, er.command, er.wait_type,
er.last_wait_type, er.wait_resource, er.wait_time
FROM sys.dm_exec_requests er
INNER JOIN sys.dm_exec_sessions es
ON er.session_id = es.session_id
AND es.is_user_process = 1;
```

2. Load another query to observe resource usage.

In another session for SSMS in the context of the database, load a query to monitor a Dynamic Management View (DMV) unique to Azure SQL Database called **sys.dm_db_resource_stats** from a script called **dmdbresourcestats.sql**:

```
SELECT * FROM sys.dm_db_resource_stats;
```

This DMV will track overall resource usage of your workload against Azure SQL Database such as CPU, I/O, and memory.

3. Edit the workload script.

Edit the script **sqlworkload.cmd** (which will use the ostress.exe program).

I'll substitute my server, database, and password. The script will look like this (without password substitution):

```
ostress.exe -Sbwazuresqlserver.database.windows.net
-itopcustomersales.sql -Uthewandog -dbwazuresqldb -P<password>
-n10 -r2 -q
```

4. Examine the T-SQL query we will use for the workload. You can
    find this T-SQL batch in the script **topcustomersales.sql**:

```
DECLARE @x int
DECLARE @y float
SET @x = 0;
WHILE (@x < 10000)
BEGIN
SELECT @y = sum(cast((soh.SubTotal*soh.TaxAmt*soh.TotalDue)
as float))
FROM SalesLT.Customer c
INNER JOIN SalesLT.SalesOrderHeader soh
ON c.CustomerID = soh.CustomerID
INNER JOIN SalesLT.SalesOrderDetail sod
ON soh.SalesOrderID = sod.SalesOrderID
INNER JOIN SalesLT.Product p
ON p.ProductID = sod.ProductID
GROUP BY c.CompanyName
ORDER BY c.CompanyName;
SET @x = @x + 1;
END
GO
```

This database is not large, so the query to retrieve customer and
their associated sales information ordered by customers with
the most sales shouldn't generate a large result set. It is possible
to tune this query by reducing the number of columns from the
result set, but these are needed for demonstration purposes of this
activity. You will note in this query I don't return any results to the
client but assign values to a local variable. This will put all the CPU
resources to run the query to the server.

5. Now let's run the workload and observe its performance and results
    from queries we loaded earlier. Run the workload by executing the
    sqlworkload.cmd script from a command shell or PowerShell. The
    script uses ostress to simulate ten concurrent users running the
    T-SQL batch. You should see output that looks similar to this:

```
[datetime] [ostress PID] Max threads setting: 10000
[datetime] [ostress PID] Arguments:
[datetime] [ostress PID] -S[server].database.windows.net
[datetime] [ostress PID] -isqlquery.sql
[datetime] [ostress PID] -U[user]
[datetime] [ostress PID] -dbwazuresqldb
[datetime] [ostress PID] -P********
[datetime] [ostress PID] -n10
[datetime] [ostress PID] -r2
[datetime] [ostress PID] -q
[datetime] [ostress PID] Using language id (LCID): 1024 [English_
United States.1252] for character formatting with NLS: 0x0006020F
and Defined: 0x0006020F
[datetime] [ostress PID] Default driver: SQL Server Native
Client 11.0
[datetime] [ostress PID] Attempting DOD5015 removal of
[directory]\sqlquery.out]
[datetime] [ostress PID] Attempting DOD5015 removal of
[directory]\sqlquery_1.out]
[datetime] [ostress PID] Attempting DOD5015 removal of
[directory]\sqlquery_2.out]
[datetime] [ostress PID] Attempting DOD5015 removal of
[directory]\sqlquery_3.out]
[datetime] [ostress PID] Attempting DOD5015 removal of
[directory]\sqlquery_4.out]
[datetime] [ostress PID] Attempting DOD5015 removal of
[directory]\sqlquery_5.out]
[datetime] [ostress PID] Attempting DOD5015 removal of
[directory]\sqlquery_6.out]
```

```
[datetime] [ostress PID] Attempting DOD5015 removal of
[directory]\sqlquery_7.out]
[datetime] [ostress PID] Attempting DOD5015 removal of
[directory]\sqlquery_8.out]
[datetime] [ostress PID] Attempting DOD5015 removal of
[directory]\sqlquery_9.out]
[datetime] [ostress PID] Starting query execution...
[datetime] [ostress PID]  BETA: Custom CLR Expression support
enabled.
[datetime] [ostress PID] Creating 10 thread(s) to process queries
[datetime] [ostress PID] Worker threads created, beginning
execution...
```

6. Now use the DMVs that you loaded to observe performance
    while this runs. First, run the query from **dmexecrequests.sql**
    five or six times in the query window from SSMS. You will see
    several users have status = RUNNABLE and last_wait_type =
    SOS_SCHEDULER_YIELD. This is a classic signature of not having
    enough CPU resources for a workload.

7. Observe the results from the query **dmdbresourcestats.sql**. Run
    this query a few times and observe the results. You will see several
    rows with a value for **avg_cpu_percent** close to 100%. sys.dm_db_
    resource_stats takes a snapshot every 15 seconds of resource usage.

8. Let the workload complete and take note of its duration. For me, it
    measured around 1 minute and 30 seconds.

9. Let's use the Query Store now to dive deeper into the performance
    the queries in this workload. In SSMS in the Object Explorer, load
    the Top Resource Consuming Queries as seen in Figure 7-6.

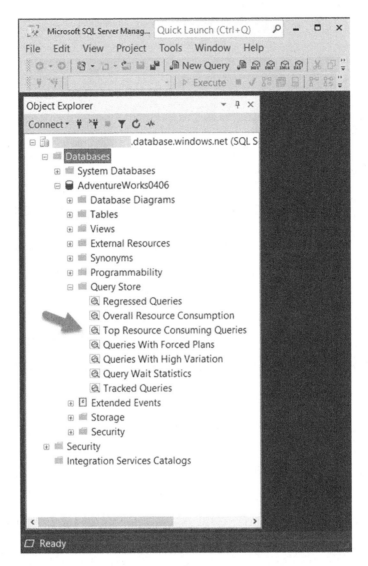

Figure 7-6. *Finding the Top Consuming Queries report for Query Store*

10.   Dive into the details of this report to see the performance of the
workload.

Select the report to find out what queries have consumed the most
average resources and execution details of those queries. Based on
the workload run to this point, your report should look something
like Figure 7-7.

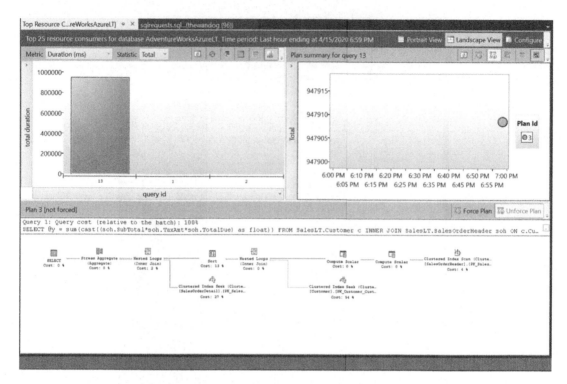

Figure 7-7. *The Top Consuming Queries Report in SSMS*

The query that is shown is the one from our workload. If you click
the bar chart, you will see details about the query including the
query_id which should look like Figure 7-8 (your query_id will
likely be different).

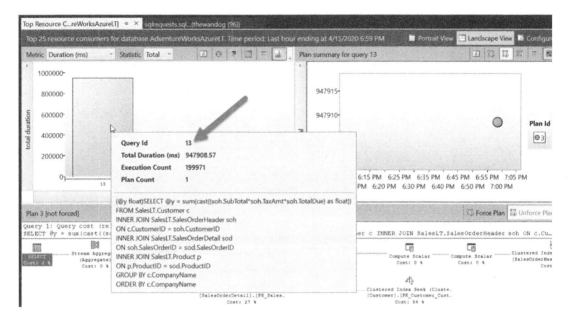

Figure 7-8. *query_id from the Top Resource Consuming Query report*

If I hover over the dot on the right-hand side of this report, you will see performance statistics about the query which will look like Figure 7-9.

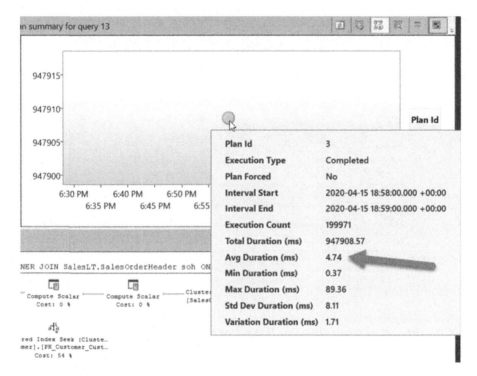

Figure 7-9.   Query stats for a query plan

Your times may vary some. You can see here the average duration
was around 5ms for each query. You can also look at the bottom
of this report to see the query plan. There are not many rows in
these tables, so there is not much to tune for the query plan. 5ms
doesn't sound bad for performance for each execution, but let's
keep analyzing to see if it could be faster.

11.   Look at the Query Wait Statistics Report for the Query Store.

Based on the decision tree earlier in this chapter, this appears to
be a **running** scenario. If the query plan can't be tuned, how can
we make the query *run faster*? The Query Wait Statistics report
could help give us a clue (along with the DMV results we have
already observed).

If you then select Query Wait Statistics report from the Object
Explorer and hover over the Bar Chart that says CPU, you will see
something like Figure 7-10.

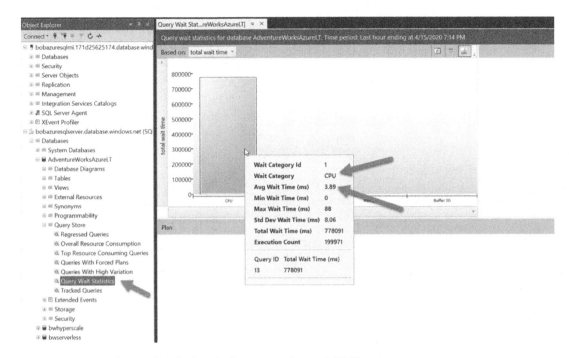

Figure 7-10. *Query Wait Statistic report from SSMS*

So the top wait category is CPU, and the average time waiting for this wait type is almost 4ms. A wait category of CPU is equivalent to a wait type = SOS_SCHEDULER_YIELD.

If you click the bar chart, you see the same query_id from our workload. Notice the average wait time is just the same as the average wait time for all CPU waits. And this average wait time is *almost the entire duration* of the query as seen in Figure 7-11.

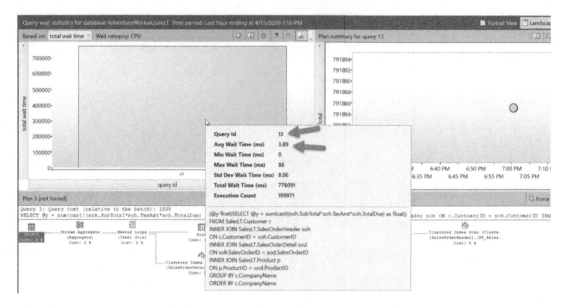

Figure 7-11. *Average wait time for CPU for a specific query*

Now consider the evidence. The workload consumes CPU resources for the database at almost 100%. The status of many requests is RUNNABLE, and the top wait type for the workload is SOS_SCHEDULER_YIELD. If the query cannot be changed, then the most likely scenario is that you don't have enough CPU resources for your workload. Later in this chapter, we will use Azure interfaces to make this query run faster.

12.   Use Azure Monitor and metrics.

Let's look at this performance scenario through the lens of Azure Monitor and metrics. I'll navigate to my database using the Azure portal. In the monitoring pane is an area called Compute utilization. After my workload has run, my chart looks similar to Figure 7-12.

Note   I grabbed these numbers from a different test I had already done using databases just like bwazuresqldb called AdventureWorks0406 and AdventureWorksLT.

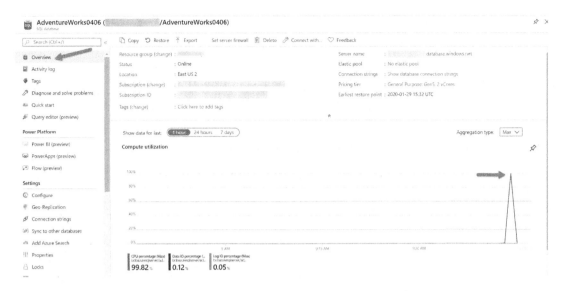

Figure 7-12. *Viewing CPU utilization from the Azure portal*

This view comes from Azure Metrics. You can get a different angle
on this if you select Metrics from the resource menu and choose
CPU percentage as seen in Figure 7-13.

Figure 7-13. *Azure metrics for an Azure SQL Database*

As you can see in the screenshot, there are several metrics you
can use to view with Metrics Explorer. The default view of Metrics
Explorer is for a 24-hour period showing a 5-minute granularity.
The Compute Utilization view is the last hour with a 1-minute
granularity (which you can change). To see the same view, select
CPU percentage and change the capture for 1 hour. The granularity
will change to 1 minute and should look like Figure 7-14.

Figure 7-14. *Granular view of Azure Metrics*

13. Use Azure Monitor Logs.

I've mentioned Azure Monitor includes another capability called
Azure Monitor Log. Azure Monitor Logs can provide a longer
historical record than Metrics.

Note   There is a delay in seeing results in Logs, so it may take several minutes
for you to see results like this figure.

I can choose Logs from the Resource menu and run a Kusto Query
as seen in Figure 7-15 to see the same type of CPU utilization.

Figure 7-15. *Using Kusto to view resource usage from Azure Monitor Logs*

I've talked about Kusto in the book before, but here is a link for you to learn more: `https://docs.microsoft.com/en-us/azure/data-explorer/kusto/concepts/`. There is another tool you can use to run Kusto queries is Kusto Explorer which you can read more about at `https://docs.microsoft.com/en-us/azure/data-explorer/kusto/tools/kusto-explorer`. At the time I was writing this chapter, we plan to bring the Kusto query experience to Azure Data Studio!

Azure SQL Specific Performance Scenarios

Based on the Running vs. Waiting scenario, there are some scenarios which are specific to Azure SQL.

Log Governance

Azure SQL can enforce resource limits on transaction log usage called *log rate governance*. This enforcement is often needed to ensure resource limits and to meet promised SLA. Log governance may be seen from the following **wait types**:

LOG_RATE_GOVERNOR – Waits for Azure SQL Database

POOL_LOG_RATE_GOVERNOR – Waits for Elastic Pools

INSTANCE_LOG_GOVERNOR – Waits for Azure SQL Managed Instance

HADR_THROTTLE_LOG_RATE* – Waits for Business Critical and Geo-Replication latency

Log rate governance is enforced inside the SQL Server engine before transaction log blocks are submitted for I/O. The documentation has a good description of how this works at https://docs.microsoft.com/en-us/azure/azure-sql/database/resource-limits-logical-server#transaction-log-rate-governance. Scaling your deployment to a different service tier or vCore choice can give you more log rate for your application.

Worker Limits

SQL Server uses a worker pool of threads but has limits on the maximum number of workers. Applications with a large number of concurrent users may need a certain number of workers. Keep these points in mind on how worker limits are enforced for Azure SQL Database and Managed Instance:

- Azure SQL Database has limits based on service tier and size. If you exceed this limit, a new query will receive an error like

  ```
  Msg 10928
  The request limit for the database is <limit> and has been
  reached.
  ```

- Azure SQL Managed Instance uses "max worker threads" so workers past this limit may see THREADPOOL waits.

Note   Managed Instance in the future may enforce worker limits similar to Azure SQL Database.

Business Critical (BC) HADR Waits

Let's say you deploy a Business Critical service tier for Azure SQL Managed Instance or Azure SQL Database. Now you start running transactions that modify data and therefore require logged changes.

You look at a DMV like sys.dm_exec_requests and see wait types like HADR_SYNC_COMMIT. What? This wait type is only seen when you deploy a sync replica for an Always On Availability Group (AG).

It turns out Business Critical service tiers uses an AG behind the scenes. Therefore, it is not surprising to see these wait types normally, but it may surprise you if you are monitoring wait types.

You can also see HADR_DATABASE_FLOW_CONTROL and HADR_THROTTLE_LOG_RATE_SEND_RECV waits as part of Log Governance to ensure we can meet your promised SLA.

Hyperscale Scenarios

I've talked about the Hyperscale architecture briefly in Chapter 4 of the book. I'll go even deeper in Chapter 8. While Hyperscale has log rate limits just like other deployment options, there are cases where we must govern transaction log generation due to a page server or replica getting significantly behind (which would then affect our ability to deliver our SLA). When this occurs, you may see wait types that start with the word **RBIO_**.

Even though we don't dive into the details of how to diagnose various aspects of the Hyperscale architecture in this book, there are interesting capabilities for you to take advantage of. For example, reads from page servers are now available in DMVs like **sys.dm_exec_query_stats**, **sys.dm_io_virtual_file_stats**, and **sys.query_store_runtime_stats**. In addition, the I/O statistics in sys.dm_io_virtual_file_stats apply to RBEX cache and page servers since these are the I/O files that mostly affect Hyperscale performance.

Get all the details for Hyperscale performance diagnostics at `https://docs.microsoft.com/en-us/azure/azure-sql/database/hyperscale-performance-diagnostics`.

Accelerating and Tuning Performance

You have seen performance capabilities for Azure SQL including monitoring tools. You have also seen an example of how to apply your knowledge of monitoring and a performance scenario to recognize a possible performance bottleneck. Let's apply that knowledge to learn how to accelerate and tune performance in the areas of scaling CPU capacity, I/O performance, memory, application latency, and SQL Server performance tuning best practices.

Scaling CPU Capacity

Let's say you ran into the performance problem with high CPU as I showed you in the previous exercise *in your data center*. What would you do? If you were running SQL Server on a bare-metal server, you would have to potentially acquire more CPUs or even move to another server. For a virtual machine, you may be able to reconfigure the VM to get more vCPUs, but what if the host server didn't support that? You are possibly facing a scenario to migrate your database to another VM on another host. Ouch.

For Azure SQL, you have the ability to *scale* your CPU resources with very simple operations from the Azure portal, az CLI, PowerShell, and even T-SQL. And you can do all of this with no database migration required.

For Azure SQL Database, there will be some small downtime to scale up your CPU resources. It is possible with larger database sizes this downtime could be longer, especially if we need to move your deployment to another host with enough resources for your request. We also have to ensure your replicas have the same new resources for Business Critical service tiers. Hyperscale provides a more constant scaling motion regardless of database size.

Azure SQL Managed Instance can be a concern for duration of scaling. We may need to build a new virtual cluster, so scaling operations can be significantly longer. This is something to keep in mind and is why deploying with the right resources for Managed Instance can be important. Managed Instance pools are much faster but still significantly longer than Azure SQL Database in most cases.

Azure SQL Database Serverless compute tier provides the concept of autoscaling as I described its implementation in Chapter 4 of the book.

Let's go back where we left off in our exercise where we determined it is likely we didn't have enough CPU resources for our workload. Let's scale it up and see if workload performance improves:

1. Look at scaling options in the Azure portal.

   I'll navigate to my database in the Azure portal and select Pricing tier as seen in Figure 7-16.

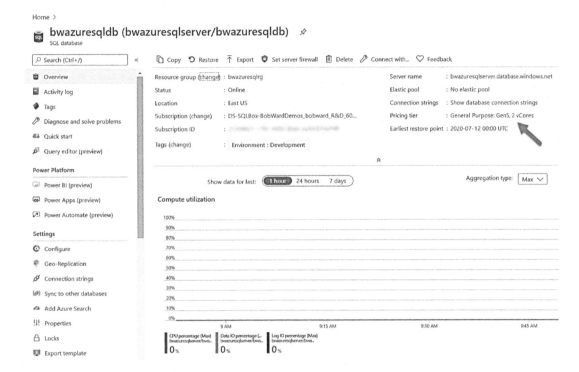

Figure 7-16. *Choosing a pricing or service tier for a General Purpose database*

You are now presented with a screen to make changes to your deployment. I showed you a screen similar to this in Chapter 4 as I described all the options after you deploy. My options look like Figure 7-17 where I can use a slider bar to increase the number of vCores for my General Purpose deployment.

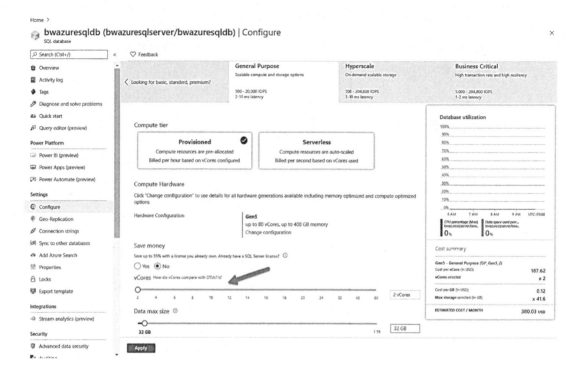

Figure 7-17. *Using the Azure portal to increase vCores*

2. Scale vCores using T-SQL.

Let's use a more familiar method to make changes to SQL Server.
The T-SQL ALTER DATABASE statement has been enhanced for
Azure SQL Database to scale CPUs for the deployment.

To properly show a performance difference with Query Store
reports, I'm going to flush the current data in memory in the
Query store using the script **flushquerystore.sql** which executes
this T-SQL statement:

```
EXEC sp_query_store_flush_db;
```

Now let's use other T-SQL queries to view the current service or
pricing tier for our deployment. Execute the T-SQL script **get_
service_objective.sql** which uses the following T-SQL statements
(you need to substitute in your database name):

```
SELECT database_name,slo_name,cpu_limit,max_db_memory,
max_db_max_size_in_mb, primary_max_log_rate,primary_group_max_io,
volume_local_iops,volume_pfs_iops
FROM sys.dm_user_db_resource_governance;
GO
SELECT DATABASEPROPERTYEX('<databasename>', 'ServiceObjective');
GO
```

The results from these queries look like this for my deployment:

```
database_name   slo_name                    cpu_limit  max_db_memory
max_db_max_size_in_mb  primary_max_log_rate  primary_group_max_io
volume_local_iops  volume_pfs_iops

bwazuresqldb    SQLDB_GP_GEN5_2_SQLG5   2          7836980
4194304                7864320               640
8000               1000
```

```
(No column name)
GP_Gen5_2
```

You are seeing the same information you saw in the Azure portal regarding CPUs, but **sys.dm_user_db_resource_governance** effectively gives us a way to programmatically look at resource limits you would read in our tables in the documentation.

The system function DATABASEPROPERTYEX has also been enhanced to show you the **ServiceObjective** for a database.

You can *decode* the information from the **slo_name** column (slo = service-level objective) or the system function. For example, SQLDB_GP_GEN5_2_SQLG5 is equivalent to General Purpose Gen5 Hardware 2 vCores. SQLDB_OP... is used for Business Critical.

We can use the T-SQL ALTER DATABASE documentation to see all possible values for the service objective at https://docs. microsoft.com/en-us/sql/t-sql/statements/alter-database-transact-sql.

Using this documentation, let's change the tier or objective to 8 vCores using the script **modify_service_objective.sql** or the T-SQL statement:

```
ALTER DATABASE <databasename> MODIFY (SERVICE_OBJECTIVE =
'GP_Gen5_8');
```

This statement executes immediately because the modification to scale to 8 vCores is an option that happens in the background.

If you navigate to the Azure portal, you will see a notification that the operation is in progress as seen in Figure 7-18.

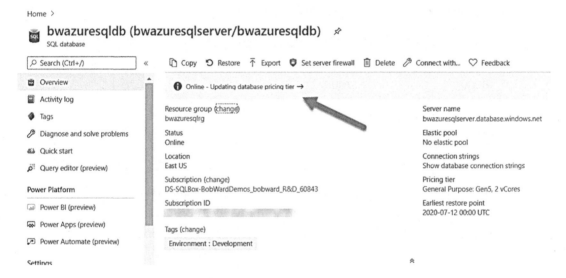

Figure 7-18. *Scaling of Azure SQL Database in progress*

In addition, you can use the T-SQL statement in the context of the master database of the logical server to see operations against databases:

```
SELECT * FROM sys.dm_operation_status;
```

For my logical server, I got the following results:

```
session_activity_id                     resource_type
resource_type_desc    major_resource_id    minor_resource_id
operation     state        state_desc     percent_complete
error_code     error_desc     error_severity
error_state     start_time                  last_modify_time

D22C1CB5-C164-4BB5-BC18-EE593C1759AF    0
Database                  bwazuresqldb           ALTER DATABASE
2              COMPLETED   100         0
0             0
                2020-07-19 15:21:40.670   2020-07-19 15:22:14.423
```

You can read more details about **sys.dm_operation_status** at https://docs.microsoft.com/en-us/sql/relational-databases/system-dynamic-management-views/sys-dm-operation-status-azure-sql-database.

3. Run the workload again.

   Let's run the workload again to see if there is any performance differences. I'll use the same scripts, queries, and SSMS reports as I did in the previous example in the chapter.

   Run the script **sqlworkload.cmd** again from the command prompt.

4. Observe resource usage with **sys.dm_db_resource_stats**.

   Just as you did before running this query, several times should show a lower overall CPU usage for the database.

5. Observe active queries with **sys.dm_exec_requests**.

   You should see more RUNNING requests and less SOS_SCHEDULER_YIELD waits.

6. Observe the overall workload duration.

   Remember this ran in around 1 minute and 30 seconds before. Now it should finish in around 25–30 seconds – clearly, a significant performance improvement.

7. Observe performance with Query Store Top Consuming Reports.

Using the same report as before, you can see two queries in the
report with a new query_id as seen in Figure 7-19.

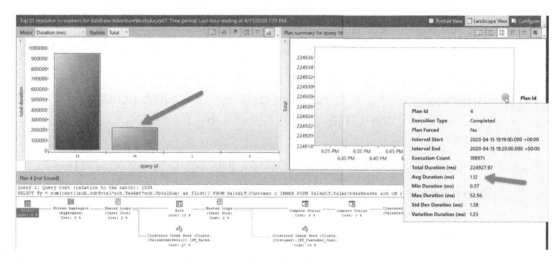

Figure 7-19. *Top Consuming Query report with a faster query*

Even though there is a new query_id, it is the exact same query.
Because the SQL Server that hosts our database was restarted
for scaling (or a new SQL Server used), the query had to be
recompiled, hence a new query_id. This scenario is also where
the power of Query Store comes into play. Query performance is
stored in the user database, so even if we had to migrate your SQL
Server behind the scenes to a new node, no query performance
information is lost.

Note   The behavior of a different query_id is actually very interesting. The query
was recompiled, but in many cases, the same query_id would appear in the Query
Store. However, in this case, the first execution of the query was against a 2 vCore
deployment. In a 2 vCore deployment, maxdop is fixed at 1. When the back-end
server has a fixed maxdop of 1, queries will use a *context setting* with a bit that
is NOT set for **Parallel Plan**. With a deployment of 8 vCores, maxdop is fixed at 8.
In this case, the context_setting will include the bit set for Parallel Plan. Parallel
Plan is not an option set by the application but rather by a negotiation with the

server and indicates the query can use a parallel plan. In this case, the query_id is different because the context_settings_id (see the catalog view **sys.query_store_query**) is different for each execution. You can view context settings in the Query Store using the catalog view **sys.query_context_settings**. You can see more about context settings "bits" in the DMV **sys.dm_exec_plan_attributes**.

You can see from this figure a significantly faster average duration for the query than before.

8. Look at Query Wait Statistics report.

   If you use the Query Wait Statistics report, you can see a significant less time waiting on CPU for the query as seen in Figure 7-20.

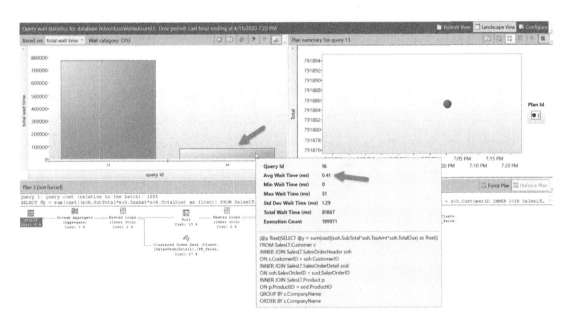

Figure 7-20. *Faster query with less waiting on CPU*

9. Look at differences with Azure Metrics and Logs.

   Let's navigate to the Azure portal to see the difference in compute utilization. Figure 7-21 shows the example.

Figure 7-21. *Azure compute after scaling CPUs*

If you run the same Kusto query as before (there will be a lag in seeing these results), you can see the performance difference as well from Azure Logs like Figure 7-22.

Figure 7-22. *Using Kusto with Azure logs after scaling CPUs*

What happens if we were to use the **Serverless** compute tier option for our workload? Remember Serverless offers the ability to autoscale workloads and also pause idle compute.

I deployed a new Serverless database with a min vCore = 2 and max vCore = 8. Turns out in most cases (not guaranteed), a Serverless database is deployed with the number of SQL Schedulers = max vCores. So provided the Serverless database is not paused, running the same workload as in this example gives you approximately the same performance as the scaled General Purpose 8 vCore deployment. Here is the big advantage of Serverless over the General Purpose deployment. Let's say over a period of two hours, this workload only consumes compute for 15 minutes of the 120 minutes. For a General Purpose deployment, you will pay for compute for the entire 120 minutes. For a Serverless deployment, you would pay for the 15 minutes of compute usage for 8 vCores, and for the remaining 90 minutes, you would pay for the equivalent compute usage for the min vCores. In addition, if you have AutoPause enabled, you will not pay for any compute costs for the last 60 minutes of that two-hour period (this is because the smallest time before a Serverless deployment is paused if idle is one hour).

Figure 7-23 shows an example of CPU utilization for a Serverless deployment and below it a graph of actual compute billed. Notice the highest average CPU billed is during high compute utilization. After the utilization, a lower static billing is for min vCores. Then following this is no compute is billed as the deployment is paused.

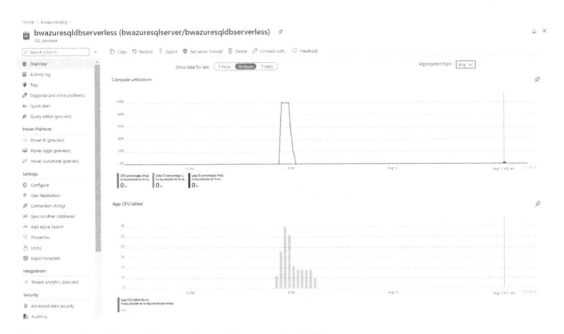

Figure 7-23. *Serverless scale and compute billing*

I/O Performance

I/O performance can be critical to SQL Server applications and queries. Azure SQL abstracts you from physical file placement, but there are methods to ensure you get the I/O performance you need.

Input/Output Per Second (IOPS) may be important to your application. Be sure you have chosen the right service tier and vCores for your IOPS needs. Understand how to measure IOPS for your queries on-premises if you are migrating to Azure (Hint: Look at Disk Transfers/sec in Performance Monitor). If you have restrictions on IOPS, you may see long I/O waits. Scale up vCores or move to Business Critical or Hyperscale if you don't have enough IOPS.

I/O latency is another key component for I/O performance. For faster I/O latency for Azure SQL Database, consider Business Critical or Hyperscale. For faster I/O latency for Managed Instance, move to Business Critical or increase file size or number of files for the database.

Let's take a minute to examine this last statement a bit more closely for Managed Instance and file size or number of files. I've pointed you to this blog post from Jovan Popovic before on the topic at `https://medium.com/azure-sqldb-managed-instance/ increasing-data-files-might-improve-performance-on-general-purpose-managed- instance-tier-6e90bad2ae4b`.

The concept is that for the General Purpose tier, we store database and log files on Azure premium storage disks. Turns out that for premium disks, the larger the size of disk we use, the better performance we can get. So as you increase the size of your files, we will use a level of Premium storage to meet those needs, which can result in more IOPS or better throughput. I love Jovan's blog post because he backs up his statements with data using the popular open source tool HammerDB.

Configuration isn't your only choice. Improving transaction log latency may require you to use multi-statement transactions. Learn more at `https://docs.microsoft.com/ en-us/azure/azure-sql/performance-improve-use-batching`.

Increasing Memory or Workers

Memory is also an important resource for SQL Server performance and Azure SQL is no different. The total memory available to you for buffer pool, plan cache, columnstore, and In-Memory OLTP is all dependent on your deployment choice. As I described earlier in this chapter, your highest memory capacity comes from an Azure SQL

Database Business Critical tier using the new M-Series hardware generation (around 4TB). For a Managed Instance, you can get around 400Gb of memory using the 80 vCore deployment for Business Critical. Also keep in mind that In-Memory OLTP, which is only available for Business Critical service tiers, has a maximum memory as a subset of the overall maximum memory.

One key statement about memory that holds true for SQL Server or Azure SQL: If you think you don't have enough memory, be sure you have an optimal database and query design. You may think you are running out of buffer pool after you scan a massive table. Maybe indexes should be deployed to enhance performance of your query and use less memory. Columnstore indexes are compressed, so use far less memory than traditional indexes.

Note   The Hyperscale vCore choice not only affects the amount of memory available to the compute nodes but also the size of the RBEX cache which can also affect performance.

I've described worker limits in this chapter already which is set to a maximum value for Azure SQL Database, but Managed Instance uses "max worker threads" (but this is something we may limit less than this in the future). As with SQL Server, running out of workers may be an application problem. A heavy blocking problem for all users may result in an error running out of workers when the problem is fixing the blocking problem.

Improving Application Latency

Even if you configure your deployment for all your resource needs, applications may introduce latency performance issues. Be sure to follow these best practices with Azure SQL applications:

- Use a redirect connection type instead of proxy.

- Optimize "chatty" applications by using stored procedures or limiting the number of query round trips through techniques like batches.

- Optimize transactions by grouping them vs. singleton transactions.

Take a look at this documentation page for tuning applications for Azure SQL Database: https://docs.microsoft.com/en-us/azure/azure-sql/database/performance-guidance.

Tune Like It Is SQL Server

Azure SQL is still SQL Server. Even though you will see capabilities to help you with performance built into the engine, there is almost never a substitute for ensuring you tune your SQL Server queries and look at the following:

- Proper index design.

- Using batches.

- Using stored procedures.

- Parameterize queries to avoid too many cached ad hoc queries.

- Process results in your application quickly and correctly (avoid the dreaded ASYNC_NETWORK_IO waits).

Let's use an exercise to demonstrate how in some cases, while it may seem natural to try and change a service tier to improve performance, a change in your queries or application can show benefits.

For this exercise, I'll use all the same tools, the same Azure SQL database deployment (which now has 8 vCores), and the same VM to look at a performance scenario for I/O. The scripts for this exercise can be found in the **ch7_performance\tuning_applications** folder for the source files included.

Let's consider the following application scenario to set up how to see this problem. Assume that to support a new extension to a website for AdventureWorks orders to provide a rating system from customers, you need to add a new table for a heavy set of concurrent INSERT activity. You have tested the SQL query workload on a development computer with SQL Server 2019 that has a local SSD drive for the database and transaction log. When you move your test to Azure SQL Database using the General Purpose tier (8 vCores), the INSERT workload is slower. You need to discover whether you need to change the service objective or tier to support the new workload or look at the application.

Important   I ran all of my tests for this exercise in an Azure VM which will use
the Redirect connection type by default. If you run this outside of Azure, the default
is Proxy. You will not see the same significant performance increase I observed if
you use Proxy, but you will see some gains. This is because the simulation of the
application requires enough round trips that Proxy can affect overall performance.

1. Create a new table in the database.

    I'll use SSMS in my Azure VM that is connected to Azure SQL
    Database to add this table into the database based on the script
    order_rating_ddl.sql:

    ```
    DROP TABLE IF EXISTS SalesLT.OrderRating;
    GO
    CREATE TABLE SalesLT.OrderRating
    (OrderRatingID int identity not null,
    SalesOrderID int not null,
    OrderRatingDT datetime not null,
    OrderRating int not null,
    OrderRatingComments char(500) not null);
    GO
    ```

2. Load queries to monitor execution.

    Using SSMS, load up queries in separate query windows to look
    at DMVs using scripts in the context of the user database with
    sqlrequests.sql, **top_waits.sql**, and **tlog_io.sql**. You will need to
    modify tlog_io.sql to put in your database name.

    These scripts use the following queries, respectively:

    ```
    SELECT er.session_id, er.status, er.command, er.wait_type,
    er.last_wait_type, er.wait_resource, er.wait_time
    FROM sys.dm_exec_requests er
    INNER JOIN sys.dm_exec_sessions es
    ON er.session_id = es.session_id
    AND es.is_user_process = 1;
    ```

```
SELECT * FROM sys.dm_os_wait_stats
ORDER BY waiting_tasks_count DESC;

SELECT io_stall_write_ms/num_of_writes as avg_tlog_io_write_ms, *
FROM sys.dm_io_virtual_file_stats
(db_id('<database name>'), 2);
```

The DMVs used in these queries are a great example of showing
you diagnostics in the context of a database based on instance-
level DMV diagnostics. It is one of the benefits when we moved to
the V12 architecture I mentioned in Chapter 1 of the book.

Tip   You can also find your session_id and use the DMV **sys.dm_exec_session_
wait_stats** to see only the waits for your session. Note that this DMV will not show
waits for any background tasks. Learn more at https://docs.microsoft.
com/en-us/sql/relational-databases/system-dynamic-management-
views/sys-dm-exec-session-wait-stats-transact-sql?view=sql-
server-ver15.

---

3. Run the workload.

    The workload to insert database can be found in the script **order_
    rating_insert_single.sql**. The batch for this script looks like this:

```
DECLARE @x int;
SET @x = 0;
WHILE (@x < 500)
BEGIN
SET @x = @x + 1;
INSERT INTO SalesLT.OrderRating
(SalesOrderID, OrderRatingDT, OrderRating, OrderRatingComments)
VALUES (@x, getdate(), 5, 'This was a great order');
END
```

We will use ostress.exe to run this query with a script as found in **order_rating_insert_single.cmd**. For you to run this, you will need to edit the script to put in your correct server, database, login, and password.

Run this script from a command or PowerShell prompt.

4. Observe query performance and duration.

   Using the DMV you loaded, you will likely observe the following:

   • Many requests constantly have a wait_type of WRITELOG with a value > 0.

   • The WRITELOG wait type is one of the highest counts for wait types.

   • The avg time to write to the transaction log is somewhere around 2ms.

   The overall duration of running this workload on SQL Server 2019 on a computer with fairly normal SSD storage is around 10–12 seconds. The total duration of running thins using Azure SQL Database with my deployed General Purpose 8 vCore database is around 25 seconds. The latency of WRITELOG waits is affecting the overall performance of the application.

Note   The documentation states that the expected latency for General Purpose is 5–7ms for writes. Our diagnostics showed better performance, but it won't be the same as using an SSD storage system.

---

5. Decide on a resolution.

   You could look at changing your deployment to Business Critical or Hyperscale to get better I/O latency. But is there a more cost-effective way? If you looked at the batch for order_rating_insert_single.sql, you will notice that each INSERT is its own commit or singleton transactions. What if we grouped INSERTs into transactions?

6. Change the application workload.

You can see a new workload method to group INSERTs into a transaction with **order_rating_insert.sql** like the following:

```
DECLARE @x int;
SET @x = 0;
BEGIN TRAN;
WHILE (@x < 500)
BEGIN
SET @x = @x + 1;
INSERT INTO SalesLT.OrderRating
(SalesOrderID, OrderRatingDT, OrderRating, OrderRatingComments)
VALUES (@x, getdate(), 5, 'This was a great order');
END
COMMIT TRAN;
GO
```

Notice the use of BEGIN TRAN and COMMIT TRAN to wrap the loop of INSERT statements.

You can now edit the order_rating_insert.cmd script with your server, database, login, and password to run this workload change.

7. Run the new workload change.

When you run the new script (which is executing the same number of INSERT statements), you will see

•   Far less WRITELOG waits with lower average wait time

•   A much faster overall duration

The workload runs even faster now (I've seen as fast as 3 seconds overall).

This is a great example of ensuring you are looking at your application when running it against Azure SQL vs. just assuming you need to make a deployment option change and pay more in your subscription.

Intelligent Performance

I mentioned earlier in this chapter our intention to build into the database engine intelligent capabilities based on data and your application workload to get you faster with **no code changes**.

Let's take a look in more detail to these areas of Intelligent Query Processing, Automatic Plan Correction, and Automatic Tuning.

Intelligent Query Processing

In SQL Server 2017, we enhanced the query processor to adapt to query workloads and improve performance when you used the latest database compatibility level. We called this Adaptive Query Processing (AQP). We went a step further in SQL Server 2019 and rebranded it as **Intelligent Query Processing (IQP)**.

IQP is a suite of new capabilities built into the Query Processor and enabled using the latest database compatibility level. Applications can gain performance with no code changes by simply using the latest database compatibility level. An example of IQP is *table variable deferred compilation* to help make queries using table variables run faster with no code changes. Azure SQL Database and Managed Instance support the same database compatibility level required to use IQP (150) as SQL Server 2019. IQP is a great example of a cloud-first capability since it was first adopted by customers in Azure before it was released in SQL Server 2019.

I covered this topic extensively in the book *SQL Server 2019 Revealed*. You can go run any of these examples from `https://github.com/microsoft/bobsql/tree/master/sql2019book/ch2_intelligent_performance` against Azure SQL to see how this works in action.

In addition, the documentation covers this topic extensively at `https://docs.microsoft.com/en-us/sql/relational-databases/performance/intelligent-query-processing`.

At the time of the writing of this book, Scalar UDF inlining was not yet available in Azure SQL Database, but probably by the time you are reading this, it will be available.

I asked Joe Sack who is not only the technical reviewer of this book but also the program manager lead for IQP about the significance of IQP for Azure SQL. According to Joe, "Over the last four years, the query processing team delivered two waves of Intelligent QP features – all with the objective to improve workload performance automatically with minimal changes to application code. Today we're already seeing millions of databases and billions of queries using IQP features. Just as one example, we already have millions of unique query execution plans being executed hundreds of millions of times per day that use the memory grant feedback feature. In Azure SQL on a daily basis, this ends up preventing terabytes of query spills and petabytes worth of overestimations for user queries. The end result is improved query execution performance and workload concurrency."

This area of improving our query processor to help your application is significant for Azure SQL. As Joe tells it for the future, "We have a long-term plan and active engineering investments to keep alleviating the hardest query processing problems that customers face at-scale. We look at a myriad of signals in order to prioritize features – including telemetry, customer support case volume, customer engagements and SQL community member feedback. We have eight separate Intelligent Database-related efforts underway in "wave 3", and our plan is to light these efforts up in Azure SQL Database first over the next few years."

Automatic Plan Correction

In 2017, I stood on stage with Conor Cunningham at the PASS Summit and showed off an amazing piece of technology for SQL Server 2017 to solve a performance problem using automation with Query Store. Query Store has such rich data; why not use it with automation?

What I showed on stage was a demonstration of a **query plan regression** problem that can be automatically fixed.

Note   You can see the code I used for this demonstration at `https://github.com/microsoft/bobsql/tree/master/demos/sqlserver/autotune`.

A query plan regression occurs when the same query is recompiled and a new plan results in worse performance. A common scenario for query plan regression are *parameter-sensitive plans* (PSP), also known as parameter sniffing.

SQL Server 2017 and Azure SQL Database introduced the concept of **Automatic Plan Correction** (APC) by analyzing data in the Query Store. When the Query Store is enabled with a database in SQL Server 2017 (or later) and in Azure SQL Database, the SQL Server engine will look for query plan regressions and provide recommendations. You can see these recommendations in the DMV **sys.dm_db_tuning_recommendations**. These recommendations will include T-SQL statements to manually force a query plan when performance was "in a good state."

If you gain confidence in these recommendations, you can enable SQL Server to force plans automatically when regressions are encountered. Automatic Plan Correction can be enabled using ALTER DATABASE using the AUTOMATIC_TUNING argument.

For Azure SQL Database, you can also enable Automatic Plan Correction through *automatic tuning options* in the Azure Portal or REST APIs. You can read more about these techniques in the documentation. Automatic Plan Correction recommendations are always enabled for any database where Query Store is enabled (which is the default for Azure SQL Database and Managed Instance). Automatic Plan Correction (FORCE_ PLAN) is enabled by default for Azure SQL Database as of March 2020 for **new** databases.

You can read more about Automatic Plan Correction at `https://docs.microsoft.com/en-us/sql/relational-databases/automatic-tuning/automatic-tuning`.

Automatic Tuning

Technically, Automatic Plan Correction is part of a suite of services to use automation to improve query performance with no code changes called **Automatic Tuning**. Automatic Plan Correction works in SQL Server, Azure SQL Managed Instance, and Azure SQL Database.

In Chapter 1 of this book, I talked about the history of how Automatic Tuning was created. Azure SQL Database offers a unique feature of Automatic Tuning to help automate creating and dropping indexes called **automatic indexing**.

Note   Today automatic indexing is not available for Azure SQL Managed Instance.

This capability is known as **Automatic Tuning for Azure SQL Database** (also known in some parts of the documentation as SQL Database Advisor). These services run as background programs analyzing performance data from an Azure SQL Database and are included in the price of any database subscription. Automatic Tuning will analyze data from telemetry of a database including the Query Store and Dynamic Management Views to recommend indexes to be created that can improve application performance. Additionally, you can enable Automatic Tuning services to automatically create indexes that it believes will improve query performance. Automatic Tuning will also monitor index changes and recommend or automatically drop indexes that do not improve query performance. Automatic Tuning for Azure SQL Database takes a conservative approach to recommend indexes. This means that recommendations that may show up in a DMV like **sys.dm_db_missing_index_details** or a query show plan may not show up immediately as recommendations for Automatic Tuning. Automatic Tuning services monitor queries over time and use machine learning algorithms to make recommendations to truly affect query performance.

One downside to Automatic Tuning for index recommendations is that it does not account for any overhead performance an index could cause insert, update, or delete operations.

Note   You can read an excellent paper for how automatic indexing is built by our engineering team at `www.microsoft.com/en-us/research/uploads/prod/2019/02/autoindexing_azuredb.pdf`.

One additional scenario in preview for Automatic Tuning for Azure SQL Database is parameterized queries. Queries with non-parameterized values can lead to performance overhead because the execution plan is recompiled each time the non-parameterized values are different. In many cases, the same queries with different parameter values generate the same execution plans. These plans, however, are still separately added to the plan cache. The process of recompiling execution plans uses database resources, increases the query duration time, and overflows the plan cache. These events, in turn, cause plans to be evicted from the cache. This SQL Server behavior can be altered by setting the forced parameterization option on the database (this is done by executing the ALTER DATABASE T-SQL statement using the PARAMETERIZATION FORCED option). Automatic tuning can analyze a query performance workload against a database over time and recommend forced parameterization for the database. If over time performance degradation has been observed, the option will be disabled.

Let's see an example of automatic indexing in action. I'll use a database I deployed based on the AdventureWorks example to show this capability. You can try this out yourself using the scripts found in the **ch7_performance\tuning_recommendations**. You will need to edit the **query_order_rating.cmd** script to put in your server, database, login, and password. These scripts assume you have completed the previous exercise for concurrent INSERT execution as it uses the OrderRating table created in that exercise.

Here is the main issue when using these scripts. It takes time and patience. Why? Our algorithms don't just recommend indexes based on a single query and single execution. We look at query workloads over time and for frequent executions to decide if an index makes sense. Therefore, when you try this yourself, you will need to let this script run to completion (it runs thousands of iterations). When I did this within 24 hours, I saw the information I'm about to show you from the Azure portal:

1. See recommendations in the Azure portal.

   After running the workload and waiting for 24 hours, I saw recommendations how up in the Azure portal similar to Figure 7-24.

Figure 7-24. *Index recommendation notification in the Azure portal*

   I can click Performance overview in the Resource menu of the database to visually see information from the Query Store and a look at Recommendations. This looks similar to Figure 7-25.

Figure 7-25. *Performance overview from the Azure portal*

The Azure portal offers another visualization for query
performance called Query Performance Insights from the
Resource Menu as seen in Figure 7-26.

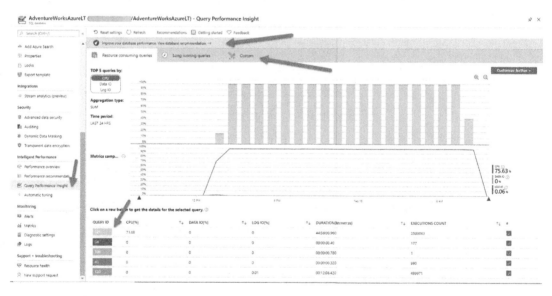

Figure 7-26. *Query performance insights from the Azure portal*

You can see in this figure a list of top queries consuming resources
and a suggestion at the top of the screen to improve performance.

The Azure portal can also take you directly to Performance recommendation from the Resource menu as seen in Figure 7-27.

Figure 7-27. *Performance recommendations from the Azure portal*

You can see here specific recommendations for indexes, possible impact on performance, and history of any automatic tuning actions. You can also see in the command bar an option to select **Automate**.

To this point, everything is a recommendation. If you select Automate, you will be presented options to enable automation of automatic plan correction force plans, creating, and dropping indexes. This screen will look like Figure 7-28.

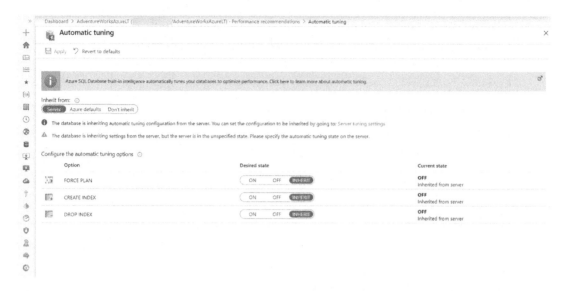

Figure 7-28.   *Setting automatic tuning options*

You can configure Automatic Tuning options at the logical server or database level. You can also view automatic tuning options through the catalog view **sys.database_automatic_tuning_options**. You can view all the columns for this catalog view at https://docs.microsoft.com/en-us/sql/relational-databases/system-catalog-views/sys-database-automatic-tuning-options-transact-sql?view=sql-server-ver15.

If you would have had create index turned on for this database, an index would have been automatically created.

If you go back and look at the recommended index, you can view more details as seen in Figure 7-29.

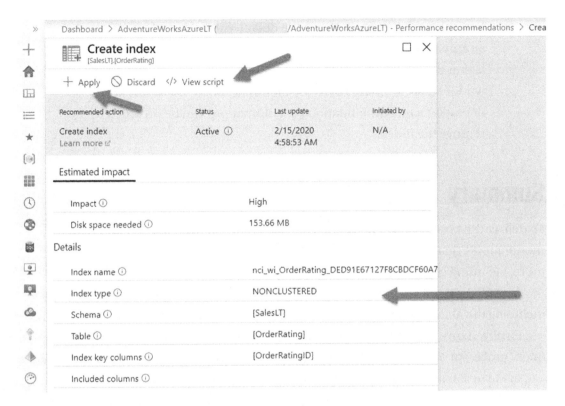

Figure 7-29. *Details of a create index recommendation*

You can apply the index recommendation or even view the T-SQL
script behind the operation as seen in Figure 7-30.

Figure 7-30. *T-SQL script for index recommendations*

You can see an online index is the default method used for
automatic indexing. One thing I love about automatic indexing
is that the service will run behind the scenes to monitor your
workload performance after the index is applied. If performance
degrades, a recommendation (or automation) can be provided to
remove the index.

Summary

To deliver the best performance for you application, you need the capabilities and
monitor tools that are tried and proven from SQL Server. Azure SQL gives you that and
more, including capabilities and tools specific to Azure.

Azure SQL gives you the controls and options to accelerate and tune performance
including the ability to scale easily with no database migration required.

Finally, Azure SQL comes with Intelligent Performance capabilities built into the
query processor and services that leverage the power of Query Store from your database.

In the next chapter, we will explore and dive deep into the final core engine
capability of Azure SQL to ensure your deployment is **highly available** and ensure you
have the tools you need for disaster recovery.

CHAPTER 8

Availability for Azure SQL

You have now made the journey from deploy to configure to security and then to monitor and tune performance. The final piece of the core of Azure SQL is **availability**. I have rarely talked to a SQL Server customer over the years that didn't need their database to be highly available. I also almost never talk to a customer who doesn't care about being able to recover from a disaster. Therefore, this chapter is really about **High Availability and Disaster Recovery (HADR)** for Azure SQL. I will tell you that in my opinion after now assessing and using Azure SQL over this last year, the built-in capabilities for HADR for Azure SQL are one of the great stories of the service. In fact, I believe after you go through this chapter you will be convinced that looking at Azure SQL as a target for your deployment is worth it just on the HADR capabilities alone.

In this chapter, we will spend the majority of time diving into the details of HADR capabilities including Backup and Restore, built-in HA, Azure capabilities to go farther, and database availability and consistency. Then I'll finish the chapter on how to monitor HADR for your deployment.

This chapter will contain examples for you to try out and use as you read along. For you to try out any of the techniques, commands, or examples I use in this chapter, you will need

- An Azure subscription.

- A minimum of Contributor role access to the Azure subscription. You can read more about Azure built-in roles at `https://docs.microsoft.com/en-us/azure/role-based-access-control/built-in-roles`.

- Access to the Azure Portal (web or Windows application).

- A deployment of an Azure SQL Managed Instance and/or an Azure SQL Database as I did in Chapter 4. The Azure SQL Database I deployed uses the AdventureWorks sample which will be required to use some of the examples.

373

© Bob Ward 2021
B. Ward, *Azure SQL Revealed*, https://doi.org/10.1007/978-1-4842-5931-3_8

- To connect to Managed Instance, you will need a *jumpbox* or virtual machine in Azure to connect. I showed you how to do this in Chapter 4 of the book. One simple way to do this is to create a new Azure Virtual Machine and deploy it to the same virtual network as the Managed Instance (you will use a different subnet than the Managed Instance).

- To connect to Azure SQL Database, I'm going to use the Azure VM I deployed in Chapter 3, called **bwsql2019**, and configured for a private endpoint in Chapter 6 (you could use another method as long as you can connect to the Azure SQL Database).

- Installation of the **az** CLI (see `https://docs.microsoft.com/en-us/cli/azure/install-azure-cli?view=azure-cli-latest` for more details). You can also use the Azure Cloud Shell instead since az is already installed. You can read more about the Azure Cloud Shell at `https://azure.microsoft.com/en-us/features/cloud-shell/`.

- Installation of Azure PowerShell. Use the following documentation on how to install Azure PowerShell for your client: `https://docs.microsoft.com/en-us/PowerShell/azure/install-az-ps`. I installed Azure PowerShell in my Azure VM.

- You will run some T-SQL in this chapter, so install a tool like SQL Server Management Studio (SSMS) at `https://docs.microsoft.com/en-us/sql/ssms/download-sql-server-management-studio-ssms?view=sql-server-ver15`. You can also use Azure Data Studio at `https://docs.microsoft.com/en-us/sql/azure-data-studio/download-azure-data-studio?view=sql-server-ver15`. I installed both SSMS and ADS in the bwsql2019 Azure Virtual Machine.

- For this chapter, I have script files you can use for a few of the examples. You can find these scripts in the **ch8_availability** folder for the source files included for the book. I will also use the very popular tool ostress.exe for exercises in this chapter which comes with the RML Utilities. You can download RML from `www.microsoft.com/en-us/download/details.aspx?id=4511`. Make sure to put the folder where RML gets installed in your system path (which is by default C:\Program Files\Microsoft Corporation\RMLUtils).

HADR Capabilities

I want to first review with you the amazing HADR capabilities that come with Azure SQL before we dive deeper with examples into each topic.

Automatic Backups and Point-In-Time restore

Azure SQL is SQL Server, so the full complement of BACKUP and RESTORE functionality is possible. However, the promise of PaaS is to provide **managed capabilities**. Therefore, Azure SQL provides an automated backup system for both Managed Instance and Databases to meet your Recovery Point Object (RPO) and historical data needs. In fact, for Azure SQL Database, you are completely abstracted from the BACKUP T-SQL statement. Managed Instance will allow a COPY_ONLY backup to Azure Storage.

All backups from Azure SQL are kept on separate storage from your database and log files with automated geo-redundant mirrors. Azure SQL also offers a long-term backup retention option.

Azure SQL will use full, differential, and log backups supporting a complete Point-In-Time restore interface. In addition, you have these restore capabilities:

- Restore deleted databases.

- Managed Instance supports the RESTORE T-SQL statement from Azure Blob Storage which could be from an on-premises SQL Server backup or a COPY_ONLY backup from a Managed Instance.

Built-In High Availability

You may be used to using an Always On Failover Cluster Instance (FCI) or Always On Availability Group (AG) with SQL Server to give you high availability and achieve a desired Recovery Time Object (RTO).

As part of **every** Azure SQL deployment, you get a complete built-in High Availability system, just by deploying Azure SQL. This is included in your Azure subscription and fees for your deployment.

As you will see in this chapter, a General Purpose deployment will behave similar to FCI and Business Critical will be similar to AGs. Hyperscale uses a unique architecture that will feel like a combination of both. In all cases, the power of the Azure Service Fabric is used for automatic failover capabilities.

Azure Redundancy

Why rely on a single data center when you have three? Azure SQL can integrate with a capability called **Availability Zones in Azure**. Each zone is a set of one or more datacenters (so actually more than three) within an Azure region that has independent power, cooling, and networking. Azure SQL can deploy a high available solution across zones to provide you even more availability should there a failure in a particular data center.

All Azure SQL deployments are created as part of an **Azure Availability Set** which includes using different fault and update domains. Fault domains define the group of virtual machines that share a common power source and network switch. Update domains are groups of virtual machines and underlying physical hardware that can be rebooted at the same time. Only one update domain is rebooted at a time. A rebooted update domain is given 30 minutes to recover before maintenance is initiated on a different update domain. You can read more about this concept at `https://docs.microsoft.com/en-us/azure/virtual-machines/windows/manage-availability#configure-multiple-virtual-machines-in-an-availability-set-for-redundancy`.

Geo-replication and Auto-failover Groups

You might want to provide even higher levels of availability by synchronizing your deployments across Azure regions. Azure SQL provides two methods for this capability called Geo-replication and Auto-failover groups. We will go into each option in this chapter and why you may want to choose one vs. the other.

Database Availability and Consistency

With SQL Server, you are used to using various techniques to make your database available and checking consistency. Azure SQL eliminates the need for heavy "emergency" recovery options and provides many built-in consistency checks. I'll explore more in this chapter specific comparisons for database availability, recovery, and consistency for Azure SQL as compared to SQL Server.

SQL Server Replication

SQL Server Replication has been a popular method to provide a level of availability and database synchronization over many SQL Server releases. I won't dive into the details of using SQL Server Replication in this chapter, but point out these capabilities:

- Azure SQL Managed Instance gives you the full capabilities to set up a transaction or snapshot replication system including publisher, distribution, and subscribers. A subscriber can be another Managed Instance database, an Azure SQL Database, or even a SQL Server in Azure VM or on-premises. Read more about Azure SQL Managed Instance and Replication at `https://docs.microsoft.com/en-us/ azure/azure-sql/managed-instance/replication-transactional- overview`.

- An Azure SQL Database can be a subscriber from an on-premises SQL Server, SQL Server in Azure VM, or Managed Instance for transaction and snapshot replication. This might be an interesting migration option when moving to Azure SQL Database because it can provide a type of "online" migration strategy. Read more at `https://docs.microsoft.com/en-us/azure/azure-sql/database/ replication-to-sql-database`.

Backup and Restore

Imagine you needed to set up an automated backup system for your SQL Server deployment. You basically want a system to abstract even other DBAs from worrying about performing backups. You want these backups to run regularly; use a combination of full, differential, and log backups; and be placed on storage separate from your database for full protection. And, you would also like the storage for your backups to be mirrored even across data centers in your company.

Guess what? When you deploy an Azure SQL Managed Instance or Azure SQL Database, we just do all of this by default and more. Let's look at various aspects to the automated backup system and how to use restore with these backups.

Automatic Backups

When you deploy an Azure SQL Database or create a new database for an Azure SQL Managed Instance deployment, we monitor this activity and kick in the following schedule of backup activity:

- A full database backup once a week.

- A differential backup every 12 hours.

- A transaction log backup every 5–10 minutes. The actual frequency of log backups is based on number of vCores and database activity.

Note   We may vary the implementation of how we do this. The concept is that provided we give you Point-In-Time restore and meet your RPO objective.

All backups are done using standard T-SQL statements in the background and stored separately from your data and log files (even if they are on Azure Storage). In fact, your backup files are stored on Azure Storage using RA-GRS. RA-GRS stands for **read-access geo-zone-redundant storage**. This means that backup files are copied across three Azure availability zones in the primary region and also copied asynchronously to a single physical location in a different region. Read more about RA-GRS at `https://docs.microsoft.com/en-us/azure/storage/common/storage-redundancy#redundancy-in-a-secondary-region`.

When you deploy or create a new database, we schedule a full database backup almost immediately. We perform integrity checks on your backups using CHECKSUM and restore techniques. Read the complete story of automated backups for Azure SQL at `https://docs.microsoft.com/en-us/azure/azure-sql/database/automated-backups-overview`.

Backup Retention

By default, we keep enough backup files to allow you to perform a Point-In-Time restore (PITR) within the last 7 days at any point in time. For Azure SQL Database, you can change this retention lower to 1 day or up to 35 days. This is called **short-term backup retention**. You have the same option for any database created for a Managed Instance.

Note   You cannot configure the retention of 7 days for Hyperscale deployment. We are looking in the future to allow this.

Retention policies affect how far back you can restore from a point in time but also how much storage space your backups consume. You can configure the short-term retention policy for Azure SQL Database backups through the Azure portal (I'll show you an example when I discuss long-term retentions later in this section of the chapter), az CLI (**az sql db ltr-policy**), or PowerShell (**Set-AzSqlDatabaseBackupShortTermRetentionPolicy**).

Note   Anytime there is az CLI or PowerShell support, there is also REST API support because that is what az and PowerShell use. For backup retention, you can read about REST API support at `https://docs.microsoft.com/en-us/rest/api/sql/backupshorttermretentionpolicies`.

Short-term backup retention can be configured for databases for Managed Instance using the Azure portal as seen in Figure 8-1 for one of the databases I deployed on my Managed Instance.

Figure 8-1. *Configuring short-term backup retention for a Managed Instance database*

The portal only allows configuration on a database level, so for the instance you may want to use scripts for automation. Therefore, you can also manage the short-term retention policy for Managed Instance backups with az CLI (**az sql midb short-term-retention-policy**) and PowerShell (**Set-AzSqlInstanceDatabaseBackupShortTermRetentionPolicy**).

Backup Storage Consumption and Costs

As part of your deployment, you get free storage for backups equivalent to the maximum size of your database or Managed Instance storage size. This includes the space for all full, differential, and log backups. Even though we compress all backups, the size you need will depend on the size of your data, how many changes you make (affects size of differential and log backups), and your number of backup retention days.

If you exceed the backup storage you get for free with your managed instance maximum storage size or maximum Azure SQL Database size, you can incur extra costs for backups.

In most cases, we have found customers that use the default retention period of 7 days rarely incur extra charges. For Azure SQL, you can track if you are using extra space that is being charged on your subscription by using the Azure portal and viewing billing information with your subscription. Learn more at `https://docs.microsoft.com/en-us/azure/azure-sql/database/automated-backups-overview?tabs=single-database#storage-costs`.

For Azure SQL Database, Azure Metrics allow you to track and even get alerts on backup storage consumed for full, differential, and log backups. Figure 8-2 shows an example of using Azure Metrics through the portal to see what is available.

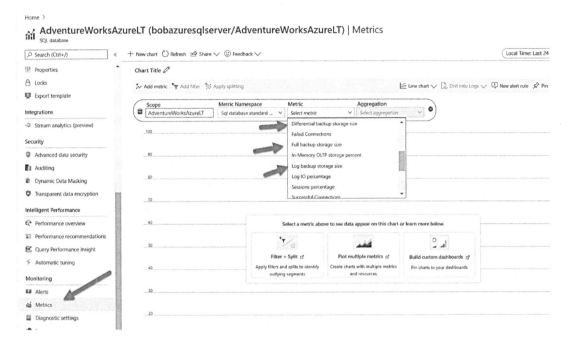

Figure 8-2. *Metrics for backup storage consumption for Azure SQL Database*

Here are some tips to help you on consuming backup storage space:

- Reduce the retention period to the shortest possible number of days per your requirements.

- The larger modifications you make (e.g., index rebuilds), the larger the space needed for differential and log backups. Take a look to ensure these operations are all needed.

- It is possible that you can increase your maximum storage size so you get more backup space, but the increase in storage size could cost less than backup storage costs.

Point-In-Time restore

Now that you know about the automated backup strategy we use, you may have a need to use backups to perform a restore. In some cases for SQL Server, you may run into a situation where an accident has occurred that affects availability like a database owner dropping a table.

Since we deploy a combination of full, differential, and log backups, we allow you to pick a *point in time* and restore back to that state using these backups. This concept is called **Point-In-Time restore (PITR)** and is available in SQL Server (provided you deploy the right backup strategy).

If you look at the SQL Server documentation at `https://docs.microsoft.com/en-us/sql/relational-databases/backup-restore/restore-a-sql-server-database-to-a-point-intime-full-recovery-model`, the method to restore to a point in time is to use a series of backups to restore from a log backup using the T-SQL RESTORE statement. For Azure SQL, PITR is supported for the automated backups we create for Azure SQL Managed Instance and Databases. Therefore, to perform a Point-In-Time restore, you must use Azure interfaces such as the portal, az CLI, or PowerShell.

Note   Even though the RESTORE statement is supported for a Managed Instance, your syntax is limited and you cannot perform a Point-In-Time restore. This is only to restore full backups from the COPY_ONLY option or from a SQL Server.

Azure SQL Managed Instance supports PITR through the Azure portal (navigate to the database in the portal and select the Restore option from the command bar), az CLI (**az sql midb restore**), and PowerShell (**Restore-AzSqlInstanceDatabase**). A PITR operation is asynchronous and creates a *new database* (in fact a new deployment) based on the date and time you select for the restore. Your date and time choices are based on your backup day retention.

Azure SQL Database also supports PITR through the Azure portal, az CLI (**az-sql-db-restore**), and PowerShell (**Restore-AzSqlDatabase**).

Let's look at an example of how to use PITR for the database I deployed called **bwazuresqldb** in Chapter 4 of the book. I created this database some time back as I was writing the chapters of the book, so by now at least 7 days has gone by for a series of backups. Let's go through an exercise where I accidentally drop a table in my database and then use PITR to restore the database to a new database name before the drop so I can merge that data back into my current database:

1. Drop the table.

    I'll use the Azure VM **bwsql2019** I deployed in Chapter 3 and have used in the last two chapters to connect with SSMS and run the following T-SQL statement against the **bwazuresqldb** database connected as the server admin I used during deployment (remember it is based on the AdventureWorks sample):

    ```
    DROP TABLE SalesLT.OrderRating;
    GO
    ```

Note   This is the table I created as part of an example in Chapter 7. I left around 1500 rows in the table before I dropped it. So, if we restore it correctly, we should have it back with 1500 rows.

---

2. Audit when the table was dropped.

    I dropped the table to show the example but imagine the scenario is that someone else dropped the table and no one remembers exactly when. In order to find out when to restore the database to a point in time, we need to know when the table was dropped. If you remember, we set up auditing for this database in Chapter 6 of the book. Let's take advantage of that auditing to see when the table was dropped. I showed you in Chapter 6 of the book how to navigate to find Audit records for a database. The records for my database just after the DROP statement look like Figure 8-3.

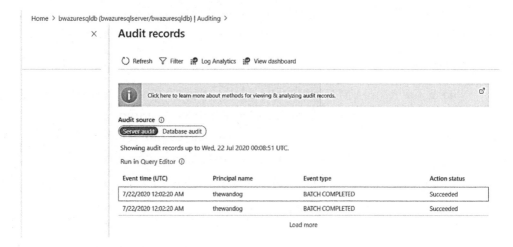

Figure 8-3. *Audit records after a DROP statement*

If I click the first BATCH_COMPLETED record, I see the DROP
statement including date and time and the user like in Figure 8-4.

Home > bwazuresqldb (bwazuresqlserver/bwazuresqldb) | Auditing > Audit records >

Audit record   ×
bwazuresqldb

Event time (UTC)
7/22/2020 12:02:20 AM

Event type
BATCH COMPLETED

Server name
bwazuresqlserver

Database name
bwazuresqldb

Application name
Microsoft SQL Server Management Studio - Query

Principal name
thewandog

Client IP
172.16.6.4

Status
Succeeded

STATEMENT

```
DROP TABLE SalesLT.OrderRating;
```

Figure 8-4. *An audit record for a DROP statement*

3. Restore the database to the time before the DROP.

I purposely waited overnight from when I dropped the table to simulate a real-world scenario where someone could realize the drop happened at an earlier point in time. Based on the preceding audit record, I know I need to restore to a point in time before 7/22/2020 at 12:02 AM UTC time. Let's use the Azure portal to perform a restore. I'll navigate to my database, **bwazuresqldb**, in the Azure portal and choose Restore from the command bar as seen in Figure 8-5.

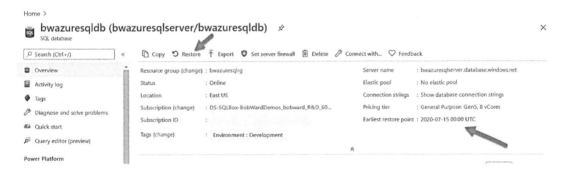

Figure 8-5. *Choosing to Restore a database with PITR*

Notice in the working pane for this database, you can see what the earliest time you can restore.

Note   The earliest point in time is based on the first transaction log backup after the database is created. A full backup must first complete before the log backup is taken.

After I select Restore, I'm presented with a screen where I can fill out the time I want to restore to as seen in Figure 8-6.

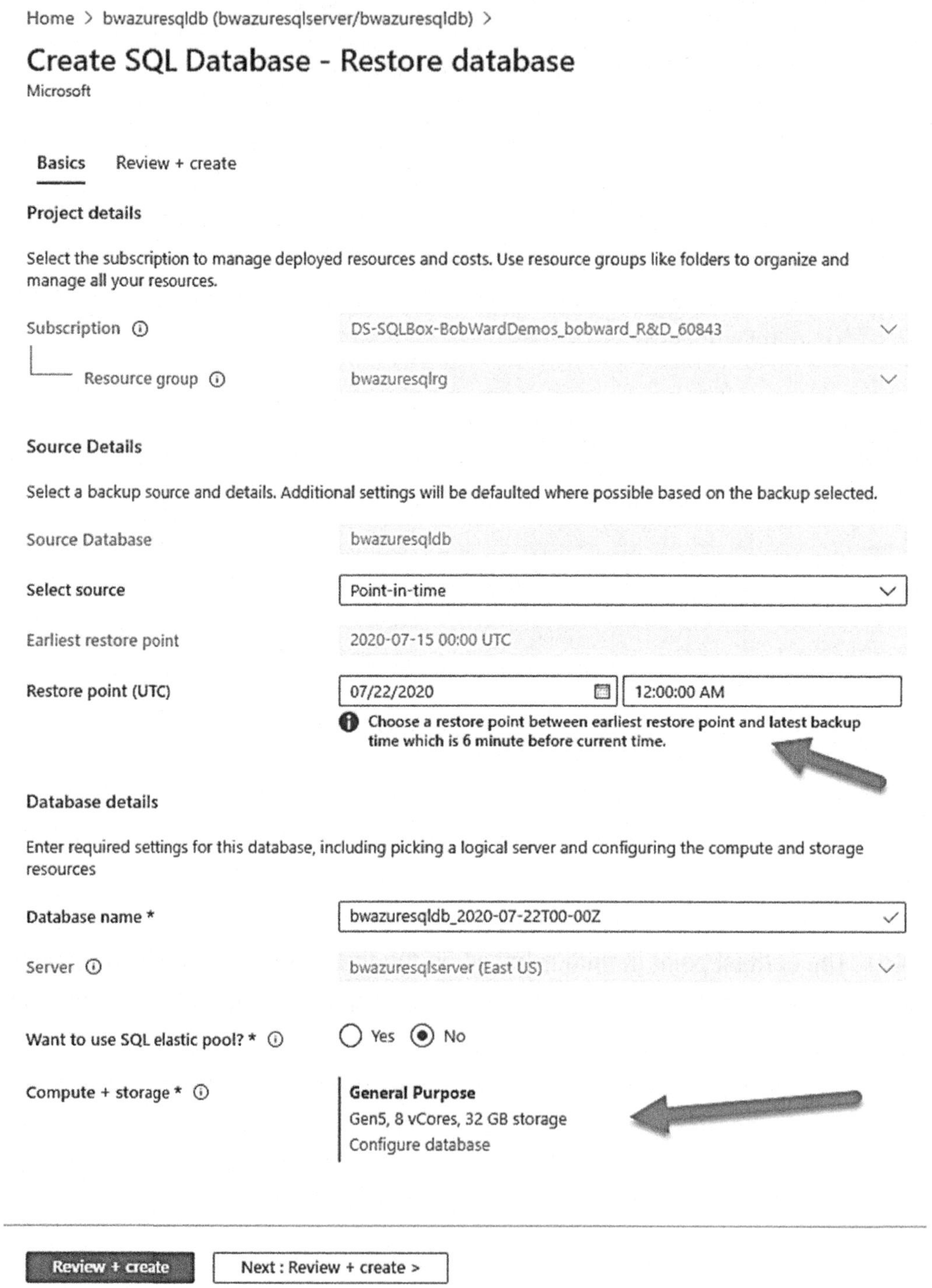

Figure 8-6. *Restoring to a point in time for Azure SQL Database*

You will notice where I can select a date and time and then I get
options for Database name, whether I want this to be part of
an elastic pool, and compute and storage options (e.g., service
tier). You wonder why you can choose compute and storage?
This is because a restore will create a new database and you can
choose that database to have the same options (General Purpose,
Serverless, Business Critical, Hyperscale, vCores, etc.) as when
you create a new database or different ones. I clicked **Review
+ create** and a new deployment was started. You need to set
some expectations on time here to deploy. This is not just a new
database. We must do all the things to deploy a new database
and restore a full database backup and a series of differential and
log backups up to the time you selected. For me, this restore took
around 10 minutes. I can do all the activities we talked about in
Chapter 4 of the book to look at the activity log and see how the
restore deployed a new database. I recommend customers try out
various scenarios here to see expected recovery times for their
workload. Just remember that higher RTO and RPO objective can
be achieved with concepts like geo-replication and auto-failover
groups which will be discussed later in this chapter.

Note   Your recovery time will depend on what we need to restore to get you to the
desired point in time. Learn more at `https://docs.microsoft.com/en-us/`
`azure/azure-sql/database/recovery-using-backups#recovery-time`
including limits on the number of concurrent restores.

---

4. Verify the new database has the dropped table.

    I went back to my Azure VM, **bwsql2019**, where I had connected
    as an admin to the logical master. Object Explorer in SSMS now
    shows the new database as in Figure 8-7.

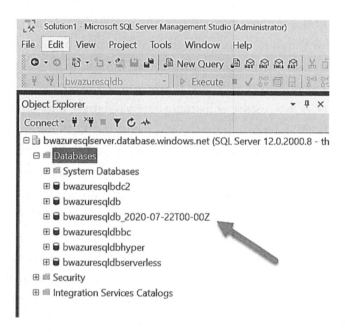

Figure 8-7.   *A restored Azure SQL Database in SSMS*

If I navigate to this database and run the following T-SQL statement:

```
SELECT COUNT(*) FROM SalesLT.OrderRating;
GO
```

I get back 1500 rows. I now have two choices:

- Drop **bwazuresqldb** and rename this new database so my applications would lose any changes since the time for PITR.

- Merge the data from this new database from SalesLT.OrderRating into my original database. I realize this may not be a simple operation if foreign keys exist.

Long-Term Retention Backups

You have seen we can keep backups for your databases from 1 to 35 days to meet your RPO requirements. However, what if your business needs to meet certain regulations and keep a longer history of backups? You may not need these backups to recover from a disaster, but rather need them to access historical data to meet some type of compliance. Azure SQL offers a concept called **long-term backup retention (LTR)**. This allows you to keep backups for up to **10 years**. All LTR backups that are kept *are full database backups*.

Note   At the time of the writing of this book, Azure SQL Managed Instance offers LTR in a limited preview, and you must use PowerShell to configure LTR. See this documentation page `https://docs.microsoft.com/en-us/azure/azure-sql/managed-instance/long-term-backup-retention-configure` for more details. You could as an alternative use the COPY_ONLY backup feature of Managed Instance to create any schedule for backups to your Azure Storage account for any period of time you like.

Here is how the concept works. You configure a retention period > the maximum of short-term retention of 35 days. You do this by selecting the frequency of how long you want LTR backups to be kept on a weekly, monthly, and yearly basis. You can select all three options if you like. Azure SQL will take short-term retention backups and copy them to a different Azure storage account (it also uses RA-GRS so is geo-redundant) based on the choices you make. LTR is not included as part of the subscription fee for your database but is charged a less expensive rate than excess short-term backup retention storage over what is included with your deployment.

Let's look at one of my databases and see an example of how you could configure LTR. In order to configure LTR in the Azure Portal, I need to navigate to my logical server vs. directly to the database. Figure 8-8 shows how I can select the Manage Backups from the Resource menu of the logical server, select a database I want to configure, and select the Configure retention option.

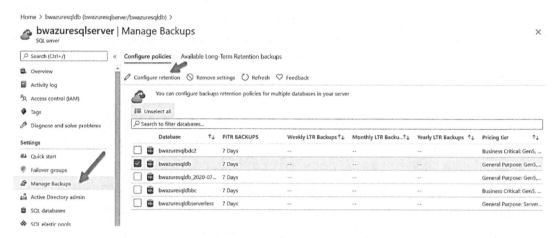

Figure 8-8. *Configuring backup retention for Azure SQL Database*

When I select Configure retention, I'm presented with a screen where I can configure short-term backup retention and LTR. Figure 8-9 shows the choices you can make.

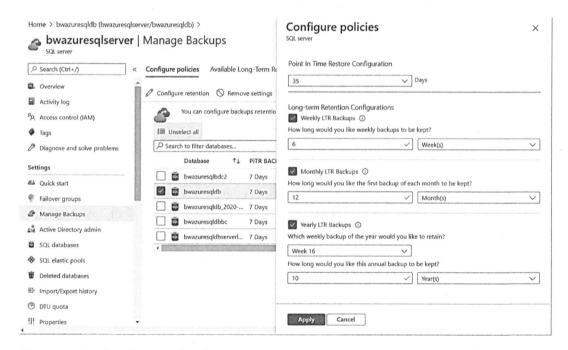

Figure 8-9. *Configuring backup retention policies for Azure SQL Database*

Let me explain how the choices I've made affect backup retention for this database:

- I modified the short-term backup retention for the database to 35 days.

- I chose that each full database backup taken weekly be kept for six weeks.

- I chose that the first full backup taken for a month be kept for 12 months.

- I chose that the full backup taken on the 16th week of the year be kept for 10 years.

You don't have to choose all three options as I did. You can choose various combinations or just one of them. We have a chart in our documentation that can help you sketch out a schedule for LTR at `https://docs.microsoft.com/en-us/azure/azure-sql/database/long-term-retention-overview#how-long-term-retention-works`.

You can also configure LTR for Azure SQL Database using az CLI (**azsqldbltr-policy**) or PowerShell (**Set-AzSqlDatabaseBackupLongTermRetentionPolicy**).

Note   If you use geo-replication or auto-failover groups, which I will discuss later in this chapter, you can configure LTR for those databases, but LTR backups are not taken unless that database becomes a primary.

Geo-restore of Databases

Let's say that your database from Azure SQL Database or Managed Instance is unavailable due to a data center outage. While these situations are rare, it would be nice to able to restore a backup from a geo-redundant backup from another region that does not have an outage.

The process is called **geo-restore** and is outlined at `https://docs.microsoft.com/en-us/azure/azure-sql/database/recovery-using-backups#geo-restore`. The concept is that you will deploy a new Azure SQL Database or create a new database for a Managed Instance based on a backup. When you select this option, you will be presented with all the known backups that exist for your existing Azure SQL deployments. If the data center is down where your backups are normally stored, we will retrieve the geo-redundant copy of the backup from a different region.

Restore Backups from Deleted Databases

The built-in HADR options just keep coming with Azure SQL. Let's say you *accidentally* delete a database for an Azure SQL Database or Managed Instance.

Note   Deleting a database for Azure SQL Database or Managed Instance does more behind the scenes than a traditional SQL Server given we have all types of services and operations tied to the database. This is why you can delete a database through Azure interfaces or the DROP DATABASE T-SQL statement.

I realize this may not be something you almost never see, but one of the great stories for built-in HADR is that when you delete a database, you can restore from backups associated with the deleted database using PITR based on the retention period you configured. If your retention period is 7 days and you delete a database, we can't perform any more backups, but you can restore to a point in time from the earliest backup point to the time of database deletion.

Note   You cannot recover from a deleted logical server or Managed Instance. However, if you have configured LTR backup retention, you can create new databases based on these backups. You may be asking since LTR backups are not free, how do I ever remove LTR backups? You can use the PowerShell cmdlets **Remove-AzSqlDatabaseLongTermRetentionBackup** or **Remove-AzSqlInstan ceDatabaseLongTermRetentionBackup** *even if the logical server or Managed Instance has been deleted.*

You can restore deleted databases through the Azure portal, az CLI, or PowerShell. Read more about how to do this at https://docs.microsoft.com/en-us/azure/azure-sql/database/recovery-using-backups#deleted-database-restore.

Restore in Azure SQL Managed Instance

I've mentioned that it is possible to execute a BACKUP T-SQL statement for an Azure SQL Managed Instance earlier in this chapter. We have referred this capability as a *native* database backup. The term native is used because you can perform a full database backup using the BACKUP T-SQL statement to disk storage. This disk storage must be an Azure storage account and uses the "backup to URL" capability that SQL Server has supported for several releases.

You must use the WITH COPY_ONLY option to back up a database for a Managed Instance. SQL Server has supported a *copy-only* backup for several releases. A copy-only backup does not affect the backup sequence of full, differential, and log backups. Our team has posted a nice blog about how to set up a native backup with Managed Instance at `https://techcommunity.microsoft.com/t5/azure-sql-database/native-database-backup-in-azure-sql-managed-instance/ba-p/386154`.

Since you can perform a native backup with a Managed Instance, you can also restore these backups using the T-SQL RESTORE statement. You can only restore copy-only backups from a Managed Instance to an existing or new Managed Instance. Just remember it is a new database. For example, you will get an error (Mg 41901) if you try to use the WITH REPLACE syntax of RESTORE. You cannot restore these backups to SQL Server or Azure SQL Database.

Note   The reason you cannot restore a backup from Managed Instance to a SQL Server is because Managed Instance is versionless.

In addition, you can take any full database backup from any supported version of SQL Server and restore it to a Managed Instance. This is actually the process you use to perform an offline or online migration from SQL Server to a Managed Instance. Learn more at `https://docs.microsoft.com/en-us/azure/dms/tutorial-sql-server-managed-instance-online`.

The following documentation page walks you through the process of performing a native restore with a Managed Instance: `https://docs.microsoft.com/en-us/azure/azure-sql/managed-instance/restore-sample-database-quickstart`.

Built-In High Availability

SQL Server has a great tradition of providing the necessary capabilities and software to keep your database highly available. The tradition started with Always On Failover Cluster Instance (FCI) using shared storage and integrating with technologies such as Windows Server Failover Clustering (WSFC) for automated failover. In SQL Server 2012, we introduced Always On Availability Groups to allow a non-shared storage approach, read replicas, and still integrated with WSFC for automatic failover decisions. SQL Server Linux also supports these capabilities but is integrated with Linux technologies such as Pacemaker.

One of the aspects of Azure SQL the engineering wanted to provide was a public commitment to a Service-Level Agreement (SLA) included availability. They also wanted the deployment process for a database or Managed Instance to "just do it" when it came to configuring and setting up availability. Finally, since Azure SQL was deployed with Azure Service Fabric (SF), we needed to integrate with SF for failover decisions.

The result is truly an amazing story. Every Azure SQL deployment option you choose has a built-in High Availability. Let's take a look at each deployment option and the architecture of availability that makes it all happen. You can also use the following documentation page as a reference: https://docs.microsoft.com/en-us/azure/azure-sql/database/high-availability-sla. The details of this chapter for General Purpose and Business Critical service tiers apply to both Azure SQL Managed Instance and Database.

I asked Girish Mittur Venkataramanappa, a Principal Group Software Engineering Manager, who has worked on SQL availability for many years on the importance of our investment in built-in availability for Azure. According to Girish, "Our customers are increasingly migrating mission critical workloads to SQL DB. Availability outages not only impact our customer's business, operations, and bottom line, it also erodes their own customer trust putting their business at risk. At Microsoft, our mission is to empower every person and every organization on the planet to achieve more. We offer strong Availability SLAs and stand behind them. We have built very effective High Availability technologies that offer redundant stand by replicas, multiple Availability Zones, and GeoDR which protect Databases against a variety of failures. In addition we have sophisticated monitoring, alerting and self-healing capabilities, and a well-trained 24x7 live site DevOps team. We take Availability very seriously. Most recently we invested a couple of years reengineering our Database Crash Recovery algorithms so that crash recovery is near instant as opposed to several minutes prior to that. We have a continuous development cycle of measuring and improving availability for the millions of Databases that we run today."

General Purpose High Availability

I've described the overall concept of a General Purpose (GP) service tier several times in this book. Your databases are stored on Azure Storage, while tempdb is stored on local SSD storage. Let's use a visual to describe more about the General Purpose architecture and how availability and failover work. (these figures are based on diagrams in the documentation at `https://docs.microsoft.com/en-us/azure/azure-sql/database/high-availability-sla#basic-standard-and-general-purpose-service-tier-availability`).

First, let's look at Figure 8-10.

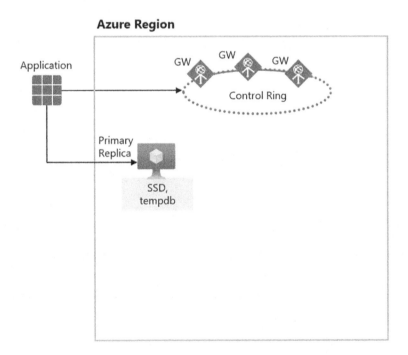

Figure 8-10. *Application connects to a General Purpose deployment using Gateways*

An application will connect to the primary replica (there is only one replica with General Purpose) by using Gateways in the control ring in an Azure region. If you remember, we talked about connection types of proxy and redirect with gateways in Chapters 4 and 6 of the book. In either case, the gateways provide a connection abstraction for the application. Notice the local SSD storage for the deployment is where tempdb is stored.

Figure 8-11 shows the next piece of the architecture.

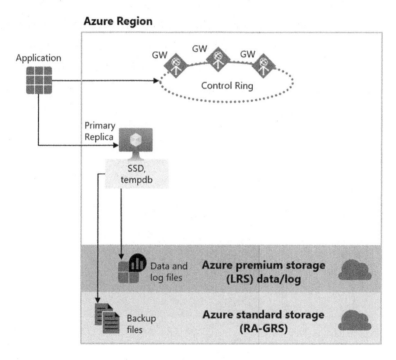

Figure 8-11. *Storage for a General Purpose deployment*

The Database and transaction log files are put on Azure premium storage using LRS (Locally Redundant Storage). This means your database and transaction log files are replicated three times within a physical location of the data center. You can read more about LRS at https://docs.microsoft.com/en-us/azure/storage/common/storage-redundancy#redundancy-in-the-primary-region.

As I've described earlier in this chapter, your backup files are stored in a different storage location within the data center but using RA-GRS so they are geo-redundant.

The Azure SQL deployment is integrated with Service Fabric (SF) to detect problems (e.g., a node failure) and initiate a *failover* if necessary. If a failover is required, we will find a new node with spare capacity to host your deployment as seen in Figure 8-12.

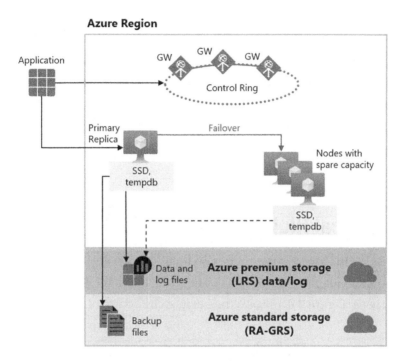

Figure 8-12. *A failover for a General Purpose deployment*

The local storage of the new node hosts SQL Server including tempdb. The new SQL Server will be directed to your database and log files on Azure storage. This type of architecture is very similar to how an FCI works for SQL Server. Your downtime is based on how fast we can find a new node with enough capacity to host your deployment choices (vCores, etc.). In addition, SQL Server that is hosting your database on the new node has just started up with a cold buffer and plan cache, so normal startup activities will affect your performance (recovery of the database will be extremely fast since we use Accelerated Database Recovery).

You may be wondering how does the application connect to the new node after a failover? The gateways are the answer. The application never changes any names to connect to the new node. The gateways take care of that logic. The application must simply retry a connection and is off and running.

You can learn more about the GP availability architecture at `https://docs.`
`microsoft.com/en-us/azure/azure-sql/database/high-availability-sla#basic-`
`standard-and-general-purpose-service-tier-availability`.

Note   The Serverless compute tier uses the same high availability architecture since today it is only available for General Purpose service tiers. Some HADR features such as Long-Term Backup Retention will prevent the autopause feature of Serverless to be used. Learn more at `https://docs.microsoft.com/en-us/azure/azure-sql/database/serverless-tier-overview#autopausing-and-autoresuming`.

Business Critical High Availability

A Business Critical (BC) deployment relies on local storage and a series of replicas, much like an Always On Availability Group (AG). Let's look at the BC architecture as compared to General Purpose. Figure 8-13 shows the basic architecture of a BC deployment.

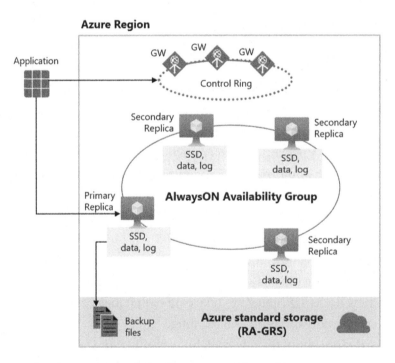

Figure 8-13. *A Business Critical deployment with replicas*

You can see from this figure that gateways are still an important part of connectivity and that a primary replica exists. Local storage is used for tempdb but also for database and log files. In addition, like an Always On Availability Group, there are secondary replicas. For a BC deployment, we always keep four replicas up and running (one primary and three secondaries). From a transaction point of view, a commit cannot proceed on the primary replica until *at least one* of the secondary replicas has acknowledged the changes are hardened.

You can also see that backup files are stored in Azure storage with RA-GRS just like a General Purpose deployment.

If a failover is necessary, we simply need to choose a secondary replica that is synchronized and make that the primary replica just like an AG as seen in Figure 8-14.

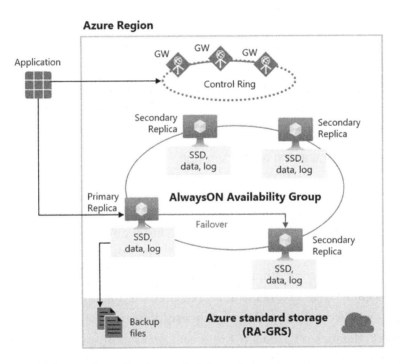

Figure 8-14. *A failover for a Business Critical deployment*

Downtime is significantly less General Purpose since the new primary replica simply has to run undo recovery to become available. Since Accelerated Database Recovery (ADR) is enabled, undo recovery can be very fast. I'll discuss more about the important of ADR later in this chapter. You can read the entire Business Critical high availability story at `https://docs.microsoft.com/en-us/azure/azure-sql/database/high-availability-sla#premium-and-business-critical-service-tier-availability`. If the old primary replica is not usable, we will need to spin up a new secondary replica (and synchronize it) to keep four available.

Just like General Purpose service tier, applications just need to reconnect and start running again due to the use of gateways. In addition, a BC deployment will allow you to use *one* of the secondary replicas as a *read-only replica* as part of your monthly free for using BC. Our gateways help provide the redirection logic. You simply just ensure application supplied the correct "read intent" option. You can learn more at `https://docs.microsoft.com/en-us/azure/azure-sql/database/read-scale-out`.

Note   Read Scale-Out supports session-level consistency. It means if the read-only session reconnects after a connection error caused by replica unavailability, it may be redirected to a replica that is not 100% up to date with the read-write replica. Likewise, if an application writes data using a read-write session and immediately reads it using a read-only session, it is possible that the latest updates are not immediately visible on the replica. The latency is caused by an asynchronous transaction log redo operation.

Let's take a look at an example to show you that even though GP provides good built-in availability to your application, BC can truly be faster and provide higher availability.

For this example, I'm going to use the same General Purpose database I deployed in Chapter 4 and have used in other chapters called **bwazuresqldb**. I deployed a BC database in Chapter 4, but it was empty. So I deleted this database and deployed a new Business Critical database called **bwazuresqldbbc** using 8 vCores and the sample AdventureWorks database (I used 8 vCores because bwazuresqldb was scaled to 8 vCores in Chapter 7 of the book).

You will also need the ostress.exe program I've used in previous chapters as described and in the prerequisites in the beginning of the chapter. As I also stated at the beginning of this chapter, you will need Azure PowerShell.

I also have scripts you will use in the **ch8_availability\gp_vs_bc** folder.

For a client, I'll use the Azure VM **bwsql2019** which is already set up to connect to the logical server for these databases:

1. Log in to Azure with PowerShell and set your subscription context. I first had to log in to Azure with PowerShell using the command

   ```
   Connect-AzAccount
   ```

   This prompts me for MFA which is required at Microsoft.

   I then need to set the context to my correct subscription with these commands

   ```
   Set-AzContext -SubscriptionId $subscriptionId
   ```

   where $subscriptionId is set to the subscription associated with the resource group of the database deployment.

2. Prepare and run scripts to test General Purpose availability.

   In order to see these results correctly, I recommend you have two PowerShell windows displayed side by side.
   In the left-hand window, you will want to run the script **querybase_gp.cmd**. This script looks like the following:

   ```
   ostress.exe -S<server>.database.windows.net -Q"SELECT COUNT(*)
   FROM SalesLT.Customer" -Uthewandog -dbwazuresqldb -P<password>
   -n1 -r50000
   ```

   You should substitute in your server name, login, database, and password for your deployment. You can see this script uses ostress to find the count for a table in the database with a single user over 50,000 iterations. The idea here is to query the table over and over. ostress.exe is smart enough to retry a connection should a failover occur.

   In the right-hand window, you will be running the script **failoverbase_gp.ps1** which looks like the following:

   ```
   $resourceGroup = "<resource group>"
   $server = "<server>"
   $database = "<database>"
   ```

```
Invoke-AzSqlDatabaseFailover -ResourceGroupName $resourceGroup
-ServerName $server -DatabaseName $database
```

You will substitute in your resource group, server, and database. Note the server is not the fully qualified DNS name, just the logical server name.

Now execute the script in the left-hand window **querybase_ gp.cmd**. You should see results scroll across your screen like this:

```
-----------
847

(1 row affected)

-----------
847

(1 row affected)
```

We are just repeating this query over and over.

Now run in the right-hand window the script **failoverbase_ gp.ps1**. Very quickly in the left-hand window, you will notice errors like these:

```
07/22/20 21:44:17.444 [0x00001E6C] Attempt to establish connection
failed.  See the detailed errors that follow:
07/22/20 21:44:17.444 [0x00001E6C] SQLState: HY000, Native Error:
40613
[SQL Server]Database 'bwazuresqldb' on server 'bwazuresqlserver'
is not currently available.  Please retry the connection
later.  If the problem persists, contact customer support, and
provide them the session tracing ID of '{CC39135B-D638-4A51-BB25-
EABB8A5315A0}'.
```

Then within about 30 seconds, you will see the count of rows appear again. This shows a failover occurred and the application was down for a short period of time but then can reconnect and just get the same results. You can exit the script by hitting <ctrl>+<c> and typing in "Y" to quit.

We only allow manual failovers for Azure SQL Database (except Hyperscale and is not allowed for Managed Instance) and only allow them every 30 minutes. A manual failover requires a lot of things in the background to ensure you are available, so if we allowed you to do this anytime you want as much as you want, it could overwhelm our infrastructure systems. Therefore, if you tried to run failoverbase_gp.ps1 immediately again, you will get this error after a few seconds:

```
Invoke-AzSqlDatabaseFailover : Long running operation failed with
status
'Failed'. Additional Info:'There was a recent failover on the
database or
pool if database belongs in an elastic pool.  At least 30 minutes
must pass
between database failovers.'
```

You can read more about testing high availability at https://docs.microsoft.com/en-us/azure/azure-sql/database/high-availability-sla#testing-application-fault-resiliency.

3. Test failover for Business Critical.

   Perform the same tests as with General Purpose, but this time use the scripts **querybase_bc.cmd** and **failoverbase_bc.ps1**. You will this time substitute all the same information except the database should be your Business Critical database (mine was called **bwazursqldbbc**).

   Then using the same concept as in step #2, run the script to query the database and then run the script to invoke a failover. See any differences? The result set of rows should come back in seconds with a Business Critical failover.

This demonstrates both General Purpose and Business Critical have built-in availability, but Business Critical provides the highest level of availability.

Hyperscale High Availability

I've described the unique characteristics of the Hyperscale service tier for Azure SQL Database in several chapters of the book so far. Let's dive further into the pieces of the Hyperscale architecture including the interesting way availability is handled. For a complete reading on Hyperscale high availability, see the documentation at `https://docs.microsoft.com/en-us/azure/azure-sql/database/high-availability-sla#hyperscale-service-tier-availability`.

First, let's look at how compute nodes and replicas are part of the architecture as in Figure 8-15.

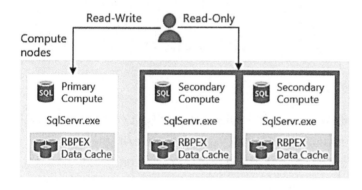

Figure 8-15. *Compute nodes for Hyperscale*

The **primary compute node** is a primary replica for a Hyperscale deployment. Hyperscale has **zero to four secondary replicas** which are represented as **secondary compute nodes.** I'll discuss more about how replicas work shortly. The primary compute node hosts a SQL Server for your database. This SQL Server has the standard components like a buffer pool to host database pages. Additionally on this primary compute node is your tempdb databases on local storage plus an RBEX *cache*. Caches in Hyperscale are all files on local SSD storage. RBEX stands for **Resilient Buffer Pool Extension**. It is similar but not exactly the same as the Buffer Pool Extension (which you can read more about at `https://docs.microsoft.com/en-us/sql/database-engine/configure-windows/buffer-pool-extension`). The concept is that if a query needs a database page and it is not in buffer pool, it will first try to read that page from RBEX.

What if a page is not available in either the compute buffer pool or RBEX cache? Figure 8-16 shows that we deploy a set of **page servers**.

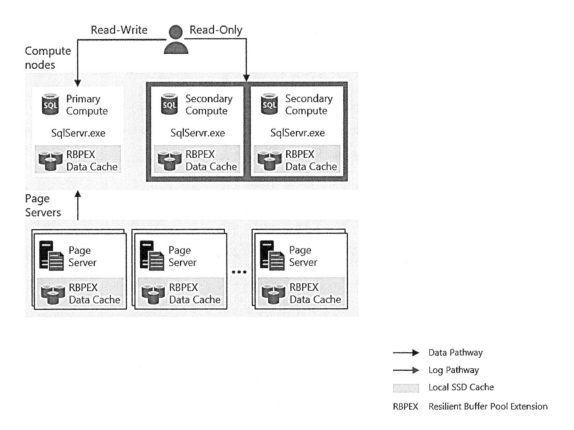

Figure 8-16. *Page servers in a Hyperscale deployment*

Page servers are nodes with SQL Servers that host database pages in memory and are covered by another RBEX cache. Page servers are *paired* for redundancy and high availability. Azure SQL determines the proper number of page servers to support the deployment and database size. Remember, for Hyperscale you don't choose a maximum database size. We just keep growing and scaling the system through page server and Azure storage to meet your database size.

What if the database page the query needs is not on the compute node or a page server? Figure 8-17 shows that the database files that back your database are stored in Azure standard storage.

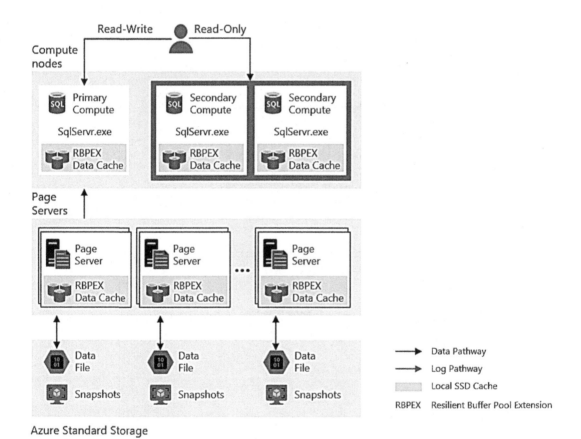

Figure 8-17. *Data files for Hyperscale on Azure storage*

In order to maximize performance, this architecture works best when we rarely have to go to Azure storage to retrieve a page for a database. When page servers first start up, they are seeded with pages from database files on Azure Storage. Page servers then will populate RBEX caches on the primary node (and secondaries if they exist). If a page is not on the primary compute buffer pool but we find it in the RBEX cache of the node, that is considered a *cache hit*. If the page is not in RBEX, we attempt to get the page from a page server (or its RBEX cache) but is considered a *cache miss*.

Having database files on Azure storage has one major advantage for automated backups and Point-In-Time restore for Hyperscale. Because the data files are infrequently accessed once the Hyperscale caching system is *warm*, we can back up the database using **snapshot backups**. This capability is very similar to using file snapshot backups with Azure Virtual Machine as documented at `https://docs.microsoft.com/en-us/sql/relational-databases/backup-restore/file-snapshot-backups-for-database-files-in-azure`. Snapshot backups are a huge advantage for Hyperscale because it doesn't affect application operations and a restore of a database is extremely fast. Just like other Azure SQL options, backups are stored on geo-redundant storage separate from the data and log files.

There is another piece I haven't discussed yet from this model. What about the transaction log?

Hyperscale redirects a transaction log I/O from the primary node to a **Log Service** as seen in Figure 8-18.

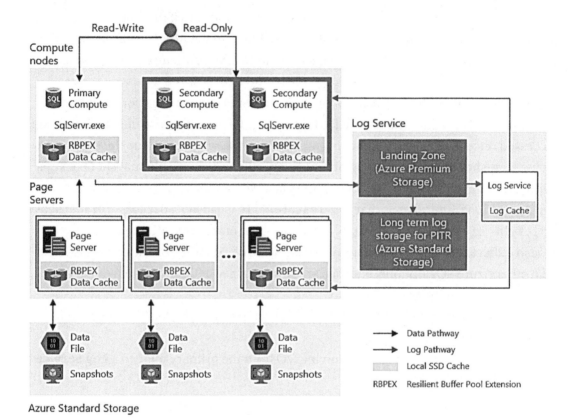

Figure 8-18. *The Log Service in Azure SQL Database Hyperscale*

Compute nodes still have a log cache, but when an I/O is needed to flush log records, they are directed by the SQL Server engine to the Log Service. The Log Service runs on a different node. It has its own log cache (local SSD storage), log storage with Azure Premium Storage called the *landing zone*, and redundant storage with Azure Standard Storage called long-term log storage. We never have to back up the transaction log. A combination of snapshot backups and long-term log storage can be used to restore to a point in time.

The Log Service receives logged changes and then feeds these changes to update page servers and replicas (if they exist). This means that while Hyperscale uses logged changes to feed replicas, it doesn't use the exact underlying technology of Always On Availability groups to keep replicas in sync.

One interesting aspect to Hyperscale is database pages I/O. For the compute node, dirty pages are not written to a database file. Hot pages on the compute node are written to RBEX cache so they are readily available. Page servers are updated though logged changes with the Log Service. Therefore, any type of checkpoint I/O happens from a page server to database files on Azure storage. This is very nice as it off-loads any database file I/O from the compute node.

I mentioned earlier the concept that you can have zero to four secondary replicas. You may be asking how can this architecture support built-in high availability with zero replicas? Because the underlying database and transaction log files are on Azure storage (and not on local storage), if we need to execute a failover, we simply provision a new node and data will be synchronized from underlying page servers (which are backed by Azure storage). Furthermore, like all of Azure SQL, Accelerated Database Recovery (ADR) is enabled, so when the new compute node comes online or a secondary replica becomes the primary, recovery to get to a consistent state is extremely fast. Every aspect of the Hyperscale distributed architecture is fault tolerant.

If we have secondary replicas provisioned, failover (which like other Azure SQL architectures is integrated with Azure Service Fabric) is of course must faster because we can just switch to one of those nodes to become the new primary node. In addition, if your application connects to the database with read intent, Azure SQL will load balance across all available secondary replicas. Read more about using read-scale replicas with Hyperscale at https://docs.microsoft.com/en-us/azure/azure-sql/database/service-tier-hyperscale#connect-to-a-read-scale-replica-of-a-hyperscale-database.

Want to learn more about Hyperscale? Watch my colleague Kevin Farlee demonstrate the architecture of Hyperscale including an amazing restore demonstration at www.youtube.com/watch?v=Z9AFnKI7sfI.

Tip   Remember, because of the unique architecture of Hyperscale, you cannot change the service tier back to General Purpose or Business Critical once you deploy or change to Hyperscale. You would have to export out your data and import into the new tier.

Go Further with Azure

While the built-in high availability of Azure SQL is really a major advantage for you to consider moving to the cloud, there are ways to go even further and build in more availability to your plans.

This includes zone redundancy, geo-replication, and auto-failover groups. In addition, it is important to understand how the promise of the Azure SQL Service-Level Agreement meets your needs. This includes how we govern and limit certain activity and deploy innovative technologies like hot patching to maximize uptime.

Zone Redundancy

I mentioned in Chapter 2 of the book features of the Azure ecosystem including regions and datacenters. One of the capabilities you can take advantage of to infuse higher availability is to deploy with **Azure Availability Zones**. Availability zones are a collection of unique physical locations within a region. Each zone in the collections is made up of multiple data centers. Today, availability zones are available only to Azure SQL Database Business Critical service tiers and is free of charge.

Note   We are working to expand availability zones to other Azure SQL deployment options.

You can choose an availability zone during deployment or configure it later. Figure 8-19, from the documentation at `https://docs.microsoft.com/en-us/azure/azure-sql/database/high-availability-sla#zone-redundant-configuration`, shows a visual example of how availability zones are implemented with a Business Critical service tier deployment.

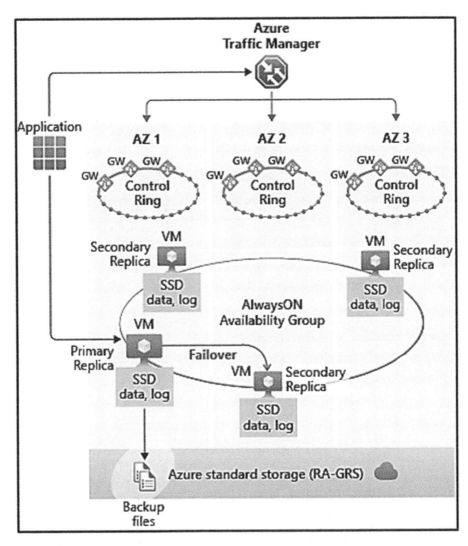

Figure 8-19. *An availability zone implementation with an Azure SQL Database Business Critical deployment*

Notice that each secondary replica is deployed in a different zone. Each zone has its own set of gateways for connection. Additionally, an Azure Traffic Manager service is deployed automatically to redirect traffic to each set of gateways. Your application is completely abstracted for worrying about the traffic manager.

Let's see how to configure an existing database to be zone redundant (if you remember back to Chapter 4 this was a choice I could have made when creating a business critical tier database but I did not enable it).

If I navigate to my database **bwazuresqldbbc** and select Configure from the Resource menu, I see an option to make my database zone redundant as seen in Figure 8-20.

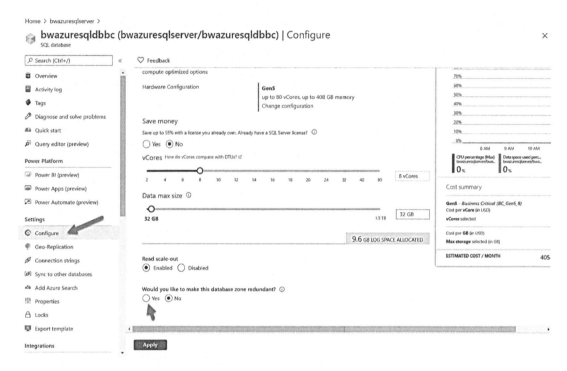

Figure 8-20. *Making a database zone redundant*

Note   This option may only be available in certain Azure regions. Keep up with the latest support for regions at `https://docs.microsoft.com/en-us/azure/availability-zones/az-region`.

I selected Yes on this screen and hit the Apply button. As you can imagine, moving to zones is not completely trivial as we have to redeploy your replicas across zones within the region. However, for my deployment which is a small database, the operation only took a few minutes. You can also configure zone redundancy with the az CLI (**az sql db update**) and PowerShell (**Set-AzSqlDatabase**). Availability zones are not available in all regions. Check your region availability at `https://docs.microsoft.com/en-us/azure/availability-zones/az-region`.

> **Note**   Because replicas are now in different datacenters, you may experience some increased latency for workloads, especially write-intensive OLTP applications. You will have to balance the benefit of availability with the performance needs of your application. You can always easily switch back to a single zone deployment.

You may be wondering whether you even need a zone redundant deployment. I mean how often does a datacenter have a major issue. I asked Emily Lisa, lead program for Azure SQL over Availability Zones, about her thoughts. She gave me an interesting perspective: "As I am writing this quote I am working from home at my desk after several months in quarantine due to the COVID-19 pandemic. After the world suddenly and unexpectedly shut down I had to find new ways and places to stay "available" for my job. Through this experience I've realized how important it is to recognize that nothing is perfect, unexpected things happen and being ready to adapt to new circumstances is crucial. At any moment, a natural disaster can take out an entire datacenter, a network failure can impact the functionality of servers, and many other unexpected events can occur potentially jeopardizing the availability of your database. We embrace this reality by actively working to minimize the effects of a single failing component with as little downtime as possible. With Azure Availability Zones, databases can be replicated within the same region across several unique physical locations with independent power, cooling, and networking. The zone redundant configuration which is currently available for Azure SQL Database Premium, Business Critical, and General Purpose (coming soon) tiers makes databases resilient to a large set of failures, including catastrophic datacenter outages, without any changes of the application logic. With this feature enabled, even a meteor can crash and destroy an entire datacenter and your database will still be up and running in a different Availability Zone within the same region (too bad the dinosaurs didn't have a zone redundant configuration). This gives peace of mind by ensuring low downtime and no loss of committed data, while automatically handling virtually all maintenance and failovers. Zone redundancy is the future of HA in the cloud!"

Geo-replication

Let's say you want to go even further and make your database resilient *across* Azure regions. Azure SQL Database supports a concept called **geo-replication**. Geo-replication uses Always On Availability Group technology to *asynchronously* transmit log changes to another Azure SQL Database deployment on a different logical server. The secondary database can be in a different Azure region or the same Azure region. Secondary databases can be used for read replica purposes.

Note   Using a geo-replicated database in the same region can give a General Purpose service tier a read replica or expand the number of replicas for a Business Critical service tier (which by default gets one).

Geo-replicated databases can be used for failover purposes, which include unexpected Azure region events or to support an application upgrade with minimal downtime. However, failover is a manual process initiated by an administrator through Azure interfaces or through T-SQL (ALTER DATABASE).

Let's see how to take the Business Critical deployment I just enabled for availability zones and create a geo-replicated secondary database in another Azure region. I'll navigate to my database, called **bwazuresqldbbc**, in the Azure portal and select Geo-Replication from the Azure portal like in Figure 8-21.

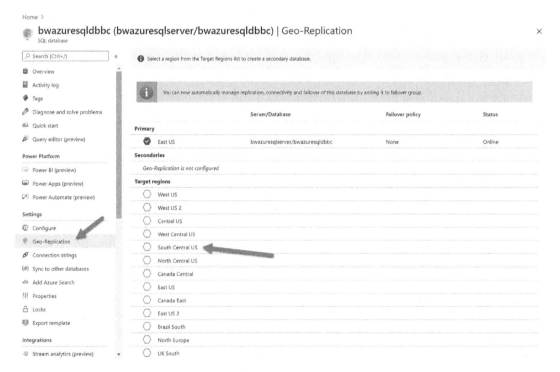

Figure 8-21. *Configuring geo-replication for Azure SQL Database*

414

Note   You see a message on this screen about using auto-failover groups. I will discuss auto-failover groups in the next section of the chapter.

I want to replicate the database in the South Central US region so will select that region. I now get a new screen to configure the new logical server to use (could be an existing server in that region) and choose a Pricing tier. You can see in Figure 8-22 I created a new server as part of the process called **bwazuresqlserver2** (on that screen I was allowed to choose "Allow Azure services to access server").

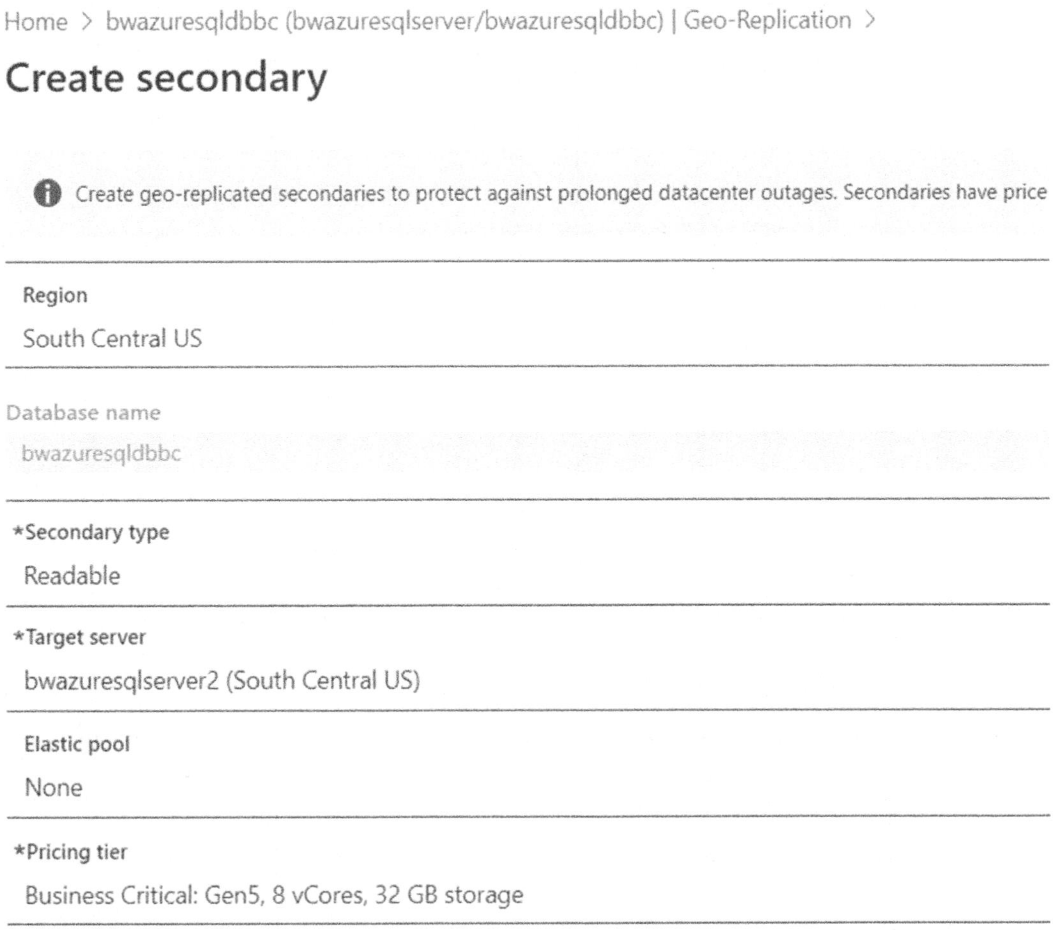

Home > bwazuresqldbbc (bwazuresqlserver/bwazuresqldbbc) | Geo-Replication >

Create secondary

ⓘ Create geo-replicated secondaries to protect against prolonged datacenter outages. Secondaries have price

Region
South Central US

Database name
bwazuresqldbbc

*Secondary type
Readable

*Target server
bwazuresqlserver2 (South Central US)

Elastic pool
None

*Pricing tier
Business Critical: Gen5, 8 vCores, 32 GB storage

Figure 8-22.   *Choices for creating a geo-replicated database*

Notice the Pricing tier matches the deployment, vCore, and storage of my current database. You do have the option of increasing or decreasing vCore capacity for the secondary, but you can't use other service tiers. It may be tempting to use a lower capacity for the secondary, but there could be consequences for this choice including

- A secondary that gets significantly out of sync

- Transaction log governance on the primary to ensure a secondary doesn't get too far out of sync

- An improperly sized new primary if a failover has to occur (although you could change it after a failover)

The deployment creates a new database of the same name as the primary on the new logical server and then performs an initial synchronization called **seeding**. When this operation is complete, you can see the status of the new secondary like Figure 8-23.

Figure 8-23. *A geo-replicated secondary database after seeding*

Any changes from my primary are asynchronously sent to the secondary. In addition, I can now connect to bwazuresqlserver2.database.windows.net and perform read operation against the bwazuresqldbbc database. The database is read-only, so any modification operations would fail. Remember I also have access to a secondary read replica in my primary region since I used Business Critical. In the case of the secondary replica in the primary region, I need to use a connection string option (as documented at `https://docs.microsoft.com/en-us/azure/azure-sql/database/read-scale-out#connect-to-a-read-only-replica`). When I connect to the geo-replicated secondary database, I don't need this special connection string option. Azure SQL supports up to four secondary databases configured with geo-replication. By implementing a geo-replication architecture for a Business Critical database, I've effectively set up a deployment similar to a distributed availability group in SQL Server (learn more at `https://docs.microsoft.com/en-us/sql/database-engine/availability-groups/windows/distributed-availability-groups`).

Tip   You are allowed to create geo-secondary databases based on a geo-replicated secondary database, thus giving you even more read replica. This is called *chaining*, but know that these chained secondaries will likely have a lag of data synchronization the further you build the chain.

Applications can use Azure technology like Azure Traffic Manager to set up abstraction to connect to a primary even after failover. Learn more from our documentation about building applications for global Azure SQL Database deployments at `https://docs.microsoft.com/en-us/azure/azure-sql/database/designing-cloud-solutions-for-disaster-recovery`. Our documentation at `https://docs.microsoft.com/en-us/azure/azure-sql/database/active-geo-replication-overview` has a nice visual showing what a fully deployed Azure SQL Database with geo-replication can look like as seen in Figure 8-24.

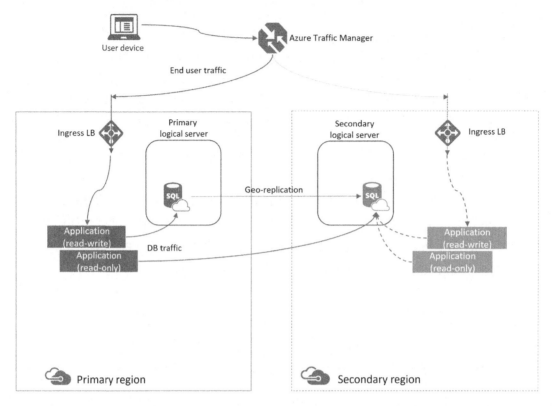

Figure 8-24. *A fully deployed Azure SQL Database using geo-replication*

Here are some important points to consider when using geo-replication:

- You can set up a geo-replicated database on another Azure subscription with a little work. Learn more at `https://docs.microsoft.com/en-us/azure/azure-sql/database/active-geo-replication-overview#cross-subscription-geo-replication`.

- Server-level firewall rules on the primary are not replicated, so consider using database firewall rules or other methods to connect to the secondary.

- Using contained database users (even with Azure Activity Directory) has a huge advantage as they are replicated.

- Geo-replication uses asynchronous replication of data. Therefore, if you fail over to a secondary, you might experience data loss (but not consistency). However, if you require a secondary to be completely in

sync before a failover, you can use the **sp_wait_for_database_copy_
sync** stored procedure. Learn more at `https://docs.microsoft.
com/en-us/azure/azure-sql/database/active-geo-replication-
overview#preventing-the-loss-of-critical-data`.

- Az CLI supports creating and configuring geo-replication (e.g., **az sql
  db replica**), and PowerShell cmdlets exist to support geo-replication
  (e.g., **New-AzSqlDatabaseSecondary**).

Auto-failover Group

While geo-replication is a great capability, what about Azure SQL Managed Instance? Also, it would be nice to have an option where failover is automatic and for an abstraction on the connection to the primary database wherever it exists. That is a nutshell what **auto-failover groups** provide.

Figure 8-25 shows a visual of an auto-failover group so you can compare to geo-replication.

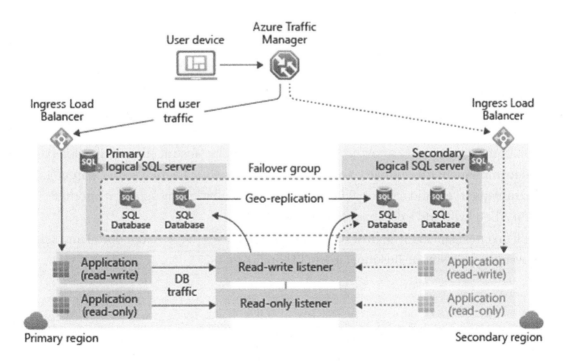

Figure 8-25. *Auto-failover groups for Azure SQL Database*

Notice here that unlike geo-replication, auto-failover groups operate at the logical server level (and then you place databases in the failover group).

Figure 8-26 shows the architecture for auto-failover groups for Azure SQL Managed Instance.

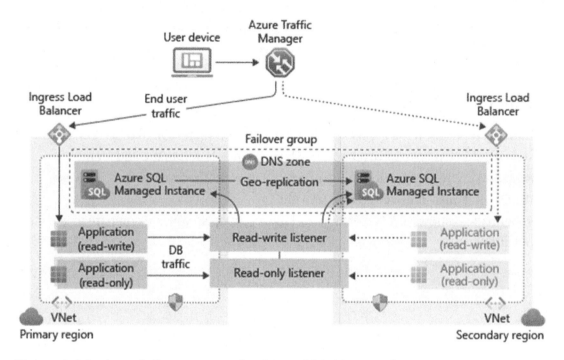

Figure 8-26. *Auto-failover groups for Azure SQL Managed Instance*

In both figures, notice an Azure Traffic Manager helps abstract the application (you need to implement this though). Let's take the logical server I deployed in Chapter 4, **bwazuresqlserver**, and create a failover group with a new logical server in another region. Then I will add a database to the failover group.

I'll first navigate to my logical server bwazuresqlserver in the Azure portal and select Failover groups from the Resource menu like in Figure 8-27.

Figure 8-27. *Creating a failover group for a logical server*

I'll select Add group to create the new failover group. Figure 8-28 shows my selections to create the failover group, which includes creating a new logical server in the South Central US region called **bwazuresqlserversouth**. I also chose to add the bwazuresqldb General Purpose database to the group.

Home > All resources > bwazuresqlserver | Failover groups >

Failover group   ✕

ⓘ Create a failover group to automatically failover databases in it.

Failover group name *

bwazuresqlww	✓

.database.windows.net

*Secondary server

bwazuresqlserversouth (South Central US)   >

Read/Write failover policy

Automatic	⌄

Read/Write grace period (hours)

1 hours	⌄

Database within the group

1 / 4   >

`Create`

Figure 8-28. *Choices to create a failover group*

Notice the first field is the **Failover group name**. You are going to love this aspect to auto-failover groups. This is effectively the *virtual logical server* name to connect. You specify this logical server name in your application, and you will always be connected to the primary logical server for read-write purposes. I'll discuss shortly how to use the failover group name to connect to read replicas for secondaries.

I selected **Create** which fires off a new deployment for the failover group. When the deployment finished (which includes seeding like geo-replication), Figure 8-29 shows the update screen for the status of the failover group.

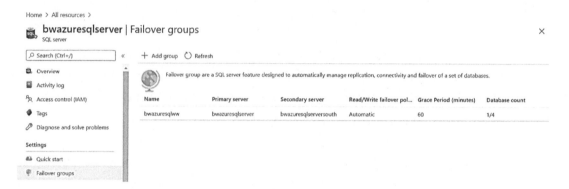

Figure 8-29. *Failover group after deployment*

If you click the failover group, you get a very nice global map visual with options to manage the failover group and connection information for both the primary server and read-only replicas like Figure 8-30.

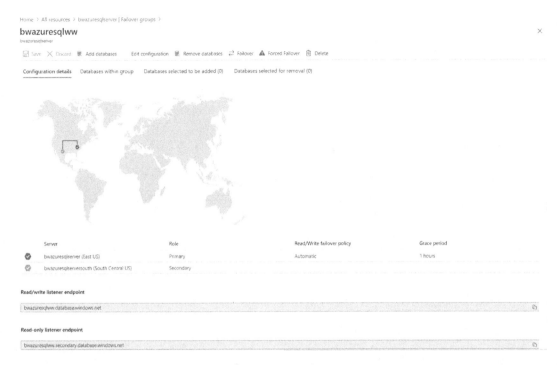

Home > All resources > bwazuresqlserver | Failover groups >

bwazuresqlww
bwazuresqlserver

Save   Discard   Add databases   Edit configuration   Remove databases   Failover   Forced Failover   Delete

Configuration details   Databases within group   Databases selected to be added (0)   Databases selected for removal (0)

	Server	Role	Read/Write failover policy	Grace period
✓	bwazuresqlserver (East US)	Primary	Automatic	1 hours
✓	bwazuresqlserversouth (South Central US)	Secondary		

Read/write listener endpoint

bwazuresqlww.database.windows.net

Read-only listener endpoint

bwazuresqlww.secondary.database.windows.net

Figure 8-30. *Configuration and managing a failover group in the Azure portal*

I'll come back to this screen shortly to look at failover.

Both servers in the failover group are configured to allow connectivity from my
virtual machine **bwsql2019** I deployed in Chapter 3 and have been using in the book.
The current primary server is configured using private link, and when I created the
secondary server as part of the failover group deployment, I chose Allow Azure services
to access server.

Using SSMS in my Azure VM, I connected to the standard logical server
(**bwazuresqlserver**) and can see all databases, the **failover group server name
(bwazuresqlww)**, the secondary logical server directly (**bwazuresqlserversouth**),
and the **failover group logical server for read replica (bwazuresqlww.secondary)**.
Figure 8-31 shows all these options.

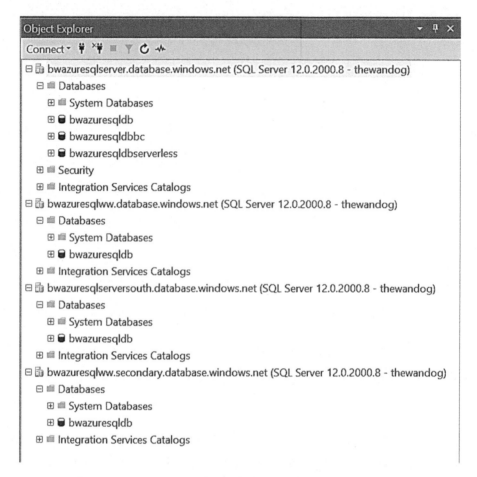

Figure 8-31. *Connecting to servers for a failover group with SSMS*

I only connected to bwazuresqlserver and bwazuresqlserversouth to show you in SSMS. When I deploy an auto-failover group, it only makes sense to use the failover server and failover server secondary names.

Let's now test a failover using the failover group name. I'll use the scripts from the **ch8_availability\gp_vs_bc folder** and modify the **querybase_gp.cmd** script to use the server name **bwazuresqlww.database.windows.net** and leave everything else the same:

1. Run the workload.

    Run the script **querybase_gp.cmd** from PowerShell. As before, you should see a stream of row counts like this:

    ```
    -----------
    847
    ```

```
(1 row affected)

-----------

847

(1 row affected)
```

2. Navigate back to the Azure portal to failover.

    Using the Azure portal, I'll navigate back to the bwazuresqlserver
    logical server and select Failover groups from the Resource Menu.
    Then as you can see in Figure 8-32, I'll select Failover and Yes.

Figure 8-32. *Failing over a failover group for Azure SQL Database*

3. Check the workload status.

    For a short period of time, ostress will hit some connection errors
    such as these:

```
07/26/20 22:13:13.945 [0x000007E0] Attempt to establish
connection failed.  See the detailed errors that follow:

07/26/20 22:13:13.946 [0x000007E0] SQLState: 42000, Native
Error: 40613
[SQL Server]Database 'bwazuresqldb' on server
'bwazuresqlserver' is not currently available.  Please
retry the connection later.  If the problem persists,
contact customer support, and provide them the session
tracing ID of '1C2C1472-3C6D-4EE7-AB1D-073D3009409E'.
```

    Notice the error to connect is for the actual logical server, not the
    failover group name.

4.   Check the Azure portal.

The Azure portal shows in this map a visual of the failover action occurring to make bwazuresqlserversouth the new primary as seen in Figure 8-33.

Figure 8-33. *A failover in progress for a failover group*

After the failover has occurred, the portal shows the new primary as seen in Figure 8-34.

Figure 8-34. *Failover group status after a failover*

5. Check the workload status.

    You will see the workload has already started showing row counts
    proving the application doesn't need to change its connection
    properties to stay available.

Here are a few other important points about auto-failover groups for Azure SQL:

- Auto-failover groups can also be managed using the PowerShell
  (**Add-AzSqlDatabaseToFailoverGroup** and **Switch-
  AzSqlDatabaseFailoverGroup**).

- Because auto-failover groups use asynchronous replication data
  when a failover occurs automatically, data loss could occur.
  Therefore, if you require no data loss with auto-failover groups,
  applications can call the **sp_wait_for_database_copy_sync**
  procedure after committing a transaction to ensure all data is
  synchronized. Learn more at `https://docs.microsoft.com/`
  `en-us/azure/azure-sql/database/auto-failover-group-`
  `overview?tabs=azure-PowerShell#preventing-the-loss-of-`
  `critical-data`.

- One of the options you can configure with an auto-failover group is
  called a *grace period* using the **GracePeriodWithDataLossHours**
  parameter (the default is 1 hour). This parameter defines the time
  we will wait to do an automatic failover should the primary be down
  and we believe data loss may occur. If no data loss would occur, the
  automatic failover takes place immediately.

Tip   There could be a scenario where the primary comes back online or is
available even after one hour. Therefore, if you cannot accept data loss and are not
using the **sp_wait_for_database_copy_sync procedure**, you may want to set
the grace period to something like 24 hours.

- A great example of how to use an application with an auto-failover
  group is available in our documentation with a Java application at
  `https://docs.microsoft.com/en-us/azure/azure-sql/database/`
  `geo-distributed-application-configure-tutorial`.

- A tutorial about how to add an Azure SQL Managed Instance to a failover group can be found at `https://docs.microsoft.com/en-us/azure/azure-sql/managed-instance/failover-group-add-instance-tutorial`.

The important limitations for auto-failover groups are system databases. System databases are **not** replicated. Therefore, any instance-level data, such as SQL Server Agent jobs, must be manually created on the secondary instance.

Auto-failover groups use geo-replication technology behind the scenes but are different. My colleague Anna Hoffman created this very nice table as seen in Figure 8-35 to compare geo-replication and auto-failover groups.

	Geo-replication	Auto-failover groups
Automatic failover	No	Yes
Fail over multiple databases simultaneously	No	Yes
Update connection string after failover	Yes	No
Managed instance supported	No	Yes
Can be in same region as primary	Yes	No
Multiple replicas	Yes	No
Supports read-scale	Yes	Yes

Figure 8-35. *Geo-replication vs. auto-failover groups*

Azure SQL SLA

One of the advantages to deploy SQL Server with Azure SQL Managed Instance and Database is the promise of availability. Our architecture which I've described in this chapter helps us achieve this promise. The promise for you is in the form of a **Service-Level Agreement (SLA).** You can view the official SLA for Azure SQL at `https://azure.microsoft.com/en-us/support/legal/sla/sql-database`.

The Azure SQL SLA means that Microsoft will ensure we maintain a **service level** or you will be eligible for a credit for your account. Service levels are stated in terms of *nines*. Nines are a percentage of uptime or availability you are guaranteed for your deployment.

As an example, if you deploy an Azure SQL Database with the Business Critical or Premium service tier and use Zone Redundancy, your SLA is 99.995%. If you look at a table like `https://en.wikipedia.org/wiki/High_availability`, you can see that 99.995% is defined as "four and a half nines" and means you could experience at maximum 26.30 minutes per year or 2.19 minutes per month of *downtime*. Other deployment options have different service-level promises.

If you look at our SLA documentation, downtime is defined as "...the total accumulated Deployment Minutes across all Databases in a given Microsoft Azure subscription during which the Database is unavailable. A minute is considered unavailable for a given Database if all continuous attempts by Customer to establish a connection to the Database within the minute fail."

We also include in our SLA promises for Recovery Point Objective (RPO) and Recovery Time Objective (RTO) if you use Azure SQL Database with a Business Critical service tier and use geo-replication (or auto-failover).

Note   Even though Managed Instance is not specifically listed in the SLA documentation (we are working to add it explicitly), the following SLA applies to databases for a Managed Instance. "Azure SQL Database Business Critical or Premium tiers not configured for Zone Redundant Deployments, General Purpose, Standard, or Basic tiers, or Hyperscale tier with two or more replicas have an availability guarantee of at least 99.99%."

There are certain aspects to Azure SQL which allow us to make these SLA promises including but not limited to

- Built-in availability and integration with the Azure Service Fabric

- Enforcing resource limits such as log governance

Note   There are several reasons why log governance is needed to manage PaaS services. This includes database recoverability, high availability, disaster recovery, and predictable performance. Learn more at `https://azure.microsoft.com/en-us/blog/resource-governance-in-azure-sql-database/`.

- Enabling database options such as Accelerated Database Recovery

One innovative technology we use in Azure SQL to maximize availability is **hot patching**. Hot patching allows us to patch the SQL Server engine code without restarting SQL Server. Read the amazing story of hot patching from my colleague Hans Olav Norheim at `https://azure.microsoft.com/en-us/blog/hot-patching-sql-server-engine-in-azure-sql-database/`.

Database Availability and Consistency

For SQL Server, you may be familiar with features and tools to make or restrict the availability of your database or perform advanced recovery scenarios. In addition, SQL Server provides tools to ensure the database is consistent, both from a physical and logical perspective.

Azure SQL in general does not provide the same level of advanced capabilities in this area mainly because they are not needed given the high level of redundancy and availability built into the service.

Let's examine a few of these areas, so your knowledge can be more complete when comparing to SQL Server.

Database Availability

You may have needed with a SQL Server to change the database state with ALTER DATABASE to OFFLINE or EMERGENCY for advanced recovery scenarios. You don't have access to use these options, but after reading about all of the built-in capabilities of Azure SQL and our SLA, you have to ask "Does it matter?" In my opinion (and believe me I've used these options to help customers over the years in support), the answer is no.

With Azure SQL Database and Managed Instance, while you cannot put the data in single user mode, Azure SQL Database allows you to use the option RESTRICTED_USER. Learn more at `https://docs.microsoft.com/en-us/sql/t-sql/statements/alter-database-transact-sql-set-options`.

In SQL Server 2005, my colleague Robert Dorr and I were in Microsoft Support and convinced the engineering team to create a simple method to connect into a "hung server." The result was a feature called Dedicated Admin Connection (DAC). DAC is supported for Azure SQL. Learn more at `https://docs.microsoft.com/en-us/sql/database-engine/configure-windows/diagnostic-connection-for-database-administrators?view=sql-server-ver15`.

Accelerated Database Recovery (ADR)

In my book, *SQL Server 2019 Revealed*, I covered the amazing story of Accelerated Database Recovery (ADR). No longer will a SQL Server administrator worry about long-running database recovery times or out-of-control transaction logs. ADR is not just a feature; it is part of the Azure SQL availability story! In fact, for Azure SQL, it is just part of the engine and not really something you turn on or off. You can learn more how ADR works in our documentation at `https://docs.microsoft.com/en-us/azure/azure-sql/accelerated-database-recovery` or in the white paper written by our engineering team at `www.microsoft.com/en-us/research/publication/constant-time-recovery-in-azure-sql-database/`.

Database Consistency

All Azure SQL databases are configured using the CHECKSUM option for database consistency. One of the benefits of using a PaaS service is that our engineering team has automation to check for any inconsistencies due to issues like a checksum problem and take correction action. For example, if you are deploying a Business Critical service tier, we can issue an online automatic page repair (learn more how this works at `https://docs.microsoft.com/en-us/sql/sql-server/failover-clusters/automatic-page-repair-availability-groups-database-mirroring?view=sql-server-ver15`).

In addition, keep in mind these facts if you are concerned about any database inconsistency issue:

- General Purpose and Hyperscale store database and log files on Azure storage which is mirrored by default with three copies.

- Business Critical tiers have three other replicas always available with their own storage.

- Our engineering team has built-in data integrity and consistency alert monitoring in our service. If automation can't solve the problem, we will directly notify a customer and take necessary steps to ensure data is restored and consistent. If we think we can repair a problem with no data loss, we might take this action and you never have to be notified.

- Azure SQL does support DBCC CHECKDB (but not repair option) for you to manually check your database consistency at any time.

- We've added checks for databases for "lost write" and "stale read" detection which we have seen in some situations occur due to an underlying I/O system issue.

Peter Carlin, a Distinguished Engineer at Microsoft who I mentioned as part of Azure SQL history in Chapter 1, has a very nice blog post outlining all the things we do to manage data integrity for your database in Azure. Read his post at `https://azure.microsoft.com/en-us/blog/data-integrity-in-azure-sql-database/`.

Monitoring Availability

As with any set of capabilities, you will no doubt want to monitor various aspects of availability for Azure SQL. This includes server and instance availability, database availability, backup/restore history, status of replicas, and failover reasons. In addition, since Azure SQL runs in the Azure ecosystem, knowing the status and health of Azure services in regions and datacenters can also be important.

Azure SQL provides you similar interfaces to SQL Server to monitor availability, including catalog views, Dynamic Management Views (DMV), and Extended Events (XEvent). In addition, Azure interfaces such as the Azure portal, az CLI, PowerShell, and REST provide additional capabilities to monitor the availability of your deployment.

Let's dive into a few examples of using these interfaces and monitoring capabilities.

Instance, Server, and Database Availability

Aside from Azure service-impacting events, you can view the availability of your Azure SQL Managed Instance or Azure Database Server and databases through the Azure portal. One of the primary methods to view a possible reason for a Managed Instance or Database to not be available is by examining **Resource Health** through the Azure portal or REST APIs.

You can always use standard SQL Server tools such as SQL Server Management Studio to connect to a Managed Instance or Database server and check the status of these resources through the tool or T-SQL queries.

In addition, interfaces such as az CLI can show the status of Azure SQL such as

az sql mi list – List the status of managed instances.

az sql db list – List the status of Azure SQL Databases.

PowerShell commands can also be used to find out the availability of an Azure SQL Database such as

Get-AzSQLDatabase – Get all the databases on a server and their details including status.

REST APIs, although not as simple to use, can also be used to get the status of Managed Instances and Databases. The complete REST API reference is at `https://docs.microsoft.com/en-us/rest/api/sql/`.

Note   For a SQL Server, I often look at past ERRORLOG files or the system_health XEvent session files for service availably and health. Azure SQL Managed Instance supports these tools. However, these files are not copied to replicas, so if a failover occurs, the history of these files is lost.

Backup and Restore History

Azure SQL automatically backs up databases and transaction logs. Although standard backup history is not available, long-term backup retention history can be viewed through the Azure portal or CLI interfaces. Learn more at `https://docs.microsoft.com/en-us/azure/azure-sql/database/long-term-backup-retention-configure`.

Additionally, Azure SQL Managed Instance supports using XEvents to track backup history. See a blog post describing how to do this at `https://techcommunity.microsoft.com/t5/azure-database-support-blog/lesson-learned-128-how-to-track-the-automated-backup-for-an/ba-p/1442355`.

Any restore of a database using Point-In-Time restore results in the creation of a new database so the history of restore can be viewed as looking at the creation of a new database. All operations to create a new database can be viewed through Azure Activity Logs.

Region, Data Center, and Service Availability

To get a global view of the status of Azure regions and datacenters, use the **Azure Status** dashboard which you can find at https://status.azure.com. Figure 8-36 shows an example of the Azure Status dashboard.

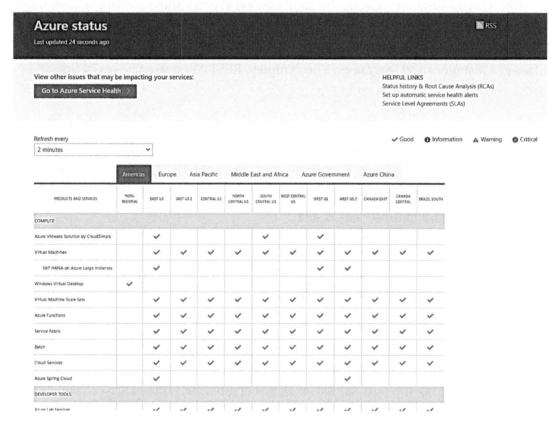

Figure 8-36. *The Azure status dashboard*

Azure status shows the status of all Azure services in all Azure regions. The status shows all services independent of your use of a specific service. To get notified of Azure status, you can use the RSS feed at the top of the page. In addition, you can see a complete history of Azure status through Azure status history at https://status.azure.com/status/history.

You can also get more information about the health of Azure services specific to your subscription through the Azure portal for a capability called **Azure Service Health**. Through Service Health, you can see current issues for Azure services, planned maintenance that could affect availability, and health history. Figure 8-37 shows an example of Service Health for my subscription.

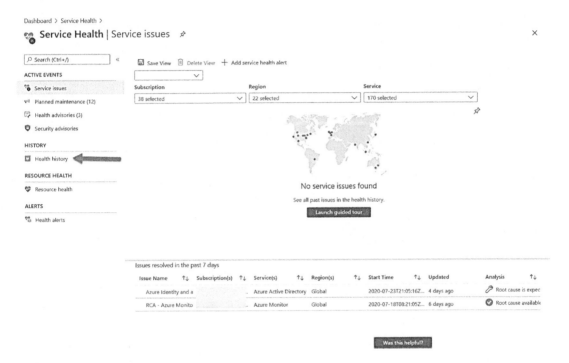

Figure 8-37. *Azure Service Health*

The default view shows any active incidents that could affect availability of your Azure resources in addition to incidents over the last week. If you select Health History, you can get more details of past issues for up to the last 3 months. You can select Service Health from your Azure portal in the dashboard. You can also view history of the health of a specific Azure resource, such as a database or Managed Instance. I'll show you an example of resource health later in this section.

Replica Status

To monitor the state of replicas in Azure SQL, you can use the DMV **sys.dm_database_ replica_states**. This DMV could be used for example to look at the status of replicas for a Business Critical service tier. You could also use this DMV to check the status for replicas for a deployment with geo-replication or auto-failover groups.

If you remember, I deployed in Chapter 4 of this book a Business Critical service tier database called **bwazuresqldbbc**. I can connect with SSMS to this database and run the following T-SQL statement:

```
SELECT is_primary_replica, synchronization_state_desc, synchronization_
health_desc, last_received_time, last_redone_time
FROM sys.dm_database_replica_states;
GO
```

I get the following results from this database on the logical server:

```
is_primary_replica    synchronization_state_desc    synchronization_health_
desc    last_received_time    last_redone_time


1                     SYNCHRONIZED                  HEALTHY
NULL                  NULL
```

I then connected to the same logical server with the database bwazuresqldbbc with applicationintent=readonly (to connect to a read replica) and ran the same query. The results look like this:

```
is_primary_replica    synchronization_state_desc    synchronization_health_
desc    last_received_time      last_redone_time


0                     SYNCHRONIZED                  HEALTHY
2020-07-28 01:22:24.813    2020-07-28 01:22:13.880
```

For geo-replication and auto-failover groups, there are additional DMVs to check on the status of replication between logical server and instances. This includes **sys.geo_replication_links** (run in the context of the logical master) and **sys.dm_geo_ replication_link_status** (run in the context of the user database). One example of using these DMVs is seeding (the initial sync of the geo-secondary). sys.geo_replication_ links can show the state of the seeding process as it progresses and completes.

In this chapter, I configured an auto-failover group. Let's connect to both the primary and secondary failover group server and see what these DMVs look like.

I connected to the failover group server **bwazuresqlww.database.windows.net** and ran the following T-SQL statement:

```
SELECT partner_server, partner_database, replication_lag_sec, replication_
state_desc, role_desc
FROM sys.dm_geo_replication_link_status;
GO
```

I got the following results:

partner_server	partner_database	replication_lag_sec	replication_
state_desc	role_desc		
bwazuresqlserversouth	bwazuresqldb	0	CATCH_UP
PRIMARY			

A **replication_state_desc** = CATCHUP means the servers are synchronized.

I then connected to the secondary failover group server of **bwazuresqlww. secondary.database.windows.net** and ran the same query. I got these results:

partner_server	partner_database	replication_lag_sec	replication_
state_desc	role_desc		
bwazuresqlserver	bwazuresqldb	NULL	CATCH_UP
SECONDARY			

You can see this is the secondary server paired with the primary logical server. **replication_lage_sec** can be used to see if there is a delay in synchronizing the servers.

You can see the full documentation of sys.dm_geo_replication_link_status at https://docs.microsoft.com/en-us/sql/relational-databases/system-dynamic-management-views/sys-dm-geo-replication-link-status-azure-sql-database?view=azuresqldb-current.

All of these DMVs to check replica status work for both Azure SQL Managed Instance and Database. az CLI can be used to check on replica status (**az sql db replica**). PowerShell cmdlets exist to support checking replica status, for example, **Get-AzSqlData baseReplicationLink**.

Failover Reasons

There are various reasons why a failover can occur, planned and unplanned, for Azure SQL Managed Instance and Database. Because the reasons for failover could vary, the best method to track if a failover occurred for your database is to use Resource Health for your Managed Instance or Database. Figure 8-38 shows an example of Resource Health for one of my Azure SQL Database deployments and a health event which resulted in a failover.

Figure 8-38. *Resource health history for an Azure SQL Database*

Note   Resource health is reported at the database level for both Azure SQL Managed Instance and Database deployments.

You can also use REST APIs to check resource health for an Azure resource. Learn more at `https://docs.microsoft.com/en-us/rest/api/resourcehealth/`.

System Center Management Pack for Azure SQL

System Center Operations Management (SCOM) packs are software modules that help a user of System Center monitor applications and services. You can learn more about SCOM packs at `https://docs.microsoft.com/en-us/system-center/scom/manage-overview-management-pack`. We have built SCOM packs for both Azure SQL Database and Managed Instances.

My colleague Ebru Ersan leads our team on the design of SCOM packs. You can read her blog post about SCOM packs for Managed Instance at `https://techcommunity.microsoft.com/t5/sql-server/released-azure-sql-managed-instance-management-pack-7-0-22-0/ba-p/1503931`. You can download the SCOM pack for Azure SQL Database at `www.microsoft.com/en-us/download/details.aspx?id=38829`.

Summary

In this chapter, you learn the amazing built-in availability capabilities for Azure SQL, including automatic backups, Point-In-Time restore, and built-in availability architectures of General Purpose, Business Critical, and Hyperscale.

You also learned how to use the power of Azure for further redundancy with Azure Availability Zones, geo-replication, and auto-failover groups. You learned how Azure provides built-in data integrity capabilities and processes and how to monitor the availability of your Azure SQL deployments.

Availability is the last part of the meat and potatoes of Azure SQL. In the next chapter, you will complete your knowledge of Azure SQL to learn capabilities not specifically related to security, performance, or availability.

CHAPTER 9

Completing Your Knowledge of Azure SQL

You have been through the journey of deploying and configuring Azure SQL Managed Instance and Databases. You have then seen all the capabilities and tasks you need to secure your deployments, make and keep Azure SQL fast, and ensure your data is highly available. In this chapter, we will complete your knowledge for Azure SQL by looking closer at a feature comparison with SQL Server, understanding options for job management, see how ways you can help support your deployments, and review best practices for using Azure SQL.

This chapter will contain examples for you to try out and use as you read along. For you to try out any of the techniques, commands, or examples I use in this chapter, you will need

- An Azure subscription.

- A minimum of Contributor role access to the Azure subscription. You can read more about Azure built-in roles at `https://docs. microsoft.com/en-us/azure/role-based-access-control/built- in-roles`.

- Access to the Azure Portal (web or Windows application).

- A deployment of an Azure SQL Managed Instance and/or an Azure SQL Database as I did in Chapter 4. The Azure SQL Database I deployed uses the AdventureWorks sample which will be required to use some of the examples (I only briefly show Azure SQL Managed Instance in this chapter, so it is not a problem if skip this step. If you still have your Managed Instance deployed from previous chapters, you can use that).

© Bob Ward 2021
B. Ward, *Azure SQL Revealed*, https://doi.org/10.1007/978-1-4842-5931-3_9

- To connect to Managed Instance, you will need a *jumpbox* or virtual machine in Azure to connect. I showed you how to do this in Chapter 4 of the book. One simple way to do this is to create a new Azure Virtual Machine and deploy it to the same virtual network as the Managed Instance (you will use a different subnet than the Managed Instance).

- To connect to Azure SQL Database, I'm going to use the Azure VM I deployed in Chapter 3, called **bwsql2019**, and configured for a private endpoint in Chapter 6 (you could use another method as long as you can connect to the Azure SQL Database).

- You will run some T-SQL in this chapter, so install a tool like SQL Server Management Studio (SSMS) at `https://docs.microsoft.com/en-us/sql/ssms/download-sql-server-management-studio-ssms?view=sql-server-ver15`. You can also use Azure Data Studio at `https://docs.microsoft.com/en-us/sql/azure-data-studio/download-azure-data-studio?view=sql-server-ver15`. I installed both SSMS and ADS in the bwsql2019 Azure Virtual Machine.

- For this chapter, I have script files you can use for several of the examples. You can find these scripts in the **ch9_completingazure** folder for the source files included for the book.

Surface Area of Azure SQL

Throughout this book, I have compared the features and capabilities of SQL Server with Azure SQL Managed Instance and Database. Let's review a few capabilities I often get asked about that are not specifically related to security, performance, and availability.

As you read through this section, consider these documentation references:

- T-SQL differences between Managed Instance and SQL Server at `https://docs.microsoft.com/en-us/azure/azure-sql/managed-instance/transact-sql-tsql-differences-sql-server`

- T-SQL differences between Azure SQL Database and SQL Server at `https://docs.microsoft.com/en-us/azure/azure-sql/database/transact-sql-tsql-differences-sql-server`

- Feature comparison between Azure SQL Managed Instance and
  Azure SQL Database at `https://docs.microsoft.com/en-us/azure/`
  `azure-sql/database/features-comparison`

Linked Servers and Cross-Database Queries

SQL Server users in some cases execute queries for objects (and joining them) that
reside in other databases on the same SQL Server instance (cross-database query)
or another instance (linked server query). Linked servers for SQL Server also allow
queries against other data providers (through OLE-DB) such as Oracle. Cross-database
queries and linked servers allow read queries (SELECT) but also (assuming the provider
supports it) distributed transactions.

Cross-database queries are supported in Azure SQL Managed but not with Azure
SQL Database.

Note   Azure SQL Database does support the concept of elastic database query (in
preview) which can allow joining data across databases. Learn more at `https://`
`docs.microsoft.com/en-us/azure/azure-sql/database/elastic-`
`query-getting-started-vertical`.

Linked Servers are supported for Azure SQL Managed Instance but not with
Azure SQL Database. There are limitations though for how you can use Linked Servers
with Azure SQL Managed Instance. For example, you cannot use a linked server for
distributed transactions and only SQL Server–based providers are supported. See the full
list of differences for Linked Servers on Managed Instance at `https://docs.microsoft.`
`com/en-us/azure/azure-sql/managed-instance/transact-sql-tsql-differences-`
`sql-server#linked-servers`.

Note   You can create a Linked Server from a SQL Server on-premises, in Azure
Virtual Machine, or Managed Instance, where the *remote server* is an Azure
Database Logical Server.

External Tables

In SQL Server 2016, we introduced a capability called Polybase using a T-SQL object EXTERNAL TABLE to be directed to Hadoop file systems. In SQL Server 2019, we expanded this capability to include other data sources such as SQL Server, Oracle, MongoDB, Teradata, and other sources that support an ODBC Driver.

Note   To see examples of Polybase with SQL Server 2019, check out Module 8 of the SQL Server 2019 Workshop at `https://github.com/microsoft/sqlworkshops-sql2019workshop` or Chapter 9 of the book *SQL Server 2019 Revealed*.

At the current time, we do not support Polybase as feature for Azure SQL Managed Instance or Databases.

However, Azure SQL Database supports external tables to use for elastic scale query. This means that you can technically set up an **external data source** to another Azure SQL Database logical server and database and define an external table with that data source. So you can now query the remote database as an external table or even join a local table with the remote database table. You can review the T-SQL reference for external data source for Azure SQL Database at `https://docs.microsoft.com/en-us/sql/t-sql/statements/create-external-data-source-transact-sql?view=azuresqldb-current`. The external table reference for Azure SQL Database can be found at `https://docs.microsoft.com/en-us/sql/t-sql/statements/create-external-table-transact-sql?view=azuresqldb-current`.

Take a look at a cool example of using this capability from my colleague Dimitri Furman where he uses external tables to look at Hyperscale read-scale monitoring. You can find the source at `https://github.com/dimitri-furman/samples/tree/master/azure-sql-readscale-monitoring`.

Database Mail

SQL Server has supported a built-in *mail* capability since back in the days of SQL Server 4.21 for Windows NT. The latest version of this feature is called **Database Mail**. The concept is that you can use T-SQL to send mail messages based on the Simple Mail

Transfer Protocol (SMTP). If you have never used Database Mail before, you can learn more at `https://docs.microsoft.com/en-us/sql/relational-databases/database-mail/database-mail`.

We introduced support for Database Mail as a feature for Azure SQL Managed Instance as this was a capability many customers who were trying to use Azure SQL Database desired as part of their migration. Database Mail is an *instance* feature which makes sense why it is part of Azure SQL Managed Instance.

One of the common scenarios for using Database Mail is for alerts for SQL Server Agent jobs. There are a few configuration differences to use Database Mail for SQL Server Agent jobs. Read more at `https://docs.microsoft.com/en-us/azure/azure-sql/managed-instance/transact-sql-tsql-differences-sql-server#sql-server-agent`. Just about everything else is the same to use Database Mail with Azure SQL Managed Instance except for these two differences as called out in the documentation:

- sp_send_dbmail cannot send attachments using @file_attachments parameter. Local file system and external shares or Azure Blob Storage are not accessible from this procedure.

- The @query parameter in the sp_send_db_mail procedure doesn't work.

Service Broker

Back in SQL Server 2005, we heard from our customers that they wanted to build service-oriented applications using asynchronous messaging techniques. We designed and built a system called Service Broker that uses the power of SQL Server tables, programming, and communication to implement a messaging system within the SQL Server engine. If you have never used Service Broker, you can get started at `https://docs.microsoft.com/en-us/sql/database-engine/configure-windows/sql-server-service-broker`.

Service broker is another example of an instance feature, and we did not support this capability with Azure SQL Database. CloudLifter to the rescue again. We support Service broker applications with Azure SQL Managed Instance. One major exception is that we only support service broker within the Managed Instance and not cross-instance. See the full set of differences at `https://docs.microsoft.com/en-us/azure/azure-sql/managed-instance/transact-sql-tsql-differences-sql-server#service-broker`.

Full-Text Search

Full-text search has been an integrated component of the SQL Server engine for many releases. Full-text search provides searching capabilities through T-SQL against *text* data stored in the database. Even though full-text search is technically an instance-level feature for SQL Server, we support this for both Azure SQL Managed Instance and Databases. You can read about how to get started with full-text search at `https://docs.microsoft.com/en-us/sql/relational-databases/search/full-text-search`.

There are a few limitations with full text when it comes to Azure SQL:

- "Third-party filters" are not supported (examples are Office and .pdf filters).

- You cannot manage aspects to the services that support full text like fdhost.

- Semantic search (learn more at `https://docs.microsoft.com/en-us/sql/relational-databases/search/semantic-search-sql-server`) is not supported.

There is another angle to integrate searching capabilities with Azure SQL. That is to use **Azure Search** which I'll discuss in Chapter 10 of the book.

Machine Learning Services

In SQL Server 2016, we introduced R Services for SQL Server. The concept is that we would use a new architecture to allow you to run R programs in a secure, isolated, and scalable manner *on the same computer* as SQL Server. In SQL Server 2017, we added Python support and rebranded this capability as **Machine Learning Services**.

Up until the end of calendar year 2019, we did not offer this capability in Azure SQL. So I was very excited to see us announce in 2020 the preview of Machines Learning Services in Azure SQL Managed Instance. Machine Learning Services is an instance-level feature, so Managed Instance is the perfect fit.

Keep track of the progress of the preview program and eventual general availability of Machine Learning Services for Azure SQL at `https://docs.microsoft.com/en-us/azure/azure-sql/managed-instance/machine-learning-services-overview`. To gain a deeper understanding of Machine Learning Services, start at `https://docs.microsoft.com/en-us/sql/machine-learning`.

What Is Missing?

While the documentation links I've provided in this chapter show you some of the feature differences between Azure SQL and SQL Server, there are two areas that stand out where I've had several customers ask me about a capability they had in SQL Server but don't have with Azure SQL.

Distributed Transactions (DTC)

Distributed transactions with SQL Server require the support and execution of the Microsoft Distributed Transaction Coordinator (MSDTC). DTC support currently doesn't exist in Azure SQL Managed Instance and Database. I suspect one of the reasons is the complexity of supporting MSDTC in the Azure SQL infrastructure. I also believe that if we add support for DTC, it would first come to Azure SQL Managed Instance.

It is possible to develop application with distributed transactions across databases in Azure, but it won't use the DTC capabilities with SQL Server. You can learn more at https://docs.microsoft.com/en-us/azure/azure-sql/database/elastic-transactions-overview.

xp_cmdshell

xp_cmdshell is a system-supported extended stored procedure (xproc) in SQL Server. This xproc runs as a DLL in the process space of SQL Server but creates a new process on the SQL Server computer to run the command you provide as a parameter. While a nifty feature of SQL Server for years, some administrators disable the use of this procedure because it can open up security concerns. For that reason, we don't support xp_cmdshell in Azure SQL.

There really isn't anything equivalent for Azure SQL to run commands from a T-SQL procedure that is invoked by the engine. You would need to bring this code outside of your server-side programming logic into a script or application.

Job Management

As part of managing a SQL Server environment, you will no doubt want to schedule *jobs* to perform various activities related to your SQL Server. Let's review what options you have to perform various aspects for job management with your Azure SQL deployment.

SQL Server Agent

For years, users of SQL Server have used the built-in capabilities of SQL Server Agent. SQL Server Agent is a job scheduling system that is integrated with SQL Server. SQL Server Agent is another example of an instance-level feature we have not supported with Azure SQL Database but now support with Azure SQL Managed Instance.

Figure 9-1 shows SSMS within my jumpbox VM I deployed in Chapter 4 connected to my Azure SQL Managed Instance.

Figure 9-1. *SQL Server Agent with Azure SQL Managed Instance*

You will start using SQL Server Agent, and it will feel very much like job management with SQL Server. There are a few limitations, and we document these at `https://docs.microsoft.com/en-us/azure/azure-sql/managed-instance/transact-sql-tsql-differences-sql-server#sql-server-agent`.

Probably the biggest difference you will see is that we do not support CmdExec or PowerShell job step types. SQL Agent for Managed Instance is mostly used for T-SQL jobs, SSIS jobs, and jobs used to support Replication.

Elastic Jobs

If Azure SQL Database is your preferred and best deployment option, you do have an alternative to scheduling jobs that execute T-SQL statements using **Azure Elastic Jobs**. You can get started by reading at `https://docs.microsoft.com/en-us/azure/azure-sql/database/elastic-jobs-overview`.

One of the cool features of elastic jobs is that I can run jobs in parallel. Let's see it in action. I'll use elastic jobs to schedule a reorganization for an index in d*atabases concurrently* using elastic jobs. I'll use two of my example databases that I deployed in Chapter 4 and have used in several other chapters **bwazuresqldb** and **bwazuresqldbbc** from the logical server **bwazuresqlserver** (if you have deleted this by now, just deploy two new Azure SQL databases, General Purpose, 2 vCores).

Here are the outlined steps of how to create and execute elastic jobs:

- Deploy a job database.

- Deploy an Elastic Job Agent service referring to the job database.

- Create job credentials, logins, and users.

- Define a target group.

- Create the job.

- Add job steps.

- Run the job.

- Monitor job execution.

Another term you should be familiar with is target logical server and target database(s). These are the logical server and database(s) you want to run your jobs against. In my example, **bwazuresqlserver** is the **target logical server** and **bwazuresqldb** and **bwazuresqldbbc** are the **target logical databases**.

Let's go through each step in detail and see how this works. All the scripts for this example can be found in the **ch9_completingazure\elasticjobs** folder:

1. Deploy an elastic job database.

   Elastic Job is an Azure service and needs a database to store information about jobs and scheduling. I'll call this database the **elastic job database** in this example. This is similar to how SQL Server Agent uses the msdb database. There is no special requirement for this database. The documentation says you can use a "S0 or higher" Azure SQL Database. S0 stands for Standard Service tier (DTU model) and is the lowest of that level. S0 is actually equivalent to less than one vCore. You could also choose any vCore-based deployment option including Serverless. Just know that with Serverless there could be warm-up time that affects how fast your jobs are executed.

   I created a new resource group (**bwelasticjobrg**), a new logical server (**bwazuresqljob**), and a Serverless database (**bwelasticjobdb**) with a min of 0.5 cores and max of 1 core to save costs.

2. Deploy an Elastic Job Agent Service.

   Now you need to deploy the Azure Elastic Job service called **Elastic Job Agent Service**.

   Search for Elastic Job agent through portal. To create an Elastic job agent, you will need to choose your elastic job database like in Figure 9-2.

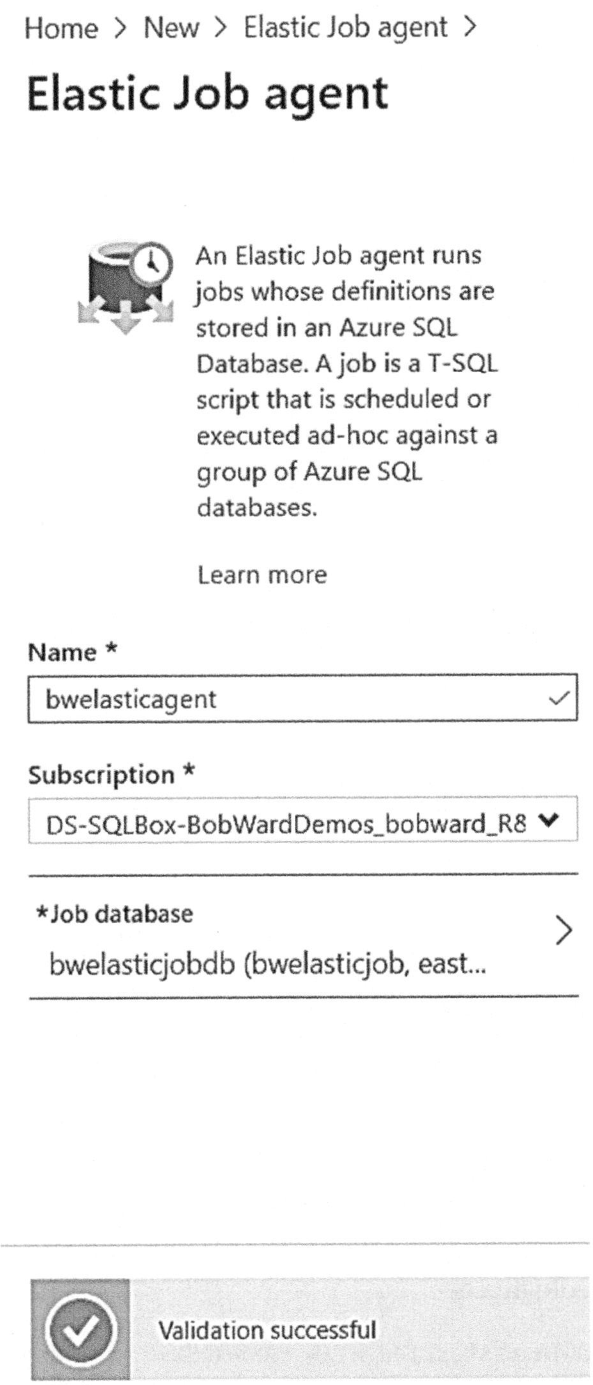

Home > New > Elastic Job agent >

Elastic Job agent

 An Elastic Job agent runs
jobs whose definitions are
stored in an Azure SQL
Database. A job is a T-SQL
script that is scheduled or
executed ad-hoc against a
group of Azure SQL
databases.

Learn more

Name *

| bwelasticagent   ✓ |

Subscription *

| DS-SQLBox-BobWardDemos_bobward_R8 ⌄ |

*Job database   >

bwelasticjobdb (bwelasticjob, east...

⊘ Validation successful

Figure 9-2. *Deploying Elastic job agent through the portal*

3. Ensure connectivity between the Elastic job agent service and
    your target logical server.

    In Chapter 6 of the book, I configured my logical server to use
    Private Link and to disable any public access. To use elastic jobs,
    I'll need to enable **Allow Azure services and resources to access
    this server**.

4. Create job credentials, logins, and users.

    In order for the Elastic Job Agent service to execute jobs against
    a target logical server and database, it needs a login and users
    to have permissions. In the elastic job database, you will create
    credentials to map to logins and users.

    You will need two credentials that will map to logins and users in
    the target logical server and database. The credentials can be any
    name, but I'll use a term to describe them:

    mastercred – This will map to a login for the logical server and a
    user in the target logical master.

    jobcred – This will map to a different login in the target logical
    server and a user in the target database(s).

    You are responsible for creating the logins and users in the target
    logical server and database. The *jobcred* login and user must have
    permissions to run the T-SQL code that is part of the job. In my
    case, I'm rebuilding indexes so I'll need this login and user to have
    permissions to rebuild the index. I won't use the server admin
    login for the logical server I deployed.

    I'll first create the login and user for mastercred in the logical
    master database (I am connected using the server admin
    account) with these T-SQL statements as found in the script
    mastercredlogin.sql:

```
CREATE LOGIN mastercred WITH PASSWORD = 'Strongpassw0rd';
GO
```

```
CREATE USER mastercred FROM LOGIN mastercred;
GO
```

Now I'll create the login for the jobcred in the context of the logical master database as found in the script **jobcredlogin.sql**:

```
CREATE LOGIN jobcred WITH PASSWORD = 'Strongpassw0rd';
GO
```

Next, I'll create a user mapped to the jobcred login in *both* target databases, bwazuresqldb and bwazuresqldbbc, as found in the script **jobcreduser.sql**:

```
CREATE USER jobcred FROM LOGIN jobcred;
GO

exec sp_addrolemember 'db_owner', 'jobcred';
GO
```

Now in the *context of the elastic job database*, I need to create credentials that map to these logins.

Azure SQL (and SQL Server) provides a concept called **database scoped credentials** for this purpose. Furthermore, since database scoped credentials contain password information, they can be protected by a master key encryption.

Since my elastic job database logical server has Allows Azure access I can also use bwsql2019 to connect to it can run the following T-SQL statements to create these credentials as found in the script **createcreds.sql**:

Note   You may already have a master key in which you don't need the first step.

```
-- Create a db master key if one does not already exist,
using your own password.
CREATE MASTER KEY ENCRYPTION BY PASSWORD='Strongpassw0rd';
GO
```

```
-- Create a database scoped credential for the master
database of server1.
CREATE DATABASE SCOPED CREDENTIAL mymastercred WITH
IDENTITY = 'mastercred', SECRET = 'Strongpassw0rd';
GO

-- Create a database scoped credential.
CREATE DATABASE SCOPED CREDENTIAL myjobcred WITH IDENTITY =
'jobcred', SECRET = 'Strongpassw0rd';
GO
```

5. Create target groups and members.

    A target group is a logical collection of target members. A target
    member is a target logical server and databases. I used the
    following T-SQL in the context of the elastic job database to create
    the target group and member in the elastic job database as found
    in the script **createtargetgroup.sql**:

```
-- Add a target group containing server(s)
EXEC jobs.sp_add_target_group 'bwazuresqlgroup'

-- Add a server target member
EXEC jobs.sp_add_target_group_member
'bwazuresqlgroup',
@target_type = 'SqlServer',
@refresh_credential_name='mymastercred', --credential
required to refresh the databases in a server
@server_name='bwazuresqlserver.database.windows.net';
GO

-- Add a server target member
EXEC jobs.sp_add_target_group_member
'bwazuresqlgroup',
@membership_type = 'Exclude',
@target_type = 'SqlDatabase',
@server_name='bwazuresqlserver.database.windows.net',
@database_name = 'bwazuresqldbhyper';
GO
```

```
EXEC jobs.sp_add_target_group_member
'bwazuresqlgroup',
@membership_type = 'Exclude',
@target_type = 'SqlDatabase',
@server_name='bwazuresqlserver.database.windows.net',
@database_name = 'bwazuresqldbserverless';
GO

--View the recently created target group and target group
members
SELECT * FROM jobs.target_groups WHERE target_group_
name='bwazuresqlgroup';
SELECT * FROM jobs.target_group_members WHERE target_
group_name='bwazuresqlgroup';
GO
```

The default is that all databases for the logical server will be part of the target group. Since I only want the job to apply to two of my databases, you notice I use a syntax to exclude some databases.

6. Create the job.

Now I'll create the job which includes a job step (those familiar with SQL Server Agent will recognize the concept of a job step) to reorganize an index with the following T-SQL statements in the context of the elastic job database as found in the script **createjob.sql**:

```
--Add job for create table
EXEC jobs.sp_add_job @job_name='ReorganizeIndexes',
@description='Reorganize Indexes';
GO

-- Add job step for create table
EXEC jobs.sp_add_jobstep @job_name='ReorganizeIndexes',
@command=N'ALTER INDEX PK_SalesOrderDetail_SalesOrderID_
SalesOrderDetailID
ON SalesLT.SalesOrderDetail REORGANIZE;',
```

```
@credential_name='myjobcred',
@target_group_name='bwazuresqlgroup';
GO
```

Notice in this case, I use the jobcred credential which is used to execute the command from the job step. Job can have multiple job steps, but I'll only use one for this example.

7. Run the job.

    Now I'll execute the job with the following T-SQL statement in the context of the elastic job database as found in the script **startjob.sql**:

    ```
    -- Execute the latest version of a job
    EXEC jobs.sp_start_job 'ReorganizeIndexes';
    GO
    ```

Note   The sp_add_job procedure supports parameters to schedule job execution on the frequency of your choice. You can also update an existing job with sp_update_job to add in a schedule. Learn more at `https://docs.microsoft.com/en-us/azure/azure-sql/database/elastic-jobs-tsql-create-manage#schedule-execution-of-a-job`.

---

8. Monitor job execution.

    I can monitor the execution of the job using the following T-SQL statement in the context of the elastic job database as found in the script **jobhistory.sql**:

    ```
    SELECT * FROM jobs.job_executions;
    GO
    ```

    The results will show the successful or failed execution of steps of the job.

9. View jobs via the Azure portal.

You can also view properties of target groups, credentials, job, and job history through the Azure portal of the Elastic job agent. Figure 9-3 shows an example.

Figure 9-3. *Elastic job agent properties and job history*

Use the tutorial at `https://docs.microsoft.com/en-us/azure/azure-sql/database/elastic-jobs-tsql-create-manage` to learn more about creating elastic job.

PowerShell provides interfaces as well to create and manage elastic jobs. Learn more at `https://docs.microsoft.com/en-us/azure/azure-sql/database/elastic-jobs-powershell-create`.

Other information about elastic jobs can be found at `https://docs.microsoft.com/en-us/azure/azure-sql/database/elastic-jobs-overview`.

Azure Automation

Azure automation is an Azure service that allows you to automate cloud management tasks which can include integration with Azure SQL. This includes executing tasks using languages like PowerShell or Python with a concept called a *runbook*. Learn more about Azure automation at `https://docs.microsoft.com/en-us/azure/automation/automation-intro#process-automation`.

Check out our documentation for specific information on how to use Azure automation with Azure SQL Database at https://docs.microsoft.com/en-us/azure/azure-sql/database/automation-manage.

Supporting Azure SQL

I have spent the majority of my career at Microsoft in technical support, and many of the details of SQL Server I have compared in this book are based on knowledge I gained while in support.

There are a few topics regarding supporting your Azure SQL deployment that are different than SQL Server worth calling out in this chapter including error handling, stack dumps, using resources in the Azure portal to assist in troubleshooting, and providing feedback with UserVoice.

Handling Errors

Most errors that you can encounter with Azure SQL Managed Instance and Database will be common with SQL Server. Our documentation has a complete list of engine errors at https://docs.microsoft.com/en-us/sql/relational-databases/errors-events/database-engine-events-and-errors.

For Azure SQL, you may encounter some new errors, and they usually center around *connectivity*, *resource governance*, and *support*. You can find a list of some of these scenarios in our documentation at https://docs.microsoft.com/en-us/azure/azure-sql/database/troubleshoot-common-errors-issues.

For example, in Chapter 8 of the book, you saw a scenario when an application could not connect during a failover and encountered an error like this:

```
07/22/20 21:44:17.444 [0x00001E6C] Attempt to establish connection
failed.  See the detailed errors that follow:
07/22/20 21:44:17.444 [0x00001E6C] SQLState: HY000, Native Error: 40613
[SQL Server]Database 'bwazuresqldb' on server 'bwazuresqlserver' is not
currently available.  Please retry the connection later.  If the problem
persists, contact customer support, and provide them the session tracing ID
of '{CC39135B-D638-4A51-BB25-EABB8A5315A0}'.
```

Msg 40613 is an example of a connectivity error because a *valid* logical server is not available, but your network connectivity is fine. What this error effectively means is that your connectivity is fine to our gateways, but the resource we need to redirect you to (your logical server or instance) is not available.

Let's say the problem is that a network error has occurred for your application. You would get a more traditional SQL Server error like this:

```
10053: A transport-level error has occurred when receiving results from the
server. (Provider: TCP Provider, error: 0 - An established connection was
aborted by the software in your host machine)
```

An example of a resource governance type of error is exceeding a resource limit as specified by your deployment option. For example, for Azure SQL Database, if you exceeded the maximum number of workers, you might get an error like this:

```
Msg 10928
The request limit for the database is <limit> and has been reached.
```

The limit you may encounter could be storage. The following code is an example of an error when you have exceeded the maximum storage limit for a Managed Instance:

```
Msg 1133
The managed instance has reached its storage limit. The storage usage for
the managed instance cannot exceed (%d) MBs.
```

Finally, you may encounter an error because you are trying to use a feature or a T-SQL statement that is not supported. For example, if you tried to change the "max server memory" option with sp_configure in Managed Instance, you would get an error like this:

```
Msg 5870
Changes to server configuration option max server memory (MB) are not
supported in SQL Database Managed Instances
```

An error may not be so obvious as to the problem. If you tried to execute sp_configure when connected to Azure SQL Database, you would get an error like as follows, indicating this system procedure is not supported for Azure SQL Database:

```
Msg 2812, Level 16, State 62, Line 1
Could not find stored procedure 'sp_configure'.
```

In some cases, you will encounter an error because you don't have access to a feature due to your deployment option. For example, In-Memory OLTP is only available in Business Critical service tiers. Therefore, if you try to create a memory-optimized table in a General Purpose service tier, you will encounter the following error:

```
Msg 40536, Level 16, State 2, Line 1
'MEMORY_OPTIMIZED tables' is not supported in this service tier of the
database. See Books Online for more details on feature support in different
service tiers of Windows Azure SQL Database.
```

Stack Dumps

In some cases, the SQL Server engine encounters a fatal error (e.g., ACCESS_VIOLATION) that results in a termination of the connection of the application and the creation of a *stack dump* on the server. If this type of problem is persistent, users of SQL Server are used to working with Microsoft technical support to examine these dump files to determine the cause of the problem. Here is a link to a Microsoft article that describes an example of this type of problem: https://support.microsoft.com/en-us/help/4519796/fix-stack-dump-occurs-when-table-type-has-a-user-defined-constraint-in.

For Azure SQL, you don't have access to the underlying file system to look at these files. The good news is that it doesn't matter. Stack dumps are conditions that Azure SQL automatically handles. It is possible your application may encounter one of these types of problems, but our back-end systems have alerts to monitor these types of issues automatically. Our engineers get notified, and an immediate investigation is initiated. If the problem is severe enough to require SQL Server to be restarted, we may initiate a failover. One of the benefits to this type of monitoring is that we may recognize a pattern to a problem like this that affects multiple users and initiate a code fix on the next *train* – another example of the benefits of a versionless SQL Server.

Troubleshooting Resources in the Azure Portal

My longtime friend and colleague at Microsoft Keith Elmore pivoted his career in support several years ago to focus on Azure SQL. Keith and his team in support worked with our engineering team to build in tools to assist you in troubleshooting your own problems in the Azure portal.

There are two paths in the Azure portal to get assistance for troubleshooting:

- The Troubleshooting tool through Resource Health

- Assisted path by opening a support request

I mentioned using the Resource Health option in the Resource Menu to look for possible failovers that affected availability. Figure 9-4 shows this screen for my Azure SQL Database bwazuresqldb with a reference to select a Troubleshooting tool.

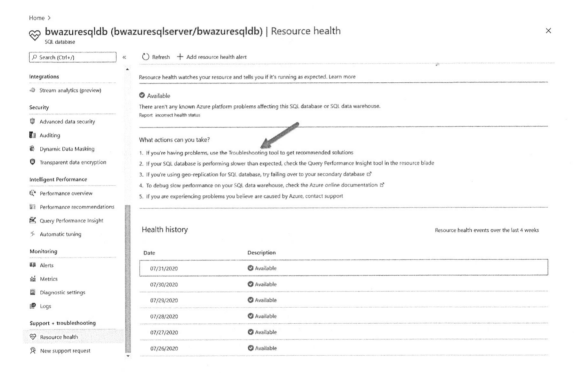

Figure 9-4. *Accessing the troubleshooting tool from Resource Health*

If you select Troubleshooting tool, you will see a set of Common Problems based on the top issues Microsoft support sees from customer support requests like Figure 9-5.

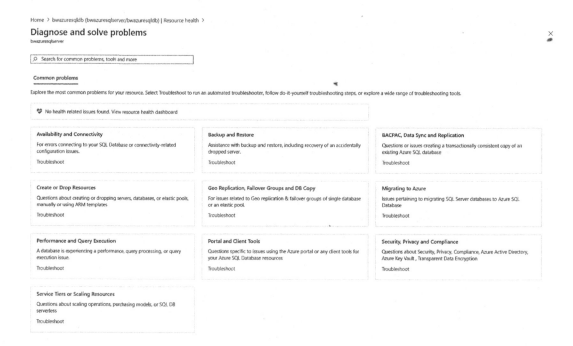

Figure 9-5. *Common problems for Azure SQL*

Note   This screen is also available from **Diagnose and Solve Problems** in the Resource Menu in the Azure portal.

If I select a topic like **Availability and Connectivity**, I'm presented with a screen like Figure 9-6 that has options to run a *troubleshooter* or look at possible manual troubleshooting steps based on known common issues related to the topic.

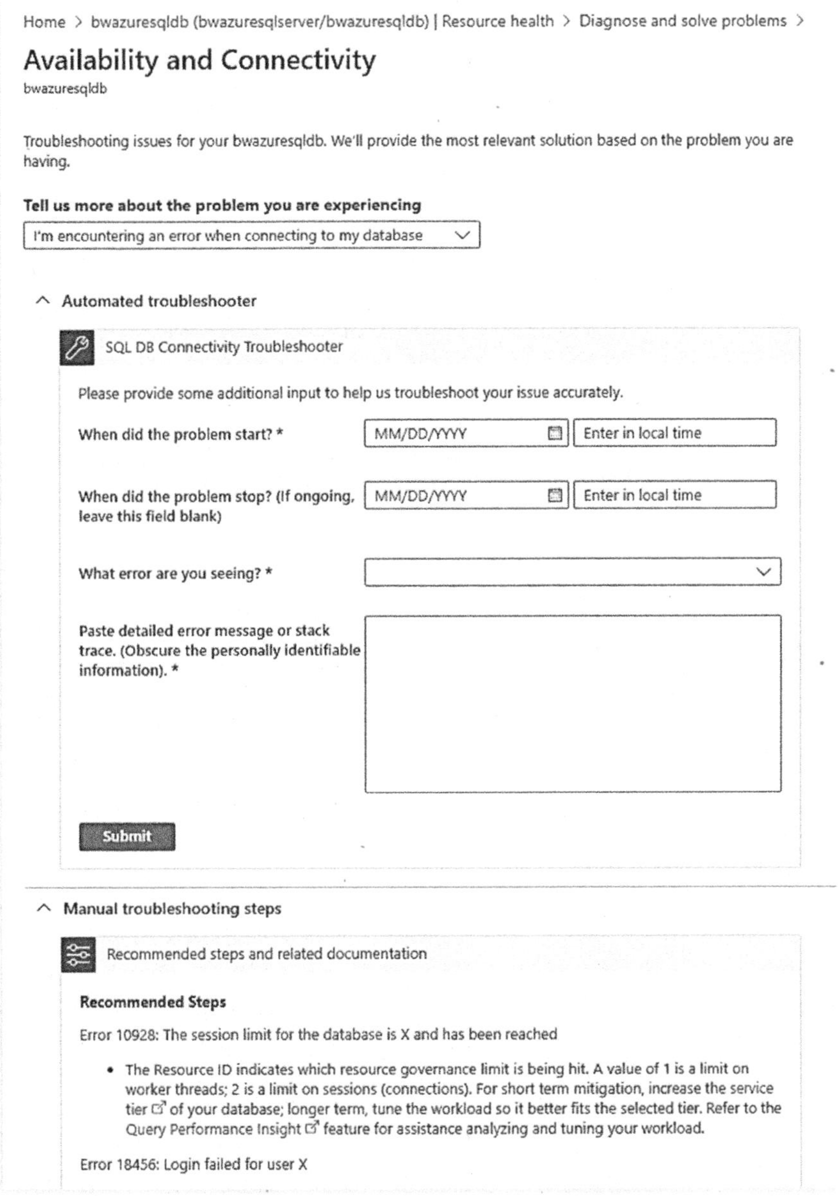

Home > bwazuresqldb (bwazuresqlserver/bwazuresqldb) | Resource health > Diagnose and solve problems >

Availability and Connectivity
bwazuresqldb

Troubleshooting issues for your bwazuresqldb. We'll provide the most relevant solution based on the problem you are having.

Tell us more about the problem you are experiencing

| I'm encountering an error when connecting to my database   ∨ |

∧ Automated troubleshooter

🔧 SQL DB Connectivity Troubleshooter

Please provide some additional input to help us troubleshoot your issue accurately.

When did the problem start? * | MM/DD/YYYY   📅 | | Enter in local time |

When did the problem stop? (If ongoing, | MM/DD/YYYY   📅 | | Enter in local time |
leave this field blank)

What error are you seeing? * | ∨ |

Paste detailed error message or stack
trace. (Obscure the personally identifiable
information). *

[Submit]

∧ Manual troubleshooting steps

⚙ Recommended steps and related documentation

Recommended Steps

Error 10928: The session limit for the database is X and has been reached

- The Resource ID indicates which resource governance limit is being hit. A value of 1 is a limit on worker threads; 2 is a limit on sessions (connections). For short term mitigation, increase the service tier ⬀ of your database; longer term, tune the workload so it better fits the selected tier. Refer to the Query Performance Insight ⬀ feature for assistance analyzing and tuning your workload.

Error 18456: Login failed for user X

Figure 9-6. *An Azure SQL troubleshooter*

In the top section, you can put in details like when the problem happened and errors you are seeing. If you select Submit, then a process is run to check telemetry available about your deployment (not your data) to see if any issues were detected. It is possible there was a known problem during the time you selected that has been resolved or point you to resources to solve it.

At the bottom of the screen (you will see more if you scroll down) are a series of common errors or scenarios related to the topic with pointers to documentation to assist you.

You also may want to try and create a support request online about your problem. Figure 9-7 shows how you can select **New support request** from the Resource Menu to be provided with a list of questions.

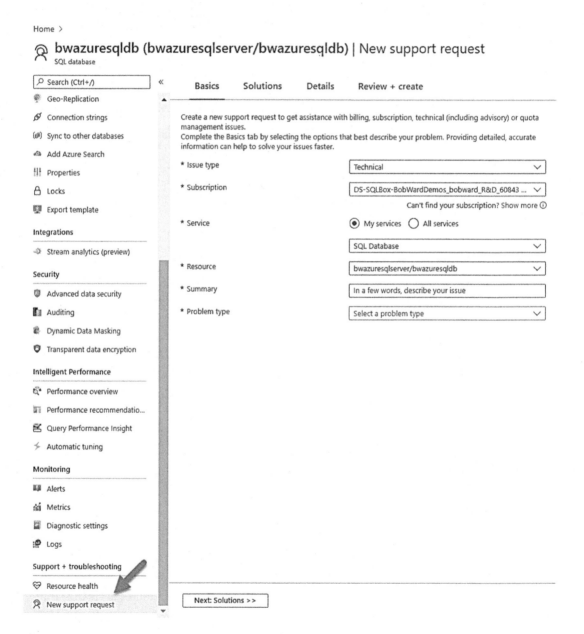

Figure 9-7. *Creating a support request for Azure*

Notice on this screen we can recognize what resources you have deployed. Having more context on your resources could potentially allow us to find a known problem. Furthermore, if we don't find a known problem, having this context allows Microsoft Support to resolve your issue faster. You can read more about the complete support request experience at `https://docs.microsoft.com/en-us/azure/azure-portal/supportability/how-to-create-azure-support-request`.

Microsoft has various support plans to help you with your Azure deployments. All Azure customers for no charge get a fundamental set of support options. However, there are also options to pay for support to increase your level of availability for Microsoft Support to handle business critical issues 24x7. Learn about all the Azure support plans at `https://azure.microsoft.com/en-us/support/plans/`.

UserVoice

You may be using Azure SQL and have a suggestion, not necessarily a problem that needs support. Microsoft provides a forum for your feedback for Azure SQL through a concept called *UserVoice or Azure feedback*. You can access the feedback sites for Azure SQL Database and Managed Instance at

`https://feedback.azure.com/forums/217321-sql-database`

`https://feedback.azure.com/forums/915676-sql-managed-instance`

I can assure you that as an engineering team we do look at these requests and how customers vote on them, so find something you are passionate about and get others to vote for your idea.

Azure SQL Best Practices

To wrap up this chapter, let's take a look at resources that can help you with best practices for your Azure SQL deployment.

Security Playbook

About a year ago, Jakub Szymaszek, a Principal Program Manager on our team who specializes in security (and one of the nicest people you will ever meet), approached me about an idea the team was working on. He said, "Bob, you have worked with SQL Server for many years. Can you take a look at a *security playbook* we are working on?" I gave him some feedback and looked forward to how the project would progress.

The result of this effort has been infused into our documentation at `https://docs.`
`microsoft.com/en-us/azure/azure-sql/database/security-best-practice`. This
document covers the collective knowledge of our team for best practices for you to
secure Azure SQL. This includes authentication, access management, data protection,
network security, monitoring and auditing, common security threads, and security
aspects for availability. This is your "de facto" guide to read and learn as you deploy and
secure your Azure SQL deployments. You will find many of the concepts you learned in
Chapter 6 of the book line up with these best practices.

One of the best practices recommended in this document (as well as in Chapter 6
of the book) is to take advantage of the Azure Security Center. You can read more about
the Azure Security Center at `https://docs.microsoft.com/en-us/azure/security-`
`center/security-center-intro`. Figure 9-8 is an example of the dashboard that comes
with the Azure Security Center across all Azure resources.

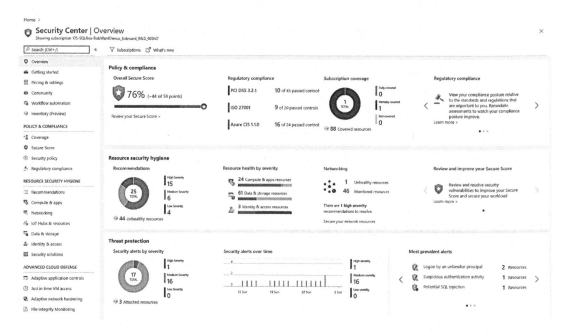

Figure 9-8. *The Azure security center*

Best Practices for Performance

In Chapter 7 of the book, you saw a comprehensive look at performance for Azure SQL. There are some best practices to follow as you saw in that chapter. We also have a very nice summary of performance best practices for you to read at `https://docs.microsoft.com/en-us/azure/azure-sql/database/performance-guidance`. This includes guidance for monitoring, query design, and application development.

Another excellent resource comes from my longtime colleague Jack Li who now works in our engineering team. Learn more at `https://docs.microsoft.com/en-us/azure/azure-sql/identify-query-performance-issues`.

Azure Advisor

Given that in the Azure ecosystem there is much telemetry about your deployments (but not your data), why not build in some automation to give you advice? That is **Azure Advisor**. Azure Advisor is the collective knowledge of the Azure engineering team all up to give you advice about your deployments in the topics of Cost, Security, Reliability, Operational Excellence, and Performance. You can read more about Azure Advisor at `https://docs.microsoft.com/en-us/azure/advisor/advisor-overview`. Figure 9-9 shows an example of Azure Advisor for my subscriptions.

Figure 9-9. *Azure Advisor*

Here is a nice blog post outlining what Azure Advisor can do you for: `https://azure.microsoft.com/en-us/blog/your-single-source-for-azure-best-practices/`.

Notice in Azure Advisor the area of *saving costs*. Our documentation calls out some of these cost saving ideas at `https://docs.microsoft.com/en-us/azure/advisor/advisor-cost-recommendations`. For me, saving costs are very important balanced with the needs of your application for security, performance, and availability. Keep these cost saving ideas in mind for Azure SQL:

- Monitor your performance for Azure SQL Database and right-size your vCore and storage choices over time. You saw in Chapter 7 of the book how easy it is to scale databases. However, Hyperscale (as of today) is a one-way choice and Managed Instance scaling can take time.

- Take a hard look at the Serverless compute tier. Serverless comes with autoscaling, pay per second, and pause for compute when idle.

- Shut down Azure Virtual Machines when you don't need them. Remember the advice Anna Hoffman gave me I discussed in Chapter 3 about using *burstable* Azure virtual machines (`https://docs.microsoft.com/en-us/azure/virtual-machines/sizes-b-series-burstable`).

- Our General Manager of Data Marketing, John "JG" Chirapurath, has a very nice blog post on how to optimize costs for Azure SQL including taking advantage of Azure Hybrid Benefit. Read more at `https://azure.microsoft.com/en-us/blog/eight-ways-to-optimize-costs-on-azure-sql/`.

Note   Another way to analyze costs is to use the Cost analysis option in the Azure portal. This provides a nice breakdown of costs and helps forecast future costs. Learn more at `https://docs.microsoft.com/en-us/azure/cost-management-billing/costs/quick-acm-cost-analysis`.

Stay in Touch with Our Team

I have some resources for you to use to keep track of various aspects of Azure SQL, gain more knowledge, and learn more best practices:

- Follow the Twitter handle @AzureSQL. This is the official twitter handle for our Azure SQL engineering team. Also we often use #azuresql to post interesting announcements, presentations, and facts about Azure SQL. My colleague Marisa Brasile does an amazing job of keeping the community and industry up to date with these resources.

- Want to keep track of the latest updates on Azure SQL (especially when it comes to performance)? Follow my colleague Joe Sack (who is the technical reviewer of this book) for his blog posts at `https://azure.microsoft.com/en-us/blog/author/josack/`. You can also follow future blog posts from Joe and other members of our engineering team at `https://techcommunity.microsoft.com/t5/azure-sql-database/bg-p/Azure-SQL-Database`.

- Several engineers who used to work for the famous CAT team now work as my colleagues. There are excellent blog posts from people like Dimitri Furman and Denzil Ribeiro you can find at `https://techcommunity.microsoft.com/t5/datacat/bg-p/DataCAT`.

- My colleague Anna Hoffman and I built a series of training materials for self-paced study and hands-on learning. The content for these materials spans labs, videos, and open source. Check out more at these links:

`https://aka.ms/azuresqlfundamentals` – This is a self-paced course you can take on Microsoft Learn. The cool part of this course is that you don't need an Azure subscription. A free sandbox is provided for you to try out Azure SQL!

`https://aka.ms/azuresql4beginners` – This is a series of short videos on YouTube (some 60+ videos) for you to learn Azure SQL at your own pace. The videos line up with the Azure SQL Fundamentals labs (but there is even more here).

https://aka.ms/sqlworkshops – This website directs you to GitHub repos built by the engineering team. My colleague Buck Woody shepherds this site, and we have an Azure SQL Workshop tied off this site. The workshop is open source and includes a slide deck that you will see on the YouTube videos. The content here is free. Take the content, deck, and source code and fork it for your own training needs. Since this is GitHub, the latest version of the training will be here.

- Anna also hosts a video series called **Data Exposed** where members of the engineering team talk about various aspects of Azure SQL and SQL Server. Take a look at this series at `https://channel9.msdn.com/Shows/Data-Exposed`.

Summary

In this chapter, you completed your knowledge of Azure SQL by looking at features compared to SQL Server such as linked servers and Database Mail, understanding options for job management, exploring ways to support your deployments, and reviewing best practices for using Azure SQL.

If your knowledge is complete, is that it? Not quite. If you are going to make the move to Azure, why not go bigger? In the final chapter of this book, we will explore how to take advantage of the fact that you have deployed your database in the world's computer.

CHAPTER 10

Go Big with the Cloud

I wanted readers of this book to finish with a feeling of comfort. Azure SQL is SQL Server in the cloud, and you have read in this book details on what is the same and what is different. I also wanted readers to not just think Azure SQL is just about deploying an instance or a database. I want you to learn how to take advantage of the world's computer and all the services that come with it.

This chapter will contain examples for you to try out and use as you read along. For you to try out any of the techniques, commands, or examples I use in this chapter, you will need

- An Azure subscription.

- A minimum of Contributor role access to the Azure subscription. You can read more about Azure built-in roles at `https://docs.microsoft.com/en-us/azure/role-based-access-control/built-in-roles`.

- Access to the Azure Portal (web or Windows application).

- A deployment of an Azure SQL Database as I did in Chapter 4. The Azure SQL Database I deployed uses the AdventureWorks sample which will be required to use some of the examples.

Integration with Azure Services

Because you have deployed in Azure, you have access to the world's computer through your Azure subscription. You have already seen examples of this so far in the book including

- Azure interfaces like the Azure portal, az CLI, PowerShell, and REST APIs

- Connecting to Azure SQL Managed Instance and Databases from an Azure Virtual Machine

- Kerberos authentication with Azure Active Directory

471

© Bob Ward 2021
B. Ward, *Azure SQL Revealed*, https://doi.org/10.1007/978-1-4842-5931-3_10

- Managing your own encryption keys with Azure Key Vault

- Azure services to give you the advice you need with Azure Advisor
  and Azure Security Center

- Azure Elastic Job Agent to schedule T-SQL jobs for your Azure SQL
  Database

Basically, if any Azure Service has the ability to connect using the *TDS protocol*, it
can integrate with Azure SQL Managed Instance or Databases. I'll discuss a few possible
options for Azure services for you to consider in the next section on Azure solutions.

Consider first taking a look at some of the designed integrated services by looking at
the Azure portal for a deployed Azure SQL Database.

Power Platform

Figure 10-1 shows integration with the **Power Platform** (https://docs.microsoft.com/
en-us/power-platform/) from the Resource menu.

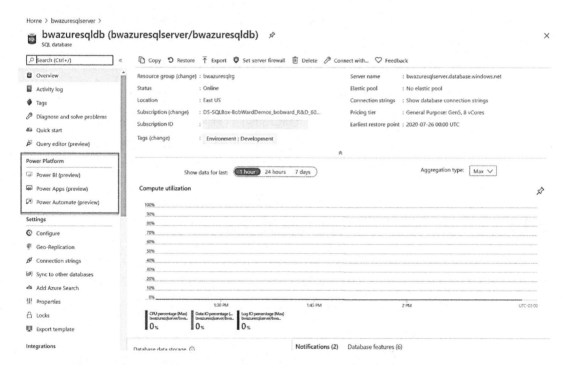

Figure 10-1. *Power Platform integration with Azure SQL*

Let's examine each of these integration points in more detail.

Power BI

Power BI is the most popular reporting platform in the world. Selecting this integration point will point you to documentation on how to build Power BI reports to connect to your Azure SQL Database and the ability to *point and click* to get a Power BI Desktop file (a .pbids file) which has connection information built in to connect to your logical server and database.

If you are interested in looking at Power BI reports connected to Azure SQL, consider these resources:

- Get started with Power BI at `https://powerbi.microsoft.com/`.

- Get started with Power BI with Azure SQL Database at `https://powerbi.microsoft.com/en-us/blog/using-power-bi-to-visualize-and-explore-azure-sql-databases/`.

- Learn from one of the world's experts on Power BI (and a close friend of mine) Adam Saxton at `https://guyinacube.com/`. Adam is joined on this site by another amazing expert (and another great friend) Patrick LeBlanc, `https://guyinacube.com/author/pleblanc/`.

Power Apps

Power Apps is a new rapid *low-code* system to build new applications. Think of visual-based development. I love trying new technology, so I selected Power Apps from the Resource Menu from my database. On the next screen, I selected Get Started and was presented with a screen like Figure 10-2.

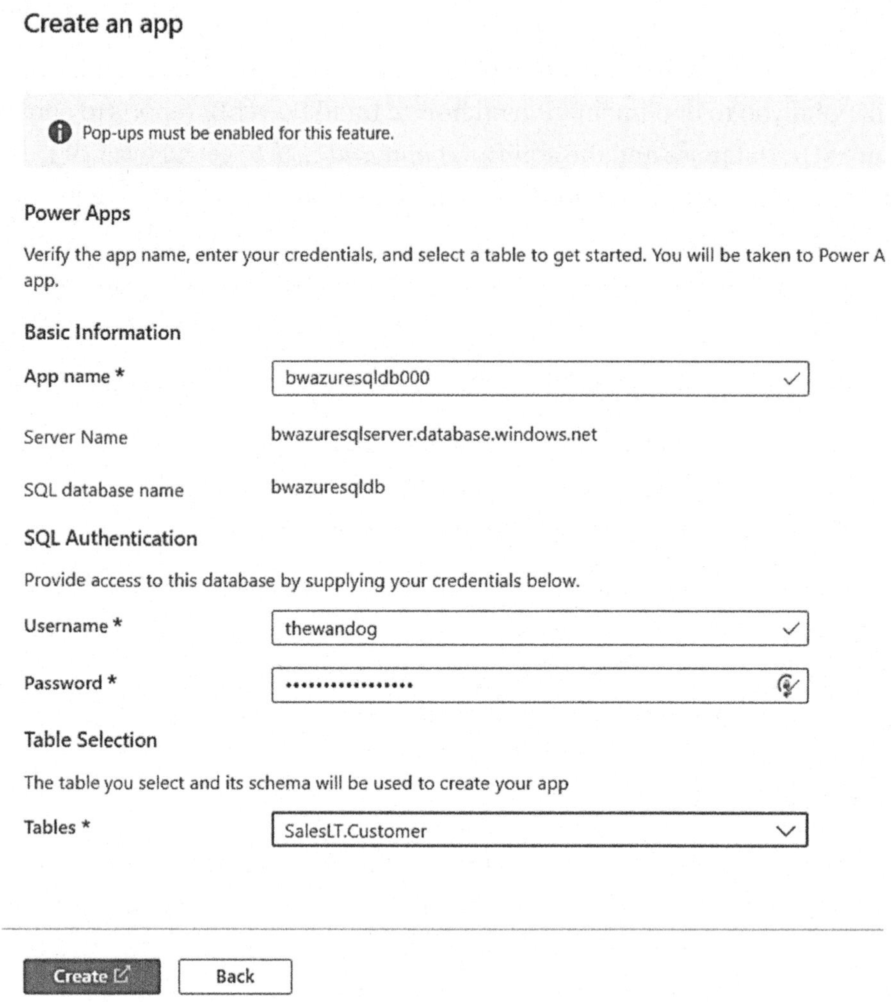

Create an app

🛈 Pop-ups must be enabled for this feature.

Power Apps

Verify the app name, enter your credentials, and select a table to get started. You will be taken to Power A app.

Basic Information

App name * | bwazuresqldb000   ✓ |

Server Name   bwazuresqlserver.database.windows.net

SQL database name   bwazuresqldb

SQL Authentication

Provide access to this database by supplying your credentials below.

Username * | thewandog   ✓ |

Password * | •••••••••••••••••   🔏 |

Table Selection

The table you select and its schema will be used to create your app

Tables * | SalesLT.Customer   ⌄ |

[Create ⬀]   [Back]

Figure 10-2. Creating a Power App application with Azure SQL Database

When I selected Create, I was brought to a new browser window (pop-ups must be enabled) that looked like Figure 10-3.

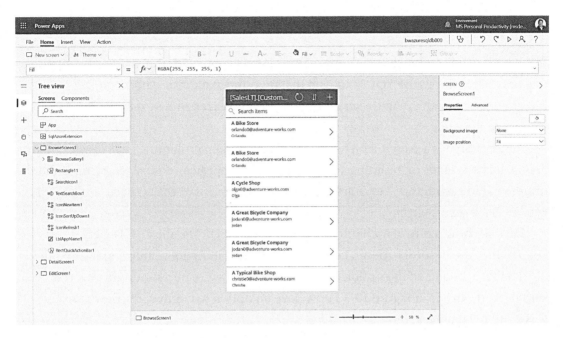

Figure 10-3. *A Power App application*

The visual in the middle of the screen is a pre-built object in Power Apps to view Customer data from my database. I can then use the Power App designer to customize to my needs.

Power Apps could be a very attractive way for your organization to build new applications, especially using Azure resources. Get started with Power Apps at `https://powerapps.microsoft.com/en-us/build-powerapps/`.

Power Automate

Power Automate, formerly known as Microsoft Flow, is a no-code/low-code platform for building flows to automate business processes. Get started with Power Automate at `https://docs.microsoft.com/en-us/power-automate/getting-started`. If you select Power Automate form the Resource menu of your database, you will be presented with a series of flow templates to integrate Power automation with Azure SQL Database. An example of a flow template is building automation to send email when an Azure SQL Database table is refreshed. You can see this example at `https://flow.microsoft.com/en-us/galleries/public/templates/2040562fd8d0432d97673715051841ac/send-office-365-email-and-mobile-notification-when-sql-table-is-refreshed`.

475

Azure Search

In Chapter 9, I discussed how full-text search is integrated with the SQL Server engine and is available for Azure SQL Managed Instance and Database. Another option is to integrate search with an Azure service called **Azure Search**, newly renamed to **Azure Cognitive Search**.

Azure Search is a *search-as-a-service* cloud solution. Similar to a PaaS service, Azure Search lets you focus on building search indexes and applications vs. worrying about the underlying infrastructure. Get started with Azure Search at `https://docs.microsoft.com/en-us/azure/search/`.

Let's see how Azure Search integrates with Azure SQL Database. If I select Azure Search from the Resource menu, I get a screen to add an Azure search service to index my database. I selected the option on this screen to first create a new Azure search service. You can see in Figure 10-4 I now have an option to connect my new search service to my database.

Figure 10-4. *Connect Azure search with Azure SQL Database*

Now as seen in Figure 10-5, I add in details for my database and table to index with the search service.

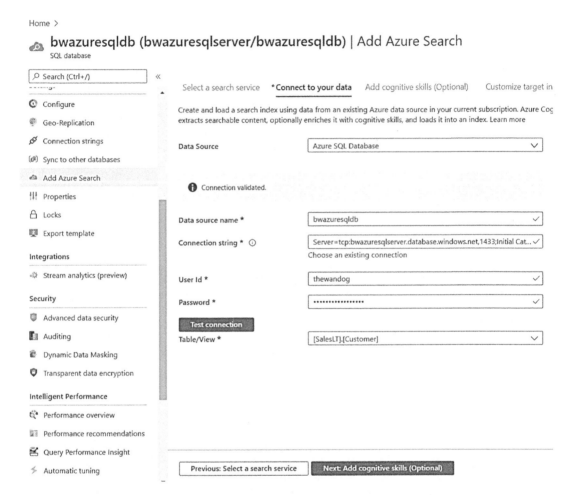

Figure 10-5. *Connect Azure search with a database and table*

Next, there is an optional step to add in *AI enrichment* into the search index. This is where the *cognitive* part of the name comes into play. Learn more how to add these options at `https://docs.microsoft.com/en-us/azure/search/cognitive-search-concept-intro`. I'll skip this step to get a screen like Figure 10-6 to customize the index for searching.

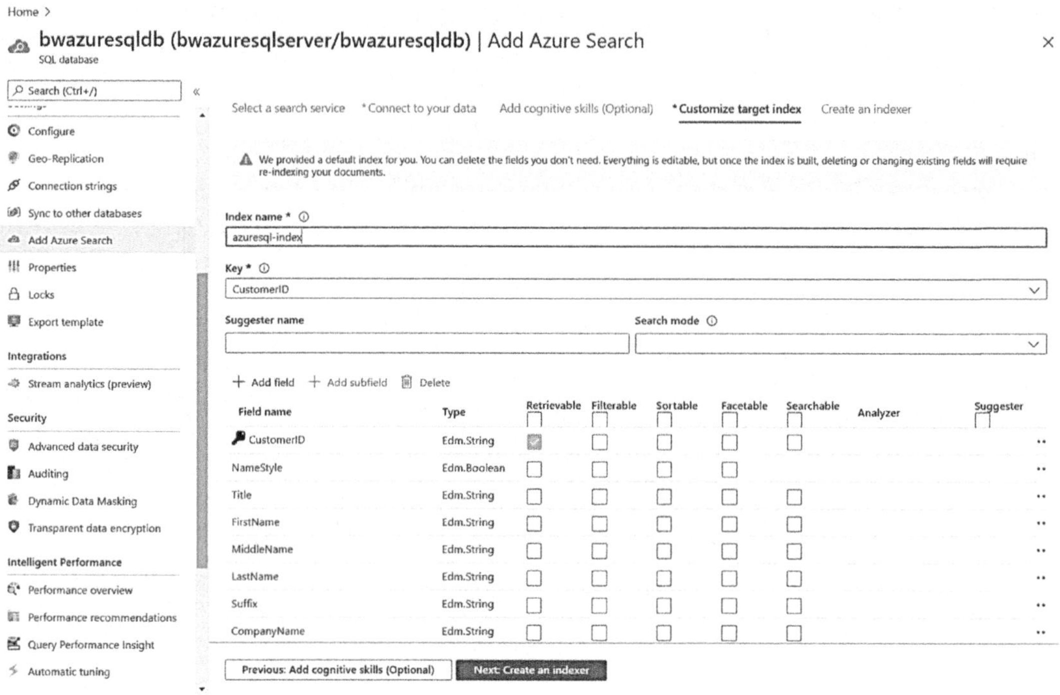

Figure 10-6. *Customizing the search index*

This is where I can select different columns to index with different indexing techniques. I then select Create an indexer to pick a one-time build or a schedule like in Figure 10-7.

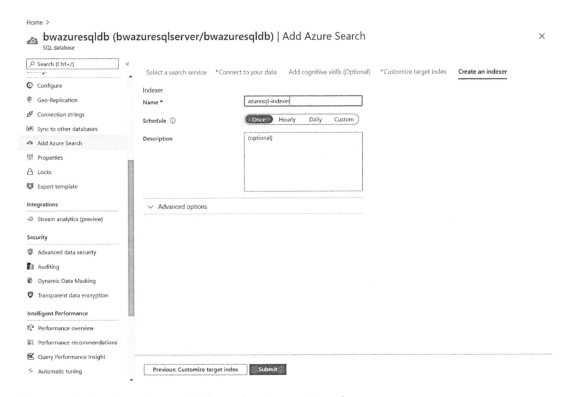

Figure 10-7. *Creating an indexer for Azure Search*

After I hit Submit, an index population is started asynchronously like in Figure 10-8.

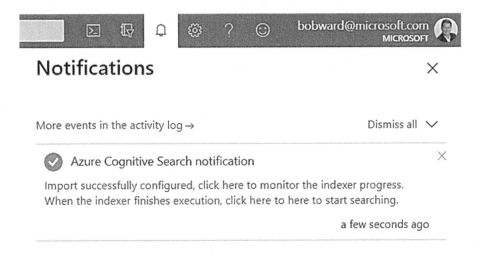

Figure 10-8. *Index build notification*

I can see in the Notifications links to check the progress of the index. When the build is done, I chose a link to search on the index (click here to start searching) using Search Explorer as seen in Figure 10-9.

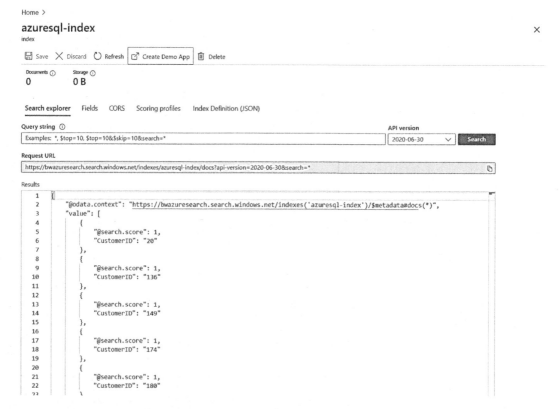

Figure 10-9. *Azure Search Explorer*

Learn more how to use Azure Search Explorer in the portal at `https://docs.microsoft.com/en-us/azure/search/search-explorer`.

Here are other resources to help you go further with Azure Search and Azure SQL:

- Learn more how to get started with Azure Search at `https://docs.microsoft.com/en-us/azure/search/search-what-is-azure-search#how-to-get-started`.

- Check out this tutorial to connect to a Managed Instance at `https://docs.microsoft.com/en-us/azure/search/search-howto-connecting-azure-sql-mi-to-azure-search-using-indexers`.

- Here is more information on how to use Azure Search with Azure
  SQL Database at `https://docs.microsoft.com/en-us/azure/`
  `search/search-howto-connecting-azure-sql-database-to-`
  `azure-search-using-indexers`.

- Read this comparison of Azure Search with other search services and
  techniques including full-text search at `https://docs.microsoft.`
  `com/en-us/azure/search/search-what-is-azure-search#how-it-`
  `compares`.

Stream Analytics

Azure Stream Analytics as its name implies is a real-time event-processing engine to
analyze and process high volumes of streaming data. Get started with Azure Stream
Analytics at `https://docs.microsoft.com/en-us/azure/stream-analytics/stream-`
`analytics-introduction`.

Stream Analytics uses a *job system*. From the Azure portal, you can select Stream
Analytics to assist you in creating a job that will take input data from **Azure IOT Hub** or
Azure Event Hub and stream the data into Azure SQL Database. Learn more the process
of how to do this at `https://docs.microsoft.com/en-us/azure/azure-sql/database/`
`stream-data-stream-analytics-integration`.

I love examples to learn a topic, so check out our documentation for Streaming
Analytic solutions such as Read-time fraud detection at `https://docs.microsoft.com/`
`en-us/azure/stream-analytics/stream-analytics-real-time-fraud-detection`.

Azure Architectures and Solutions

Because Azure is the world's computer, just connecting an Azure service to Azure
SQL Database is just the tip of the iceberg. Connecting Azure services into a complete
solution architecture is not only possible but very real. Microsoft has put together (and
continually adds) solutions based on architectures for real-world business scenarios.
Start with the Azure Architecture Center at `https://docs.microsoft.com/en-us/`
`azure/architecture/`. Here you will find **Azure architectures** you can browse for
solutions at `https://docs.microsoft.com/en-us/azure/architecture/browse/`.

One example is Internet of Things (IOT) solutions. An example solution architecture to build an IOT solution is at `https://docs.microsoft.com/en-us/azure/architecture/reference-architectures/iot`. The documentation shows a visual of how Azure services are connected like Figure 10-10.

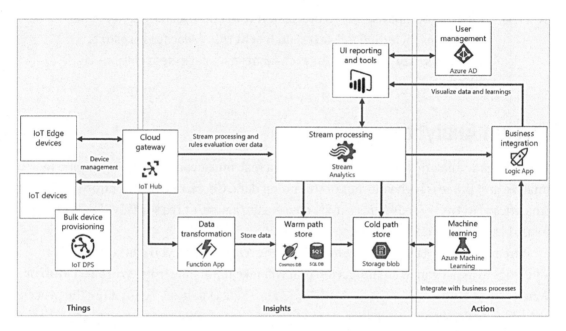

Figure 10-10. *Azure IOT reference architecture*

You can see from this visual that data is processed from IOT Hub into a *Warm path store* which can be Azure SQL Database. We have even built sample code on GitHub at `https://github.com/mspnp/iot-guidance` to show you how to build a solution like this. The code to implement the Azure SQL Database part of this solution can be found at `https://github.com/mspnp/iot-guidance/tree/master/src/WarmPath/WarmPathDeployment_SqlDb`. If you look closely at this solution, Azure SQL Database is used to store telemetry events generated by drones. The code uses technology like clustered columnstore indexes, JSON functions in T-SQL, and geo-spatial functions built into the SQL Server engine for Azure SQL.

Azure Synapse

Azure Synapse (formerly called Azure SQL Data Warehouse) is an *analytics as a service*. Synapse combines the power of data warehousing with Big Data analytics. Azure Synapse deserves its own book, but I wanted to call it out in this chapter so you know it is not technically part of the Azure SQL suite. Azure Synapse is amazing technology, and if you are looking for a cloud service for large-scale analytics, Synapse could be a good choice for you. Get started with Azure Synapse at `https://docs.microsoft.com/en-us/azure/synapse-analytics/sql-data-warehouse/`.

One interesting component of Synapse is **SQL on-demand**. SQL on-demand is a *serverless query service* against your data lake. There is a database to store metadata (e.g., external tables) but not data. You use the query service to query data against other data sources such as your warehouse or Big Data filesystem. Learn more about SQL on-demand at `https://docs.microsoft.com/en-us/azure/synapse-analytics/sql/on-demand-workspace-overview`.

Azure Arc

Not long after our team had built SQL Server Big Data Clusters (see Chapter 10 of the book *SQL Server 2019 Revealed*), we realized our investments in automation with Kubernetes could be used in other ways. At the same time, other teams at Microsoft were discussing how we could connect the world of Azure with on-premises. The result is a series of products under a family called **Azure Arc** (in this case, the word *arc* is like an electrical arc that connects two points).

Azure Arc was announced at the Microsoft Ignite conference in 2019, and our team was a big part of it. At the time of the writing of this book, it is still in Preview and we are working to refine the architecture and the solutions behind it. You can get started with Azure Arc at `https://azure.microsoft.com/en-us/services/azure-arc/`.

When it comes to SQL, Azure Arc has two flavors:

- **Azure Arc enabled SQL Server**

- This is a set of software components that run on your existing SQL Server installation (Azure Arc Agent) to connect your server to Azure for billing, subscription, and inventory purposes. In addition, we can now connect you to services traditionally found in the cloud like

Advanced Threat Protection. Read more about the Azure Arc enabled for SQL Server announcement at `https://devblogs.microsoft.com/azure-sql/preview-of-azure-arc-enabled-sql-server-is-now-available/`.

- **Azure Arc enabled data services**

- Instead of connecting your existing deployments, Azure Arc enabled data services is a complete solution that runs on top of Kubernetes (K8s). This is where our work on Big Data Clusters is paying off since it is also a platform based on K8s.

- One of the solutions that comes with Azure Arc enabled data services is an Azure SQL Managed Instance. Even though the architecture is different than how we deploy Azure SQL Managed Instance in the Azure ecosystem, the concept of abstracting you from the underlying infrastructure is part of the solution. Concepts like versionless, built-in HADR, and security services are all part of the vision.

- We are still working on Azure Arc enabled data services, but to learn more, check out this video from my colleague Travis Wright: `https://youtu.be/eEipBtXV78I`.

Summary

There are great benefits in deploying Azure SQL in the world's computer. You now have access to a wealth of other services to open up new possibilities for your application and business. I had hoped that as part of writing this book in 2020, I would be able to visit an Azure data center and give you insights into the incredible innovation and security and thought that we have built to host your resources in the cloud. That could not happen because of the COVID-19 pandemic. I hope to visit one in the future when possible. For now, check out our videos and information about the power you are harnessing when you use Azure at `https://azure.microsoft.com/en-us/global-infrastructure/`.

You may be a DBA or a SQL Server professional and after reading this book wondering "Do my skills still matter?" Is there a future for me in a cloud world? I was going to add in my own comment here, but my technical reviewer Joe Sack said it better than I, "...your DBA readers can see that gaining cloud skills are very much within their grasp. And with a future with cloud front-and-center, these are valuable AND critical skills to pick up." If you know SQL Server, Azure SQL is for you and it can be your future too.

The future of Azure SQL is bright. We will continue to build new capabilities into SQL Server for Azure Virtual Machine, Azure SQL Managed Instance, and Azure SQL Database. We will keep pushing the limits of scale and size balanced with costs to meet the demands of customers both large and small.

I asked Asad Khan, my manager and the Partner Director of Program Management for Azure SQL, about his thoughts for the future. He told me, "As we look into the future, here are few areas where we are heavily investing: We want to empower the developers by taking away the worry of managing databases. Whether it be the infrastructure or the query processor or the database engine, all three should automatically adapted to the application needs, without the developer or DBA intervention. Today we are already making heavy use of AI to offer better database service to our customers. The first one is in intelligent Query processing. Customers don't have to worry about writing performant queries or query performance degradation. We have machine learning models that automatically optimize the query plan and add or drop indexes to provide the best query performance. The second area where we are using AI is in Azure SQL Serverless. SQL Serverless offers the same SQL Server that developers love but we have taken away the worry of managing the infrastructure. You only pay when you run the query; but on top of that, the underlying infrastructure management layer is intelligent; it continuously monitors the usage. The system detects as soon as the application needs more resources, we will scale up and scale down the both the underlying compute as well as the memory resources. The machine learning models that govern the resource allocation get retrained over time and become more intelligent. Azure SQL Serverless lets you cost optimize in unpredictable usage patterns.

In the next couple of years, we will take the use of AI to a whole new level by offering 'AI governed' databases. A database that is self-managed at all three levels, database core, query processing, and at the infrastructure layer. Second is our commitment towards limitless databases. In the last 2–3 years we have made a huge investment into making Azure SQL limitless. Today Azure SQL Hyperscale is the only relational database in the world that can scale one database to support 100TB plus size of data. Next, we will bring Hyperscale to every deployment option of SQL Server. Developers should not worry about the size of data or compute needed to process that data. In additional to a limitless database, we are also looking at enabling capabilities that will make Azure SQL a globally distributed relational database. Third is our investment for enterprise security. Today Azure SQL has the most comprehensive security features, all the way from network security, access management, threat detection, and information protection. Year over year, industry analysts and security experts rank Azure SQL as the most secure data platform. We will continue to do innovations in this area. You will see us innovate towards immutability of SQL tables and temper proof auditing. This will allow us to solve 80% of the scenarios for which customers use blockchain but struggle with the complexity of the tech. One more area under security where we are investing is 'always protected'; we are looking at how to protect the data even when the data leaves Azure SQL. Think of it as the DRM capability in Office 365 coming to Azure SQL. Lastly, we will remove any differences that exist between cloud and on-prem deployments. When you deploy SQL, it doesn't matter where it runs; we will bring the same versionless, cloud managed, and centrally governed SQL databases everywhere."

I remember early in the writing of this book when I interviewed Rohan Kumar about the future of Azure SQL. His vision is more capability with a simpler path for choice and deployment. Rohan says we want to move to a model of "…You declare what you want and we pick the right Azure SQL option for you. We will continue to build SQL as cloud first but not cloud only. Azure SQL is SQL Server." For me, Azure SQL *is the world's database*, and I hope this book will put you on a path to maximize its potential.

Index

A

Accelerated database recovery (ADR),
208, 399, 409, 431
Accelerated networking, 97
Accelerating and tuning performance
AdventureWorks, 358–362
application latency, 357
increasing memory/workers, 356, 357
I/O performance, 356
scaling CPU capacity, 346–355
SQL Server, 358–362
Access, 266
Access control list (ACL), 134
Access to sensitive data, 294
Active directory authentication, 237
Activity log, 50, 274–276
Administrator account, 258
Advanced data security (ADS), 28, 63, 127,
179, 238
ASC, 301, 302
ATP, 299–301
Azure SQL Database, 288
configuration, 287, 288
data classification (*see* Data
classification)
vulnerability assessment, 295–299
Advanced threat protection (ATP), 28, 288,
299–301, 322
AdventureWorks, 358
AdventureWorksLT database, 179

AdventureWorks sample, 373, 441
ALTER DATABASE reference, 209
Altering databases, 212
ALTER SERVER CONFIGURATION, 217
Always Encrypted, 238, 272
Always On Availability Groups (AG),
25, 137, 215
Always on failover cluster instance, 137
Amazon elastic compute cloud (EC2), 16
Amazon web services (AWS) suite, 16
Analytics as a service, 483
Application programming
interface (API), 46
ARM template, 120
Asynchronous messaging techniques, 445
Auditing, 238
Azure SQL Database
configuration, 279
log analytics dashboard, 285
log analytics workspace, 281
query editor, view data, 284
security insights dashboards, 285
selection, 282
storage account, creation, 280
storage details, configuration, 280
tracking connections, 277, 278
viewing audit, 283
managed instance
SQL Server Audit, 276, 277
tracking logins, 276

487

Made in the USA
Coppell, TX
19 March 2022

75222231R00293